Congress and U.S. Veterans

Recent Titles in Conflict and Today's Congress

Congress and the War on Terror: Making Policy for the Long War
Darren A. Wheeler

Congress and U.S. Veterans

From the GI Bill to the VA Crisis

Lindsey Cormack

Conflict and Today's Congress

An Imprint of ABC-CLIO, LLC
Santa Barbara, California • Denver, Colorado

Copyright © 2018 by Lindsey Cormack

All rights reserved. No part of this publication may be reproduced, stored in a retrieval system, or transmitted, in any form or by any means, electronic, mechanical, photocopying, recording, or otherwise, except for the inclusion of brief quotations in a review, without prior permission in writing from the publisher.

Library of Congress Cataloging-in-Publication Data

Names: Cormack, Lindsey, author.
Title: Congress and U.S. veterans : from the GI bill to the VA crisis / Lindsey Cormack.
Other titles: Congress and United States veterans
Description: Santa Barbara, California : Praeger, an imprint of ABC-CLIO, [2018] | Series: Conflict and Today's Congress | Includes bibliographical references and index.
Identifiers: LCCN 2018021776 (print) | LCCN 2018022008 (ebook) | ISBN 9781440858376 (ebook) | ISBN 9781440858369 (alk. paper)
Subjects: LCSH: Veterans—Legal status, laws, etc.—United States. | Veterans—Education—Law and legislation—United States | Veterans—Medical care—Law and legislation—United States. | United States. Veterans Administration.
Classification: LCC KF7709 (ebook) | LCC KF7709 .C67 2018 (print) | DDC 362.86/5610973—dc23
LC record available at https://lccn.loc.gov/2018021776

ISBN: 978-1-4408-5836-9 (print)
    978-1-4408-5837-6 (ebook)

22 21 20 19 18   1 2 3 4 5

This book is also available as an eBook.

Praeger
An Imprint of ABC-CLIO, LLC

ABC-CLIO, LLC
130 Cremona Drive, P.O. Box 1911
Santa Barbara, California 93116-1911

www.abc-clio.com

This book is printed on acid-free paper ∞

Manufactured in the United States of America

Contents

Acknowledgments		vii
Introduction		ix
Chapter 1	No Golden Era: History and Challenges of the Veterans Administration	1
Chapter 2	Connections among Veteran Populations, Legislators, and Groups	23
Chapter 3	Public Opinion: Veterans Policy and Veterans' Preferences	53
Chapter 4	Legwork: Legislative Leaders on Veterans' Policy	97
Chapter 5	A Theory of Lip Service versus Legwork	125
Chapter 6	Lip Service: Legislator Communications about Veterans	143
Chapter 7	Veterans' Education Policy: The Post–9/11 GI Bill	171
Chapter 8	Veterans' Health Care and the VA Scandal	191
Chapter 9	Conclusions and Directions for the Future of Veterans' Politics and Policies	221
Notes		231
Bibliography		261
Index		285

Acknowledgments

The journey of writing this book has been long and difficult, and therefore, I realized quite early on that this journey must be traversed with the aid of countless people, to whom I owe my heartfelt appreciation.

The first person I must thank, and the impetus for the book, is Heath Brown, a colleague of mine who sat me down and convinced me this would be a worthwhile endeavor. He was right in more ways than he knows. I also thank Jessica Gribble at Praeger for the continuous support and willingness to follow the research as it unfolded. I was fortunate to be able to turn to mentors such as Lee Vinsel, Patrick Egan, Jonathan Nagler, and Andy Russell at every stage of the process. I am also grateful to my colleagues at Stevens Institute of Technology, especially Kristyn Karl and Ashley Lytle, for offering their candid and insightful feedback.

I was greatly supported by a rotating cast of research assistants, each serving different roles at different times. In the very early stages, Stephen McArdle and Nick Monzillo helped to build the tools that would make later analyses more readily doable, and both worked to make the communications data of DCinbox available to the public. In later stages, Hannah Castello and Madison Telles worked on some of the detailed, fine-grain research details necessary to complete more comprehensive analyses. In particular, Ali Hameed worked tirelessly at the end to fill in missing details, edit, and give the whole work a read over for consistency.

I am deeply indebted to my friends. While I cut short our coffee dates and turned down invitations, they provided me with continual encouragement in their offers to read over parts, contribute new ideas, and even fix website glitches. Liz Shah, Ilana Goldfarb, Dave Bour, Jovis DePognon, and Tamir Duberstein, I especially thank you for being remarkably understanding in the face of my withering attention.

To my family, the words I write here are inadequate to express my love. My writing this manuscript made it hard for me to spend as much time as

I wanted with my daughter, Charlotte, and husband, Matt. Yet, they patiently stood by me as steadfast rocks throughout this time. It is through their endless belief in me that I gained the strength to continue work when the days were long and the end of the road seemed far.

And of course, I am thankful for the veterans who protect our nation and their families that endure all that comes with service. Their service is in many ways relegated to background noise in the minds of many, but the very gift of mental quiet is one that we would not enjoy without their work and sacrifice.

Introduction

This past Sunday I had the pleasure of riding with my fellow Veteran bikers. We stopped at the Stand Down House in Lake Worth for Homeless Vets. The fact that we have to have a shelter for Homeless Vets in America is reprehensible. We then stopped at the Veterans Administration Hospital in West Palm Beach. At both stops I read a poem "Have They Been Forgotten," written by American Legion Rider Post 318, Samson A. DeVille, aka Sad Sack, from Port St. Lucie, Florida. The poem begins:
Have they been forgotten? We can't know what they've been through!
They were fighting for our Freedom, and to this Country, they stood true.
. . .
On Veteran's Day and every day . . . thank you.
—Representative Allen West (R-FL), October 31, 2011,
"West's Weekly Wrap-Up," *Official Constituent Communication*

This book came about through a series of observations and a desire to make sense of what seemed like oddities around veterans' politics and policies in the United States. In the process of writing, making sense became theory building and casual observations were replaced with empirical assessment. In this book I present a background of veterans' politics in the United States, analyses of some of the curious features of how legislators approach veterans' policies, and a theory of why those curiosities are explained by party politics. Along the way I explore insights on how public opinion has changed around veterans and veterans' policies and pull from two in-depth case studies representing the best and worst of veterans' policies to detail the nuances of veterans' politics.

In 2009, I began collecting all official constituent e-newsletters sent by representatives and senators in the Congress and created a database now known as DCinbox. One of my initial observations in setting up the database was that many official communications make references to veterans. In fact, veterans are discussed in over one-fifth of all official legislator-to-constituent communications. Every day members of Congress write to constituents to let them know their offices are happy to help obtain benefits from the Veterans Administration; they send pictures of their staffs assembling care packages for veterans and pictures of themselves holding in-district veterans listening sessions and professing their reverence for the dedication of our service members.

At first glance I thought the prevalence of veterans in constituent communications was not related to party and instead offered a rare similarity between the communication styles of Democrats and Republicans. Without a more robust assessment, a partisan pattern to these communications was not obvious; it seemed like both Democrats and Republicans referred to veterans at similar rates. Yet, given the new ability to readily assess e-newsletters within the new DCinbox database, I discovered that 67 percent of all messages referring to veterans came from Republican members of Congress.

This was somewhat interesting and understandable. After studying the issue ownership literature, I knew Republicans "owned" military policy, or at least voters seemed more willing to trust Republicans to administer military policy in public opinion surveys.[1] Yet, veterans' issues are not the same as military issues, and in many ways the social and economic policies in place to help veterans such as VA hospitals and higher education support seemed "owned" by the Democratic Party.

Compared to other populations, veterans and their families are some of the greatest recipients of government welfare. Nearly 50 percent of the Department of Defense budget goes to providing assistance to veterans and their dependents in the form of housing, health care, child care, counseling, legal assistance, education benefits, and more.[2] And these sorts of government-administered and government-provided support programs are much more at home in the ideological underpinnings of the Democratic Party rather than the Republican Party.

At this point in my interest in veterans' politics, I considered the result of lopsided attention to veterans to be a small descriptive finding. When I told others in the field that Republicans were out-communicating Democrats on veterans' issues, everyone seemed to accept that as an expected outcome. My reservations about veterans' policies being more aligned with Democratic political ideology were brushed aside with arguments about how the Republican Party is the "patriotic" party and that veterans themselves were far more likely to identify as Republicans. When I discussed this research with friends outside of academia, I was met with similar responses. One friend keenly noted, "Well, I've never heard a pop song about veterans, but they are in plenty of country music—not surprising that Republicans talk about them more in official channels."

Introduction xi

There is a narrative inside and outside of academia that ties Republicans to veterans and vice versa. When I began to discuss my small, descriptive finding, I was not familiar with any specific research on veterans' policy issue ownership; thus, I had no further research to rebut sentiments of unsurprised acceptance. In looking at party identification and voting statistics, I found evidence that veterans themselves tended to identify as Republicans and support Republican candidates in elections, and I too put away the project, deeming it nothing more than partisan politics as usual.

A year later, when learning how to navigate the new Library of Congress legislative issue codes on Congress.gov, a little lightbulb went off on my head. Democrats in Congress, not Republicans, were proposing and passing greater numbers of veterans' legislation by the counts offered in the revamped database on congressional legislation. This curiosity seemed to be worthwhile, but a new baby, a dissertation aimed at different ends, and a new job meant that I did not robustly attend to my long-standing interest until over four years later.

By the time I returned to the project, there was less than a year to go in the Obama presidency, and I was ready to dive into something new. After an unrelated meeting with a colleague at a nearby university, I decided to utilize all of the DCinbox data against all of the data on veterans' legislation to see just how communication and legislating efforts matched up across the parties.

What I found and present in this book are the results of that exercise. During the time period of this study, 60 percent of the over 3,000 pieces of veterans' legislation offered came from Democrats.[3] I somewhat expected this finding, but it is odd with the public narrative that Republicans are the party for veterans.

I anticipated that someone else had investigated this discrepancy, but I knew that access to large amounts of text data was somewhat new, so there might still be room to contribute to the discipline. To my surprise, I found the opposite; veterans' politics and policies are unusually understudied from academic political science perspectives. Very little political public opinion survey research treats veterans as a separate class of interest either to survey or to ask others their opinions about. There are relatively few studies of veteran representation in Congress. As a rough metric of comparison, Google Scholar searches including the terms "black" or "women" along with "representation," "politics," and "congress" return six times as many results as a search using "veterans" in place of "black" or "women."

This is not to say there is not good political science on veterans; in fact this is quite to the contrary. In *Protecting Soldiers and Mothers: The Political Origins of Social Policy in United States*, Theda Skocpol painstakingly describes the evolution of the social welfare system in the United States using the expansion of veterans' policies as a way to understand the comparatively slow spread of government support policies relative to Western European countries. In an edited collection of papers, *Veterans' Policies, Veterans' Politics: New Perspectives on Veterans in the Modern United States*, Steven Ortiz provides the discipline with a detailed understanding of how our current veterans' policies came to be and the power of inertia in slowing down change. Other political historians and sociologists offer deep dives into specific legislation, pressure groups, the administration of benefits, and more.[4]

In the past 10 years, there have been targeted studies from a variety of social science disciplines, covering a wide scope of study. There is research on how policies that create an incentive to hire veterans in government roles change the way other government policies are implemented;[5] how military service plays a crosscutting role for populations who are otherwise thought to prefer Democratic political candidates;[6] and how service influences political preferences generally.[7] Yet compared to other subfields in political science, there is not a lot of work on veterans. Consequently there are many questions left unasked and unanswered. In this book, I attempt to fill some of those gaps.

Book Plan

This book seeks to square two seemingly contradictory political realities by proposing and testing a theory, using newly available political communications data. The two basic starting points are the following:

- Despite a somewhat scant political science landscape, there is a sense that Republicans are the party of veterans, and public opinion and voting data of veterans support this general sense.
- Democrats in Congress exert more legislative effort to enhance veterans' benefits, yet the narrative sense of the first point persists.

How can this be? What is it that the Republican Party does to engender greater support from veterans while those in the Democratic Party propose and successfully pass more veterans' legislation? I argue that there are large and newly quantifiable party differences between legislators who talk about veterans' policy and those who work to create policy.

To assess my claims, I marshal the latest data on how members of Congress communicate to constituents as well as data on the legislative accomplishments of legislators in the 111th–114th Congresses. After considering veterans' politics and policies broadly, I narrow the focus to look at the issues of veterans' health care and educational benefits.

The limit on the data range and issue foci is driven both by data constraints and historical context. Prior to the 111th Congress, the Congress

Introduction xiii

passed the greatest expansion of the veterans' educational entitlements with the Post–9/11 GI Bill. This is considered one of the greatest achievements in the veterans' policy space in the past decade. At the other end of the spectrum, as the Obama presidency wound down, there was a high-profile scandal in the realm of veterans' health care in which over 40 veterans died due to alleged misconduct within the Veterans Administration. Therefore, I study the best and the worst of veterans' policy implementation.

In the first chapter, I familiarize readers with the Veterans Administration (VA) and veterans' policy. In Chapter 2, I provide an overview of three critical players in veterans' politics: veterans themselves, members of Congress who serve veteran constituencies, and veterans' pressure groups. In Chapter 3, I combine and report on the extant public opinion data on veterans and veterans' politics. In this chapter I also include the public opinion *of* veterans in terms of their party preferences and specific issue areas and lay out the evidence linking veterans to the Republican Party.

In Chapter 4, I present the data on legislative efforts to change veterans' policies from the 111th to 114th Congresses. I consider legislation broadly and then in finer ways recognize the differences between different types of bills. I find that even controlling for other elements that are related to bill introduction and success in other theories of law making, partisanship is strongly related to the amount of legislative effort legislators expend on veterans' policies.

In Chapter 5, I offer a theory of lip service over legwork as the way to make sense of the way party politics plays out in regard to veterans' policy. I identify the weaknesses of this theory and explain the analysis strategy that I employ in Chapter 6. In Chapter 6, I use original data on the strategic communication of legislators and a set of increasingly rigorous analyzing techniques to test the theory explained in Chapter 5.

In Chapters 7 and 8 I turn to the specific case studies of the Post–9/11 GI Bill and the 2014 Phoenix area VA hospital scandal to show how lip service and legwork play out in more specific veterans' policy realms. I conclude in Chapter 9 with an eye to the future and offer some discussion on how veterans' policies and politics might be positioned to change in the coming years.

Contributions and Impact

In the polarized and sometimes frenzied nature of U.S. politics, there is an urge to throw one's hands up and declare that both parties are equally at fault for X, Y, and Z. In online discussion communities of veterans, this line of reasoning is observed with good frequency.[8] But one of the duties of scholars is to rigorously investigate claims of party politics and attempt to elucidate the differences between actors so that political discourse and the attentive public can have a rooted way to move forward.

Veterans' policies in the United States require that both parties give a little, but the programmatic needs of veterans' policies demand more ideological flexibility from Republicans. To care for veterans under the architecture built over the past 100 years requires government-provided health care, government spending, and government meddling in multiple economic sectors. Veterans' policies are not wholly unlike the social policies for disabled or poor individuals that provide basic necessities such as medical treatment, job assistance, and housing programs. Yet while many in the GOP would balk at funding a robust general social assistance program, there is generally very little visible pushback from Republicans within Congress as long as veterans are the recipients of such aid. Moreover, there is a difference between Republican members of Congress expressing support for veterans' benefits and actively legislating to accomplish it.

I only analyze a snippet in the greater history of veterans' politics, and this is a limitation. Data limitations aside, this book offers an assessment of an important historical era, and the theory and conclusions drawn from the empirical analyses still provide value in understanding how our politics operate in the area of veterans' benefits.

The challenges of providing veterans' health benefits are widespread, but there is no lack of voices inside and outside of government seeking to continually improve our systems. Fortunately, the attempts and eventually successes in the Congress have been detailed and recorded in ways that are easier for scholars to access and analyze than ever before. It is my hope that by bringing various sorts of political, behavioral, and communications data together, our understanding of the curiosities of U.S. politics will be somewhat more understandable than they were before.

CHAPTER ONE

No Golden Era: History and Challenges of the Veterans Administration

The Importance of Veterans' Policies and Politics

The relationship between civilians, legislators, and soldiers is of fundamental importance in a democracy. Civilians are represented by legislators and protected by soldiers, legislators are elected by civilians and control many elements of how soldiers conduct their lives during and after active duty, and soldiers are tasked with protecting both civilians and legislators and must also rely on civilians and legislators to advocate for and pass policies that support soldiers.

The stakes in producing supportive veterans' policy are very high. With exclusive reliance on an all-volunteer military, the care the U.S. government provides on the back end of active duty must be sufficient to ensure that we continuously recruit high-caliber people to this integral role. And yet, the politics and policies around veterans oftentimes take a backseat to other questions of interest to academic social scientists.

In an era marked by high levels of mistrust of government, the military and veterans are the most respected and revered government entities in public opinion.[1] Polls indicate that the public consistently supports government efforts to do more for veterans. This public sentiment is echoed in the official statements of federal legislators. Veterans and the politics around veterans represent a rare point of bipartisan agreement. Both Democrats and Republicans seek the approval of veterans. In a way unlike politics of the Vietnam

War era, there are virtually no voices in opposition to any sort of expansion of benefits to veterans; since the 1990s onward veterans have been nearly universally revered both by the public and by politicians.

While there is not high-level, partisan opposition to more generous government policies toward veterans, a closer examination of the veterans' policy space makes clear the nuances and limits of policy versus political support for veterans. The reasons for quieter, ideological divisions underlying arguments for providing more generous veterans' benefits are complicated in some ways and quite simple in others.

The task of this book is to lay bare the differences in how public and government actors approach the *policies* of veterans' benefits and *politics* of veterans' benefits in looking at both the simple questions and the more complicated issues. In order to cover ground on both sorts of questions, I approach veterans' politics and policies used as a broad strategy and use more in-depth case studies of veterans' health and education benefits.

The responsibility, willingness, and capacity for government to take care of armed service members once they have exited duty and become veterans are not specified in the Constitution. The provisions for veterans are not a set matter of government but rather are a creation of policy and politics. Arguments around the proper role and scope of government actors, the specific execution of laws, who earns benefits, who scores political points, and how the U.S. public perceives each step in the process are all large topics to grapple with.

The simple parts are where most politicians and citizens agree. Everyone understands that veterans and their families sacrifice their own qualities of life so that others may continue to enjoy freedom and privileges of living in the United States. That is, we all recognize that people who enter the armed services take on a burden and, in doing so, perform a grand task that serves the rest of the country.

Military service involves physical and mental health risks as well as educational and industry opportunity costs that most in the civilian population never face. The economic and educational trade-offs are especially difficult given the timing at which most service members join the U.S. forces. Right as civilian counterparts enter the work force or higher education, service members ship off for duty, oftentimes moving away from their homes and sometimes uprooting their families in the process.

The mental and physical health impacts of service are different and oftentimes more impactful than those experienced in the civilian population. Physically wounded veterans must learn to redo common tasks that most civilians take for granted. Mentally wounded veterans fight more complex internal battles than most of the public has insight into. But again, while the costs of service are intense, the simple part of the politics around veterans' care is that each responsible actor recognizes that the government owes veterans fair treatment and consideration when active duty comes to a close.

The more complicated considerations for veterans' politics reside in questions like *what* the government owes to veterans for the rest of their lives and *how* to deliver on those promises, questions about eligibility for veteran status, how much assistance ought to be provided for veterans, and the role of the federal government versus private charity or industry as actors. There are a multitude of variations of these questions and many more potential answers. What is owed to veterans and their families? How much does the country and government owe to veterans after their service? If a member serves for 2-6 years, does the government owe that person another potential 80 years of health care? What if someone "games the system" by faking an injury or spends away a pension on nonessentials? To what extent is a veteran owed training in order to make him or her more suited for civilian jobs? To what extent are families of veterans owed some sort of protection if their parents, spouses, or children die or are injured while in service? These are questions of policy, and in policy there are inevitable trade-offs and complications that make even the most agreed-upon goals more complicated in practice.

There are also greater ideological questions about government and the role it ought to have in helping individuals. Should government provide lifelong health care to veterans, or does that represent an unjustified "socialized" strategy that would be better left to private industry? At what cost should the government be willing to finance efforts to aid veterans? Are veterans rightfully considered as a separate, privileged, or deserving group of government welfare recipients over teachers, construction workers, and other necessary tradespeople and service workers who do the essential work of maintaining and bettering free society? The politics of government policy has many questions to reckon with on this front.

Veterans' care is a political process. There is no simple cause and effect for why some policies are implemented and some are not. There are many opinions and considerations that influence the way veterans are cared for in the United States. Citizens, veterans groups, medical professionals, administrative bureaucrats, and elected officials all have a role to play. As an issue of politics, there are puzzles and conundrums that take research and thought to parse together. In this book I *describe* the role of medical professionals and administrative bureaucrats, but I dedicate the bulk of my attention to *analyzing* policy makers and the U.S. public.

Using the frame of veterans' policies and specifically veterans' health care and education policy, I start with the following broad questions:

1. Which political actors do the public and veterans trust to legislate on behalf of veterans?
2. Which political actors offer legislative solutions for veterans?

The answers to these questions are not aligned, and thus a puzzle emerges. The U.S. public generally, and veterans specifically, trusts and thinks that members of the Republican Party do more on behalf of veterans. Yet the realities of public policy indicate that members of the Democratic Party have done much of the legislative work on veterans' policy. How can this be? That question underlies the development of this book.

Using detailed analyses pulled from multiple and some new forms of data, I put forth a possible explanation. The shorthand I use for the explanation is *lip service* versus *legwork*. Members of the Republican Party in Congress do a great deal of discussing veterans issues, vowing to work to improve the system, and publicly thanking veterans; that is, they pay a lot of *lip service* to veterans relative to Democratic members in Congress. Democrats are largely responsible for the *legwork* of introducing veterans' policy yet lag behind in efforts to speak to their work on behalf of veterans in public statements.

The U.S. public has an understandably difficult time discerning the intricacies of who is responsible for what sorts of policies but can more easily process the repetition of an issue heard from one side more than the other. This theory and subsequent empirical research are not criticisms of either the Republican or the Democrat style of governing and politicking, but rather it is an empirical assessment of the differences in strategies used on each side of the aisle.

Veterans' Politics and Policy as a Focus

Veterans' politics are important to understand yet largely understudied. While the United States has hundreds of women's studies and race studies programs throughout institutions and universities, only six higher education institutions have dedicated veterans' studies programs.[2] Veterans' politics are also under attended to in political academia. As later chapters show, while we have a lot of data on the locations, health, and educational outcomes of veterans, we know far less about their political preferences and relationships to legislators than we know about other groups of voters.

In this chapter I briefly outline the history of the federal entities tasked with administering veterans' policy, and then I point to the long-standing challenges of administered veterans' benefits as well as the more recent challenges in the contemporary era. I situate the contributions of this book among the extant literature on veterans' policy and politics. At the end of this chapter, I identify the population of interest, and how the designation of veteran has evolved over time.

What Is the Veterans Administration?

What started as a patchwork of family, local, and state care became the federal Veterans Bureau in 1920, an executive agency known as the Veterans

Administration in 1930, and the current cabinet-level U.S. Department of Veterans Affairs (VA) in 1989.[3] In this section I detail the major developments related to the expansion of veterans' care in the United States.[4]

Today the VA is comprised of three basic administrative systems, the Veterans Health Administration (VHA), Veterans Benefits Administration (VBA), and the National Cemetery Administration. In this book the illustrative low light happens under the administration of the VHA when veterans' hospitals fell short on their promises to veterans; the highlight happens with the VBA implementation of the GI Bill. In what follows I focus on the development of the VA primarily in health policy and secondarily in educational policy. For readers interested in the history and current scope of the National Cemetery Administration, see the sources in the endnotes.[5]

The political issue of how much the U.S. government owes to service members after active duty has been debated since before the Revolutionary War (1775–1783). But once the U.S. experiment began in earnest, government officials faced hard questions about what do to for those who served. Caring for veterans is costly and difficult. The young Republic confronted large questions, such as who deserves care, for how long, and at what cost.

In large part, military service at the founding of the Republic was considered a duty owed of those who wanted a freer society. This is in contrast to the modern notion that military service involves some back-end guarantee of health care and educational assistance from the government. This is not to say the government of the time did not dedicate resources to former military members; by 1818 Congress granted pensions to those who served for nine months or more in the Revolutionary army who required assistance.[6] Even then, questions of eligibility turned on political notions of deservingness with veterans having to prove that they were poor enough to qualify for a pension. Since then, opinions and politicking around veterans' care have evolved in many different ways.

Once the early Congresses began to appropriate monies to care for veterans in the form of pensions, the federal government continued to do so and sometimes at incredible levels. By the 1890s more than 40 percent of the entire federal budget went to paying veterans' pensions.[7] The point of a sizeable pension system prior to the creation of the federal Veterans' Bureau was to eliminate the need for government to run specifically dedicated institutions to veterans' care. Yet, for many veterans, pensions were the only source of income and thus were insufficient for those who required greater levels of care due to injury or disability. In the absence of a federal system of health and educational programs, veterans instead relied on privately hired caretakers and a patchwork system of state and local health services to meet their needs. This cobbled together amalgamation of veterans' care eventually transformed into the Veterans Administration that we know today.

Each war created larger veterans populations, and in response the government infrastructure tasked with caring for veterans grew. At the end of the Civil War there were an estimated 2.7 million veterans among the total U.S. population of 38 million.[8] The federalized veterans' care system was born out of legislative action in the first Congress after the Civil War (1861–1865). Despite stated preferences for laissez-faire government and a valorization of heroic individualism, Congress passed National Asylum for Disabled Volunteer Soldiers Act in 1865. This act was one of the clearest official recognition that veterans were in a class of their own regarding the appropriate use of federal government funds to aid individuals. Financial, medical, and educational assistance to other classes of people such as the poor, the disabled, and orphaned children largely happened at a community and, in rarer cases, the state level.[9]

The National Asylum for Disabled Volunteer Soldiers Act created the first standardized, nationalized federal responsibility for creating veterans' centers, known at the time as *asylums* and then later as *homes*. The asylum system was to provide veterans with shelter, food, and a greater ability to rejoin society with vocational training programs. This was a marked difference in government approach. Veterans of the Revolutionary War as well as those from the Barbary Wars (1803–1815), the War of 1812, and the Mexican-American War (1846–1848) were offered no more than small pensions upon exiting service, and even then these were not guaranteed to all.[10]

The debate surrounding this post–Civil War legislation included many of the thorny questions posed when considering any new government program. Who is eligible? How much assistance should the government offer? For how long? Should the government provide or just pay for the actual care? Further complicating these questions, every version of nationalized veterans' policy entails public outcry from some political actors claiming scandal, mismanagement, or ineptitude of those tasked with administering the programs.

The initial veterans' asylum system consisted of three locations, all established within a year of congressional appropriations. They were in Togus, Maine; Milwaukee, Wisconsin; and Dayton, Ohio. The intention in locating these facilities outside of city centers was to provide veterans with an area of respite and to placate local populations by putting some distance between the facilities and already-established communities so that veterans would be less tempted by outside vices. By 1900 the system spread to serve populations throughout the country, with eight locations ranging from the original location in Maine to a West Coast facility in California.[11]

With the understanding that benefit demands would grow in the face of a growing veteran population, members in Congress and President Grover Cleveland attempted to push back against calls for more government spending on veterans' care by appealing to norms of frugality.[12] After the Spanish-American

War (1898–1902), some 300,000 more members joined the aging Civil War veteran population, and the stresses on the newly established system began to show. Civil War veterans were the first organized veterans' groups to successfully extract government benefits from Congress; returning Spanish American vets looked toward continuing that tradition.[13]

From 1910 to 1930, members of the legislative and executive branches aired concerns about government largesse toward veterans. They argued that continued spending would lead to inefficient and unnecessarily gluttonous government waste. One of the last things the exiting president Herbert Hoover did in office was to pocket veto a bill that would have increased veterans' pension benefits.[14] This act is almost unthinkable in the contemporary political climate. Yet it is important to note that veterans at this time did not enjoy the widespread support they do today. Instead, most rank-and-file members of the army were considered to be members at the margins of polite society rather than people to be revered and honored by civilians.[15] Fiscally concerned legislators worried about burgeoning appropriations in the name of veterans' care. A secondary concern arose regarding the inability for Congress to exert reasonable oversight on the outcomes of any programs. And third, legislators feared free-for-all pork barrel races where each would try to secure as much money as they could for their own districts without regard of the overall federal budget.[16]

Yet other activities of the era benefited veterans for years to come. One of the most influential changes was with shift in how veterans' care ought to be conceived of. Rather than viewing veterans as a group of men who ought to be cared for as wards of the state or left to their own devices to manage reentry into society, progressive voices argued for a framework of rehabilitation. Journalist Samuel Hopkins Adams wrote against the expensive and troubled "homes" system and argued that policy ought to take a new direction. He declared that the American public was,

> no longer content to accept for our maimed and crippled a future which will commit them to the life of fungi. A place in the social and economic world must be found for them.[17]

In 1918 as the extent of World War I (1914–1918) was realized by policy makers, Congress passed the Vocational Rehabilitation Act (Public Law No. 65–178).[18] After World War I, the ranks of veterans swelled by an additional 4 million. This bill provided medical care and job training for returning disabled veterans. Supporters of the bill argued that veterans were owed physical reconstruction in the form of therapy and limb prosthetics as well as vocational and educational rehabilitation to increase the likelihood that former military men would reintegrate back into society successfully.

Those against the bill argued that the government was not equipped to assess the efforts to rehabilitate veterans meaningfully, and thus, it would be foolish to invest the sums required to take on such a large responsibility.

The debates around post–World War I veterans' care were different from those concerning Civil War and other smaller interim wars. World War I involved both more gruesome weaponry and more advanced medical care. These factors meant that returning veterans suffered injuries from war technologies not previously used. At the same time, injuries that would have previously been fatal were now possible to treat in the field with better amputation strategies and medical practices. This led to a quick increase in the demand for rehabilitative physical therapies and limb prosthetics. Losing fewer soldiers in war was an accomplishment, but providing lifelong care for returning disabled veterans required more foresight and intervention than the pre–World War I system could provide.

At this time, there was no executive agency dedicated to the enforcement and oversight of laws and programs on behalf of veterans. Instead the loosely connected system of Veterans Homes run in various combinations of federal, state, and private configurations had largely become the health and elder care centers for veterans. There was no strictly centralized system of care, but there were still sizeable governmental resources poured into veterans' pensions.

The architects of the Vocational Rehabilitation Act of 1918 opted to keep the medical responsibility within government systems but recognized the limited capacity for the government to provide exclusive and efficient veterans' educational programs. The educational components of the bill were outsourced to extant schools and private-sector enterprises. As word spread about the willingness for the federal government to pay schools and vocational training centers for veteran rehabilitation, the number of pop-up or fly-by-night companies allegedly providing such services grew. Within three years of the end of World War I, the government had entered into 3,500 contracts with educational providers and 30,000 contracts with specialized academic or vocational training businesses. This sort of expansion occurred without robust checking systems and unsurprisingly rankled Congress members keen to not waste federal dollars.[19]

Amid the growth of direction and size of federal programs for veterans, the calls to create some sort of centralized agency or bureau to coordinate all the different components grew louder. While most policy makers recognized the desirability for Congress to assess the programs it had authorized, creating an executive agency specifically to do so was not a universally held goal. Opponents of federal control or government expansion pushed back. Some argued that a medical system specifically created for veterans and administered by the government represented a dangerous experiment with socialism that was highly counter to the premise of a private, capitalist America. Others argued that veterans' specific needs did not justify government expansion and would snowball into greater government responsibilities.

In 1919, Representative James R. Mann (R-IL) offered the following point in a floor speech on expanding government agencies as a caution about creating a new federal agency tasked with delivering health benefits to veterans:

> It is very rare that any bureau or department of the government does not seek to increase its authority and jurisdiction rather than decrease it.

Despite the contingent of legislators against the idea of a new agency, the vastness and rapid expansion of both the veteran population and the intricacies of the programs established to help veterans eventually led to the establishment of an executive bureau tasked with developing and overseeing veterans' care policies.

In 1921, Congress created the Veterans Bureau. The newly created bureau oversaw veterans' housing, health care, and disability pensions. Representative Mann's concerns of federal government expansion materialized quite quickly and have been proven true repeatedly since. What started as a congressionally approved bureau with 1 D.C. and 14 regional offices became an elevated federal administration in 1930 when President Herbert Hoover signed Executive Order 5398, which formalized the bureau into an executive agency to be known as the Veterans' Administration or VA for short.

The Congress passed the World War II GI Bill in 1944 after rancorous debate about increasing the role of the federal government into the lives of returning soldiers.[20] Opposing legislators argued that paying for veterans' schooling would rob them of a personal incentive to better their situations. There was also an ugly racial component of the opposition with members such as John Rankin of Mississippi arguing that returning black and white veterans ought not to receive the same sorts of education benefits.[21]

Each of the chambers ended up passing slightly different versions of the bill, and once a conference version had been set, the final draft passed the Senate conference committee by just one vote.[22] This bill not only offered veterans a way to reintegrate back into civilian life, but it also broadened the scope of VA responsibilities. Previously the primary focus of the VA was health care and pension disbursement, but when President Franklin D. Roosevelt signed the first GI Bill into law, the VA charge expanded to education and training, loan guaranty for homes, farms or businesses, and unemployment pay.

With a more robust and dedicated government system in place to care for veterans, gains that would change the entire medical field were realized. At the end of World War II, VA head Omar Bradley argued that the system needed to be upgraded to care for the impending volume of veterans. He worked to create strong linkages with the nation's top medical schools during his tenure and funneled VA money into medical research.[23] With the size and targeted research funds, VA doctors invented the first implantable cardiac pacemaker in 1958, the first computed tomography (CT) scanners in 1960, the nicotine patch in 1984, and the first computerized ventilators in 1989.

Beyond invention VA doctors also pioneered practices used for the first successful liver transplants in the 1960s; in the 1970s and 1990s, two Nobel Prizes for Medicine were awarded to VA doctors who developed better screening techniques for blood donors and breakthroughs in circulatory medicine.[24] While the politics around veterans in the 1960s–1970s took a more negative tone in light of the Vietnam War, the VA itself was experiencing notable advances in medical care, and wide success of the educational benefits put in place with the first GI Bill.

After 30 or so years of federalizing and centralizing VA care, in the 1980s, the VA followed broad industry trend to decentralize systems of care.[25] Specifically around the maintenance of data and the development of practices, the VA of the 1980s permitted more leeway for individual facilities to implement policy directions and manage patient data as individual locations thought best. This trend was later reversed as the reputation of the VA dimmed when different standards of care and practice left some veterans feeling shortchanged with the offerings from their closest points of care.

In the 1980s, the VA underwent the largest change in organization and became the cabinet-level department it is today. While President Reagan had railed against President Carter's creation of the Departments of Education and Energy as a part of government expansion, in late 1987 he took on the task of elevating the Veterans Administration to a formal VA.[26] He announced his plans on the day before Veterans Day:

> This is a personal decision that I have thought about for some time. . . . Veterans have always had a strong voice in our government. It's time to give them the recognition they so rightly deserve.

By 1987, the spending and size of the VA would make it the second-largest U.S. government department, following the Department of Defense. By the summer of 1988, both the House and the Senate had passed legislation over the protestations of Republicans in Congress.[27] In 1989, then president George H. W. Bush reappointed Ed Derwinski to lead the department, and Derwinski opted to keep the shortened version "VA," which is still in use today.

In the 1990s, many of the practices of the VA were reengineered, focusing especially on management accountability, care coordination, resource allocation, and information technology and data systems.[28] Counter to the decentralization of the 1980s, the VA created 22 consolidated Veterans Integrated Service Networks as an attempt to improve health care practices in a more uniform manner. This change is credited with broad improvements to the system in terms of procedures and outcomes.[29] This strategy of consolidation and systems integration continued through the 2000s, and to this day, legislators continue to advocate for greater coordination among veterans' care centers.

What started as private efforts to care for veterans has expanded today into one of the largest coordinated systems in the world. Besides Walmart, the VA employs more people than any *Fortune* 10 company, totaling 377,805 in 2016. The $153 billion budget for the VA consistently exceeds the gross sales totals of many of the most successful companies in the United States. And most important, the VA is tasked with caring for the 21.4 million veterans residing in the United States.[30]

Who Leads the VA?

From the very beginning the leadership of the VA has been politicized and marked by occasional scandal. In fact, the very first leader of the Veterans Bureau, Charles R. Forbes, ended up in prison following a public affair in which he was convicted of accepting private kickbacks from contractors in return for government contracts to build veterans' hospitals as well as permitting the fraudulent resale of postwar materials.[31]

Leading the VA is not easy. The charge involves pleasing the executive responsible for appointment in the first place, the members of Congress who exert oversight on the agency, veterans, and veterans pressure groups who can wage public relations campaigns against VA heads who do not heed their demands. Despite the difficult nature of the role, the Senate has unanimously confirmed every man ever appointed to lead the department.[32] That is to say that even though the department has been repeatedly marred by controversy, Senate confirmation proceedings have not drifted into the partisan division that marks the confirmation hurdles that are observed for other appointed positions.

Out of the 23 heads of the VA, 8 have resigned in the face of scandal or accusations of misdoings. In Table 1.1, I provide a glimpse into the details of the 23 men who have led the Veterans Bureau, Veterans Administration, and the Department of Veterans Affairs.

All but one of the leaders of the VA had previous military service. Trump's choice of David Shulkin never served, yet his confirmation was not widely opposed on those grounds. Prior to his appointment he was the VA's under secretary for health, and on February 13, 2017, he too was unanimously confirmed.

While the individual at the helm of the VA is important in executing the policies to aid and assist veterans, the power to create and change policies rests

Table 1.1 Leaders of the VA

Name	Years	Veteran	President	Departure
Veterans Bureau				
Charles Forbes	1920–1923	Yes	Harding	Resigned—Conviction and prison
Frank T. Hines	1923–1930	Yes	Harding	
Veterans Administration				
Frank T. Hines	1930–1945	Yes	Hoover, Roosevelt	Became ambassador to Panama
Omar Bradley	1945–1947	Yes	Truman	Resigned—Veterans' pressure group(s)
Carl R. Gray Jr.	1947–1953	Yes	Truman	New administration
Harvey V. Higley	1953–1957	Yes	Eisenhower	Retired
Sumner G. Whittier	1957–1961	Yes	Eisenhower	New administration
John S. Gleason	1961–1964	Yes	John F. Kennedy/ Lyndon B. Johnson	New administration
William J. Driver	1965–1969	Yes	Lyndon B. Johnson	Resigned—Congressional opposition
Donald E. Johnson	1969–1974	Yes	Nixon	Resigned—Congressional opposition
Richard Roudebush	1974–1977	Yes	Ford	New administration
Max Cleland	1977–1981	Yes	Carter	New administration
Robert P. Nimmo	1981–1982	Yes	Reagan	Resigned—Financial scandal
Harry N. Walters	1982–1986	Yes	Reagan	Resigned
Thomas K. Turnage	1986–1989	Yes	Reagan	New administration
Ed Derwinski	1989	Yes	H. W. Bush	

(*continued*)

Table 1.1 (continued)

Name	Years	Veteran	President	Departure
Department of Veterans Affairs (Cabinet Level)				
Ed Derwinski	1989–1992	Yes	H. W. Bush	Health concerns (Merkel cell carcinoma)
Jesse Brown	1993–1997	Yes	Clinton	Health concerns (Amyotrophic lateral sclerosis)
Togo D. West Jr.	1998–2000	Yes	Clinton	Resigned—Veterans' pressure group(s)
Anthony Principi	2001–2005	Yes	W. Bush	Resigned—Age
Jim Nicholson	2005–2007	Yes	W. Bush	Resigned—Veterans' pressure group(s)
James Peake	2007–2009	Yes	W. Bush	New administration
Eric Shinseki	2009–2014	Yes	Obama	Resigned—Veterans' pressure group(s) and congressional opposition
Robert A. McDonald	2014–2016	Yes	Obama	New administration
David Shulkin	2017–2018	No	Trump	Presidential dismissal

Note: Biographical data are maintained by the Department of Veterans Affairs and may be accessed online.[33]

with members of Congress. In both the high point of the GI Bill and the low point of the VHA scandal, many members of Congress are eager to blame the agency. The point of providing this brief biographical history of VA leaders is to show that this strategy is not new. Leaders of the VA have repeatedly borne the ire of members of Congress, and some have left in the face of that ire.

Historical Challenges and Scandals within the Veterans Affairs System

The challenges in meeting veterans' expectations for postservice care predate the establishment of the Veterans Bureau and Veterans Administration.

The 2014 VA Hospital scandal, detailed later in this book, revolved around claims of excessively long wait times, far distances of travel required for veteran treatment, and subpar quality of care. These complaints are not new; in the century or so of the modern VA, there have been a number of scandals stemming from the same sorts of shortcomings. There was no golden era in veterans' benefits in the United States. Each era has been marked by its own scandals and challenges. I now provide a few examples of the most notable difficulties in administering veterans' benefits.

In return for their service, Civil War veterans oftentimes reported that the country was not doing enough or not making appropriately respectful efforts to care for veterans. Until 1880 veterans living in facilities of the initial National Homes program were known as "inmates" rather than beneficiaries.[34] As such, there were mobility and decision-making limitations placed on veterans within government-administered homes. Veterans Homes administrators argued that the task of housing, feeding, and providing services to a population of returning men who were prone to vices at rates higher than civilians necessitated and justified the limitations put on behavior in order to deliver services in a productive way.

In 1909, there was a series of petitions sent to Washington, D.C., about the rules and accommodations provided for wounded and deceased veterans in the care of the Army Hospital at Fort Bayard, New Mexico.[35] The commander of the home, Col. George E. Bushnell, was forced to answer the claims of these protestations and within his response lies one of the basic truths of the balancing act of government-provided veterans care. His counter included the following passage about expectations of veteran patients and his tactics of requiring order as not counter to his responsibilities to veterans,

> The government is disposed to provide bountifully for patients of this Institution and entertains a benevolent interest in their welfare, but that the Commanding Officer of this Hospital renders nugatory this benevolence by insisting upon a hard and rigid military discipline which is unnecessary and uncalled for.

He continued explaining his restrictive rules noting that

> experience proved them necessary, because given complete freedom the gamblers get together and it is almost impossible to prevent gambling.[36]

Policies slowly changed as personnel turnover dictated, but veterans and veterans' groups still argued that care in government facilities was too rigid. In the 1920s veterans complained that they had to obey certain rules regarding their whereabouts and habits while receiving care. They contended that they ought to be given more autonomy on account of their prior service and they perceived continuous government interference as an undue overreach.

While veterans and their families found this state of affairs distasteful, the general population did not hold veterans in the high regard exhibited in our national discourse of today. By design, the first federal veterans homes were located far from city centers. This was under the auspices of providing a place a refuge from the challenges of daily life but also allayed concerns that the communities of veterans might taint otherwise wholesome civilian hospitals and institutions with the vices and indecency thought to be widespread among ex-soldiers.[37]

These distances oftentimes meant that veterans could not realistically access the sorts of care that were dedicated to the particular needs of ex-soldiers. In fact, in the states that had the greatest populations of veterans, there were insufficient veteran facilities because those also tended to be places of high civilian population centers.[38] Veterans and veteran families began to call on their representatives to relocate and better plan the geographies of any care expansion efforts. Public outcry did appear to influence the expansion of veterans' health facilities. What started as 3 veterans' "asylums" in 1865 expanded to 11 facilities and then were referred to as "homes" by 1929.

In the 1940s, with the greater needs for treating war-wounded amputees, the government opened seven army hospitals dedicated to amputees. These facilities served veterans and importantly incentivized a new fleet of doctors and engineers to develop better prosthetics. The VA retained much of the control over the purchasing of veterans' prosthetics, taking bids each year from private manufacturers and buying artificial limbs in bulk.[39] Serious defects were found in many limbs, and veterans' groups began to complain that the government was willing to pour technology and money into weapons systems but not into prosthetics for veterans.[40] These individual complaints blossomed into national attention when the press and veterans pressure groups began to publish stories using images of disabled veterans to motivate action.[41] While the VA maintained that it was doing all it could to purchase adequate prosthetics, the Department of Justice launched an investigation into purchasing practices on the prompting of congressional committee hearings into the matter. The Justice Department eventually indicted 75 percent of the prosthetics companies in operation at the time for engaging in a price-fixing scheme to inflate the costs of limbs while delivering subpar qualities to the VA. The indictments resulted in convictions that were later overturned, but the most lasting impact was the public scrutiny and backlash leveled at the VA.[42] The VA of today faces very similar, if not greater, levels of public scrutiny than before. Politicians are more keenly aware of the potential for fallout and public dismay if the VA missteps. This lesson was on display in 2014 when the Phoenix area VA hospital wait-time scandal came to light.

Between 1970s and 1990s the VHA had developed a reputation for low-quality care. Following public outcry, the VHA underwent a series of reforms. These reforms involved internal assessments, target setting for treatment times, and the development of more routine "best practices" to be shared across different hospital facilities.

After reforms were implemented, there was an interesting effect. As the reputation of VHA care rebounded, more veterans sought care within the system. While this should be taken as a success of the initial attempts to reform the VHA, new problems emerged. The system that successfully reformed with a smaller patient load could not handle the influx of veterans who used the revamped system rather than seeking private care. This led to problems of patient overuse and underfunded facilities with understaffed medical teams.[43] This pattern of overburdened VA facilities partially explains the 2014 Phoenix area crises that I take up in Chapter 8.

Why Are Veterans' Benefits Difficult to Administer Today?

The health care component of the VA, the VHA, is enormous. One of the greatest difficulties in coordinating health care and benefits today is the wide scope and spread of institutions included under the umbrella of the VA. The VHA provides care at 1,245 health care facilities of varying complexity making it the largest health care system in the United States. As many as one-sixth of all medical doctors in the United States will have spent some training time in a VA facility, and each year between 7 and 9 million veterans are patients. As of 2016, the VHA employed more than 300,000 full-time employees, yet despite the size of the department, not all health care needs of veterans are met within the governmental systems; private providers administer approximately one-third of all veteran health care.[44]

Veterans' care covers all treatments associated with injuries sustained while in service as well as the general health care needs of veterans. For a comprehensive listing of conditions covered and treatments provided, the VA maintains an A–Z list of health topics online.[45] VA health benefits include "all necessary inpatient hospital care and outpatient services to promote, preserve, or restore" veterans' health status. In order to deliver on all these promises, VHA facilities provide a broad range of services ranging from critical care and surgery to mental health care and lifelong physical therapy. In addition to state-provided care in state-run facilities, there are many veterans' benefits that allow for home health aides or virtual telehealth check-ins for eligible members.[46] In what follows I describe the basic provisions of health care for veterans in the system today.

Veterans' health care facilities are specialized to care for the mental and physical wounds of war as well as general health care difficulties faced by veterans.[47] For veterans service-connected conditions are cared for free of charge. For other more general health care needs, there are nominal co-pays like other health care systems in the United States. In cases in which veterans cannot pay for medical care, there are provisions to provide general care free of charge, but in order to qualify veterans must meet means testing financial standards.

All prescription drugs prescribed for treatment of service–related conditions are provided to veterans free of charge; for drugs indicated for other occasional illnesses or conditions not related to military service, veterans are expected to contribute a co-payment.

Some of the most complex and costly forms of care for veterans are old age and end-of-life care. Because of the geographical dispersion of veterans as well as the multifaceted needs of veterans in advanced age, there are various programs to address different modes of care. Under the broad umbrella term Community Living Centers, previously known as VA nursing homes, veterans are cared for in multiple setting types across the country.

For longer-term care for elderly veterans, there are non–VA operated but VA-recognized, assessed, and standardized "State Veterans Homes." State Veterans Homes are owned and managed by state governments to provide nursing home, domiciliary, and adult day care. These institutions were born out of Civil War State Homes tasked with doing the same type of work and continue to do so today. There are 162 State Homes in existence today with each state having at least one, but numbers on occupancy are kept individually and hard to obtain consistently. Because these Homes are not run by the federal government, federal legislators have limited abilities to augment the services offered; despite this limitation some members seek funding for Homes in their own states, and one of the policy changes in the 111th Congress led to an increased scope of eligibility for State Home care.

In terms of cost to the federal government, the State Veterans Home system is the least expensive way to provide long-term care for elderly veterans. Using average cost per veteran per year, the VA spends $332,000 in VA nursing homes, $88,000 in community nursing homes, and about $45,000 a year in per diem payments to veterans in State Veterans Homes.[48]

Medical foster homes are smaller than state veterans' homes but are not places that exclusively serve veterans. These sorts of facilities act as an alternative to the larger institutional setting homes as they are run privately and often have fewer residents. The VA must approve and conduct routine inspections of any medical foster home that wishes to serve and be reimbursed for veterans' care.

For non-full-time care, VA-regulated adult day care facilities offer a place for veterans to spend time during the day in order to receive assistance with activities such as eating and bathing as well as socialization with other veterans. These facilities also offer training for family members or home health care professionals who spend time with veterans on weekends and overnights.

Respite care is similar to adult day care but is temporary in nature and is intended to allow primary caregivers and opportunity to attend to other demands. Respite care may be used for a few hours at a time if a caregiver needs to run an errand, or for a few days or weeks at a time if a primary caregiver has to attend to more extended demands such as work travel and other vacations. Those seeking to utilize respite care can do so either by enrolling their veteran charge into a veteran adult day care or by employing round-the-clock home health care in the absence of the primary caregiver. Each veteran is limited to 30 days a year of respite care.

While not exclusively an issue of health, federal programs that serve homeless veterans are almost all funded through the VHA.[49] Generally these services are broken into short-term rehabilitation care and long-term maintenance care for veterans who may not have extraordinary health care needs but cannot provide for their own housing.

For veterans with an expected six months or less of life, there are provisions for VHA-provided or reimbursed hospice care. Hospice care covers a variety of needs, but in contrast to other medical provisions, the focus of care is comfort rather than treatment.

In August 2014, Obama signed into law the Veterans Access, Choice, and Accountability Act (VACAA). This program expanded reimbursement options for veterans who sought medical services with community providers rather than within a VA facility. Payments to these outside providers still run through federal systems and thus are a point of logistics that VA members must navigate and organize. The calls to privatize segments of veterans' health care have grown in recent years. I return to this topic in the closing chapter of the book with the anticipation that the future of politics around veterans' health care will continue to take up the issue of privatization.

The responsibility to provide health care to veterans does not begin with the doctors and nurses working in the VHA hospitals; this responsibility begins with the political actors in charge of creating policies, authorizing funding, and prioritizing assistance for veterans' care in Washington, D.C. In the United States, the primary political actors responsible for veterans' care are the 441 representatives in the House, the 100 senators in the Senate, and the president. The Congress is responsible for formulating policy, the VA is responsible for administering the policy, and day-to-day workers must carry out the varied tasks of caring for veterans.

Providing health care for veterans is complicated, time-consuming, and expensive. The complications are wide in that veterans are geographically dispersed, have diverse needs, come from different backgrounds, hope for different futures, and need different forms of assistance. The expense of veterans' care is hard to understate but is oftentimes underappreciated. Any military entanglement is financially costly upfront, but the costs of waging war are sometimes rivaled on the other end with the costs associated with veterans care. For each countable military engagement involving U.S. troops, one-third to one-half of all expenses come from caring for veterans after active duty.[50]

The time-consuming and costly nature of health care comes from the types of injuries sustained by veterans. Each era in war produces veterans with different sorts of medical needs that are markedly divergent from those of the general population. World Wars I and II relied on artillery shells at rates never seen in past wars. This resulted in shrapnel wounds and subsequent limb amputations at unprecedented levels, and a fleet of caregivers who had to quickly adapt techniques to new sorts of wounds. The Korean War and Vietnam War saw the use of the toxic herbicide Agent Orange and new neurological, epidemiological, and carcinogenic diseases in veterans. The Gulf Wars, North African, and Middle Eastern U.S. military activities such as those in Afghanistan and Iraq of the 1990s, 2000s, and 2010s have resulted in an increase of mental health difficulties such as posttraumatic stress syndrome, known as PTSD, for short. Caregivers today still grapple with determining the best practices for treating the mental wounds that oftentimes are harder to diagnose and address than the physical ravages that defined veterans care of previous eras. On top of wounds specific to active duty, like the general population, veterans too suffer from heart disease, diabetes, cancer, and later in life mental deterioration. Under the architecture of our current VA system, these more pedestrian health needs must also be met within veterans' hospitals. It is easy to see the enormity of the challenges policy makers and physicians face.

Policy makers have to create solutions to prepare the medical field to be able to handle the numbers and sorts of cases of the veteran population. Great advances in both body armor and treatment options mean that veterans who previously may have died in battle now come away with their lives, thanks to new protections. But these returning soldiers are more severely wounded and thus require greater and more expensive levels of care. This sort of care is time-consuming; rehabilitation is often a multiyear and sometimes a lifelong process for wounded veterans. These are all difficult realities that the political system and medical professionals must face.

Previous Academic Analyses of Veterans' Policies and Politics

There are a multitude of books that survey wars and the plights of veterans in different historical contexts. These studies vary in focus from in-depth case research on specific laws, time periods, activist groups, and political responses to veterans' issues. But far fewer take on and empirically assess the politics and political communications surrounding veterans' issues. This book contributes to both of those realms.

The two most prominent academic books on veterans' policy and politics are Theda Skokpol's *Protecting Soldiers and Mothers: The Political Origins of*

Social Policy in United States (1995) and Stephen Ortiz's edited volume of *Veterans' Policies, Veterans' Politics: New Perspectives on Veterans in the Modern United States* (2012). Both provide systematic historical evidence of veterans' care in the United States. Both offer brilliant insights to why veterans' politics are so unlike other parts of politics: notions of deservingness, the personal histories of many members of Congress, the willingness for veterans' political action groups to fight for policy change, and more.

But for all that these seminal pieces provide, they do not squarely focus on the roles of political parties within Congress and the specific mechanisms for proposing and communicating about veterans' policies. Of course, there are examples of more targeted research on the relationship between partisan priorities and veterans' politics, but much of that work focuses on the spending outlays sought when different parties control the Congress.[51]

Virtually every journal article on veterans' politics notes that analytic attention to veterans' issues from academia is scant compared to other contemporary topics. I do not detail the dearth of scholarly research on the issue. But I—as well as others in the discipline—conclude that the field is underattended to, despite the importance of the subject matter.

As with any endeavor, there are limitations and cautions to be aware of. I focus my attention on the contemporary efforts of the 111th–114th Congresses spanning 2009–2017. I also find limits within public opinion data availability on some of the more nuanced questions that would make for a clearer explanation. With the limitations as they are, I have done my best to put all the pieces out in view. The research involves additional inputs that might not seem directly relevant to the thesis but are offered in order to provide context. I have done my best to connect the dots in a way that tells a cohesive story, but one that also lays bare potential criticisms and shortcomings.

To these ends I hope that I have provided a compelling explanation for why the politics around veterans' care in the United States is so complicated and contentious. The lives of veterans ought not to be a rope to be used in a game of political tug of war. But given the reality of limited resources, competing ideologies, and a democratic system linking voters to their legislators, we ought to do our best to understand complicated truths. While the Republican Party is given much of the public credit for doing work on behalf of veterans, legislatively the Democratic Party has done far more. I argue that one reason for this discrepancy lies in the difference between lip service and legwork, and the ways in which the public interprets lip service to mean actual service.

Who Is a Veteran?

I conclude this chapter with a simple question that does not have a simple answer: Who is a veteran? In the most general sense, a veteran can be *any* person who served for *any* length of time in *any* military service branch. However, through the lens of government, there are different eligibility criteria for veterans benefits. These criteria are not static and instead change as social norms and public policy dictate.

Government programs relying on veteran status for eligibility have a history of denying people of color, women, gays, and reservists the same privileges afforded to others. The following details are not exhaustive but do show some of the VA privileges bestowed upon some veterans and not others on account of status modification made not from service differences but from individual race, sex, and orientation differences.

After World War I, nonwounded women who returned from being nurses or assistants in the army were not provided with discharge pay that was typical for a man and were not considered veterans even though people who fill these roles today are.[52] This is despite the fact that over 30,000 women served as nurses. By World War II women filled more than nursing roles and made up over 350,000 positions through the course of the war.[53] Women continued to serve in all of the intervening military engagements after World War II, but it was not until the 1980s that the VA established an Advisory Committee on Women Veterans.[54] When the original GI Bill passed, states and localities retained a lot of enforcement authorities allowing political actors in the Jim Crow South to selectively accommodate white veterans' claims over blacks. As a part of the bill provisions creating home loan guaranties, out of the first 67,000 loans taken out, fewer than 100 went to veterans of color.[55] As recently as 2014, the VA clung to policies that denied gay veterans the same rights as others. In states that had not yet legalized same-sex marriage, the VA could and did deny requests for gay veterans to be interred together in veterans' cemeteries.[56]

There are other delineations that some use to describe veterans: combat versus noncombat, wartime versus peacetime, disabled or not. These sorts of modifications add a level of descriptive accuracy, but for most intents and purposes under legal protections and benefits, these designations do not amount to meaningful differences.

Today we have the broadest understanding of veterans that the United States has ever held. Veterans who run into trouble with the law still maintain their status and eligibility for many programs; these veterans are known as "justice-involved" veterans.[57] Generally speaking, veterans must serve an active-duty career of no less than 24 months and leave under any condition other than dishonorable to qualify for benefits.[58] If active duty is cut short due to injury or if the soldier is taken as a prisoner of war, veteran status follows in all but the most exceptional circumstances.

Veteran terminology is not strictly central to the thesis of this book, but given the historical limits of the status, there is merit in considering the ways political communication can influence policy. When I use the term "veteran,"

I mean any former armed service member who identifies as such and is entitled to government benefits. Having sketched the functions of our governmental apparatus dedicated to serving veterans, and having noted how this population has been regarded historically, I now turn to current veterans living in the United States and the political connections between veterans as a part of an electoral constituency and veterans within Congress.

CHAPTER TWO

Connections among Veteran Populations, Legislators, and Groups

Veterans' politics has many different actors, inputs, and connections. First, there are veterans themselves, a widely distributed group of individuals who remain connected by their history of service. Second, there are legislators tasked with representing the needs of their districts—all of which contain veterans. Finally, there are pressure groups dedicated to electing favorable legislators and crafting veterans' policies.

The interconnectedness of these actors is easy to appreciate theoretically, but little academic research considers these linkages. We know that in the United States the current veteran population accounts for just 7 percent of the total population.[1] We know that far fewer veterans currently serve in Congress than during previous eras.[2] And in contrast to dwindling numbers in the population and in Congress, there are now multiple veterans' pressure groups that are active in politics.

There is research that veterans tend to hold different policy preferences than civilians in some political areas, especially in the use of military force and nuclear security.[3] Yet very little work has attempted to connect the presence and opinions of veterans in the public, veterans' pressure groups, and veterans elected to Congress. There are of course scholars who dive deep on other neglected pockets of veteran politics, but there is still much to be done.

In this chapter, I provide a descriptive landscape of veterans, the sorts of members of Congress who represent veterans, the largest and most influential pressure groups in the veterans' space, and the links between each of these pieces. Veterans, like any other group, do not completely share the same characteristics or political preferences, but there are patterns about the types of legislators that districts with more veterans tend to elect. In a related way, the multitudes of veterans' organizations speak to the various interests and political desires of different sorts of veterans, but again there are comparisons to be made and inferences to draw from a more complete understanding of the different players. Over the following pages I focus on the contemporary configurations of these different elements in veterans' politics.

Political Geographies of Veterans

Across the United States approximately 7 percent of the population is veterans.[4] Veterans live in every congressional district. Every member of Congress is tasked with representing their needs, and each seeks to earn veterans' approval. Members of Congress are often keen to note the levels of veterans in their districts as a point of pride and argue for the prioritization of veterans' issues. This consideration is not just sentimental; veterans are also known to be much more politically participatory than others, and thus, there are instrumental benefits to engaging the community.[5] Consider this passage from Republican representative Curt Clawson of Florida-19,

> Supporting the approximately 100,000 veterans and active military personnel in our district, amongst the highest number in any of America's Congressional districts, is one of my highest priorities.—December 19, 2015[6]

The share of the veterans in Clawson's district is 10.7 percent, which is well above the average that serves as the basis for his appeal and stated priority. But this prioritization of veterans in communications is present in a great deal of legislator-to-constituent communications even for those with few veterans in a constituency. Representative Jose Serrano (NY-15) represents the district with one of the lowest share of veterans, just 1.8 percent, and yet his official calendar and constituent communications show his reverence and prioritization for veterans,

> Earlier this month, Congressman Serrano met with members of the Military Officers Association of America and discussed current issues affecting military retirees. The Congressman thanked them for their service to our Nation and expressed his strong support for our veterans.[7]

These two examples are illustrative, but there are more systemic linkages to be uncovered by considering veterans' populations more systematically.

Where are the highest concentrations of veteran populations? Do those areas tend to elect Democrats or Republicans? And how much do members of those districts talk about veterans in their constituent communications?

The share of veterans in a district is the number of people in a district who are veterans over the number of people in a district who are 18 years or older. This strategy is the method the U.S. Census uses when calculating official statistics about veterans' populations and allows for a more fair comparison of district-to-district adult populations. Florida's first congressional district has the greatest share of veterans at 18 percent, and California's 40th district has the lowest share at 1.4 percent.[8]

States with the greatest concentrations of veterans are Alaska at 12.5 percent, Montana 9.65 percent, Maine 9.57 percent, Virginia 9.32 percent, and West Virginia 9.08 percent. The states with the smallest share of veterans, but sometimes with high raw counts of veterans, are New York with 4.51 percent, California 4.73 percent, Utah 5.06 percent, Massachusetts 5.59 percent, and Illinois 5.61 percent. Looking at the extremes is illustrative but fails to recognize the many more districts and states that occupy the middle and have comparable levels of veterans.

Figure 2.1 displays the distribution of population shares of veterans across U.S. congressional districts and states. The figure is of two overlapping histograms done by the party of the elected member of Congress. Veteran status

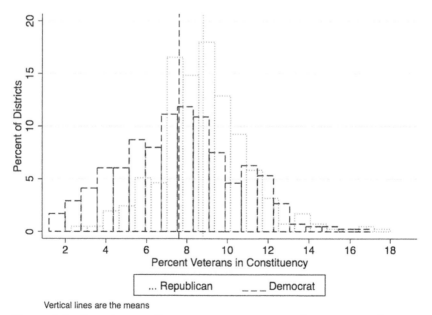

Vertical lines are the means

Figure 2.1 Distribution of veterans as a percentage of constituency for Democrat and Republican legislators (111th–114th Congress).

within a constituency was obtained from annual updates in the Veterans' Affairs Veteran Data Portal, other constituency measures come from the data of the 2010 Census, and veteran status of a legislator comes from the Brookings Institute, the House Committee on Veterans' Affairs, and Veterans Campaign.

Binning all congressional districts and states over the 111th–114th Congresses, I find that both parties represent constituencies of different levels of veterans, but the average share of veterans in a constituency is somewhat higher for Republican legislators than Democrat legislators.

Republican members of Congress tend to represent larger veterans' constituencies than Democrats, but Republican representatives do not have an exclusive hold on highly concentrated veteran population centers. As a different way to display district voting preferences, veterans' constituencies, and the partisanship of representatives and senators in Congress, Figure 2.2 provides a breakdown of districts and legislator partisanship by the share of veterans within a district and the percentage of voters voting for President Barack Obama in 2008. This figure not only shows the extremes from Figure 2.1 but also shows the vast middle ground where districts of both moderate veteran populations as well as moderate Obama support exist and a good mix of Democrats and Republicans represents those constituencies.

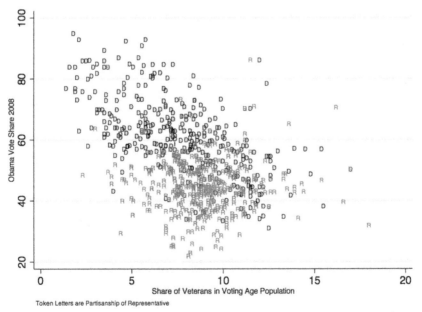

Figure 2.2 Veterans as a percentage of constituencies by Obama vote share in 2008.

Having presented the political geography of veterans within the United States, I now discuss the distribution of veterans *within* Congress. Once a frequent pathway to a career in federal government, former service members now make up far fewer members of Congress than they did in the past.

Veterans in Congress

In the late 1970s and into the early 1980s, nearly 80 percent of all representatives and 75 percent of senators were veterans.[9] By 2009 just over 20 percent of representatives and senators were veterans.

The contemporary share of veterans in Congress is roughly 20 percent and is greater than the share of the veteran population in the United States. By that account, veterans more successfully obtain federal legislative seats than one would expect based on the overall population of veterans. Yet, current levels of veterans in Congress are the lowest ever. At the conclusion of this section, I return to possible explanations as to why there are fewer veterans than there have been in the past, but first I present some of data describing the current veterans in Congress.

Partisanship

Veterans in the most recent Congresses tend be members of the Republican Party, but this was not always the case. Table 2.1 provides a breakdown in the 111th–114th Senate and House by veteran status. As recently as the 111th Congress, veteran legislators were equally likely to be Democrats or Republicans. Starting with the 2012 general election, veterans in Congress have declined overall, but of those who hold office, greater shares come from the Republican Party. Table 2.2 provides the partisan breakdown of veterans in Congress.

This difference in the percentage of veterans in Congress from the Republican Party and the Democratic Party is an important part to consider as an element in the theory of lip service versus legwork presented in later chapters.[10]

Table 2.1   Percentages of Veterans in the House and Senate (2008–2018)

Congress	House (%)	Senate (%)
111th	22	25
112th	22	26
113th	20	18
114th	19	16

Note: Data on veterans in Congress come from the Brookings Institute, the House Committee on Veterans' Affairs, and Veterans Campaign.

Table 2.2 Partisan Breakdown of Veterans in the Congress (2008–2018)

Congress	Democrat (%)	Republican (%)	Total
111th	50	50	121
112th	47	53	118
113th	29	71	106
114th	26	84	102

Source: VeteransCampaign.org and the Brookings Institution.

Veterans in Congress on Veterans' Committees

Within Congress the most important committees for veterans' policy are the House and Senate Veterans' Affairs Committees. The distribution of committee seats is up to the party leadership within the Congress and the preference of individual legislators. Are veterans in Congress more likely to get a seat on those committees than nonveterans? There are certainly reasons to think that veterans would be more likely to be on such a committee given their own personal histories, but the assignment of committee seats is not as straightforward as matching career histories of members of Congress to available committee seats. A military veteran legislator who comes from a district with lots of farmland may be cross-pressured to seek a seat on Veterans' Affairs as well as on the Agricultural Committee. While members can sit on multiple committees in the House, one can see how the complications of matching 435 members to different committees and subcommittees would not always result in every military veteran member sitting on the Veterans' Affairs Committee.

Of the 114 unique veteran representatives and senators in office during the 111th–114th Congresses, 15 percent held a seat on the Veterans' Affairs Committee for at least one term. Of the nonveteran members, only 10 percent ever sat on those committees. But it is not clear the veteran status of an individual legislator is more important than the constituencies of members of Congress in order to secure such a seat.

As a way to assess the relative relationships of veteran status and the share of veterans in a constituency on the likelihood that someone has a seat on the Veterans' Affairs Committee, I set up a simple probit regression. The outcome measure is a seat on the Veterans' Affairs Committee, and the inputs are the veteran status of a legislator and the share of veterans in a legislator's constituency. I find that when controlling for both inputs, there is no significant relationship between being a veteran and the likelihood that one gets a seat on the Veterans' Affairs Committee, but that there is a significant and positive relationship between the share of veterans in a district and the likelihood that a legislator secures such a seat.[11] Members on the committee have an average veteran population of 9.1 percent, whereas those not on the committee have an average population of 8.1 percent.

This finding corresponds to old and new research that indicates that members are not always placed on committees for substantive expertise, but more often than not there is a determination of which committee is the best fit for a member's constituency concerns.[12]

Service Branch

Veterans in 111th–114th Congresses come from four of the five major branches of the U.S. Armed Forces. There are no former Coast Guard members, but the other branches are represented in similar amounts to their divisions within the greater military apparatus. In the time period under study, military personnel were divided such that 42 percent were in the army, 32 percent in the navy, 27 percent in the air force, 6 percent in the Marine Corps, and 1 percent in the Coast Guard.[13] In the Congress, 50 percent of veterans come from the army, 21 percent from the air force, 16 percent from the navy, 13 percent from the Marine Corps, and none from the Coast Guard. The army and air force are overrepresented in Congress, whereas the other service branches are each a bit underrepresented.

Gender

Women make up 10 percent of all U.S. veterans.[14] This is a historic high, as military policies have relaxed to allow women to serve in a greater variety of roles than in the past. Women have served in every military operation since the Revolutionary War and have continued to do so in greater numbers in each successive engagement. The proportion of women serving in Operation Enduring Freedom and Operation Iraqi Freedom was the highest ever at 14 percent.[15] With the gender composition of the military changing, we will likely see more women veterans in Congress, but this is not yet a reality. Of the veterans in Congress over the past 10 years, just 2 percent were women.

Veterans in Constituencies and Veterans in Congress

What sorts of legislators tend to represent districts made of greater shares of veterans? Are districts with more veterans prone to elect veterans to Congress? Are there other generalizable findings that describe the types of legislators preferred by districts with more veterans? In this section I consider select legislator characteristics in relation to the constituencies that elect them. To be clear, this does not assess the political preferences of individual veterans but is intended to determine if there are identifiable patterns of what sorts of legislators represent districts with greater shares of veterans. This is one part of the arc in the circle of the greater story of how veterans' policies and politics unfold in the United States.

Do Districts with More Veterans Elect Veterans to Congress?

The more veterans in a district means that eligible members to run for Congress are more likely to be veterans themselves. We know that districts with greater amounts of minorities tend to elect minorities to Congress more so than districts with smaller minority populations.[16] Does the same sort of descriptive representation linkage exist for veterans?

As a way to test this proposition, I pool all members from the House elected during the 111th–114th Congresses. This totals 670 legislators. As a first pass, I simply consider standard demographic measures of a constituency: the share of veterans, the percentage of a constituency that is white, the percentage that has a bachelor's degree, the percentage that is native born, the percentage of people unemployed, the median household income, and the percentage in poverty.[17] I consider the primary explanatory variable the percentage of veterans within a constituency.

As a second test I reproduce the model and add in the share of votes Obama earned per district in the 2008 presidential election.[18] I use the 2008 election results because this race occurs at the outset of the data and may be considered as an indicator of prior preferences of a constituency. A consideration of the greater political context is prudent; all the constituency-level indicators included in this model are elements of the explanations surrounding why some districts elect Republicans over Democrats in other lines of research.[19] Given the infrequent attention paid to veterans' populations in those sorts of analyses in general political science research, there is not an extant academic comparison of the relative importance of the share of veterans in a constituency vis-à-vis other constituency-level measures. But knowing that partisan preferences of electorates are powerful explanations for other features of American politics, including this measure as a proxy for district preference is a natural next step.

Of the 670 members of Congresses analyzed, 112 (17%) are veterans. Table 2.3 shows the direction and magnitude of the relationship between constituency characteristics and the likelihood that a member of Congress is a veteran.

This says nothing of the individual contests for each election but can be used to understand the descriptive relations between constituencies and veterans in Congress. When only considering district demographics, the percentage of veterans in a constituency is the only characteristic that exhibits any significant relationship to the likelihood that a member of Congress is a veteran. In the political identity politics literature, veterans are nearly

Table 2.3 Probit Results of Veteran Legislators as a Function of Constituency Characteristics and Other Controls (111th–114th Congresses)

	Constituency Characteristics	+ Presidential Vote Share
% Veterans	0.07*	0.05
	(0.03)	(0.03)
% White	0.00	−0.37
	(0.48)	(0.52)
% Bachelor's Degree	−0.01	−0.01
	(0.02)	(0.02)
% Native Born	0.44	0.19
	(0.80)	(0.81)
% Unemployed	−0.01	0.01
	(0.03)	(0.03)
Median Household Income	0.00	0.00
	(0.00)	(0.00)
% in Poverty	0.02	0.01
	(0.03)	(0.03)
Obama Vote Share 2008		−0.01*
		(0.00)
N	670	670
Pseudo R2	0.02	0.03

* $p < 0.05$

Note: White standard errors in parentheses.

never considered a group of people who translate strength in population numbers to political representation in the way that black and Hispanic identities are commonly considered. So in looking at the results from model 1, a possible interpretation could be that districts with more veterans tend to elect veteran representatives more than other, less veteran–dense districts. But that conclusion is undercut when looking at the second model that includes the presidential preferences of a district. When including that element of district-level variation, it appears that factors related to partisanship in a district tend to be a greater influence the likelihood that a veteran serves in Congress or not. Districts that preferred McCain to Obama in 2008 had a slight preference for veterans as representatives. This is a thread that contributes to the greater tapestry of veterans' politics in the United States, namely that there is a connection between preferences for the Republican Party that are intertwined with notions of pro-veteran politics.

Do Districts with Greater Shares of Veterans Tend to Elect Republicans?

This question is more complicated than it may seem.[20] Places with higher veterans' constituencies tend to have Republican representatives. The average share of veterans in a Republican-represented constituency is 8.8 percent compared to 7.6 percent for a Democratic-represented constituency. However, it might be the case that other considerations that are coincident in districts with greater shares of veterans better explain the partisanship of elected members of Congress.

I repeat the analyses presented in Table 2.3 with the different outcome variable of legislator partisanship. I do not display the full table of results for this model, but when placed in comparison with other constituency variables, the share of veterans in a population is not significantly related legislator partisanship. Instead the constituency characteristics most related to the outcome of legislator partisanship in descending order of magnitude are the percent white, the percent native born, and the percent unemployed. As the percentage of white citizens increases and the percentage of native-born citizens increases, so too does the likelihood that a legislator is a Republican. The opposite effect is observed for unemployment rates. As unemployment rates increase, so too does the likelihood that a Democrat represents a district. Of course, when using the second model that includes the share of the 2008 vote that went to Obama, I find that the overall preferences for a Republican in the White House is the only significant explanatory variable related to the partisanship of a representative or senator, all else equal.

Do Districts with More Veterans Tend to Have Men or Women Representatives?

Women are not often in positions of power within the armed services. Out of the over 200 members to attain the rank of four-star general, only three have been women.[21] For the service members currently rising within the branches today, most have never worked under a woman. While internal promotion within the armed services is not conducted as an election, the elevation of women to positions of power is so infrequent that it may be reasonable to expect that service members and veterans are more comfortable with men in roles of leadership than women.

During the only general presidential election pitting a woman versus a man, a 2016 internal poll of 2,000 troops conducted by *Military Times* found that 82 percent were either dissatisfied or strongly dissatisfied by the idea of

Hillary Clinton as commander in chief.[22] A quote from the article discussing the results of that poll better elucidates the rationale for why veterans may choose men rather than women in electoral competition,

> This is a community in which no service chief has been a woman; one that has been slow to open opportunities to women. It also is a community, however, not prone to put a woman in any position, let alone as commander in chief, just for a feel-good moment.

A lack of experience with female leadership as well as stated distaste for such a leader provide the logical underpinning supposing that districts with greater shares of veterans may choose men over women for elected representation. Is that the case?

All constituencies independent of veterans' populations are more apt to have male representatives rather than female, as women only account for 20 percent of all federal legislators. However, constituencies with higher veterans' population tend to be represented by men rather than women in Congress. A two-tailed comparison of means shows that the average share of veterans in a constituency that has a male representative is 8.3 percent, whereas it is significantly lower at 7.3 percent for districts with women representatives.

I perform the same probit from relating constituency characteristics to legislator characteristics.[23] The more robust analyses including other constituency-level characteristics do not produce evidence that the share of veterans in a population is significantly related to representative's gender. In fact, out of the variables considered, only the share of white people in a constituency is significantly related to legislator gender. As the share of the white population increases, the likelihood that a district is represented by a woman is reduced. In the model including the 2008 Obama vote share measure, districts that had greater shares supporting Obama also are more likely to have women as representatives, and no other variable shows a significant relationship, all else equal.

In the absence of consideration of the political preferences in a district, I find that places with greater levels of veterans are more likely to be represented by veterans than places with fewer veterans in the population. For other measures such as the partisanship and gender of elected officials, the share of veterans is not meaningfully related one way or another once other basic demographic indicators are included.

Do veterans in Congress offer some distinct representational benefits for veteran populations? In what ways are veterans in Congress active on veterans' issues? In the next section I assess and profile the veterans in Congress who are most active on veterans' issues.

Most Active Veterans in Congress

Rather than offer a cumbersome list of all the veterans serving in the current Congress, I present the veteran office holders who (1) introduced the greatest numbers of veterans' specific pieces of legislation and (2) most often talk about veterans in their constituent communications. This is a top-level way to see what sorts of legislative and political communication activities veterans undertake.

In order to measure the first activity, I assembled a database of all veterans' legislation introduced in the 111th–114th Congresses by the sponsoring legislator. Veterans' legislation is any piece that the Library of Congress categorizes as in at least one of the five areas of veterans' legislation: (1) veterans' education, employment, rehabilitation; (2) veterans' loans, housing, homeless programs; (3) veterans' medical care; (4) veterans' organizations and recognition; and (5) veterans' pensions and compensation.[24] I employ this database throughout the book. All together, there were 3,150 pieces of veterans' legislation introduced in 111th–114th Congresses.

In order to measure the political communications of legislators, I employ the DCinbox database to analyze every official legislator-to-constituent e-newsletter.[25] Each communication that mentions the word "veteran" or "veterans" is counted as a reference to veterans. In sum, over 16,400 official legislator-to-constituent communications (20% of total communications) mentioned veterans. Veteran members of Congress sent about 2,700 of messages mentioning veterans. That is, veterans do not seem to overperform in sending more messages about veterans when assessed as a whole; their share of messages is roughly equal to their seat share.[26]

The count of legislation introduced is a measure of the effort that members of Congress exert in their capacity to change laws.[27] Theoretically, this is the central role that defines the privilege of being elected to Congress. The count of official constituent communications that mention veterans is an approximate measure for level of effort a legislator wishes to be perceived as exerting on veterans' issues.

There is variation both in the amount of legislation proposed and the amount of veteran referencing in official communications. There are also variations in the time served as a legislator for each member of Congress. For both the legislative and communication measures, I take variations in tenure into account by dividing the counts over the number of years in Congress each legislator served between the 111th and the 114th Congresses. The database of Congresses under study spans 8 years, and the average number of years a legislator served in the Congress during that time is 5.2. Table 2.4 shows the most legislatively and communicatively prolific veterans during the 111th–114th Congresses.

Connections among Veteran Populations, Legislators, and Groups

Table 2.4 Military Veteran Members of Congress Who Introduced the Greatest Numbers of Veterans' Legislation and Sent the Most Constituent Communications about Veterans (111th–114th Congress)

Veteran Legislators with the Most Pieces of Veterans' Legislation Introduced per Year in Congress			Veteran Legislators with the Most Communications about Veterans Sent per Year in Congress		
Member	Party	Pieces of Legislation per Year	Member	Service	Number of Veteran References per Year
Rep. Steve Buyer (IN)	Republican	8.5	Rep. Jeff Denham (CA)	Republican	32
Sen. Daniel Akaka (HI)	Democrat	8.25	Rep. Allen West (FL)	Republican	27
Sen. Richard Blumenthal (CT)	Democrat	4.5	Rep. Mike Coffman (CO)	Republican	25.9
Rep. Joe Sestak (PA)	Democrat	3.5	Rep. Paul Cook (CA)	Republican	20
Sen. Dan Inouye (HI)	Democrat	2.7	Rep. Geoff Davis (KY)	Republican	17
			Rep. Rodney Frelinghuysen (NJ)	Republican	17

The most legislatively active veteran in the 111th–114th Congress was Republican representative Steve Buyer from Indiana. Buyer served in the Gulf War at the rank of captain and was a military attorney in Iraq.[28] Buyer authored multiple pieces of legislation intended to improve efficiency at the Department of Veterans Affairs (VA) and incentivize businesses to hire veterans.

Senator Daniel Akaka (D-HI) offered the second greatest amount of veterans' legislation. Akaka chaired the Veterans' Affairs Committee from 2007 to 2011. That role undoubtedly influenced his amount of legislation authored on veterans. Chairing the committee provided him with additional research and resources on topics of interest to veterans as well as a special sort of responsibility to develop and propose policy solutions around veterans' issues.

Senator Richard Blumenthal (D-CT) offered the third-most veterans' legislation during the time under study. Blumenthal is a veteran, but his assertions about his involvement during the Vietnam War sparked controversy repeatedly during his tenure.[29] He served in the Marine Reserves during the Vietnam Era but never went to Vietnam.[30] His occasional public obscuration of that distinction opened him to criticism of trying to mislead voters. But ultimately for governmental categorization of veterans, he meets the criteria of serving in a branch of the U.S. military apparatus without a dishonorable discharge and hence is recorded as and entitled to call himself a veteran. His policy efforts centered on legislation designed to improve veteran access to facilities and increasing accountability of employees within the VA system.

Representative Joe Sestak (D-PA) served for 30 years in the army before joining the Congress. He served two terms in the House before unsuccessfully seeking a Senate seat. While in Congress Sestak introduced legislation to increase funding for the administration of the GI Bill, to expand the eligibility requirements for housing assistance measures offered to homeless veterans, to make the electronic medical records of veterans more accessible, and more.

Senator Daniel Inouye (D-HI) fought in World War II and lost his right arm while in the service. Once Hawaii became a state in 1959, Inouye became the first person elected to the House of Representatives from the islands, and in 1962 he was elected to the Senate. He served until his death in 2012. During that time he introduced numerous pieces of legislation on behalf of veterans. In the Congresses under study, he focused on ensuring that veterans were given protections and privileges that he thought they were owed. These privileges included the ability to travel on military aircraft and permissions to use Department of Defense commissary and exchange stores.

On the right hand side of Table 2.4 we see the veterans in Congress who most often talked about veterans in constituent communications. Each of the veterans who most often write about veterans has their own sort of "home style" or way of relating their experience and expertise to constituents.[31] In order to summarize the ways in which these members referred to veterans, I assembled a single additive record for each legislator with all the paragraphs that referred to veterans over their time in Congress. Each of these documents was processed using standard protocols to identify words, bigrams, and trigrams used by each member. This is a way to summarize how each legislator approaches veterans as a topic of official communications.

Jeff Denham (R-CA) oftentimes refers to his service and repeatedly reminds his constituents of his veteran status. One of his most used bigrams is "As a," which is followed by modifiers like fellow veteran myself, crew chief in the air force, or member of Congress and a veteran myself. When referencing veterans in communications, Denham routinely signals that he too is a veteran and uses that grounding to justify his positions on issues of importance to veterans. Sometimes this is done in the context of lawmaking and his work on the Veterans' Affairs Committee. He also regularly encourages his constituents to "thank a veteran" and even riffs on the social media call to

#TBT (Throw Back Thursday) by including a weekly #TVT (Thank a Veteran Thursday) where he thanks a specific veteran from his district.

The second-most veteran-focused legislator, Allen West (R-FL), is a former army lieutenant colonel. He most often wrote about concerns of government spending toward other programs that could have otherwise been put to use on veterans' programs. As a part of his style, he wrote to constituents to describe the details of budget appropriations for different areas with a special focus on Military Construction and Veterans Affairs appropriations.

Mike Coffman (R-CO) took aim at a different sort of issue. Most of his communications decry mismanagement within the VA and delays in building a VA hospital in his district in Aurora, Colorado. He routinely argued for more oversight from the Army Corps of Engineers to make sure that VA construction budgets and timelines were adhered to. Coffman was the chair of the House Veterans' Affairs Subcommittee on Oversight and Investigations. He oftentimes described his role in hearings and investigations into bureaucratic shortcomings with the VA. He also leveled charges of overspending on the order of "hundreds of millions of dollars" because of VA inefficiencies. Coffman wrote to his constituents about some of his most scathing exchanges with VA officials during hearings. He recounted his response to VA secretary Robert McDonald, after a heated exchange during a budget hearing,

> Let me start by telling you something I haven't done. I have never run a federal agency that tolerates corruption the way the VA has. I've never built a hospital that's years behind schedule and hundreds of millions over budget. . . . And I've never been a shill for inept bureaucrats who allowed American heroes to die on a medical waiting list while waiting for medical care.[32]

Representative Paul Cook (R-TN) prioritized veterans in communications by including a section in nearly all of his communications called the "Veterans' Corner." In these sections Cook described veterans' events in his district, veterans or veterans' groups who came to visit him in D.C., or good stories of casework where he and his staff were able to help a veteran get benefits caught up in red tape. He let constituents know that his office was "here to help" if ever they found themselves in need of an advocate to expedite the processing of veteran benefits.

Geoff Davis (R-KY) commonly introduced his opinions on VA and veterans' matters by starting with, "As a former Army Ranger" or "As a West Point graduate." He also pointed to the veterans in his community, noting that Kentucky is home to 344,000 veterans. After discussing a policy issue, Davis typically closes with a reminder that veterans put their lives on the line to defend our nation, followed by an expression of appreciation. Davis does not have a specific sort of policy-focused theme to his communications, but he did often express his gratitude for the sacrifices veterans and their families face and encouraged his constituents to do the same.

Tied with Davis, veteran representative Rodney Frelinghuysen (R-NJ) rounds out the topmost veteran-focused veteran legislators with 17 communications per year that mention veterans. Frelinghuysen was born into a politically prominent family, his father, great-grandfather, great-great-grandfather, and great-great-great-grandfather all served in office in New Jersey.[33] Frelinghuysen was poised to enter politics as he matured but was drafted to serve in Vietnam. Once returned to New Jersey, he began his career in local politics and worked his way through state and eventually to federal office. Frelinghuysen had two ways he most often communicated about veterans. His first focus was on VA health care and the ways the system could be reformed to make efficiency gains. His second focus was more local, talking about veterans fairs in the district, encouraging school children to write valentines for veterans, and making sure citizens know about celebrations and events on Veterans Day.

Collectively, these top five lists are insightful in a way that intimates some of the previously overlooked partisan dynamics of the modern Congresses. All but one of the members of Congress who top the list of offering veterans' legislation is from the Democratic Party. If the list is expanded from the top 5 to the top 10, 7 of 10 are Democrats. In fact, if you compare the mean number of veterans' legislation proposed per year by veterans in Congress, Democrat veterans average 0.94 to the Republican average of 0.67. That is, while there are more Republican veterans in Congress, it is the Democratic veterans in Congress who are responsible for proposing much of the legislation specifically for veterans. When looking at which sorts of military veterans in Congress talk the most about veterans in constituent communication a very different picture emerges. All of the top veterans-focused members via communications in Congress are Republicans.

Why Are There Fewer Veterans in Congress Now?

There are various reasons explaining the decline of veterans in Congress ranging from a smaller numbers of veterans to different sorts of people entering the military to the decreasing prestige of election seeking. While not central to the thesis of this book, a look at why veterans themselves occupy fewer congressional positions is likely part of the reason why political parties have been more successful in posturing as agents for veterans' political goals.

Most veterans in contemporary Congresses do not come directly from military service into the federal government. Instead the majority seek lower level elective office prior to launching a House or Senate campaign. All but 2 of the 164 major party veteran candidates in the 2014 congressional elections had held some form of public office previously.[34]

Connections among Veteran Populations, Legislators, and Groups 39

Share of Veterans in the Population

There are fewer veterans as a percentage of the population now than there were after the major wars and military engagements of the 20th century. According to the VA, after World War I the United States had a population of over 4 million veterans, accounting for nearly 4 percent of the total U.S. population at the time. World War II led to 15.7 million new veterans and resulted in a higher share of veterans in the U.S. population at a little over 8 percent. The Korean and Vietnam War added 3.8 million and 8.7 million veterans, respectively. Before operations were completed in Korea, the U.S. veteran population swelled to the highest percentage ever at 13.8 percent in 1970.[35]

While the Gulf Wars of the 1990s and the Global War on Terror initiated after the 2001 attacks on the World Trade Center in New York City added more veterans to the ranks of the U.S. population, the overall share of veterans declined to 7 percent in 2010. Given this general decline in population share, a decline in congressional service of veterans is not an unreasonable result.

But an explanation that simply looks at the declining veterans' population is obviously insufficient in that the rates of decline in the general population do not at all occur at similar rates to what is observed in the Congress. While declining overall numbers may be part of the reason there are fewer veterans in Congress today, this cannot be the only reason.

Time Out of District

One reason veterans face steeper hurdles than business people or party activists seeking to launch a congressional campaign is that service interferes with cultivating an in-district presence. When deployed, service members have a more difficult time getting to know the important actors in seeking ballot access and monetary support. In addition to the practical concern of not being as well acquainted with important persons in local politics, veterans are not as well attuned to the needs of their communities if they spend significant amounts of time outside of those communities while in service. There are groups that I detail later that seek to bridge those gaps for veterans, but it is undeniable that time spent outside of a district can work against someone seeking to represent that district on a national level.

Career Political Competition

As local and state politics increasingly become a pathway to national politics, people who start political careers earlier in life may have advantages over veterans in experience and time inside the civil side of government. Career politicians are able to strategically plan their entrance into certain races and do not face the sort of uncertain timeline disruptions that characterize life as an armed service member.[36] This sort of crowding of the field is relatively new but may yet wane, as the public seems to have an appetite for political amateurs for some high-profile federal roles.

Social and Economic Status

Another explanation for why we may see fewer veterans in office is the changing demographic makeup of the various armed services. The all-volunteer army of the 21st century pulls from fewer sorts of people who have the requisite connections and histories to be better able to conduct a legislative campaign after service than the variety of men drafted to serve in the efforts of the 20th century.[37] Mounting a successful run for Congress costs large sums of money and requires connections to and familiarity with the political systems and pipelines that funnel people into elected office. When the United States had a draft system of army recruitment, men from families and backgrounds that would more easily be able to run for Congress were among those serving in the military. Representative Rodney Frelinghuysen is an example of a person who otherwise would likely have launched a political career but was drafted before that happened. While somewhat simplistic, the explanation aligns with conventional wisdom that posits that people who decide to join the army have few other economic or education opportunities available. Yet it is important to note that analyses of army recruits and officers compared to the general population show that there are fewer differences than most suppose.[38]

What Is the Value of Having Veterans in Congress?

One of the best elements of having veterans serve in public office is the invaluable perspective of having policy makers who have "been there themselves" when formulating military and veterans' policy.[39] Battle experience is impossible to truly recreate for civilians, and thus, veterans offer viewpoints that only they have access to. After military service, veterans have direct personal experiences with the Veterans Administrations' programs for education and health. Having used veteran benefits before, veterans are more intimately aware of the challenges within such systems. Of course, direct personal experience of an issue is not the only qualification for understanding or attempting to solve a problem, but it does undoubtedly provide a different perspective.

Senator Daniel Inouye (D-HI), a veteran, was one of only 23 members of Congress who voted against sending troops to Iraq in 2003. Reflecting on that decision once President Obama determined to bring troop levels down,

Inouye had this to say about being a veteran and making decisions to commit troops to engagement zones,

> Having seen the costs of war firsthand, I am always very cautious when deciding to send our men and women into combat. As a veteran of World War II, I believe I can feel some of the anguish felt by the troops, the veterans and their families.[40]

He uses his status both as a unique justification for his decision and as an experience that informs his process of decision making. This is his perspective.

Veterans have unique histories of service in that they do not always select their coworkers, but they are tasked with making major decisions with different sorts of people. This is not unlike Congress. Furthermore, this history provides veterans with cooperative skills that might not be afforded to members of Congress who come from other industry backgrounds. Because of this background, veterans may be more apt to show bipartisanship and a willingness to find compromise solutions that work for everyone. Two veterans and former senators, one Republican and one Democrat, even formed an organization, With Honor, because of their strong belief and experience in seeing how veterans bring their diverse backgrounds together and compromise to form good policy.[41]

Confidence in Government

As fewer and fewer Americans express trust in government institutions, trust in veterans has remained relatively high. In 1958, when asked if they trusted the federal government to do what is right, over 70 percent of the U.S. public said the government did what was right just about always or most of the time.[42] By 2015, fewer than 20 percent said the same.[43] While we have not asked a similar question about trust in veterans, questions about how much the public trusts the military routinely result in over 70 percent positive assessments across history.[44] While confidence in other government institutions, banks, international businesses, and religious organizations has fallen in recent years, the military and those who serve remain popular. A Congress that can boast of more veterans may be more likely to inspire trust in government than one made of professionals coming from other fields suffering from trust deficits.

In the most recent Congresses some have noted that more members of each new, incoming class are veterans than in preceding Congresses.[45] This trend, if continued, could slowly inch overall numbers of veterans upward if it overcomes the amount of retiring veteran members.

Veterans' Electoral and Pressure Groups

The political landscape of veterans is not simply made of veterans in the population and veterans in Congress. Like all other interests, there are political groups that act as power brokers, lobbying arms, and candidate recruitment shops to serve the needs and wants of specific constituencies. In the United States there is no one, unified veterans' lobby or group, but rather a set of organizations, each claiming to represent veterans' interests.

While there are fewer veterans serving in Congress than there have been at most other times in our history, there is no shortage of veterans' groups that seek to influence policy by mentoring would-be candidates and lobbying sitting members. In this final section I provide descriptions and data on the largest and most active veterans' groups. It is not as straightforward to perform comparable statistical analyses as it is with populations and legislators, but there is important measurable information that provides insight into the scope and activities of the most prominent groups operating today. For each group I provide information on the year the group was founded, their reported membership, a count of their followers on Twitter, the amount of money spent on national political campaigns from 2010 to 2016, the amount of money spent on lobbying from 2010 to 2016, the stated goals of the group, and a list of their accomplishments and strategies to influence politics from 2010 onward.

The longevity of a group's existence is indicative of institutional success. Groups that can effectively enlist supporters from election to election over a long history must offer some value to their members in the form of extracting governmental policy benefits or electoral goal, lest they would fold. Reported membership is an indicator of influence and is a number pressure groups seek to increase to make their lobbying demands on elected officials more pressing. I report the number of Twitter followers to give an indication of wider public interest. Twitter followers are not numbers reported by individual groups but rather serve as a more comparable way to assess the outreach and social media efforts of competing groups. For the data on political contributions and lobbying dollars, I used the FEC listings compiled and maintained by the Center for Responsive Politics. While obviously not comprehensive, I provide examples of the important political changes each veteran's group lays claim to in the 111th–114th Congresses.

Not all of these groups are the same type of interest groups. There are differences between veterans' lobbying groups and groups that seek to recruit, train, and elect veterans into office. Traditional veterans' lobbying groups such as the Veterans of Foreign Wars (VFW) are predominantly concerned with lobbying members once in Congress rather than trying to get specific members elected in the first place. Some are nonprofit service organizations such as the Disabled American Veterans (DAV), Iraq and Afghanistan Veterans of America (IAVA), some are congressionally chartered corporations to act as a link between veterans and government services like the American Legion, and American Veterans (AMVETS), and others are exclusively political action committees (VoteVets). Some are nonprofits that also run political action committees such as the VFW. By and large the older organizations spend less directly on supporting certain members over others, but the newer organizations have explicit election-minded goals.

While the heyday of veterans in Congress may have passed, an influx of post–9/11 veterans aided by election-minded groups such as VoteVets founded in 2006 and Veterans Campaign in 2009 have worked to reverse the trend of fewer veterans participating in government. The differences between the operations of these groups are sometimes wide, but the similarity of working on behalf of veterans exists in each.

Veterans of Foreign Wars (VFW)

Founded: 1899

Reported Membership: 1.7 million

Number of Twitter Followers: 60,000

Money Spent on Congressional Campaigns 2010–2016: $0

Money Spent on Lobbying 2010–2016: $175,000

Stated Goals

To foster camaraderie among U.S. veterans of overseas conflicts. To serve our veterans, the military, and our communities. To advocate on behalf of all veterans. The motto of the group is, "No one does more for veterans."

Their vision: Ensure that veterans are respected for their service, always receive their earned entitlements, and are recognized for the sacrifices they and their loved ones have made on behalf of this great country.[46]

Notable Political Accomplishments

In terms of political ideology, the VFW claims to represent "every generation, race, religion, gender, and political and ideological viewpoint."[47] Their recent legislative accomplishments also span across the partisan aisle of Congress. The VFW has achieved numerous political victories for over a century and continues to lobby members of Congress today.[48]

Since 2010 they have successfully advocated for the passage of legislation such as the VOW to Hire Heroes Act of 2011 prioritizing active-duty and recent veterans for positions within the federal government and

Honoring America's Veterans and Caring for Camp Lejeune Families Act of 2012 to provide benefits for veteran caretakers and extend eligibility.[49] They also worked for the Stolen Valor Act of 2013, a bill to supersede a Supreme Court decision allowing people to publicly lie about military service, the Veterans Access, Choice, and Accountability Act of 2014 to fund and reform some practices within the VA, and the Clay Hunt Suicide Prevention for American Veterans (SAV) Act to increase veteran access to mental health services.[50]

American Legion

Founded: 1919
Reported Membership: 2.4 million
Number of Twitter Followers: 87,700
Money Spent on Congressional Campaigns 2010–2016: $0
Money Spent on Lobbying 2010–2016: $93,000

Stated Goals

The Four Pillars of the American Legion are Veterans' Affairs & Rehabilitation, National Security, Americanism, and Children & Youth.[51]

Notable Political Accomplishments

The American Legion prioritizes lobbying efforts for funding of VA health care, access to facilities, fair rulings on benefit claims, and economic opportunities for veterans. The post–9/11 Veterans Educational Assistance Act signed under Bush and implemented under Obama was one of their greatest recent victories. The American Legion was pivotal in forming earlier iterations of the GI Bill and takes pride in the most recent version.[52]

The Legion has a hand in many legislative activities, but during the Obama era, the role of the American Legion was less focused on legislative creation but rather on VA criticism. In the face of scandalous VA wait times, the group called for the resignation of VA secretary Eric Shinseki, and he eventually did leave his post.

Today the American Legion runs community programs and activities intended to foster patriotism and aid to military families. In order to incentivize members of Congress to push legislative reforms for veterans, the group awards certain distinctions such as the American Legion national commander's Distinguished Public Service Award on members. Members can then in turn tell their constituents about the award to indicate broader veterans' support.[53] The organization does not make specific efforts to fund certain congressional candidates over any others, but individual Legionnaires can and do donate to congressional campaigns.

Disabled American Veterans (DAV)

Founded: 1920
Reported Membership: 1.3 million
Number of Twitter Followers: 92,600
Money Spent on Congressional Campaigns 2010–2016: $0
Money Spent on Lobbying 2010–2016: $2,765,000

Stated Goals

Their motto is, "Fulfilling Our Promises to the Men and Women Who Served." As a part of that effort, DAV is a nonprofit that seeks to help veterans obtain benefits they may otherwise not know about, hosts job fairs and career training programs, and provides transportation services for veterans to get from their homes to medical care sites. In addition, DAV runs community programs like medical device donations and refurbishing and then matches those devices free of charge to veterans in need.

One major end of the DAV is navigating the bureaucracy of benefits' accessibility for veterans. They can provide these services free of cost, and over a million veterans make use of their administrative services and assistance each year.[54] Some members of Congress will have informal Veterans Advisory Board that they meet with in order to discuss policy areas of concern to the veteran population—on boards such as these, a representative of DAV will be present.

Notable Political Accomplishments

Within Congress, DAV plays a role by expressing support for certain bills or resolutions. Members of Congress will then advertise when they are on the same side of an issue with the DAV. In the most recent Congresses, DAV was able to successfully lobby for language to be included in omnibus bills in order to expand access to the VA's comprehensive caregiver program, make improvements in services such as maternity care and mental health services for veterans, and halt the practice of rounding down on various estimating procedures for veterans' benefits.

American Veterans (AMVETS)

Founded: 1944
Reported Membership: 250,000

Number of Twitter Followers: 1,324

Money Spent on Congressional Campaigns 2010–2016: $1,500

Money Spent on Lobbying 2010–2016: $952,500

Stated Goals

American Veterans or AMVETS is a congressionally chartered organization like the American Legion, and in some ways they provide similar sorts of supports and linkages. The mission of AMVETS is to enhance and safeguard the entitlements for all American Veterans who have served honorably and to improve the quality of life for them, their families, and the communities where they live through leadership, advocacy and services.[55]

AMVETS has a fleet of 74,000 national service officers who are tasked with aiding veterans in filing and processing claims to obtain benefits. They have auxiliary functions to support veterans in community hospitals and homebound veterans in need of occasional companionship and cheer.

Notable Political Accomplishments

AMVETS has explicit legislative priorities that respond to the political exigencies of certain times. Currently their priorities are mental health and suicide prevention, toxic exposure wounds, service dogs and assistive technology, and complementary and alternative medicine.[56] The group lent its support and voice to the 2014 appropriations bill to authorize money to military construction and the VA and took stances to oppose smaller style piecemeal funding measures offered by congressional Republicans during the Obama era.

Vietnam Veterans of America (VVA)

Founded: 1979

Reported Membership: 75,000

Number of Twitter Followers: 4,244

Money Spent on Congressional Campaigns 2010–2016: $1,920

Money Spent on Lobbying 2010–2016: 1,440,000

Stated Goals

This group is expressly for veterans who served on tours of active duty between 1961 and 1975. By imposing this service limitation, VVA attempts to ensure a continuity of experience throughout its community of members.

Notable Political Accomplishments

This group is election focused. Their online portals have systems for identifying political candidates, current representatives, issues and legislation of concern to veterans, as well as media coverage. While they spent lobbying dollars during the time period under study, they did not have any specific legislation that they claim to have been pivotal in supporting. The group is opposed to efforts to privatize veterans' health care; in that way they are successful in stopping rather than supporting legislation.

Iraq and Afghanistan Veterans of America (IAVA)

Founded: 2004
Reported Membership: 400,000
Number of Twitter Followers: 59,500
Money Spent on Congressional Campaigns 2010–2016: $0
Money Spent on Lobbying 2010–2016: $1,450,000

Stated Goals

The core mission of IAVA is, "Focus on ensuring veterans and their families are supported, protected, empowered and never forgotten." Programmatically the group is interested in lobbying for better access to quality care for veterans.

Notable Political Accomplishments

Like the VFW, in the 112th Congress IAVA successfully urged members of Congress to pass the VOW to Hire Heroes Act to assist returning service members in seeking employment. They also successfully lobbied for the Clay Hunt Suicide Prevention for American Veterans (SAV) Act. In the 114th Congress the group, along with the DAV, came together to support the passage of legislation introduced by Senator Barbara Boxer (D-CA), the Female Veteran Suicide Prevention Act to study and identify VA mental health programs that are most effective in preventing suicide among women veterans.

VoteVets

Founded: 2006
Reported Membership: over 500,000

Number of Twitter Followers: 91,100

Money Spent on Congressional Campaigns 2010–2016: $374,118

Money Spent on Lobbying 2010–2016: $0

Stated Goals

To elect veterans to public office; hold public officials accountable for their words and actions that impact America's 21st-century service members, veterans, and their families; and fully support our men and women in uniform.

Notable Political Accomplishments

As a group interested in electing veterans to Congress, VoteVets can credibly boast of meeting their goals with every successful election they wage. They focus on state and federal elections and to date have elected over 12 members to Congress. With each cycle they spend hundreds of thousands of dollars on direct candidate donations as well as independent communication and campaign efforts stressing the importance of electing veterans. They support both Democrats and Republicans and are very clear that their interests are not partisan but rather to infuse a veteran perspective. Yet, there is a progressive element to their independent support efforts. They argue that political issues of the day such as opening military service to lifelong Americans born to undocumented immigrants is something that demands a viewpoint that supports leftist ends and they are happy to play that role.

American Women Veterans (AWV)

Founded: 2008

Reported Membership: Not Reported

Number of Twitter Followers: 43,800

Money Spent on Congressional Campaigns 2010–2016: $0

Money Spent on Lobbying 2010–2016: $0

Stated Goals

AWV is dedicated to preserving and promoting the legacy of servicewomen, veterans, and their families. They welcome veterans and supporters from all eras and branches of service. Their programmatic goals are to advocate for policies that support women veterans, sponsor retreats and conferences focused on women veterans, conduct outreach campaigns, promote positive public images of servicewomen, commit to ongoing community service, and cultivate leadership among their ranks.

Notable Political Accomplishments

In contrast to other veterans' organizations, AWV is primarily run by volunteers, and their efforts are therefore less robust than more professionally organized efforts. Their aims are not as expressly political as other groups and instead are geared toward connecting women veterans with other women veterans to create supportive extended networks. Agreeing to interviews and writing articles for other outlets on the topics of interest to women service members meet the goals of outreach and awareness. AWV also attempts to influence members of Congress by keeping up with e-mail, Facebook, and Twitter campaigns when legislation of interest is under consideration.

Veterans Campaign

Founded: 2009
Reported Membership:
Number of Twitter Followers: 3,857
Money Spent on Congressional Campaigns 2010–2016: $0
Money Spent on Lobbying 2010–2016: $0

Stated Goals

Veterans Campaign is concerned with readying veterans for the possibility of running for public office. The group considers itself an educational nonprofit focused on teaching veterans and transitioning service members toward civic and political leadership.[57] They host precampaign workshops and ongoing support through the life cycle of a campaign for veterans seeking office. The organization prides itself on providing "non-partisan instruction with bi-partisan perspectives" to enhance the appeal of office-seeking veterans as well as the goal of filling elected positions with active-minded candidates rather than simply partisan loyalists.

Notable Political Accomplishments

Modeled after the Rutgers University program Ready to Run that trains women to run for office, former Marine Corps captain Seth Lynn started Veterans Campaign with his former commanding officer, Michael Hunzeker.

The group was originally a student group on the campus of Princeton University, but given strong institutional support and a network of former members of Congress, this group was able to hold their first workshop for veterans interested in public office in September 2009.

There are other groups than those listed here, but this listing represents most active and most accomplished set of political action groups working in the veterans' political space.[58] The importance of these groups is somewhat hard to comparatively quantify because of the diffusion of interests. There is no one "veterans' lobby." This diversity also makes using measures such as campaign donations problematic. In the first place, compared to other sorts of interests, veterans' groups donate relatively little in the way of monetary contributions to federal candidates. Second, the goals of each group are sometimes out of alignment, so there is not a clear theoretical link between donations and outcomes. Thus, I detail the major groups here as a way to make clear that there are actors at play that coordinate efforts beyond the opinions on individual, but in the later chapters the actions of these groups and their efforts are not quantified in ways that I treat other explanatory variables. As such, what precedes provides the details and most notable accomplishments of these groups as a way of sketching a more complete picture of the veterans' policy and political landscape.

Despite a low level of investing in electoral politics, veteran pressure groups have been some of the most successful groups by extracting government benefits via lobbying influence within the legislative and executive branches. From the creation of the Veterans Bureau to the expansion of the VA hospital system to the various GI bills to assisting political campaigns to even intervening on behalf of specific veteran family requests, organized veterans' groups are an integral part of veterans' politics in the United States.

Conclusion

Veterans make up about 7 percent of the U.S. population, and in some congressional districts, they account for nearly 20 percent of all eligible voters. This chapter showed that districts with more veterans are slightly more likely to have veteran representatives in Congress, but political preferences of a district are also important. Considering other characteristics of elected representatives, constituencies with lower and higher shares of veterans support both Democrats and Republicans and men and women for political office.

There are fewer veterans in office than at any other time in history, and of those who held seats in the 111th–114th Congresses, more were associated with the Republican Party. Despite the low numbers of elected officials, veterans' groups are numerous in number and focus, yet all seem to agree that having a veteran in Congress is a benefit to veteran communities as well as the nation generally.

Central to the arguments and theory I put forward in the second and third part of the book, I report that military veterans in Congress behave differently in ways that relate to party identification. Of military veterans who serve in Congress, this chapter provided evidence that Democratic veterans tend to introduce more veterans' legislation than Republican veterans, but Republican veterans more often mention veterans in their constituent communications.

CHAPTER THREE

Public Opinion: Veterans Policy and Veterans' Preferences

Veterans hold a special position in the constellation of U.S. politics. Party politics research describes issues that each political party can be said to "own." Parties own issues that they tend to prioritize and that their voters care about. Owning an issue is not merely attributed to performance on a given issue by one party or the other; the public narrative linking an issue to a party is also important. Among other issues, Democrats own social welfare, whereas Republicans own defense. Veterans' politics straddles these realms.[1] Legislators from both parties revere veterans in their official statements. Citizens of all stripes indicate broad support for funding veterans' initiatives, and over 90 percent of civilians report that they feel proud of soldiers serving in the military.[2] While many areas of contemporary politics are clearly split on party lines, both Democrats and Republicans agree that veterans ought to have access to some benefits that others do not. While public approval of Congress as a whole continues to break new record lows, the congressional committees responsible for formulating the bulk of veterans' policies are considered to be some of the most functioning within Congress and thus represent a hopeful point of study for the functions of democracy.[3] Yet, despite general agreement, there remain differences between the parties and ideological tensions that become more apparent with a closer look at how veterans' policies are created and adopted.

In the issue ownership literature, scholars look to survey research on questions posed in the form of, "Which political party, the Democrats or the

Republicans, do you trust to do a better job handling [insert issue area]?" where the issue area may be tax policy, environmental regulation, gun polices, and so on. Or variants that ask respondents which party will be able to better deal with an issue or which party would be more likely to do what the respondent wants. This sort of inquiry started in the 1970s when multiple surveys began to routinely ask these sorts of questions.[4] While we know a lot about which policy areas the public trusts the Republican or Democratic Party on, there have not been any explicit studies asking about the ownership of veterans' policy.

Ideologically, the Republican Party espouses ideals of small government, low government spending, and the self-reliance of individuals. But for veterans, these ideals are somewhat relaxed with arguments in favor of lifelong health, education, and financial support for returning veterans. Democrats tend to hold values that stress diplomacy over military might, more government spending and interjection into parts of the economy, as well as a commitment to helping individuals, including veterans, when they cannot find a way to help themselves. Veterans and veterans' policies sit at an ideological intersection between Republican and Democratic approaches.

Unlike the policy areas that scholars have used to establish literatures around partisan issue ownership, we do not have good public opinion data on which party the general population trusts to do better for veterans. Is there anything in the public opinion data that supports this supposed link between the GOP and veterans? Is this link something that comes from individuals, or do party operatives play a greater role in cultivating images of association with veterans? The link between the Republican Party and veterans may not have been established using standard social science practices, but there have been other approaches and the broader media narrative and popular culture speak to the connection.

In the late 1990s Bacevich and Kohn, two professors, one of whom is a Vietnam veteran, authored a piece in the *New Republic* that argued service members ought to stop voting because the military had grown to be a wing of the Republican Party.[5] Other research at the time indicated that there were partisan splits emergent within the armed forces, though with less forceful arguments about to curtail such partisan permeation.[6]

Shortly after the *New Republic* piece, the Triangle Institute for Security Studies released a report that captured both academic and media attention with the claim that military officers "have largely abandoned political neutrality and have become partisan Republicans."[7] General media outlets like the *New York Times* began to disseminate this story with headlines reading, "Sharp Divergence Is Found in Views of Military and Civilians," and described to the public how military service members preferred the Republican Party far more than civilians did.[8] The flurry of coverage in the 1990s focused predominantly on active military preferences rather than those of veterans.

In the 2000s links between parties and veterans somewhat quieted down after the attacks of 9/11 as the country rallied around President Bush and grappled with questions of committing to greater military activity around the globe. In 2001, Gallup conducted a poll and reported that veterans were slightly more conservative than the general public and more willing to identify as Republicans (34% v. 29%) than as Democrats (30% v. 33%) when compared to the general public. Yet, the editorial tone of the report indicated that veterans were quite similar to others other than the fact that they are held in higher public confidence than many other groups and that the events of 9/11 probably contributed to that assessment.[9]

In 2004, when military veteran John Kerry ran against President George W. Bush, the political lines of veteran support were drawn with an anti-Kerry ad aired by a group called the Swift Boat Veterans for Truth. This ad alleged that Kerry exaggerated his service in Vietnam and questioned his fitness for President. Even the famous military veteran, and former presidential candidate, Senator Bob Dole weighted in against Kerry and told him he and the Democratic Party owed veterans an apology for attempting to point to Kerry's military service as a reason to vote for him for president.[10] This ad marked a turning point in the campaign and communications scholars argued the broader frames used in the appeal were powerful and had a significant chance of changing the way people associated partisans and veterans in the future.[11]

In 2008, when military veteran Senator John McCain ran against Senator Barack Obama, veterans solidly supported McCain (56% v. 34%) further connecting the GOP to veteran voters.[12] Yet, McCain stumbled toward the end of his campaign and even went so far as to speak out against the popular, Democrat-authored, Post–9/11 GI Bill that would pass just before President Bush left office.[13]

Despite the Obama win, and the implementation of the Post–9/11 GI Bill, the Democratic Party did not make up much ground in the fight for veteran approval from 2008 to 2016. In many ways the members of the Republican Party in Congress and the campaign trial learned the lessons of the failed Kerry and McCain candidacies. It is wise to bill yourself as an advocate for veterans, the public has little ability or willingness to decipher deeper truths around veterans' issues, and coming out against veterans' policies is bad politics. It seems that in only two decades or so a constituency that was defined as being somewhat apolitical has transformed into one that is aligned with one party over another.

As the Obama presidency wound down, stories about veteran allegiances to political parties began to appear again. For instance, in 2014 a *Salon* article argued that the media and the public tend to pay close attention to acts of respect toward veterans performed by Republicans but do not as closely cover the acts of legislating that implicate Republicans as acting counter to veteran interests.[14] In the run-up to the 2016 Presidential election, some media outlets also kept with a somewhat questioning tone in headlines asking, "Why Do Veterans Support Donald Trump?"[15] Yet, these doubts and questions around why veterans continued to support Republican political candidates largely went unanswered. In the pages that follow, I show that in the contemporary period, veterans continue to identify as and prefer candidates from the Republican Party.

Before delving into how the most recent Congresses have approached veterans' policy, it is helpful to examine extant data on what the public *thinks* about the policy domain. In this chapter I present data bearing on the public's perception of veterans and how the government ought to provide for veterans. I then turn to the opinions of veterans themselves on issues of partisanship, policy preferences and assessment, and electoral choices. When the data permit, I offer direct comparisons between the veterans' population and the general population. After reviewing various indicators about general population and veteran population outlooks on veterans' policy, I conclude by laying the groundwork for a broader theory of how the parties navigate these ideological tensions in a way that corresponds with the findings on public opinions of veterans and the general population.

Public Opinion on Veterans and Government—Limitations

Public opinion data on veterans, opinions of government policy toward veterans, and opinions of veterans themselves are scanter than one might think. Despite a prioritized place in legislator-to-constituent communications, polling houses, private survey firms, and academic surveys very rarely focus exclusively on veterans' political issues. Because the veteran population is somewhat small, veterans are hardly ever polled in numbers great enough to make compelling inferences based on their limited presence in nondirectly targeted public opinion surveys. The VA does a good deal of polling, but because of the restrictions on what sorts of questions the government agency can ask, VA polls do not attempt to ascertain the political leanings or policy preferences of veterans.

There are three general sorts of gaps in public opinion data on veterans. First, there is a lack of focus on veterans' issues. Second, very few polls field their questions on a representative sample of veterans. Third, there is longitudinal variation in what questions are asked on how specific questions are worded. Each of these limitations means that public opinion work on veterans and veterans' issues is idiosyncratic and harder to make general claims from. With an understanding of the limitations of this sort of data, this chapter sets out to weave a comprehensive look at the status of political opinion toward veterans and veterans' policies as well as veterans' opinions on political issues.

Limitation 1: Nonspecific Focus

Public opinion surveys exclusively focused on veterans and veterans' issues are rare.[16] Of the over 650,000 public opinion survey questions maintained by the Cornell Roper Center dataverse, only 330 mention the word "veteran" at the time of writing. Of those, 70 percent use demographic questions establishing if a survey respondent or a member of the household is a veteran and/or if the survey respondent gets government assistance in some form from the Veterans Administration.[17] By the survey standards upheld as scientifically rigorous and nationally representative, there are only about 100 questions that describe public opinion on veterans and veterans' politics from the 1930s until today.[18]

Exclusive Focus Exceptions

In 1979, there was a survey expressly about veterans conducted by Louis Harris and Associates for the VA.[19] The sample was nationally representative and consisted of 2,563 personal interviews fielded from November 17 to December 19, 1979. This was a general population survey in which respondents were asked what they thought about veterans in terms of their character, proclivities for vices, and projected life outcomes. Most of the questions asked respondents to consider veterans versus "average young person who didn't happen to serve" during the deployment of veterans.

In 2012, this survey effort was nearly duplicated by the Mission Continues, a nonprofit organization with an aim to aid veterans in their transition to civilian life.[20] This survey was also nationally representative but was conducted via telephone on a smaller pool of 801 respondents. I use both of these surveys in the subsequent section looking at public opinion on veterans to make overtime comparisons.

Limitation 2: Sampling of Veterans

Veterans are a small proportion of the public, accounting for 7 percent of the U.S. population. As such, many surveys do not use a question to establish whether or not respondents are veterans, and for those that do, the resulting numbers of veterans are too small to do any meaningful analysis. For many lines of inquiry, researchers believe the veteran status of a respondent is not important for their measures of interest. Even the best political academic work on veterans' public opinion generally uses proxy measures of their opinions rather than survey research.[21]

This presents a few difficulties. First, we oftentimes do not know if people are veterans or not in many general surveys. Second, even when we do know the veteran status of a respondent in a nationally representative survey, their combined sample sizes are sufficiently small so that interpreting results of the subsample of veterans alone is an inappropriate indicator of veterans' opinions generally. Lastly, self-identifying as a veteran is somewhat complicated. Some people who served in a capacity that would legally afford them the entitlements afforded to veterans do not identify as veterans when asked. This happens when people see divisions between combat status, if an individual was discharged in a less than honorable way, or if someone simply does not consider their veteran status as an identifier. Any interpretations of these data should acknowledge these difficulties.

The VA itself conducts lots of surveys of veterans in order to assess the accessibility and effectiveness of different VA health, education, and business programs. Yet, these surveys sometimes do not represent scientific public opinion polling because of their sampling methodologies, question formation/style, as well as content limitations. These sorts of VA-conducted surveys are not so much geared toward measuring the greater opinions of veterans but rather to identify the needs and pressures veterans face. Additionally, none of the VA-conducted surveys may ask for the partisan identification or leanings of respondents, so their utility for addressing questions of the sort that I pursue here is limited.

However, there are a few surveys that use veterans as the sampling focus and ask opinion questions that can inform our understandings of how veterans perceive issues of public policy. Gallup conducted the earliest poll of this sort in 1946.[22] This survey was meant to be nationally representative but with a large, targeted subsample of veterans so that they could ascertain the opinions of veterans as well as the general population. The total veterans sampled made up 28 percent of the 1,500 U.S. adults sampled. In 2014, Gallup conducted another poll with an exclusive sampling frame of veterans.

Another exception is a Pew Research Center for the People & the Press/Pew Social & Demographic Trends poll of veterans and civilians conducted in 2011.[23] This survey was administered to a nationally representative sample of 1,853 military veterans and a nationally representative sample of 2,003 civilian American adults. The results from this survey offer insights into veterans' partisan preferences as well as their assessments of the VA. An additional perk of this survey is that it was conducted in parallel with a national adult general public sample, so there are ways to make clean party identification comparisons across veteran and nonveteran samples using the same questions asked at the same time periods.[24]

Lastly, from August to December 2013, the Washington Post-Kaiser Family Foundation poll surveyed a nationally representative sample of the U.S. veteran population, whereas the Washington Post/ABC News poll surveyed a representative sample of the whole U.S. population.[25] I use these exclusively focused surveys when discussing veterans' partisanship and political preferences in this chapter.

Limitation 3: Longitudinal Variation

Questions about veterans and veterans' policies reflect the times in which they are conducted. This limits the ability to track shifts in opinion overtime in a consistent way. Whenever possible I try to link questions across time in the most reasonable way, but it is often the case that specific questions are not identically repeated.

In the introduction to this book, I alluded to public sentiment holding that the Republican Party best serves veterans. This sense is born out in pop culture and in countless newspaper articles and online blog postings, but most public opinion surveys available do not address this question head on. Questions linking political parties to veterans' interest in public opinion surveys are few. To that end, when veterans themselves have opportunities to indicate a preference for one party over the other, I include it in my analyses.

Acknowledging these caveats, I now examine the actual public opinion data that we have about veterans and from veterans. The organization of the section that follows first considers historical public opinion on veterans. I use opinions about veterans' politics and present the best data we have from the 1940s through today. I then use a set of surveys that bridges historical settings to more contemporary understandings using similar questions about veterans. After that I look at the opinions of veterans themselves and make use of the surveys that ask veterans for their opinions on policies, leaders, and political parties. I conclude with a top-level look at the breadth of data here and attempt to summarize the opinions of both the general public and veterans on their perceptions of veterans, veterans' policies, and the political parties best positioned to serve the interest of veterans.

Historical Public Opinion

Veterans are generally held in high regard today, but that was not always the case. Before the era of national scientific public opinion polls starting in the 1940s, there were scholars and journalists who covered veterans and asked the public their opinions of soldiers returning from war. These accounts provide the best available historical record of public sentiment toward veterans.

With the population of veterans set to increase after World War I, communities and different levels of government had to determine how to return deployed soldiers into civilian life. Young men who had seen the ravages of war had often come of age in situations where women and alcohol were more licentiously available than in civilian populations in the United States. This caused some to worry what reintegration might mean for such men and the communities they choose to settle in. When considering how to formulate returning programs for servicemen, the War Department conducted a study and reported that the public was worried that if there were not meaningful government efforts at postwar rehabilitation, the streets might be filled with undesirable armies of "war cripples" that would beg and menace the civilian population as well as give rise to underground economies and behavior at odds with idealized polite society.[26] This is a far cry from the discourse about veterans we hear today but was of use in the development of veterans' care facilities.

As the provision of veterans' care became a more routine responsibility of the state, some segments of the population feared the introduction of a culture of welfare dependency among veterans.[27] The contrast of depending on the government for educational, medical, or financial care and the notion that economic independence was a marker of good citizenry and an era-specific sense of "manliness" put veterans in a quandary as the recipients of government assistance. That is, while public sentiment expressed admiration for the courage of those who served, there was unease about providing veterans with support systems because it cut against the very things that supposedly led soldiers to bravely serve in the first place.

These historical norms and concerns are present in the sorts of questions asked by pollsters starting in the 1940s. When considering the measurement of public opinion, a word of caution is in order. Like with any endeavor to accurately characterize the opinions and feelings of a large group of people like the population of the United States, public opinion polls are blunt instruments. But they are nonetheless instruments and do offer insights into general trends and relative opinions across time. In the next section, I offer a comprehensive analysis of all the extant, standardized polling data that we have from 1942 until the current day on the perceptions of veterans and veterans' politics.

Bridging Historical and Contemporary Comparisons

Opinions on veterans and veterans' policies are distinct, and the questions used to ascertain public opinion on the two are different. In this section I first consider opinions on veterans themselves, as we have more precisely comparable questions to pull from. Following this, I combine a variety of questions on veterans' policy to generate a historical running tally of U.S. public opinion on the topic.

Public Opinions on Veterans over Time

Two surveys were administered in the 1970s and the 2010s that explicitly focused on public opinion toward veterans. Before delving into the specifics of those surveys, it is important to note that public opinion on "veterans"

Public Opinion: Veterans Policy and Veterans' Preferences   61

generally must be contextualized by the makeup of veterans in the first place. Large numbers of veterans from the Vietnam Era served as a function of the draft rather than voluntary enlistment. When respondents took the survey in the late 1970s, the images and reality of veterans undoubtedly influenced the internal understandings they held of veterans in a way that is different than what those taking the survey in the early 2010s did. Nonetheless, this is the best possible set of time comparative questions available and thus of use in assessing views on veterans overtime.

While not all of the questions were posed in each survey, there are nine questions that were asked in identical or near-identical forms in both. As a way to infer contextual sentiment about veterans, the changes in questions indicate a difference about what survey *makers* had in mind, in addition to survey *takers'* opinions. Before discussing the nine similar questions, let us look at those questions that appeared in one wave but not the other.

Question Wording: Overtime Changes

In the survey administered in the late 1970s, there were questions about veterans that do not appear in the 2012 version. These 1970s-specific questions asked if respondents thought veterans were different than those that did not serve in terms of being: not willing to keep tradition, too interested in changing things, willing to rebel or protest, being unpatriotic, having lost respect for the family, being selfish and self-centered, being spoiled, expecting things to be given to them, being assertive, and being outspoken. While not all necessarily negative, these sorts of questions were related to the protest activity of that era and do not have a modern counterpart in contemporary polling about veterans.

To those in charge of crafting survey, and likely to other segments of the population, there were perceptions of veterans having some negative characteristics at rates that were different from the general population. That is not to say that survey makers thought veterans were worse than the general population, but that they were interested in finding differences one way or another.[28] The context of the VA contracting a survey house to run this poll in the first place is a useful clue as to what considerations may have grounded the questions. Table 3.1 displays the breakdowns of respondents across the questions asked only in 1979.

As Table 3.1 shows, while survey makers thought it useful to include these sorts of questions, a majority thought these characteristics and behaviors were equally prevalent in veteran and nonveteran populations. Those who did see differences in characteristics indicated that they occurred in nonveteran populations more than veteran population for each trait.

The very fact that some questions were posed in 1979 and not asked in 2012 speaks to the shift in discourse and underlying public opinion about

Table 3.1 Veteran Characteristics and Behaviors Asked in 1979 but Not in 2012

	More Applicable to Veterans (%)	More Applicable to Nonveterans (%)	Equally Applicable to Both (%)
Not Willing to Keep Tradition, Too Interested in Changing Things	13	22	58
Willing to Rebel or Protest	18	27	49
Unpatriotic	9	30	50
Having Lost Respect for the Family	6	18	63
Being Selfish and Self-Centered	5	24	60
Spoiled, Expect Things to Be Given to Them	7	31	54
Assertive, Outspoken	15	17	61

Source: The Veterans Administration, *Attitudes toward Vietnam Era Veterans Survey*, Louis Harris and Associates (Ithaca, NY: Roper Center for Public Opinion Research, iPOLL, Cornell University, 1979).

veterans in the intervening years. Additionally, there were three questions asked in 2012 that did not appear in the 1979 survey. These questions asked if respondents thought veterans were more stressed, more stable, and more likely to have problems with anger or rage.

Like before, the majority of respondents did not think that these characteristics applied more for veterans than for nonveterans, but rather that the prevalence of these characteristics were applicable to both veterans and nonveterans. Of those who did think one group held a characteristic more than the other, veterans were the ones respondents thought have a special claim to being more stressed, more stable, and more likely to have problems with rage or anger.

Comparing Questions from 1979 and 2012

Of the questions about veterans that were asked in both surveys, there are some notable differences in public perception but generally a good deal of

Table 3.2 Veteran Characteristics and Behaviors Asked in 2012 but Not in 1979

	More Applicable to Veterans (%)	More Applicable to Nonveterans (%)	Equally Applicable to Both (%)
Stressed	40	5	52
Stable	22	11	58
Having Problems with Anger or Rage	28	6	59

Source: The Mission Continues, *A New Generation of Leaders: Public Opinion Strategies*, Bad Robot/Greenberg Quinlan Rosner Research (Archived at the Roper Center, 2012).

stability. Each question was asked in a way that respondents had four answer options; a respondent could indicate veterans had a certain characteristic more than the civilian counterparts, civilian counterparts had the characteristic more than veterans, both veterans and civilians had the characteristic at similar rates or in similar amounts, and a nonresponsive "I don't know" option. The specific questions were worded this way,

> Now I'm going to read you the same characteristics, and for each, I'd like you to tell me if today it applies more to the average young veteran who happened to serve anywhere in the Armed Forces during the Vietnam Era, to the average young person who didn't happen to serve during that time, or that it applies equally to both groups?) . . . [Being able to hold a steady job]

Figure 3.1 shows the differences in attributions to veterans across time.[29] Of the identical questions asked in both waves, two are generally negative—those about drug and alcohol abuse while the rest are positive traits about willingness to try to get a job, stay involved in one's community, express an interest in politics, and so on. For each year I show the percentage of respondents who thought a given characteristic was more applicable to veterans or civilians. In each figure the y-axes are rendered on the same scale and the veterans' lines are always in green and the civilian lines are gray.

In 1979, the characteristics that most separated veterans from civilians in public perception were drug use and drinking problems. That is, the areas in which the greatest differences of people willing to say veterans had a characteristic more than veterans had on drug and alcohol dependency.[30] These differences are depicted in the top two frames of Figure 7.1. As you may note, anytime the lines cross to form a "X" that signals a shift in public opinion that one population was believed to have more of a specific trait in 1979, but the other population did in 2012. For drinking and drug use—there were

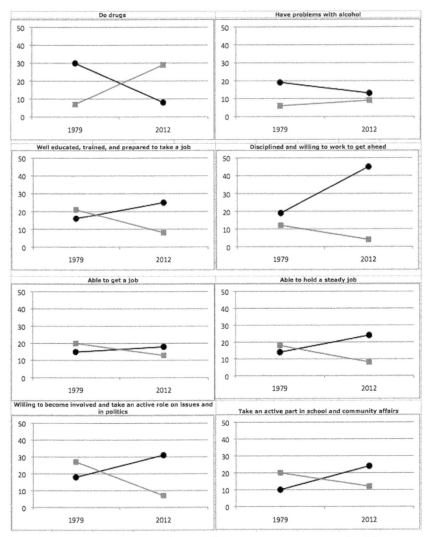

Figure 3.1 Percentages ascribing a characteristic as more applicable to veterans or civilians in 1979 and 2012

reductions in perceptions that veterans had more issues around substance abuse than their similarly suited counterparts when asked in 2012 than in 1979. In terms of drug use, people thought nonveterans were much more likely to use drugs in 2012 with differences of opinions so large as to nearly reverse the assessments in 1979.

In 2012, the greatest gaps in opinions were that veterans were more disciplined and willing to work to get ahead, as well as more likely to take an active role in politics than their civilian counterparts.[31] This speaks to the somewhat new and unique context that veterans hold today. Long gone are the post–World War I and post–World War II assessments of fearsome "war cripples" as well as the post-Vietnam views of veterans as rabble-rousing protestors into an era of esteemed veterans set apart from their counterparts in terms of their willingness to work hard and be involved in their communities.

Veterans have risen in the ranks as compared to civilians for all of the positive traits asked in each survey and are thought to hold the negative characteristics less often than civilians. According to the available survey data, perceptions of veterans truly have changed in public opinion over the past 40 years and their position in politics has changed as well.

A Note on Alcohol Abuse in Veteran Populations

When asked who is more likely to have problems with alcohol veterans or the general public, of those who ventured an opinion between the populations, more people thought veterans both of the Vietnam Era and the post–9/11 era were more apt to have alcoholism problems. When connected with posttraumatic stress disorder (PTSD), alcoholism or alcohol use disorder (AUD) is the most common associated co-occurring health disorder.[32] But the overall levels of AUD in veteran populations are generally comparable or less than that observed within similarly situated civilian populations.

Our best available research combined with the research of the VA indicates that diagnosed alcohol abuse disorder affects approximately 10 percent of veterans. The general population between 18 and 25 years old has similar alcohol abuse rate of 16 percent and the 26 and older population averages alcoholism rates around 6 percent.[33] It is important to note that men are more likely than women to abuse alcohol, and the percentages of men to women ratio in the veterans' community is 9:1 whereas the general population ratio is roughly 1:1. That is to say that when considering the nearest demographic comparison, veterans are actually less likely to abuse alcohol than the general population, but given the demographic makeup of veterans versus civilians, a perception that alcoholism is more widespread is understandable.

Public Opinion on Veterans' Policy

Having looked at the most comparable set of public opinion data on perceptions of veterans is illuminating in many ways, but there is more to the picture. We know that the public generally tends to look more favorably upon veterans today than they did 40 years ago; but what about the policies and government agencies tasked with administering veterans' policy?

There have been questions sprinkled in various surveys about veterans and veterans' politics from the 1940s until today. While few polls focus exclusively on veterans, there are insights and trends to be extrapolated from the questions scattered through different surveys. In what follows, I sort public opinion temporally and, when possible, by the partisanship of the respondent. In the aim of summarizing and presenting data in a more concise way, I have combined similar sorts of questions into unified, topic-level measures. For interested readers, the actual question wordings, as well as specific breakdowns, are in the appendix to this chapter.

In the 1950s, polling houses began to press independents and nonidentifiers with questions about which party they "leaned toward" despite the fact that a respondent might not have initially identified with a political party. I have included leaners as partisans when the option exists in the following figures. Respondents who do not identify with a party are eliminated in the partisan counts. Because of that the partisan percentages on a given topic are sometimes divergent in ways that do not always sum to the overall percentage. Unless otherwise noted all survey results presented are from samples representative of adults of the United States.

When asked in generalities what civilians think about veterans, great majorities indicate that they respect the work of veterans and support efforts to give veterans advantages in education, hiring, and home ownership. In comparison to other professions, 84 percent of Americans said veterans "contribute a lot" to society, whereas 77 percent said the same of teachers, 70 percent about scientists, and 69 percent about medical doctors.[34]

The reverence afforded to veterans is unique, as nearly all other government agents have fallen in public support. In 2017, Gallup asked respondents about the level of faith they have in different elements of the government. Seventy-two percent of Americans had either a "great deal" or "quite a lot of faith" in the military, whereas only 12 percent expressed those levels for Congress. Active military members are not yet veterans, but if the 60 percent gap between service members and legislators serves as any hint to which sort of group the U.S. public views favorable, even conservative estimates would place veterans well above members of Congress.

General Support for Veterans' Assistance

There is widespread support for government financial support to the families and caretakers of veterans. In 2008, 89 percent of the public said they favored giving family caregivers VA benefits such as tuition support, job training, and employment assistance to help provide for the veteran(s) in their family.[35] But this level of support is higher than in earlier times.

As Figure 3.2 indicates, in the 1930s–1950s, public opinion supporting an increase to or general funding for veterans' benefits was much lower. Part of

Public Opinion: Veterans Policy and Veterans' Preferences

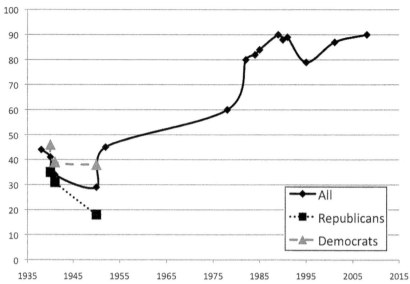

Figure 3.2 Percent supportive of general government benefits for veterans and veteran families and more government spending on vet programs (1979–2017).

Sources: Gallup Organization, *Military Pensions/Unions/Politics/Electric Power Companies* (Ithaca, NY: Roper Center for Public Opinion Research, Cornell University, 1938); Gallup Organization, *Gallup Poll (AIPO)* (Ithaca, NY: Roper Center for Public Opinion Research, iPOLL, Cornell University, 1940); Gallup Organization, *Gallup Poll (AIPO)* (Ithaca, NY: Roper Center for Public Opinion Research, iPOLL, Cornell University, 1950); Gallup Organization, *Gallup Poll (AIPO)* (Ithaca, NY: Roper Center for Public Opinion Research, iPOLL, Cornell University, 1953, accessed October 27, 2017).

the original unwillingness to support government programs for veterans was likely due to the mentality that assistance would breed an unhealthy reliance on government and rid veterans of the necessary drive to support themselves. Historians of the time note this sentiment as a hindrance to VA policy expansion.

However, in the years between World War II and Vietnam War, effects of veterans' policies such as the original GI Bill were heralded as successful interventions that both allayed concerns from civilian populations that unruly and licentious veterans would overrun their towns as well as veteran concerns that they would not be able to fully participate in the postwar economy. The importance and prestige of the VA hospital system also grew during this time period despite occasional episodes of scandal and mismanagement. The consequent rise in public opinion speaks to the increasingly positive perception of the role of government in aiding veterans.

Since the 1980s majorities of over 80 percent responded positively to questions on if the government ought to provide more benefits for veterans, spend more money on veterans' programs, and stop cuts to extant benefits even when issues of budgetary limitations are made salient in surveys. All told, public support for veterans' aid policies is as high now as it has ever been.

Opinions on the VA

Oftentimes the VA is one of the executive agencies held in the highest regard by the majority of the public. Even during the Obama era, despite scandals and a dip in opinions of how well the United States served veterans, the agency was still one of the highest ranked among those listed in surveys. The Pew Research Center conducts periodic surveys on how the public perceives government agencies. Comparing survey responses from 1997/1998 with those in 2010, public opinion held more or less constant regarding the VA. In the late 1990s, 59 percent of respondents said they approved of the job the VA was doing and 57 percent responded in the same way in 2010.[36] By comparison, the Department of Education went from a 61 percent approval to 40 percent in that time frame, the Social Security Administration went from 62 to 49 percent, and the Department of Defense went from 76 to 67 percent. That is, during a time period in which other agencies that had previously enjoyed high levels of public approval fell, the VA remained popular with nearly 60 percent of the public. Figure 3.3 shows the trends on people holding a favorable opinion of the agency.

Approving opinions about the VA are different from assessments of how well the VA and other government entities perform in serving veterans. The first time the public was polled about how well they thought the VA was serving the needs of veterans was in 1979. At that time 35 percent of respondents thought that VA was doing excellent or very well.[37] It was not until 2009 that the question was posed again on a nationally representative survey, but thereafter the question appeared more frequently. Figure 3.4 displays the percentages of people who responded that the VA was doing excellent or very good in terms of the service provided to veterans.

In 2009, a majority (62%) thought the United States and the VA were serving veterans well, and by 2010 that number fell to 41 percent and only continued to drop until 2017. The contours of public opinion have been similar for both Democrats and Republicans; both indicated that the government was not doing a good job serving veterans.[38] The measures after 2014 are reasonable as public outrage following the Phoenix area VA hospital wait-time scandal exploded.[39] But why we observed a drop prior to the 2014 scandal is somewhat harder to explain; but media coverage on the shortcomings at Walter Reed National Military Medical Center may have played some role.[40]

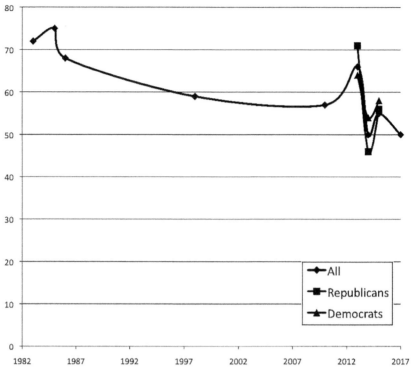

Figure 3.3 Percentage saying they hold a very or mostly favorable opinion of the VA (1982–2017).

There was the sense political leaders were ignoring the needs of veterans. In 2007, 81 percent of the public said they thought political leaders have paid "too little" attention to military veterans.[41] Additionally, both war fatigue and a transition from a Republican commander in chief to a Democrat commander in chief likely played dual roles in declining assessments of government performance. That year Jon Soltz, a veteran and leader of VoteVets.org, testified before the defense appropriations subcommittee and accused Senate minority leader Mitch McConnell (R-KY) of "aiding the enemy" by supporting failed Bush-led policies in Iraq.[42]

The numbers of people who still supported military activities in Iraq and Afghanistan fell during the first two years of Obama's term, with majorities no longer believing the activities were worthwhile.[43] In addition to the public, veterans themselves increasingly expressed doubts about Iraq and Afghanistan.[44]

Another part of the story is the transition from President Bush to President Obama. Bush did not enjoy great numbers of public support toward the

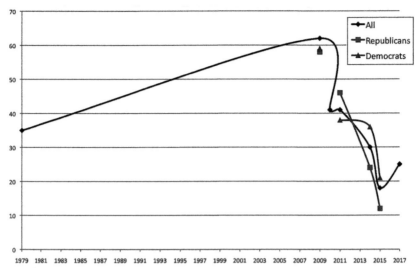

Figure 3.4 Percentage saying the VA and/or the United States is doing an excellent or pretty good job for veterans (1979–2017).

Sources: The Veterans Administration, *Attitudes toward Vietnam Era Veterans Survey*, Survey (Ithaca, NY: Roper Center for Public Opinion Research, iPOLL, Cornell University, 1979); Cable News Network, *CNN/Opinion Research Corporation Poll* (Ithaca, NY: Roper Center for Public Opinion Research, iPOLL, Cornell University, 2009); Pew Research Center for the People & the Press, *Pew Research Center for the People & the Press Poll, USPSRA.041810A.R03LF2* (Princeton, NJ: Princeton Survey Research Associates International, 2010); Pew Research Center for the People & the Press, *Pew Research Center Poll: October 2013 Political Survey, USPEW2013–10POL* (Glen Mills, PA: ABT SRBI, Inc., 2013); CBS News, *CBS News Poll: Veterans Administration, USCBS2014–05D* (Glen Mills, PA: Social Science Research Solutions, 2014); Fairleigh Dickinson University, *PublicMind Poll, USFDU.111015.R04*, Social Science Research Solutions (Ithaca, NY: Roper Center for Public Opinion Research, iPOLL, Cornell University, 2015); Pew Research Center for the People & the Press, "Pew Research Center for the People & the Press Poll, Jan, 2017)," USPSRA.011917A.R01H (2017).

end of his presidency for his role as commander in chief, but he did enjoy higher numbers than President Obama. Specifically, veterans indicated that they approved Bush as commander in chief (65%) more than those who approved of Obama in that role (42%).[45] While it is not clear why there was such a drop, the available evidence indicates that assessment of the effectiveness of the VA and government generally dropped despite decently stable general approval of the VA.

The importance of Figures 3.3 and 3.4 is not just to show how public opinion changed on the VA and assessments of VA abilities but also to show how these opinions are quite similar no matter the partisanship of respondents.

For declines and increases overtime, both Republican and Democratic respondents seem to hold the executive agency in similar regard. Both Democrats and Republicans in the public agree that veterans as a group are due government benefits and both assess the VA in similar ways.

Issue-Specific Public Opinion

Educational Benefits

Policies to allow veterans and their family members to attend college with government assistance are very popular and have been for a long time. Figure 3.5 shows how the public has responded when asked about special educational benefits for veterans.

When these questions were asked in the 1970s and 1980s, respondents were asked if they supported affirmative action for veterans as long as there

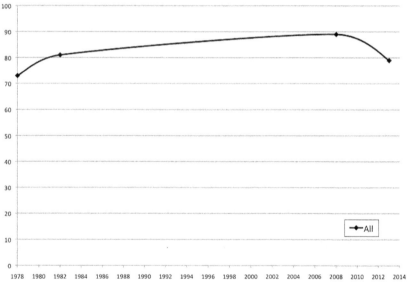

Figure 3.5 Percentage supporting veterans' tuition support and favorable higher education admissions policies (1978–2013).

Sources: 1978 (National Conference of Christians & Jews. Racial & Religious Minorities & Women 1978); Louis Harris & Associates, *Topics: DEFENSE VETERANS* (Ithaca, NY: Roper Center for Public Opinion Research, iPOLL, Cornell University, 1982); Disabled American Veterans, *Veteran's Health Care Funding Survey, USBELDEN.08VETHLTH. R03* (Ithaca, NY: Roper Center for Public Opinion Research, iPOLL, Cornell University, 2008); Lumina Foundation for Education, *USGALLUP.040714.R21D* (New York: Gallup Organization, 2013).

were no rigid quotas, and over 70 and 80 percent of respondents said they were in support of such policies. In 2008, respondents were asked if they were willing to extend tuition assistance to the family caregivers of veterans and nearly 90 percent of respondents answered in the affirmative. Finally in 2013, the specific question asked if veterans should be given special consideration in higher education admissions even if they score lower than other applicants and 77 percent thought this was acceptable.

Support for Health Benefits

Questions about veterans' health care benefits have been asked to gauge how much importance people place on the government responsibility to provide health care, how much and for how long the government owes veterans health care benefits, and assessments of the quality of care veterans received in VA hospitals.

In 2004 and 2008, nationwide surveys asked how important it was for the federal government to fund health care for veterans and how much of a priority the issue ought to be for the president and Congress.[46] Ninety-five percent said the issue was somewhat or very important, and 90 percent said that they wanted veterans' health care to be a high priority for the incoming president and Congress.

The VA conducts many polls on veterans to ascertain their opinions about the VA services and hospitals. These polls are conducted in various ways, each with the aim of better understanding the population they are charged to serve. In recent years, veterans' opinions on VA health care are mostly positive.[47] As for how the public views the responsibility of government to provide health care to veterans and the quality of care received, general assessment tends to be lower than what internal VA surveys reveal.

Veterans generally find that VA health care systems work quite well for most services, but the perceptions of the general populations are somewhat more negative.[48] In 2014, Gallup asked if people thought the VA should provide service-related health care or all related health care to veterans and if that care ought to be provided on a lifelong basis. A slight majority, 56 percent, thought that the VA ought to provide all health care to veterans for their lives, with the other 44 percent determining either that just service-related care was due or that care should not be permanent.[49]

Surveys conducted after 2014 focused on the developing Phoenix area VA hospital scandal, and in this time period very specific partisan patterns emerged in public opinion. Table 3.3 displays the nationally representative survey questions asked around VA health care in the wake of the scandal.

Public opinion was nearly unanimous that the VA scandal was serious, and similar amounts of Republicans and Democrats indicated they were aware of the allegations. Yet, when asked who was to blame, and what ought

Table 3.3 Public Opinion on Veterans' Health Care Facilities and Government Actors

Date	Question	All (%)	Reps (%)	Dems (%)
May 20, 2014–May 21, 2014	Given what you know right now, do you think Eric Shinseki, the secretary of Veterans Affairs, should have to resign as a result of the problems at some Veterans Administration medical facilities, or should he remain secretary of Veterans Affairs? (Percentage should resign)	45	56	36
May 20, 2014–May 21, 2014	Who do you blame most for the problems at Veterans Administration medical facilities—Barack Obama, Eric Shinseki and the Veterans Administration, or local VA hospitals? (Blame Barack Obama)	17	30	7
May 20, 2014–May 21, 2014	Who do you blame most for the problems at Veterans Administration medical facilities—Barack Obama, Eric Shinseki and the Veterans Administration, or local VA hospitals? (Blame Erick Shinseki)	33	31	39
May 20, 2014–May 21, 2014	Who do you blame most for the problems at Veterans Administration medical facilities—Barack Obama, Eric Shinseki and the Veterans Administration, or local VA hospitals? (Blame local hospitals)	28	20	30
May 20, 2014–May 21, 2014	Do you think the problems at Veterans Administration medical facilities are widespread or limited to just a few incidents? (Percentage widespread)	62	70	61
May 20, 2014–May 21, 2014	Do you approve or disapprove of the way Barack Obama is handling the problems at Veterans Administration medical facilities? (Percentage approve)	29	13	47
May 20, 2014–May 21, 2014	How much have you heard or read about the problems at some Veterans Administration, or VA medical facilities, including reports about long waits for treatment and the death of some patients—a lot, some, or not much? (Percentage a lot)	40	43	38
May 29–June 1, 2014	Do you approve or disapprove of the way Barack Obama is handling the situation in Veterans Affairs hospitals and medical facilities? (Percentage approve)	37	14	58
May 29, 2014–June 1, 2014	How serious is it that some military veteran hospitals did not offer timely appointments for some patients and then falsified their records to hide this fact? (Very or somewhat)	97	99	96
May 29, 2014–June 1, 2014	Do you think Eric Shinseki should have resigned because of the Veterans Administration hospital's issue? (Percentage resigned)	65	72	61

Sources: CBS News, CBS News Poll: Veterans Administration, USCBS2014–05D (Glen Mills, PA: Social Science Research Solutions, 2014); CNN/ORC International Poll, Government Veterans Leaders, USORCCNN2014–006 (Ithaca, NY: Roper Center for Public Opinion Research, iPOLL, Cornell University, 2014); ABC News/The Washington Post, ABC News/Washington Post Poll: 2016 Presidential Election/Hillary Clinton/Veterans Affairs/Global Warming, USABCWASH2014–1161 (Newyork, NY: Langer Research Associates/Capital Insight/ABT SRBI, Inc., 2014).

to be done in order to remedy the situation, partisanship more clearly entered the picture.

In the first poll administered on May 20–21, 2014, Republicans were far more likely to say that Secretary Shinseki should resign, with 56 percent in support of that action, whereas only 36 percent of Democrats thought that would be a reasonable solution. In that same survey, respondents were asked who they thought was to blame for the excessive wait times and subsequent cover-ups. For these questions the partisan splits are incredible. Of the potentially culpable actors, respondents could choose President Obama, Secretary Shinseki and the Veterans Administration, or local VA hospitals. There are arguments that could be used to justify blaming any of the actors involved. Obama nominated Shinseki and is the top of executive branch, Shinseki is the organization head of the scandalized agency and sets the culture of the VA, and local VA hospitals are the sites where the actual deception occurred. While each has points of responsibility, partisans tended to blame different actors in different ways. The greatest share of Democrats indicated that Shinseki and the VA were most at fault (39%), followed by local VA hospitals (30%), and just 7 percent indicated that Obama was to blame for the scandal. A majority of Republicans too placed the blame on Shinseki and the VA (31%), but closely behind 30 percent said Obama was to blame and just 20 percent thought local VA hospitals bore responsibility.

In a time of scandal, there is a political split in how the public perceived political actors. Republicans were much more willing to blame Obama than Democrats were. In addition to blame, two other questions asked respondents about their approval of how Obama was handling the VA situation. Only 13–14 percent of Republicans said they approved of how Obama handled the VA scandal as it unfolded, and 47–58 percent of Democrats indicated their approval. These sorts of opinion gaps on Obama in particular were common throughout his term; on a host of issues Republicans consistently rated his performance worse than Democrats did, yet the divergence is notable here because unlike other policy realms characterized by different underlying policy preferences, veterans' politics is generally a place where both parties agree. Despite this top-level agreement, it seems that negative circumstances can serve to heighten party salience in political assessments, and the VA scandal public opinion data are evidences of that. By the time Shinseki officially resigned, majorities in both parties were in favor; afterward political questions about the VA went back to being infrequent in general public opinion surveys.

Veterans' Public Opinion

In this section I turn to opinions that veterans hold. Rather than just consider what the wider population thinks about veterans, what positions do veterans themselves profess? In what ways are veteran populations similar to and distinct from civilian populations? How does political partisanship manifest itself in veterans' populations?

Since 2001 there have been over 10 nationally fielded, representative, and scientific surveys of U.S. veterans.[50] The goals of these surveys are to better understand the social, economic, housing, and health statuses of veterans. In those areas, we have a good deal of knowledge about veteran communities. What are far less researched via surveys are the specific political opinions and preferences of veterans. Despite this limitation, there have been some notable efforts to rigorously assess the opinions of veterans, and on occasion those efforts have been done in parallel with assessments of the civilian population.[51]

Partisanship and Ideology

Two surveys were fielded at the same time with samples split to be representative of veterans and the population at large. In 2011 the Pew veterans' survey asked both veterans and civilians, "In politics TODAY, do you consider yourself a Republican, Democrat, or Independent?" Figure 3.6 presents the responses of veterans compared to the general public.

Party identification is a clean way to distinguish veterans' opinions from civilians' opinions. In Figure 3.6 veterans are more likely to identify as

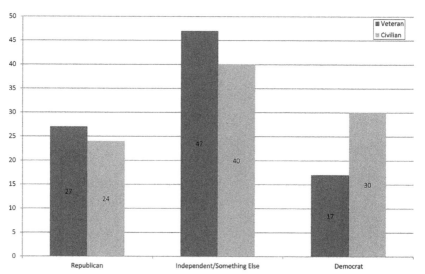

Figure 3.6 Party identification of veterans and the general public (2011).

Source: Pew Research Center, *Pew Social and Demographic Trends Poll: Veterans Survey*, conducted by Social Science Research Solutions (Washington, DC: Pew Research Center, 2011).

Republicans and Independents and far less likely to identify as Democrats than the general population. The Pew poll asked those who did not identify with one of the major parties to indicate which party they "leaned" to. When doing this, this overall share of veteran Republicans is much higher; 60 percent of the overall veterans' population says they identify or lean toward the Republican Party, with only 40 percent belonging to or leaning to the Democratic Party.

Two years later, when the second split sample poll asked civilians and veterans which of three political parties each respondent most identified with, 17 percent of veterans responded Democrat, 27 percent Republican, and 47 percent Independent. The general population responded 30 percent Democrat, 24 percent Republican, and 40 percent Independent. That is, veterans' populations appeared even more likely to identify as Republicans and Independents than members of the general population in 2013 than in 2011.[52] These results are presented in Figure 3.7.

In both samples and across both surveys, the plurality of respondents prefers not to identify with one of the major parties and instead think of themselves as Independents. But when looking at the major parties, our best survey data show that Democrats hold an edge over the general public, but Republicans lead among veterans.[53] Come election time, very few Independent candidates make it to the general election, and Independent veterans

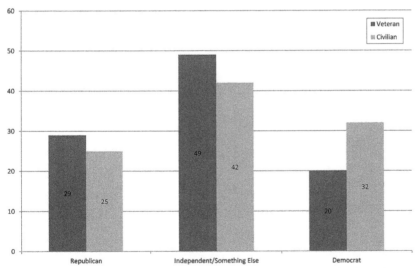

Figure 3.7 Party identification of veterans and the general public (2013).

Sources: Washington Post-Kaiser Family Foundation, "Survey of Iraq and Afghanistan Active Duty Soldiers and Veterans," Washington Post, 2013; Washington Post/ABC News Poll, "News Poll of U.S. Adults," 2013.

must select a Republican or Democrat when voting. What do our best data indicate on how veterans vote?

Voting Behaviors of Veterans

When looking at voting patterns versus identification, veterans tend to support Republican candidates more than civilian voters do. The levels as to which veterans vote for Republican candidates are even more lopsided than the divisions on party identification between veterans and civilians. In 2008, among registered voters, over 50 percent of civilians said they preferred Barack Obama to military veteran John McCain but just 35 percent of veterans did.[54] The same sort of gap was in place in 2012 when Barack Obama faced Mitt Romney; only 34 percent of veterans indicated a preference for Democrat Obama whereas 48 percent of the general public did.[55] This Republican candidate preference is not just tied to presidential politics. In the 2014 midterm elections, national exit polls reported that 59 percent of veterans voted for Republican candidates, whereas just 49 percent of the general public did.[56]

Of course, voting preferences are derived from surveys and exit polls and not from actual secret voting decisions. But looking at stated preferences for Republican or Democratic candidates offers additional information beyond the self-identification of veterans. Even more so than when responding to surveys about how veterans politically identify on their own, when asked to consider people from one party over another to represent their interests, veterans express greater levels of support for Republicans over Democrats.

Why Do Veterans Tend to Prefer the Republican Party?

What are some reasons we observe such a divergence between veterans and general public opinion in terms of partisanship and voting preferences? There is, of course, no one answer but rather many plausible, assessable reasons that combine to create an account of this reality. Previous research dedicated to a general examination of how veterans engage in the political process and the partisan nature of that behavior is provided in the notes to this chapter.[57] In order to move the extant explanations forward, I offer a new reason as to why veterans tend to support Republican candidates over Democrats.

I argue that Republican politicians pay more attention to veterans in public communications than Democrats. This is despite the fact that Democrats draft and pass more legislation for veterans. In this section I briefly review the current explanations offered as to why veterans prefer the Republican Party. Each one of these explanations has contributory power and weaknesses, but like the theory I put forward, none operates in a vacuum and instead merits consideration as parts of a greater whole.

Age

One argument offered for why veterans are more supportive of Republicans than the general public is that veterans are older and like other older parts of the population support Republicans more, collectively.[58] Setting aside the potentially problematic assertion that age is strictly determinant of or related to party affiliation, this argument is not entirely off base.

Veterans, as a group, are older than nonveterans. Comparing civilians 18 years and over versus veterans, the median age of civilian men is 41 and civilian women is 46, whereas the median age of veteran men is 64 and of veteran women is 49.[59] Given that women only make up about a tenth of the veteran population, and make up 50 percent of the civilian population, the evidence is clear that veterans are, on average, older than civilians.

But does this mean that older veterans are the reason veterans' populations tend to prefer the Republican Party? Survey data and studies using other indicators show otherwise. While analysis on the overall population indicates that there are trends of older Americans as more apt to identify with the Republican Party, a specific look at veterans shows that the story is not so clear.[60]

On average, partisan splits across age distributions of veterans are similar. Using the 2011 Pew Poll of Veterans, the mean age across all political identification classifications is 57 and the distributions are not significantly different from each other. But this may be changing; recent work cautiously indicates that younger veterans are slightly more likely to identify as Republicans than older veterans.[61] Thus, while it is clear that veterans are older than Americans on average, it is not clear that this accounts for the reasons that we tend to see more GOP identification from veterans, and in fact younger veterans are slightly more likely to identify as Republicans than older veterans.

Sex

Out of the entire current veterans' population, only 9–11 percent are women, and when looking at the population of women veterans, their political preferences tend to look more like women civilians with greater amounts of Democratic support. Figure 3.8 shows the results from the 2011 Pew veterans' survey broken down by gender.

As Figure 3.8 shows, women veterans are more likely to identify as Democrats than men veterans. When pushed to pick a major party those who are Independent or indicate something else in the initial question, the differences between men and women are even starker and the overall gains for Republicans become clearer. When including leaners, 47 percent of men veterans said they leaned toward the Republican Party to just 38 percent of

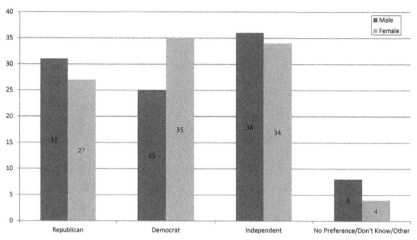

Figure 3.8 Veteran party identification by gender.

Source: Pew Research Center, *Pew Social and Demographic Trends Poll: Veterans Survey*, conducted by Social Science Research Solutions (Washington, DC: Pew Research Center, 2011).

women, while 39 percent of men veterans chose the Democratic Party and 54 percent of women did. Gender is part of the story. As veterans are 9:1 male to female, the party preferences of men come through in a clearer way when considering veterans all together.

Self-Selection to Service

One theory is that young conservatives are more likely to join the military than young liberals. If that is the case, the identification of veterans is not surprising; it simply mirrors self-selection into service in the first place. People elect to serve based on personal characteristics, family connections, and career desires. For some, personal characteristics that may contribute to having a successful military career such as deference to authority and professionalism fit better within the Republican Party. Family histories are somewhat harder to explain, but there is research that establishes the role that family plays in both political socialization and the choice to enter the armed services.[62]

This story is persuasive on face and comports with the collective wisdom that associates the GOP with military service. Research on the officer corps is very compelling in matching those who self-select into service and those who identify with the Republican Party.[63] Yet, researchers who have studied the demographic characteristics and reasons that service members who are not officers provide for joining do not support this reasoning. The most recent work on this sort of explanation from military sociologists cautions that the media narrative is overly simplified. People generally join the armed forces for personal, financial, and situational reasons, rather than partisan politics.[64]

Service Transformation

Another theory is that military life makes people more conservative, and thus, their opinions as veterans are more aligned with the Republican Party than they might have been otherwise. There are two main mechanisms put forward to account for service experience translating into political preference development.

The older of the two explanations stresses that the authoritarian nature of military order leads veterans to appreciate order and hierarchies in ways that are more at home in the Republican than Democratic Party.[65] In the general population, studies on authoritarian personality traits and subsequent affinity for Republican Party politics have been persuasively established, but none of this research developed from the study of military service.[66] That is, authoritarianism as a value or personality trait has been linked to Republican Party affinity, but there is not a body of work that describes how members of the service undergo a transformation to valuing authoritarianism and how that development then matches up with party preferences. There is no doubt that there are multiple pathways for a person to value authoritarianism—experimental research has shown that these tendencies can be induced and activated at least in the short term. Time in the military is likely one way that a person encounters more authoritarian environments, but our best research largely focuses on authoritarian traits and values as a feature of a person's childhood upbringing, or experimental manipulation.

The other suggested mechanism is that military service elevates the importance of civic duty that then spills over into greater amounts of voter turnout and political participation of veterans.[67] But this linkage need not unfold along party lines; service members could hold divergent political preferences but still tend to turn out and participate more than civilians. The research on the transformative nature of military service is scant. In many ways those in the military are encouraged to not think of their service in political terms, and the VA does not permit political survey tracking of members before, during, and after service. Yet, of the extant panel studies tracking opinions, those done in the eras of the draft did happen to get a good deal of veterans. Work of that sort shows that we do not have evidence of significant opinion differences between veterans and nonveterans due to time in service.[68]

Conclusions

To understand what it means for a party to "own" an issue in the minds of voters, scholars have noted that it is not clear if respondents are saying a party is better at performing in some policy arena, *or* if respondents mean that a party prioritizes the policy arena more than the other party, *or* if respondents associate some sort of relevant issue constituency to one party over the other.[69] Professor Pat Egan at New York University sums this complication succinctly using the example of the Democratic Party and environmentalism,

> Consider for example the environment, and issue that overwhelming numbers of Americans believe the Democrats can better handle than the Republicans. Environmentalists are today a key constituency of the Democratic Party. But we do not know if the Democrats' ownership occurs because environmentalists push Democrats to pursue environmental *policies* preferred by voters, that these activists have provided the Democratic Party with expertise to *perform* better than Republicans on achieving environmental goals, or if these activists pressure democrats to prioritize environmental issues over other national problems.[70]

The Democrats and environment example show how difficult it is to think of a causal story for why one party owns an issue, but the example assumes that parties are responsive to constituencies rather than the other way around.

When thinking about veterans' policy, I approach the linkage in a much more agnostic way. Republican citizen demands might not be the reason people tend to think Republicans can and will do better for veterans, but it could be the case that the Republican Party communications efforts more often focus on veterans' issues than the efforts from Democrats. This imbalance in focus may create the impression that Republicans do more in that policy space.

There is not a comprehensive database of citizen demands for veterans' policy. But we do have public opinion data indicating what various populations want from government, their esteem for different actors, and their thoughts on which party is better suited to deal with military issues. Everyone thinks veterans' issues should be a priority. Both Democrats and Republicans support educational and health benefits for veterans. That is, the demands are similar from partisans in the electorate to partisans in government. Yet, there is something else that accounts for why we have indications that the Republican Party is the party of veterans. In addition to the widely disseminated media and pop culture narrative linking the two groups, veterans themselves tend to identify as Republicans and support Republican candidates for office.

In the next chapter, I show that Democrats actually do more to create legislative proposal for veterans, but this finding seems at odds with the results of this chapter. For now, it is reasonable to characterize the data of veterans in the contemporary period as more supportive of the Republican Party than the Democratic Party, and for the contours of that support to look more lopsided than what we observe in the general public. That is, even if there is not an overall sense of issue ownership in the minds of the public, there is certainly a sense of party preferences in the minds of veterans.

Appendix
Public Opinion Questions and Sources

Year	Question	Overall (%)	Rep (%)	Dem (%)	Source
1938	When a World War veteran dies from causes not connected with the war, should his widow and children be given a government pension? (Percent Yes)	44			(Gallup Organization 1938)
1940	When a World War veteran dies from causes not connected with the war, should his widow and children be given a pension by the government? (Percent Yes)	41	35	46	(Gallup Organization 1940)
1940	Would you be willing to pay higher taxes to give government pensions to such widows and children? (Percent Yes)	34	31	39	(Gallup Organization 1940)
1946	Has the government given you, as a World War II veteran, all the help you think it should? (Percent Yes)	75	83	79	(Gallup Organization 1946)
1950	Should you listen to veterans' groups on how VA ought to work rather than Hoover administration? (Percentage saying listen to veterans)	44	30	52	(Gallup Organization 1950)
1950	Do you think U.S. government spending should be increased, decreased, or remain about the same on the following: veterans' benefits? (Percentage increased)	29	18	38	(Gallup Organization 1950)
1952	How about benefits for veterans—should they (the next administration) do more for veterans or less? (Percentage saying more)	45			(Opinion Research Corporation 1952)
1953	Should the government be required to give a war veteran free care and treatment at a veterans' hospital if his injury or illness was not caused by being in the service? (Percentage should)	45			(Gallup Organization 1953)
1960	Would you trust veterans' groups to determine whom to vote for? (Percentage Yes)?	16	15	15	(American National Election Study [Pre-Election] 1960)

1978	Do you favor or oppose affirmative action programs in industry for Vietnam veterans, provided there are no rigid quotas? Asked of black respondents? (Percentage favor)	83	(National Conference of Christians & Jews. Racial & Religious Minorities & Women 1978)
1978	Do you favor or oppose affirmative action programs in industry for Vietnam veterans, provided there are no rigid quotas? Asked of white respondents? (Percentage favor)	73	(National Conference of Christians & Jews. Racial & Religious Minorities & Women 1978)
1978	Do you favor or oppose affirmative action programs in higher education for Vietnam veterans, provided there are no rigid quotas? Asked of white respondents? (Percentage favor)	73	(National Conference of Christians & Jews. Racial & Religious Minorities & Women 1978)
1978	Do you favor or oppose affirmative action programs in higher education for Vietnam veterans, provided there are no rigid quotas? Asked of black respondents? (Percentage favor)	85	(National Conference of Christians & Jews. Racial & Religious Minorities & Women 1978)
1978	If cuts in federal spending have to be made and you had to choose, would you prefer to cut defense spending or federal veterans' programs? (Percentage cut vets)	40	(Louis Harris & Associates 1978)
1979	Do you think the federal government is doing excellent or pretty good at serving the needs of veterans?	26	(The Veterans Administration 1979)

(*continued*)

(continued)

Year	Question	Overall (%)	Rep (%)	Dem (%)	Source
1979	Do you think the Veterans Administration is doing excellent or pretty good at serving the needs of veterans?	35			(The Veterans Administration 1979)
1979	Do you think the Veterans Administration is now doing better than it was five years ago in serving the needs of veterans of the Vietnam Era?	25			(The Veterans Administration 1979)
1982	Do you favor or oppose affirmative action programs in industry for Vietnam veterans, provided there are no rigid quotas? (Percentage favor)	79			(Louis Harris & Associates 1982)
1982	Do you favor or oppose affirmative action programs in higher education for Vietnam veterans, provided there are no rigid quotas? (Percentage favor)	81			(Louis Harris & Associates 1982)
1982	If you had to choose, would you prefer to see sharp cuts in veterans' benefits or cuts in defense spending? (Percentage cut veterans)	20			(Louis Harris & Associates 1982)
1983	Do you think opinion of the VA is highly or moderately favorable?	72			(The Roper Organization 1983)
1984	If you had to choose, would you prefer to see more cuts in veterans' benefits or cuts in the increased defense budget? (Percentage cut veterans)	18			(Louis Harris & Associates 1984)
1985	If you had to choose, would you prefer to see sharp cuts in veterans' health benefits or additional cuts in defense spending? (Percentage cut veterans)	16			(Louis Harris & Associates 1985)
1985	Would you favor or oppose doing away for one year with the cost-of-living adjustments for veterans' pensions? (Percentage favor)	37			(Louis Harris & Associates 1985)

Year	Question	%	Source
1985	Would you favor or oppose strictly limiting cost-of-living allowances on veterans' pension programs to 2 percent, even if the cost of living goes up more than that? (Percentage favor)	23	(Louis Harris & Associates 1985)
1985	Do you think opinion of the VA is highly or moderately favorable?	75	(Roper Organization 1985)
1986	Do you think opinion of the VA is highly or moderately favorable?	68	(Roper Organization 1986)
1989	If you had to choose, would you prefer to see sharp cuts in veterans' health benefits in order to pay for the federal government's antidrug programs or not? (Percentage prefer cuts)	10	(Louis Harris & Associates 1989)
1990	You said that you want to take some money from the military budget and use it to help fund other programs. Now I'm going to read you a list of items in this year's federal budget and tell you how much money President (George W.) Bush wants to spend on each one. After each item please tell me if you would increase or not increase the budget for that item: veterans' benefits, $31 billion (Percentage would increase)	50 44 56	(Market Strategies 1990)
1990	Do you favor reducing spending on domestic programs, such as Social Security, financial aid to the needy, and Veteran's benefits (Percentage favoring reduction)	12	(Gallup Organization 1990)
1990	In your opinion, have Vietnam veterans been treated well by the people of the United States in the years since the Vietnam War or not? (Percentage yes)	26	(Gallup Organization 1990)
1991	Support government programs, such as Social Security, Medicare, and veteran's benefits, provide assistance to disabled people. (Percentage supportive)	89	(Louis Harris & Associates 1991)

(continued)

(continued)

Year	Question	Overall (%)	Rep (%)	Dem (%)	Source
1991	Currently, government benefits to disabled veterans are much more generous than government benefits to other people with disabilities. Do you support giving veterans extra benefits, or should all disabled people get about the same level of benefits? (Percentage support extra benefits for veterans)	45			(Louis Harris & Associates 1991)
1995	Favor making major spending reductions in veterans' benefits?	21			(Henry J. Kaiser Family Foundation, Harvard School of Public Health 1995)
1995	Do you favor or oppose eliminating the Department of Veterans Affairs? (Percentage favor)	22			(Business Week/ Harris Poll 1995)
1998	Do you think opinion of the VA is very or mostly favorable?	59			(Pew Research Center for the People & the Press 1998)
2000	In your opinion, have Vietnam veterans been treated well by the people of the United States in the years since the Vietnam War or not? (Percentage well)	24	26	24	(Gallup Organization 2000)
2001	Feeling thermometer Vietnam veterans (51–100%—warm)	87			(Vietnam Veterans of America Foundation 2001)

2004	Next, still thinking about the last three years, I'm going to read a list of different groups in our country and in our world, and for each one, I'd like you to tell me whether you think each has emerged as a winner or loser from this period. Military veterans (If winner/loser, ask:) Are they a big winner/loser or just a winner/loser? (Percentage winner or big winner)	40		(Mother Jones 2004)
2004	In your opinion, how important is it for the federal government to fund health care for veterans—very important, somewhat important, not too important, not important at all? (Percentage very or somewhat important)	95		(Paralyzed Veterans of America, Disabled American Veterans 2004)
2004	In your opinion, how important is it for the federal government to ensure that veterans do not have to wait to receive their benefits—very important, somewhat important, not too important or not important at all? (Percentage very or somewhat)	95		(Paralyzed Veterans of America, Disabled American Veterans 2004)
2007	Do you think the political leaders in Washington pay too much attention, about the right amount, or too little attention to the needs of each of the following groups? How about military veterans? (Percentage saying too little)	81		(Gallup Organization 2007)
2007	Do you approve of the way the Bush administration is handling the needs of active-duty troops, military families, and veterans? (Percentage some or strong approval)	29	557	8	(Los Angeles Times/Bloomberg Poll 2007)
2007	Bush administration meeting the needs of veterans (Percentage very well or well)	30		(WNBC/Marist Poll 2007)

(continued)

(continued)

Year	Question	Overall (%)	Rep (%)	Dem (%)	Source
2008	Wounded or injured Iraq War veterans generally get high-quality care for their injuries in military and Veterans Administration hospitals	31			(Harvard School of Public Health 2008)
2008	Wounded or injured Iraq War veterans generally get the same or better care for their injuries in military and Veterans Administration hospitals than they would in private hospitals	60			(Harvard School of Public Health 2008)
2008	Providing medical care to injured, sick, and disabled veterans should be top or high priority for incoming president and Congress sample: national adult.	90			(Disabled American Veterans 2008)
2008	The federal government today is doing enough or too much to support military veterans	12			(Disabled American Veterans 2008)
2008	Favor giving family caregivers VA benefits such as tuition support, job training, and employment assistance to help them provide for the veteran in their family?	89			(Disabled American Veterans 2008)
2008	Favor Congress taking action this year to increase funding specifically for the diagnosis and treatment of mild traumatic brain injuries or mental health problems such as posttraumatic stress disorder from military service?	92			(Disabled American Veterans 2008)
2009	The Veterans Administration is doing very or fairly good at serving the needs of veterans.	62	68	61	(Cable News Network 2009)
2010	Overall opinion of the Veterans Administration, the VA, very favorable/mostly favorable	57			(Pew Research Center for the People & the Press 2010)

90

2012	I am going to name a number of different groups of people and institutions in this country. I would like you to rate each as either a very valuable asset to this country, a somewhat valuable asset to this country, not a very valuable asset to this country, or not a valuable asset at all to this country. Military veterans who have served since 9/11 (September 11, 2001, the date of the terrorist attacks on the World Trade Center and the Pentagon) (Percentage very valuable)	84	(The Mission Continues 2012)
2012	I am going to name a number of different groups of people and institutions in this country. I would like you to rate each as either a very valuable asset to this country, a somewhat valuable asset to this country, not a very valuable asset to this country, or not a valuable asset at all to this country. Military veterans returning from Iraq and Afghanistan (Percentage very valuable)	86	(The Mission Continues 2012)
2012	Thinking again, would you consider military veterans returning from Iraq and Afghanistan a very valuable asset to this country, a somewhat valuable asset to this country, not a very valuable asset to this country, or not a valuable asset at all to this country? (Percentage very valuable)	77	(The Mission Continues 2012)
2012	Thinking again, would you consider military veterans who have served since 9/11 (September 11, 2001, the date of the terrorist attack on the World Trade Center and the Pentagon) a very valuable asset to this country, a somewhat valuable asset to this country, not a very valuable asset to this country, or not a valuable asset at all to this country? (Percentage very valuable)	82	(The Mission Continues 2012)

(continued)

(continued)

Year	Question	Overall (%)	Rep (%)	Dem (%)	Source
2013	In your opinion, should higher education institutions admit some applicants from the following groups even if they apply with lower grades and test scores than other applicants? How about veterans?	79			(Lumina Foundation for Education 2013)
2013	Overall opinion of the Veterans Administration, the VA, very favorable/mostly favorable	66	71	64	(Pew Research Center for the People & the Press 2013)
2014	Do you approve or disapprove of the way Barack Obama is handling the situation in Veterans Affairs hospitals and medical facilities? (Percentage approve)	37	14	58	(CNN/ORC International Poll 2014)
2014	As you may know, today/on Friday Eric Shinseki resigned as the secretary of Veterans Affairs. Do you think Shinseki should have resigned, or do you think he should have stayed in office? (Percentage should have resigned)	68			(CNN/ORC International Poll 2014)
2014	Overall opinion of the Veterans Administration, the VA, very favorable/mostly favorable	50	46	54	(CBS News 2014)
2014	Is the responsibility of the VA to only take care of health problems directly related to a military service member or veterans' service, or should it be to take care of all of military service members' and veterans' health care needs for the rest of their lives? (Percentage saying take care of everything for rest of lives)	56			(Gallup Organization 2014)
2014	(Very or somewhat) serious some military veteran hospitals did not offer timely appointments for some patients and then falsified their records to hide this fact.	97	99	96	(ABC News/The Washington Post 2014)

Year	Question				Source
2014	Do you think Eric Shinseki should have resigned because of the VA (Veterans Administration) hospitals issue?	65	72	61	(ABC News/The Washington Post 2014)
2014	Do you think Eric Shinseki should have been pressured to resign because of the VA hospitals wait times?	52			(Fox News 2014)
2014	How much have you heard or read about the problems at some Veterans Administration, or VA, medical facilities, including reports about long waits for treatment and the death of some patients? (Percentage a lot)	40	43	38	(CBS News 2014)
2014	Do you approve or disapprove of the way Barack Obama is handling the problems at Veterans Administration medical facilities? (Percentage approve)	29	13	47	(CBS News 2014)
2014	Do you think the problems at Veterans Administration medical facilities are widespread or limited to just a few incidents? (Percentage limited)	23	19	21	(CBS News 2014)
2014	Do you think the problems of long waiting times at Veterans Administration medical facilities are mostly due to the VA not having adequate resources to take care of patients?	42	42	42	(CBS News 2014)
2014	Given what you know right now, do you think Eric Shinseki, the secretary of Veterans Affairs, should have to resign as a result of the problems at some Veterans Administration medical facilities or should he remain secretary of Veterans Affairs? (Percentage should resign)	45	56	36	(CBS News 2014)
2014	How often have you or a member of your immediate family experienced problems getting appointments or access to health care at Veterans Administration medical facilities for yourself or for a family member frequently, occasionally, or almost never? (Percentage almost never)	50	50	51	(CBS News 2014)

(continued)

(continued)

Year	Question	Overall (%)	Rep (%)	Dem (%)	Source
2014	Do you blame Eric Shinseki and the Veterans Administration for the problems at Veterans Administration medical facilities?	33	31	39	(CBS News 2014)
2014	Do you blame local hospitals for the problems at Veterans Administration medical facilities?	28	20	30	(CBS News 2014)
2014	Do you blame Obama for the problems at Veterans Administration medical facilities?	17	330	77	(CBS News 2014)
2014	What is your opinion on the favorability of the VA? (Very or mostly favorable)	55	53	61	(CBS News 2014)
2015	Are the needs of veterans best served by government, such as through the Veterans' Administration versus private providers?	56	40	69	(Fairleigh Dickinson University 2015)
2015	Is Congress to blame for not providing veterans with all that they need?	42	44	45	(Fairleigh Dickinson University 2015)
2015	Is the president to blame for not providing veterans with all that they need?	11	14	9	(Fairleigh Dickinson University 2015)
2015	Is the VA to blame for not providing veterans with all that they need?	29	28	28	(Fairleigh Dickinson University 2015)
2015	Is the United States doing excellent or good in caring for its veterans?	18	12	21	(Fairleigh Dickinson University 2015)
2015	Is your overall opinion of the Veterans Administration, the VA, very favorable, mostly favorable, mostly unfavorable, or very unfavorable? (Percentage very or mostly favorable)	55	56	58	(Pew Research Center for the People & the Press 2015)

| 2016 | Thinking about some different groups, how much respect do you think Hillary Clinton has for veterans? A great deal, a fair amount, not too much, or none at all? (Percentage great deal or fair amount) | 61 | 29 | 91 | (Pew Research Center for the People & the Press 2016) |
| 2016 | Thinking about some different groups, how much respect do you think Donald Trump has for veterans? A great deal, a fair amount, not too much, or none at all? | 64 | 89 | 41 | (Pew Research Center for the People & the Press 2016) |

CHAPTER FOUR

Legwork: Legislative Leaders on Veterans' Policy

In Congress legislators cultivate reputations based on their style and legislative activity. On a continuum of legislative behavior, we have one end populated by the dedicated *workhorses* who draft legislation, hammer out compromises, and get into the weeds of complicated policy questions. On the other end, there are *show ponies* that care more about pumping out media sound bites or trying to get the next "viral" video on YouTube. In this chapter, I consider the former: the hardworking members of Congress who seek to use their office to create and influence policies that are beneficial for veterans. I call the effort of creating and introducing veterans' policy *legwork*. Legwork requires information gathering, assessment, and policy development. Researching and crafting legislation is time-consuming, costly in terms of staff efforts, and mentally demanding.

Who are these members of Congress who do this sort of work on behalf of veterans? Which members introduce the most legislation on veterans' policy? Which members are most successful in ushering legislation from the introductory stage to final passage? Are there relationships between rank, role, district, and member characteristics that can be generalized to describe those who are more apt to do this work than others? In this chapter I work to give a comprehensive look at legislation on veterans during the 111th–114th Congresses. I develop an understanding of the biggest movers on veterans' legislation using institutional explanations to assess who engages in the most legwork.

I work from the most general understanding of legwork to more refined nuanced understandings of legwork as the analyses move on. Whenever I introduce new variables, I provide a description of how each is measured, what extant research has to say about the relationship between a given variable and legwork, and then offer an empirical assessment relating a variable and my measures of veterans' policy legwork.

In this chapter, I keep things relatively simple, relating explanatory and outcome measures via comparisons of means and correlations. In Chapter 5 I propose a theory that ties together how members legislate on behalf of veterans and how legislators communicate about veterans. After the explanation of the theory and what predictions come from such an explanation, I engage in a more rigorous assessment of legwork in contrast to communication efforts in Chapter 6. Speaking of workhorses and show ponies, in an effort to not put the cart before either sort of horse, let us first start with the basics: veterans' legislation and the legislators who introduced such legislation in the 111th–114th Congresses.

The Scope of Veterans' Legislation

Starting in 2004 each bill proposed in each chamber of Congress has been made available online via www.govtrack.us. In order to facilitate issue awareness and real-time tracking of legislation, each bill is given a lead subject such as "Armed Forces and National Security," "Immigration," or "Taxation." The designation denotes the issue area of legislation and is assigned to bills by the Library of Congress. Bills are then further categorized based on area-specific subcategories. The contemporary categorization scheme started in 2009.

Veterans' legislation is concerned with health care, education, employment, rehabilitation, loans, housing, homeless programs, organizations and recognition, pensions, and compensation of veterans. To create the count for number of veterans' legislation introduced for each member of Congress, I use the number of bills introduced that fall under the veterans subcategories assigned to bills by the Library of Congress.[1]

Measuring Legwork: Introducing Legislation

All legislators may introduce legislation. All legislators make choices to draft bills in some areas and not others. The ability to think of, write up, and submit legislation is not determined by party, committee membership, seniority, or any of the other host of factors that determine how the eventual policy process proceeds. Introducing legislation is one of the only things an individual legislator exerts almost entire control over. For short, I call the effort of introducing legislation *legwork*. To measure legwork on veterans' policy, I consider the number of veterans' issue bills introduced by each legislator serving in the 111th–114th Congresses.

To make comparisons across legislators clean, I do not compare members by the raw numbers of veterans' legislation introduced, but rather by the number of legislation introduced per year in Congress. Some members serve longer terms than others; some exit mid-Congress due to resignations, health concerns, or death. In order to account for the variation in tenure, each measure of legwork is made from the count of veterans' legislation introduced divided by the number of years in Congress for the individual legislator.

One could argue that introducing legislation is not really legwork, because it does not always lead to actual policy change.[2] The overwhelming majorities of bills that are introduced fail to pass; so why would that sort of effort be valuable to measure and assess? While these concerns are reasonable, bill introduction is one of the most straightforward ways to compare legislators equally. There are many elements in the collective decision-making processes of Congress that are out of the control of an individual legislator, making bill introduction, rather than final passage, a fairer across the board measurement of individual effort.

The majority party holds many institutional levers that can create opportunities for favored legislators or hurdles for legislators in the minority. This power is broadly known as agenda control. Scholars have explored various elements of this cartel-like control of the majority party in Congress in different ways.[3] The Speaker of the House can refer bills to favorable committees, determines the allocations of seats on committees in the first place, has more resources to whip votes, and can generally set the ordering of legislation. Additionally, the majority party is able to stack and operate strict control of the Rules Committees that determines important procedural steps for favored legislation or hurdles for opposed legislation.[4]

This is all to say that while bill introductions can come from either party without regard to the overall share of power, in terms of the ability to pass legislation, majority party status matters and no individual legislator can change that. Thus, while introductions as a measure of legwork might seem restrictive, it is the most theoretically suited and empirically tractable measure to work from when considering efforts of individual members of Congress. Because of the straightforward nature of comparing individual legislators, the strategy of using bill introductions as indicators of legislative effort has become more standard in congressional research, and I too adopt this strategy to measure legwork.[5]

Institutional Constraints

During the 111th–114th Congresses, control of the House and the Senate shifted from Democrats to Republicans. Seat distribution is something to be aware of when considering the activities of party actors collectively. Majority status does not help or hinder any individual member from introducing legislation, but the more members of a party that holds seats in the first place influence the numbers of legislation that may be offered by each party.

Table 4.1 presents the percentages of seats held by each party in each of the 111th–114th Congresses and a summary over the duration of the database.

As Table 4.1 shows, Republicans controlled Congress after the 2012 elections but not in overwhelming numbers. The greatest seat margin held by Republicans is 12 percent in 2015–2016, but the average distribution is much closer to 50:50, with Democrats holding 49 percent and Republicans holding 51 percent of all seats during the 111th–114th Congresses.

Seat shares matter when thinking about how to measure overall party legwork rather than individual efforts. Consider a hypothetical Senate with 90 Republicans and 10 Democrats. The 10 Democrats could each offer 3 pieces of legislation per year, and the 90 Republicans could each offer only 1 piece per year. When comparing legwork individually, the Democrats would have greater measures of legwork because their average is 3 per year versus 1 per year for Republicans. But if we summed up the totals of legislation offered per party per year, Republicans would be ahead with 90 total pieces (1 each) while the Democrat total would be 30 (3 each from 10 seats). This is all to say that when evaluating the actions of congressional Democrats and Republicans, it is important to know if the comparisons are done by comparing individuals or party totals as well as being aware of the relevant seat shares in the first place. In the analyses to come, I look both at the actions of individual legislators and at the collective activity of political parties within Congress.

Table 4.1 Percentage of Congressional Seats Held by Democrats and Republicans (111th–114th Congress)

Year	Percentage of Democrats	Percentage of Republicans
2009	59	41
2010	59	41
2011	46	54
2012	46	54
2013	48	52
2014	48	52
2015	44	56
2016	44	56
Overall	49	51

Legwork Data

As the first way to test which legislators introduce the most veterans' legislation, I consider all legislation to be equal. After that, I consider and describe the different types of legislation that legislators may offer. In the 111th–114th Congresses, 826 different members of Congress had the opportunity to offer veterans' legislation. Of those in Congress, 586 members offered just over 3,000 total pieces of veterans' legislation. Only 6 percent, just 171 pieces of legislation from 144 different legislators made it through the arduous process and became law.

Individually, there is a good deal of variation in how many pieces of legislation members of Congress introduce. Twenty-nine percent of all legislators never introduce any veterans' legislation. Of those who introduce veterans' legislation, the average number per year in office is 0.625 and the modal number is 0.5 or about one piece of legislation for every two years in Congress. During the time of study, legislators responsible for the most legislation are Representative Bob Filner (D-CA) with 15.67 bills introduced per year, Representative Patrick Murphy (D-PA) with 15.5, and Representative Steve Buyer (R-IN) as well as Senator Daniel Akaka (D-HI) each with eight pieces of legislation introduced per year. Figure 4.1 presents the distribution

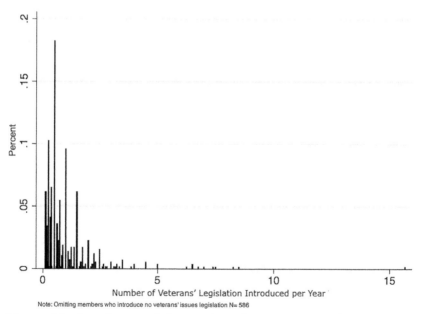

Figure 4.1 Distribution of the number of veterans' issues legislation introduced per year in service (111th–114th Congress).

Note: Omitting members who introduce no veterans' issues legislation, $n = 586$.

of legislation introduced per year in Congress for all legislators who proposed at least one veterans' bill.

Committee posts, personal history, constituency demands, and partisanship are all related to policy ownership and legislative efforts in other realms, so there is reason to believe that these ties are at work in veterans' politics as well.[6] Specifically I anticipate that Veterans' Affairs committee membership, military service, the proportion of veterans in a constituency, and partisanship will all be related to legwork. In the following sections I unpack each part by outlining why we might expect more or less legwork as each of the aforementioned variables changes and then follow up with empirical assessment.

Legislative Leaders on Veterans' Policy

In this section I consider which institutional, legislator, constituent, and party characteristics are most strongly associated with efforts to change veterans' policy by introducing relevant legislation as an indication of legwork. As one of the first stops for any piece of veterans' legislation, the Veterans Affairs' Committees in the House and the Senate play a pivotal role in ushering through policy change. This institutional feature of veterans' policy making, and those who sit on this committee, may very well be the place to look for the most legislative activity on veterans' politics.

The Veterans' Affairs Committees

Legislators ask to serve on different committees at the beginning of each congressional session, and the Speaker of the House allocates seats according to member preferences as well as the desires of the majority party leadership. The reasons for wanting a seat on a given committee are varied. Some members seek to serve because of their own background or expertise, others do so because of the relevancy of a committee to a certain constituency of their home district, and others consider the prestige and subject matter of a committee and select accordingly.[7]

The Veterans' Affairs Committees in the House and the Senate have a great amount of control of veterans' policy. By rule, bills that are introduced on the topic of veterans are referred to the committee in order to hold hearings, mark up proposed legislation, and report out bills to be considered by the greater chamber. All legislation concerning compensation, life insurance, national cemeteries, pensions, readjustment programs, civil relief, hospitals, medical care and treatment, vocational training, education, and other measures generally related to veterans are under the jurisdiction of the committee.

The members of Congress who are on the committees tasked with reviewing veterans' legislation have access to domain-specific aides and can summon additional outside expertise through the hearing process. Given their status as committee members and increased access to expertise, it is plausible that committee members would be responsible for introducing greater amounts of veterans' legislation than other members of Congress.

Data for membership on Veterans' Affairs Committee in the House and the Senate come from the committees' websites as well as archival lists maintained by Center for Responsive Politics. From the 111th–114th Congresses 91 different members served on a veterans' committee; in the appendix to this chapter, I list the specific members of Congress who served on veterans' committees.

During the 111th–114th Congresses, roughly equal numbers of Republicans and Democrats served on Veterans' Affairs Committees in the House and the Senate but the majority party held slightly more seats in accordance with the overall share of the chamber. Table 4.2 presents the average amount of veterans' legislation introduced by members who sit on the committee versus members of Congress who do not.

As Table 4.2 shows, those on the Veterans' Affairs Committee are legislative leaders. On average, committee members introduce at least one more bill than nonmembers per year in office. These differences are statistically significant when looking at just the House, just the Senate, and the Congress combined. There are subtle differences across the chambers. Noncommittee members in the Senate introduce greater amounts of veterans' legislation than noncommittee members in the House. However, for both chambers the greatest differences are between committee members and noncommittee members.

Table 4.2 Average Number of Veterans' Legislation Introduced per Year in Service by Veterans' Committee Status (111th–114th Congress)

	On Veterans' Committee		Not on Veterans' Committee		
	Legislation/Year	N	Legislation/Year	N	Difference
House	2.23	63	0.49	613	−1.75*
Senate	1.96	28	0.87	121	−1.09*
Combined	2.15	91	0.55	734	−1.60*

Two-tailed t-test

* $p < 0.05$

Veteran Status of a Legislator

Theories of descriptive representation argue that legislators who hold some sort of identification are more apt to develop and push for policies that benefit that particular identity. Theoretically, women ought to be more inclined to introduce women's issues bills, and racial minorities ought to introduce more bills attuned to the needs of minority communities. Empirical research shows that women do tend to introduce women's issues legislation more than men and provide better substantive representation for women.[8] Members of Congress who hold minority identities are far more likely to hold hearings addressing minority interest issues than others.[9] Thus, there are indications that member characteristics translate into more symbolic and substantive efforts on behalf of people who share those characteristics.

But veteran status is not like gender or race. Members of Congress who previously served in the armed services have an institutional identity as a veteran, not an inborn one. The decision to enter the armed services is not a characteristic; it is a choice. The way in which veterans came to be veterans is different than the way the majority of women become women, but there are still theoretical reasons to expect that veterans would introduce more legislation focused toward veterans than others who do not share the same history and background.

As veterans, members of Congress who have military backgrounds are better equipped to understand the needs and wants of citizens who share a history of military service. The demands that a career in the armed services puts on individual service members and their families are hard to imagine for those who have not had that experience. Do veterans introduce more legislation on veterans' issues than nonvets?[10] Table 4.3 displays the amounts of veterans' legislation introduced by year in office for veterans and nonveterans.

While the difference was clear and significant for those on the Veterans' Affairs Committees, the results by veteran status are marginal at best. In a two-tailed comparison of means test, I do not find support for the idea that

Table 4.3 Average Number of Veterans' Legislation Introduced per Year in Service by Veteran Status (111th–114th Congress)

	Veteran Legislators		Nonveteran Legislators		
	Legislation/Year	N	Legislation/Year	N	Difference
House	0.80	113	0.61	563	−0.18
Senate	1.19	31	1.05	118	−0.14
Combined	0.98	104	1.22	482	−0.24

Two-tailed *t*-test

* $p < 0.05$

veteran legislators introduce veterans' legislation at rates that are significantly different from nonveteran legislators. For veteran status, the theoretical expectation linking identity to legislative efforts on behalf of that identity is not supported by the data of the most recent Congresses. Unlike the findings in many other descriptive representation work, there does not appear to be a particular link between veteran status of a Congress person and the volume of legislation introduced on veterans' issues.

Veterans in Constituency

The numbers of veterans vary in every congressional district and state. Veterans make decisions on where to live in ways that are similar to other citizens, based on familial demands, work opportunities, climate, personal desirability, and so on. But because of the particular career paths and medical needs of veterans, there are clusters of veterans in some districts with greater percentages than others. Veterans' populations are high near military bases as these sorts of familial and cultural ties influence the decision to join the service in the first place and where to live afterwards. Another particular concern for veterans is the distance from a VA facility, where service members needing continual care oftentimes will attempt to balance other considerations with VA facility proximity.

Perhaps legislators who come from districts with greater numbers of veterans are more likely to offer veterans' legislation in an effort to match an important segment in their constituency. Research on the prevalence of certain industries finds links between the levels of the auto and steel workers within a constituency and legislative actions a member of Congress takes regarding those industries.[11] It is not too much of a stretch to surmise that a similar sort of link might connect veterans' constituencies and their legislators.

If legislators who come from districts with more veterans in their constituency ought to do more for veterans, then we would expect a positive relationship between numbers of veterans' bills introduced and the share of veterans in a district. I split the sample in two halves, those who have more than the median percentages of veterans in their constituency and those who have fewer. The median percent of veterans in any given congressional constituency is 8.27 percent. Table 4.4 shows the legislation introduced per year by veterans' constituency.

Perhaps surprisingly, when sliced this way, there is no apparent difference between the legwork efforts of members with fewer or more veterans in a constituency. Yet, the measure of veterans in a constituency is continuous; to better use this variability I present the correlation between the percent of veterans in a constituency and the numbers of legislation introduced per year. Figure 4.2 displays the relationship between these two variables.

As Figure 4.2 shows, there is a slight, positive relationship between the share of veterans in a constituency and the legwork rates of members of Congress. The correlation coefficient is a positive and significant 0.10.

Table 4.4 Average Number of Veterans' Legislation Introduced per Year in Service by Veteran Constituency (111th–114th Congress)

	Fewer Veterans in Constituency		More Veterans in Constituency		
	Legislation/Year	N	Legislation/Year	N	Difference
House	0.54	32	0.69	374	−0.15
Senate	0.95	16	1.40	43	−0.46
Combined	0.65	48	0.77	417	−0.12

Note: The median percent of veterans in a constituency is 8.27.

Two-tailed *t*-test

* $p < 0.05$

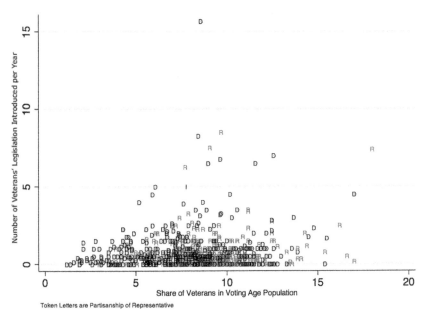

Figure 4.2 Share of veterans in voting age population by veterans' legislation introduced per year.

Party

Party matters in different policy spaces and is the organizing force behind most congressional activity.[12] Because of the importance of parties for the internal workings of Congress, it is reasonable to expect to find some patterns of activity defined by partisan divisions. In the issue ownership literature, there is no clear research on which party "owns" veterans' policies. Historically, the Republican Party is trusted to deal with issues of military readiness and foreign policy, but the Democratic Party is trusted to figure out health-care, educational, and social assistance policies.[13] No study to date has assessed specific issue ownership of veterans' politics. In many ways, veterans' politics is cross-cutting on the extant issue ownership lines as it straddles military elements and medical, education, and social welfare lines. To that end, there is no a priori reason to expect either party to have a great lead in *legwork* on veterans' policy.

The previous chapter indicated that a majority of veterans identify as Republicans and support Republican candidates in electoral contests. One reason for that may be that Republicans in Congress wield their power to legislate to *do more* for veterans than Democrats. In order to earn this support, do Republicans in Congress introduce more legislation on veterans' issues? Introduction rates by party are displayed in Table 4.5.[14]

This simple comparison shows that Democrats have significantly higher levels of veterans' legwork than Republicans. In the House, Democratic members introduce more veterans' legislation than Republicans on average, and this difference is significant. In the Senate, Democrats also introduce more pieces of veterans' legislation than their Republican counterparts, but given the small magnitude in difference and the smaller numbers of people serving in the Senate, there is not a statistically significant difference between the two parties. When combining the Congress into one set, I find that Democrats introduce 0.33 more bills per year in service than Republicans and that this difference is significant.

Figure 4.3 presents the raw counts of how much legislation was introduced collectively by members of each party during the 111th–114th Congresses. This visual representation pools all members of each party together, but the results are similar to that in Table 4.5. When considered as individual actors, Democrats introduce significantly more veterans' legislation than

Table 4.5 Average Number of Veterans' Legislation Introduced per Year in Service by Party (111th–114th Congress)

	Democrats		Republicans		
	Legislation/ Year	N	Legislation/ Year	N	Difference
House	0.80	335	0.49	341	−0.31*
Senate	1.27	78	0.87	71	−0.40
Combined	0.90	412	0.56	413	−0.33*

Two-tailed *t*-test

* $p < 0.05$

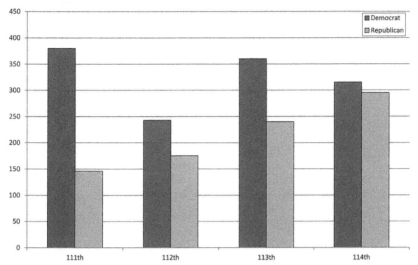

Figure 4.3 Veterans' policy—Legislation introduced by party of sponsor (111th–114th Congress).

Note: Legislation and sponsorship data from Congress.gov.

Republicans, and when pooled together, even despite the loss of the majority in the 112th Congress, Democrats collectively offered more veterans' legislation than Republicans.

Republicans had more seats in Congress and thus might be expected to introduce more legislation on issues of interest such as veterans' policy. Yet as Figure 4.3 shows, in each Congress, congressional Democrats tended to introduce more bills as a whole on veteran issues than Republicans. The legwork gap is substantial, and while it decreases somewhat overtime, in each Congress Democrats do more legwork on behalf of veterans.

Noting the finding that Democrats engage in more legwork than Republicans, I now delve into some further complexities of legwork to focus in on the sorts of legislative efforts that members of each party offer.

Further Nuances of Legwork: Types of Legislation

The previous analyses consider all veterans' bills on equal footing. The preceding section shows that committee members and Democrats are more apt to introduce legislation on veterans' issues. Yet, like any story about policy and politics, there are nuances and complications to explore and explain.

Not all legislation has the same level of impact. Some bills simply change the name of a building, some appropriate new money to create facilities, and some change the rules underlying veterans' eligibility for benefits. Some bills require presidential approval; some do not. This is all to say that there are different types of efforts, and while overall measures of introductions are illustrative, there are other features of policy that offer a more complete picture of legwork.

Bills are introduced with the titles such as "H.R." or "S." standing for House of Representatives or Senate followed by a number to signify the chamber from which they originated as well as an identifying parliamentary number. After each chamber approves bills, they are presented to the president and may then be signed into law or vetoed. Bills that are enacted become public law. Bills, unless they are very uncontroversial, will come up for a roll call where members of Congress will register their support or opposition to a bill with a recorded vote.

Resolutions are different in title, process, and outcomes. Resolutions are pieces of legislation that pertain either to the operations of the House or the Senate and are used to express some sort of sentiment of a chamber, form of recognition of an issue, or internal chamber procedures. Resolutions are introduced under the title "H.Res" or "S.Res." But these legislative vehicles are not presented to the president, and their effects are limited to the chamber that agrees to them. In some cases, resolutions are nonbinding or with little real impact other than to express a sentiment of the chamber. In other cases, resolutions are binding and change the internal procedures or personnel duties within the chamber that agrees to the resolution.

Two examples of resolutions agreed to in the 114th Congress are S.Res. 295—a resolution designating the week of November 2 through November 6, 2015, as "National Veterans Small Business Week," introduced by Sen. Jeanne Shaheen (D-NH)—and H.Res. 29—electing Members to certain standing committees of the House of Representatives introduced by Rep. Luke Messer (R-IN6).

The first resolution simply means that members of the Senate can tell constituents they named a week "National Veterans Small Business Week." This symbolic recognition may give rise to an occasion to hold some sort of veterans' round table or discussion coinciding with that week, but there is no binding effect of that resolution on any actor inside or outside of the Senate.

The second resolution is binding in the sense that it governs who is on certain committees within the House, but it has no greater impact on anyone outside of the House of Representatives. Resolutions are often agreed to by a voice vote or unanimous consent, and therefore, no members are singled out for supporting or opposing a resolution by name.

Because of both the nature and the scope of resolutions, they are less consequential for the public, but members of Congress are keen to refer to resolutions as a way of credit claiming or position taking in constituent communications. The differences between bills and resolutions are often lost on constituents not well versed in legislative procedure, and members of

Congress know this. Consequently, when minority party members are unable to pass bills, they may turn to authoring and passing *resolutions* and then highlighting those accomplishments to constituents. This is certainly easier than explaining why their party will likely not have as many substantive legislative successes as the minority.

There are even finer gradations of bills and resolutions that merit consideration. Some bills change law in a broad sense, some bills appropriate or authorize money, some bills amend current law in minor ways, and some bills or resolutions accomplish symbolic ends more than programmatic ones.

In the following analyses, I bin legislation into four types: amendments, authorization/appropriation, symbolic, and substantive. *Amendments* are bills introduced on their own to amend the text of previously agreed-to laws or to amend considered legislation. *Authorization* or *appropriation* legislation does not necessarily do the work of creating or making a new sort of policy for veterans but rather allocates or authorizes the resources to do veterans-related spending. *Symbolic* legislation is something that changes the symbols or figures around something related to veterans. For instance, naming a hospital building or ward for a certain person is a symbolic change, but there is no difference in the way health care is administered. Lastly, *substantive* bills involve a change in policy of the sort that most people would associate with legislating; new programs or new rules are made changing the ways veterans interact with the benefits system or the sorts of provisions that are offered to veterans.

I will use the activities of the 114th Congress in the specific topic of veterans' health care to provide example of the four legislative categories before considering the Congresses together for a more comprehensive look.

Amendments

During the 114th Congress, 31 pieces of legislation were enacted into public law on veterans' health care. Three made *amendments* to existing parts of U.S. code. H.R. 1755 introduced by Rep. Jeff Miller (R-FL) changed the text of Section 50302 of Title 36 of the U.S. Code by making some things clearer in the congressional charter of Disabled American Veterans (DAV). The DAV is an organization chartered by the Congress to help disabled military veterans of the armed forces, and their families navigate hardships after their time in service. The charter previously started with, "The purposes of the corporation are," and this bill changed the text to "The corporation is organized exclusively for charitable and educational purposes. The purposes of the corporation shall include . . ." and then made further grammatical changes to reflect the more concise purpose.

This does not create any great substantive changes to how veterans' health care is administered, but it does amend the way the Congress charters a body that helps veterans navigate the system. In the database of veterans' bills, amendments are easily identified because the text oftentimes starts with "To amend title X" or "To extend," meaning some time frame imposed via earlier legislation is revised.

Authorization/Appropriation

Ten pieces of legislation in the 114th Congress were fixes to or pieces of legislation rolled into much bigger *authorization or appropriation* vehicles. Authorization/Appropriation legislation tends to originate with party in control of the House via the agenda-setting power of the Speaker and the requirement that these sorts of bills start in the lower chamber. S. 2943 the National Defense Authorization Act for Fiscal Year 2017, introduced by Sen. John McCain (R-AZ), is one such bill. For the purposes of identification in the database, any bill that includes the terms "Appropriations, (re)Authorization," or is solely for the purpose of continuing the congressional authorization of some sort of veterans' program already in existence, is counted as an authorization/appropriation bill.

One consideration to note is that while majority or minority party status does not limit the ability to offer stand-alone, symbolic, or amending legislation, there are some norms and traditions around appropriation bills. Appropriations and big annual authorization bills are considered prestigious, and sponsorship of these bills is oftentimes doled out by the majority party leadership to other majority party members on relevant committees. Because of the prestige of these bills, claiming to have introduced the bill as well as the "bacon" or funding for a home district within parts of these sorts of legislation gives members something to brag about to constituents back home.[15] There are instances in which a very senior member or a member with an established reputation in a certain policy area of the minority party may be offered the opportunity to sponsor an appropriation or authorization bill, but the norm is to have majority party members offer these sorts of bills.

Symbolic

Some legislation is passed just so that members of Congress can tell constituents that they did something. Congressional scholars observe these sorts of things all the time, but more casual congressional observers tend to be a bit underwhelmed when they realize what Congress has "passed." Sometimes resolutions are passed that do not more than congratulate a hometown sports team for a recent victory. These sorts of resolutions only need introduction and passage in one chamber since they effect no change in public law.

During the 114th Congress nine pieces of legislation were *symbolic* changes in the naming or dedications of certain facilities. One was H.R. 2693: to designate the arboretum at the Hunter Holmes McGuire VA Medical Center in Richmond, Virginia, as the "Phyllis E. Galanti Arboretum" introduced by Rep. Dave Brat (R-VA).

Substantive

The remaining nine bills passed in the 114th Congress were of the sort that most people think of when they think about the work of Congress. These substantive bills are stand-alone policy proposals to change the way veterans receive or access some sort of benefit. H.R.4352: Faster Care for Veterans Act of 2016 introduced by Representative Seth Moulton (D-MA) is one such bill. This bill orders the VA to create Veterans Integrated Service Networks so that veterans can use a website or mobile phone app to schedule and confirm appointments at VA medical facilities. This changes the way veterans access health care by providing more convenient and modern ways to schedule appointments and mandates that government implement a change in the way benefits are accessed.

Do Republican and Democratic legislators offer different sorts of legislation? Given that Republicans tend to be preferred by veterans, it could be that while the GOP lags in overall legislative legwork, they focus their efforts on substantive bills, and those arguably matter more to veterans than symbolic or minor amendment efforts. In Table 4.6, I pool the 111th–114th Congresses together and show the share of different types of legislation offered by legislators of each party.

Recall the baseline expectation: if both parties engaged in legwork in ways that mirrored their seat shares, we would expect Republicans to have a slight edge. But given the results showing that Democrats offer more legislation overall, the question now changes to see if there are appreciable differences in the types of legislation offered by party. Figure 4.4 shows the breakdown of the types of legislation introduced during the 111th–114th Congresses.

The majority of bills introduced for veterans are substantive in nature. After substantive legislation, symbolic and amending legislation, each accounts for 11 percent of all bills introduced, and appropriations and authorizations account for nearly 5 percent. Do Republicans and Democrats introduce similar types of legislation? In Figure 4.5 I present a breakdown by each type of legislation by the party of the introducing sponsor.

The shares of symbolic legislation introduced are roughly equal between the parties. Democrats introduce a greater share of substantive and amending veterans' issues bills, and Republicans are responsible for the introduction of more appropriation and authorization bills. It is not the case that one party overwhelmingly relies on some types of legislation over others. There is also no evidence that the legislation Democrats introduce is of the symbolic sort that may not change the policies most important to veterans'

Legwork: Legislative Leaders on Veterans' Policy

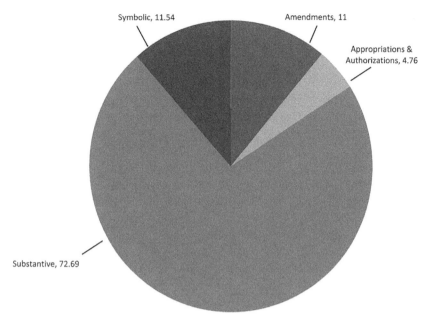

Figure 4.4 Shares of legislative types of all veterans' issues' legislation introduced (111th–114th Congress).

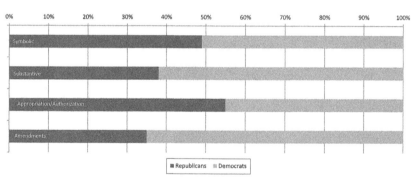

Figure 4.5 Lead sponsor partisanship across bill types introduced on veterans' issues in 111th–114th Congresses.

benefits. On the contrary, Figure 4.5 provides some evidence that Democrats have a slight edge in substantive legislation over Republicans. In the coming analyses I do not split legislation types, as there is no great theoretical development to be had, given the split results here. However, this descriptive image should serve as another piece of the somewhat curious mosaic of partisanship and veterans' issues.

Table 4.6 Average Number of Cosponsors for Veterans' Legislation Introduced (111th–114th Congress)

	Committee Membership					
	On Veterans' Affairs Committee	N	Not on Veterans' Affairs Committee	N	Difference
House	12.86	58	20.46	412	6.60
Senate	13.86	23	19.38	93	5.52
Combined	13.86	81	20.27	505	6.40
	Veteran Status				
	Veteran Legislator		Nonveteran Legislator		
House	15.80	79	20.43	391	4.63
Senate	30.74	25	14.87	91	−15.87
Combined	19.39	14	19.38	482	−0.01
	Veterans in Constituency				
	Fewer Than Average		More Than Average		
House	22.24	216	17.45	254	−4.98
Senate	16.01	82	23.79	34	7.78
Combined	20.53	298	18.12	288	−2.33
	Party				
	Democrat		Republican		
House	21.30	248	17.18	222	−3.48
Senate	17.21	63	19.57	53	2.36
Combined	20.47	311	18.15	275	−2.32

Two-tailed t-test

* $p < 0.05$

Alternate Measures of Legwork

Cosponsors

It could be the case that members with higher numbers of legislative introductions such as those on the veterans' committees, or in Democratic Party, have greater numbers of legislation introduced, but perhaps these pieces are unpopular and don't get more widespread support. How would we know? There is no universal measure of the "goodness" of legislation. Every piece has trade-offs, winners and losers, proponents and opponents. Yet, there is a measure that can be applied to all legislation that can somewhat approximate an assessment of "goodness": the number of other people who sign on to cosponsor legislation.[16]

Cosponsoring is a relatively easy thing for a legislator to do. If there is a bill that someone else spearheads, but a legislator thinks that the bill is a good idea, or that he or she would be able to impress voters by touting the bill as something he or she signed on to, then the decision to cosponsor takes nothing more than notifying the clerks of the chamber of that intent. Legislators who draft legislation want to attract cosponsors. It is a way of signaling that the sponsor has a good idea and gives credence to claims that a bill with many cosponsors ought to be more fully considered.

As before, in the following comparisons I consider committee, veteran status, veterans' constituencies, and party. For each of these analyses I only include legislators who have introduced at least one bill. If a member did not introduce any legislation, it would be impossible to attract cosponsors. This restriction eliminates 137 Republicans from the sample and 102 Democrats. That is of the legislators who offered no veterans' legislation during their time in the House or the Senate under study, 57 percent were Republicans.

The measure of average bill cosponsorship can be taken as a signal of both policy and legislative leadership, both of which are elements of legwork. Other members of Congress will want to sign on to pieces of legislation they consider to be good policy or at least good press. In a related manner, good legislative leaders will be able to enjoin other members to sign on to their bills in an effort to recruit more interested parties with preferences to see a bill ushered to final passage. Table 4.6 combines committee, veteran status, veteran constituency, and party and presents average number of cosponsors members of Congress in each category tend to get.

As Table 4.6 shows, there are no statistically significant differences across any of the posited measures relating legislator institutional status to the average numbers of other legislators willing to sign on as co-sponsors to veterans' legislation.[17] That is, if the number of cosponsors is a way to determine how good or popular legislation is, I find no appreciable differences across reasonable ways to split the data.

Final Passage

As another measure of legislative legwork, I assess the number of bills passed per year in office. This is a way to see who authors and *makes* policy change on veterans' issues. Final passage changes the status quo but is also far less in control of any one legislator, and thus, the measure does not as cleanly capture individual effort. The numbers of bills passed per year in Congress per legislator are much lower than the rates of introduction because it is much harder to pass legislation than it is to introduce it.

Table 4.7 Average Number of Veterans' Legislation Passed per Year in Service (111th–114th Congress)

	Committee Membership				
	On Veterans' Affairs Committee	N	Not on Veterans' Affairs Committee	N	Difference
House	0.09	58	0.05	412	−0.04
Senate	0.10	23	0.03	93	−0.07
Combined	0.09	81	0.05	55	−0.04*
	Veteran Status				
	Veteran Legislator		Nonveteran Legislator		
House	0.08	79	0.05	391	−0.02
Senate	0.07	25	0.04	91	−0.03
Combined	0.07	14	0.05	482	−0.02
	Veterans in Constituency				
	Fewer Than Average		More Than Average		
House	22.24	216	17.45	254	−4.98
Senate	16.01	82	23.79	34	7.78
Combined	0.04	298	0.07	289	−0.03*
	Party				
	Democrat		Republican		
House	0.07	248	0.04	222	−0.03
Senate	0.04	63	0.05	53	0.01
Combined	0.06	311	0.04	275	−2.32

Two-tailed *t*-test

*$p < 0.05$

Like cosponsorship, there are no overall consistent findings that differently situated legislators in terms of personal history, institutional positions, or constituencies are more or less successful in securing final passage for their veterans' legislation. The only statistically significant difference is that members of the Veterans' Committees when pooled together as a whole are a bit more successful in passing legislation than those not on the committee. This speaks to the importance of committee work for ushering through legislation.

Combined Influences Related to Legwork

While the previous set of simple examinations considered factors related to legwork on their own, there are undoubtedly combined influences between the institutional, legislator, and constituency characteristics that matter when legislating. On top of the four primary explanatory variables, there are sets of variables that are linked to legislative style and prowess that also likely play minor roles in the development of veterans' legwork. In Chapter 6, I present a series of statistical tests relating the variables thought to be related to legislative and communication efforts about veterans. For now, I present a few notable overlapping elements and consolidate the reporting of the larger regression analyses to Chapter 6.

Earlier analyses indicated that being on the veterans' committee is related to introducing and passing more legislation, Democrats introduce more legislation than Republicans, and there is a positive relationship between the share of veterans in a constituency and the level of veterans' legislation introduced. How do all these influences relate to each other? Figure 4.6 provides a visual comparison of veterans in a district, legislator partisanship, and committee membership.

The figure shows the distribution of differently situated legislators. Notice that the peaks of each distribution are similar to each other and nearly all

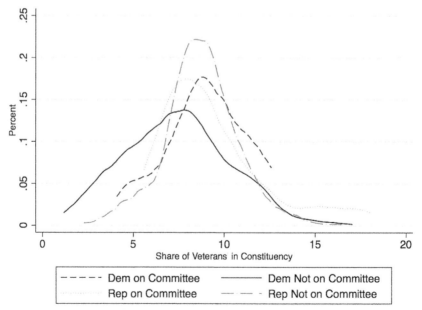

Figure 4.6 Shares of veterans in a constituency by party of legislator and veterans' committee status (111th–114th Congress).

masses have great overlap. Yet there are some details made clear by the figure. Democrat legislators who are not on the Veterans' Affairs Committee tend to have slightly lower shares of veterans among their constituents. Of committee members, Republican legislators come from constituencies with slightly greater shares of veterans.

Overall, no one configuration of party and committee status totally distinct from the others indicates that the explanatory variables considered in isolation seem to have competing rather than strictly reinforcing effects on legwork.

As a way to compare the competing influences of committee appointment, veteran status, veterans in a constituency, and party I conduct a series of analyses considering only those variables across the three measures of legwork used previously. The dependent variables are the continuous measures of legislation introduced per year in office, the average number of cosponsors, and legislation passed per year. Owing to the form and distribution of the dependent variables I employ a negative binomial regression; results are presented in Table 4.8.

Table 4.8 Legwork as a Function of Institutional, Legislator, and Constituency Characteristics (111th–114th Congress)

	Introductions	Cosponsors	Passage
On Committee	1.26**	−0.37*	0.52
	(0.14)	(0.18)	(0.32)
Veteran	0.03	0.06	0.44
	(0.12)	(0.19)	(0.32)
Veterans in Constituency	0.06**	−0.04	0.11*
	(0.02)	(0.03)	(0.04)
Democrat	0.47**	0.10	0.56*
	(0.10)	(0.16)	(0.26)
House	−0.43**	0.07	0.23
	(0.12)	(0.18)	(0.29)
Constant	−1.05	3.21	−4.61
N	823	586	586
McFadden's Adjusted R2	0.10	0.00	0.03

Negative binomial regression coefficients with white standard errors in parentheses.
* $p < 0.05$
** $p < 0.00$

As the comparisons show, for the most part the indicators that were related to legwork when considered individually also emerge as important when considered in tandem with each other. All else equal, being on the Veterans' Affairs Committee is related to introducing more veterans' legislation but is also related to having fewer cosponsors once all other variables are accounted for. On average, people on the veterans' committees offer about three more pieces of legislation for every two-year session of Congress. The percentage of veterans in a constituency is also positively and significantly related to legwork. The more veterans in a constituency, the more pieces of legislation a legislator introduces and more of their pieces are eventually passed. As before there is also a positive and significant relationship between the partisanship of a legislator and legwork. Democrats do more legwork even controlling for things like veterans' committee membership and the share of veterans in a constituency, both of which are measures that are greater for Republicans than Democrats in the first place.

Concluding Thoughts

At this first-level analyses of legwork, the key findings relating institutional status to legwork show that those on the Veterans' Affairs Committee introduce more legislation than those not on the committee and that Democratic Party legislators introduce more veterans' legislation than Republican Party legislators. When considered collectively, both of these variables still matter and are positively related to legislative introduction. The constituency measure of share of veterans in a district is also positively related to legwork.

Veteran status of a legislator is not significantly related to any measure of legwork. This is a contribution to the descriptive representation literature. Veterans in the contemporary Congress do not exert more legwork on behalf of veterans. Nor is there a link between being a veteran and one's ability to attract cosponsors on veterans' legislation, or to secure passage of veterans' legislation.

Given that committee positions are divided in a way that mirrors the partisan split of Congress, the finding that the Democrats own the policy space in terms of legislative production is somewhat striking. This is striking because it seems that in the lore of popular accounts and in the data on veterans' party identification and voting patterns, Republicans are the preferred party. To be sure there are reasons why Democrats had legislative advantages during the 111th Congress as they controlled both chambers and the presidency, but this advantage soon eroded with the midterm losses of the 112th Congress. Yet, in terms of attempting to change policy on veterans' issues by introducing legislation, Democrats do more legwork than Republicans.

Why don't Republicans introduce more veterans' legislation? Why do Republicans seem to get the share of credit from veterans despite being outdone legislatively by Democrats? Republicans and Democrats both represent veterans in Congress; Republicans even have slightly higher percentages of veterans in their constituencies than Democrats. There are more Republicans on the Veterans' Affairs Committees, and there are actually more Republican veteran members of Congress than Democratic veterans. With all these considerations, why don't we observe more legwork coming from Republicans?

One possible reason could be that Republican Party ideology stresses limited government, so the observation that members of the party offer fewer bills in the first place is just a realization of that ideological tenet. This explanation is not particularly compelling theoretically or empirically. Theoretically, even legislators wishing to cut back the role of government must be willing to introduce legislation to curb the role of government by specifically cutting or curtailing extant government powers. Empirically, Republicans do introduce legislation at rates predicted by their seat share in other policy realms, while they do not for veterans' policy.[18] In the next chapter, I put forward reasons for why veterans' policy is a particularly difficult policy space for Republicans in Congress to legislate in and I argue that there are other mechanisms to signal care about veterans without having to engage in the production of legislation.

There, of course, is no one singular reason that describes the public preference and legwork disconnect, but in the following two chapters, I put forward and test a theory that helps bridge our gap in understanding. Members of both parties are similarly incentivized to work on behalf of veterans, but Democrats legislate on behalf of veterans more. Members of both parties would like to have public recognition as agents that support veterans, yet Republicans seem to do better at cultivating that reputation. Having shown the basics of *how* legwork on veterans' politics is distributed across members of the Congress, let us now turn to considering *why* there is a political-public disconnect.

Appendix
Members of the House and Senate Veterans' Affairs Committees

114th Congress—Senate

Majority—Republican	Minority—Democrat
Chairman Johnny Isakson (GA)	Ranking Member Richard Blumenthal (CT)*
Jerry Moran (KS)	Patty Murray (WA)
Senator John Boozman (AR)	Bernie Sanders (VT)
Senator Dean Heller (NV)	Sherrod Brown (OH)
Senator Bill Cassidy (LA)	John Tester (MT)
Mike Rounds (SD)	Mazie Hirono (HI)
Senator Thom Tillis (NC)	Joe Manchin (WV)
Dan Sullivan (AK)*	

* Veteran member

113th Congress—Senate

Majority—Democrat	Minority—Republican
Chairman Bernie Sanders (VT)	Ranking Member Richard Burr (NC)
John D. Rockefeller IV (WV)	Johnny Isakson (GA)
Patty Murray (WA)	Mike Johanns (NE)
Sherrod Brown (OH)	Jerry Moran (KS)
John Tester (MT)	John Boozman (AR)
Mark Begich (AK)	Dean Heller (NV)
Richard Blumenthal (CT)*	
Mazie Hirono (HI)	

* Veteran member

112th Congress—Senate

Majority—Democrat	Minority—Republican
Chairman Patty Murray (WA)	Ranking Member Richard Burr (NC)
John D. Rockefeller IV (WV)	Johnny Isakson (GA)
Daniel K. Akaka (HI)*	Roger Wicker (MS)*
Bernie Sanders (VT)	Mike Johanns (NE)
Sherrod Brown (OH)	Scott Brown (MA)*
Jim Webb (VA)*	Jerry Moran (KS)
John Tester (MT)	John Boozman (AR)
Mark Begich (AK)	

* Veteran member

111th Congress—Senate

Majority—Democrat	Minority—Republican
Chairman Daniel K. Akaka (HI)*	Ranking Member Richard Burr (NC)
John D. Rockefeller IV (WV)	Johnny Isakson (GA)
Roland Burris (IL)	Roger Wicker (MS)*
Bernie Sanders (VT)	Mike Johanns (NE)
Sherrod Brown (OH)	Scott Brown (MA)*
Jim Webb (VA)*	Lindsey Graham (SC)*
Arlen Specter (PA)	
Mark Begich (AK)	

* Veteran member

111th Congress—House

Majority—Democrat	Minority—Republican
John H. Adler (NJ)	Brian P Bilbray (CA)
Corrine Brown (FL)	Gus Bilirakis (FL)
Deborah Halvorson (IL)	John Boozman (AR)
Joe Donnelly (IN)	Henry Brown (SC)
Glenn Nye (VA)	Vernon Buchanan (FL)*
Bob Filner (CA)	Steve Buyer (IN)*
John Hall (NY)	Douglas L. Lamborn (CO)

Tom Perriello (VA)	Jeff Miller (FL)
Stephanie Herseth Sandlin (SD)	Jerry Moran (KS)
Jerry McNerney (CA)	Cliff Stearns (FL)*
Mike Michaud (ME)	Phil Roe (TN)*
Harry Mitchell (AZ)	
Ciro D. Rodriguez (TX)	
Harry Teague (NM)	
Vic Snyder (AR)*	
Zack Space (OH)	
Timothy J. Walz (MN)*	

* Veteran member

112th Congress—House

Minority—Democrat	Majority—Republican
John Barrow (GA)	Dan Benishek (MI)
Bruce Braley (IA)	Gus Bilirakis (FL)
Corrine Brown (FL)	Ann Marie Buerkle (NY)
Russ Carnahan (MO)	Jeff Denham (CA)*
Joe Donnelly (IN)	Bill Flores (TX)
Bob Filner (CA)	Tim Huelskamp (KS)
Jerry McNerney (CA)	Bill Johnson (OH)*
Mike Michaud (ME)	Jeff Miller (FL)
Silvestre Reyes (TX)*	Jerry Moran (KS)
Linda Sanchez (CA)	Phil Roe (TN)*
Timothy J. Walz (MN)*	Jon Runyan (NJ)
	Cliff Stearns (FL)*
	Marlin Stutzman (IN)

* Veteran member

113th Congress—House

Minority—Democrat	Majority—Republican
Corrine Brown (FL)	Mark Amodei (R-Nev)*
Julia Brownley (CA)	Dan Benishek (R-Mich)
Ann Kirkpatrick (AZ)	Gus Bilirakis (R-Fla)

Ann Mclane Kuster (NH)	Mike Coffman (R-Colo)*
Gloria McLeod (CA)	Paul Cook (CA)*
Mike Michaud (ME)	Jeff Denham (CA)*
Beto O'Rourke (TX)	Bill Flores (TX)
Raul Ruiz (CA)	Tim Huelskamp (KS)
Mark A. Takano (CA)	Douglas L Lamborn (CO)
Dina Titus (NV)	Jeff Miller (FL)
Timothy J. Walz (MN)	Phil Roe (TN)*
	Jon Runyan (NJ)
	Jackie Walorski (IN)
	Brad Wenstrup (OH)*

114th Congress—House

Minority—Democrat	Majority—Republican
Corrine Brown (FL)	Ralph Abraham (LA)
Julia Brownley (CA)	Dan Benishek (MI)
Ann Mclane Kuster (NH)	Gus Bilirakis (FL)
Beto O'Rourke (TX)	Mike Bost (IL)
Kathleen Rice (NY)	Mike Coffman (CO)*
Raul Ruiz (CA)	Amata Coleman Radewagen (AS)
Mark A Takano (CA)	Ryan Costello (PA)
Dina Titus (NV)	Tim Huelskamp (KS)
	Douglas L Lamborn (CO)
	Jeff Miller (FL)
	Phil Roe (TN)*
	Jackie Walorski (IN)
	Brad Wenstrup (OH)*
	Lee Zeldin (NY)

CHAPTER FIVE

A Theory of Lip Service versus Legwork

If all we knew was what legislators told us, not their actual efforts in Congress to pass legislation, but we could only use their presentation of self to form an assessment, who would we think most cared about veterans? Would there be partisan or generational splits? What about differences between veteran and nonveteran members of Congress?

In Chapter 3 we saw that the public supports policies to help veterans. These patterns of support are not partisan, but rather span across party affiliation. Both Democrats and Republicans offer similar assessments of the VA when things are going well and when administration suffers from scandal. Yet, despite the core agreement on the importance of veterans and the desire for government to provide benefits to veterans, the Republican Party enjoys greater popular support from veterans themselves.

Yet in Chapter 4 we found that members of the Democratic Party do more in terms of legislative legwork on behalf of veterans. What are the reasons that Republicans don't introduce more veterans' legislation? How can it be that one party seems to do the majority of the legwork involved in helping veterans and yet fails to achieve the majority of support from veterans?

The way Representatives and Senators relate to constituents in official, public communications is a way to signal how much they care for veterans. But the actions that legislators take inside the chamber are much more important for generating favorable policies for veterans. Yet, the way constituents understand Congress relies more on what members of Congress *say* than on what members of Congress *do*.[1] The things members say collectively mesh together over time and are repeated across multiple media outlets to create a narrative that is overly simplistic, but understandable for constituents. Understanding Congress this way is far easier and more realistic than asking people to look through data held by the Library of Congress detailing different pieces of legislation and efforts exerted by Congress before assessing the veteran-mindedness of different political parties.

In this chapter I describe some key features of the veterans' policy landscape as related to Republican and Democratic ideology and offer a theory of *lip service* versus *legwork* to explain why this seeming discrepancy is readily understandable in light of modern U.S. politics. After describing the theory I then use the following chapter to test it using a new data set of legislator communications. In Chapters 7 and 8 I then explore two case studies that provide deeper details into how legwork and lip service play out for each party.

In describing the current elements of veterans' policies, I do not consider every U.S. veterans' program but instead focus exclusively on health care and education. By not getting into the weeds on the details of transition assistance, pension administration, favorable home loans, employment assistance, and other federal programs, I admittedly lose some richness of the story. Yet, the underlying tenets that describe how veterans' health care and educational benefits are administered are similar to the ways other programs operate. The basic understandings made clear by focusing on just these two programs are not altered by the omission of many other veterans' programs.

The key questions to be answered here are straightforward. First, if introducing legislation is a form of legwork that either party could do, why don't Republicans do more? Second, how can the Republican Party maintain more favorable public assessments on veterans' policy and from veterans despite the fact that they lag behind Democrats in legislative efforts?

I argue that introducing veterans' policy is more ideologically difficult for Republicans than it is for Democrats as a reason for why we observe fewer Republican-sponsored veterans' bills in Congress. Additionally, the theory of lip service versus legwork indicates that just talking about veterans in constituent communications may be signal enough to constituents that members of Congress care about veterans. This strategy also has the benefit of not having the expense of formulating policy. If signaling matters more than substance, Republicans could come out ahead among veterans in term of public support if they do more of it than Democrats despite the reality of legislative effort.

Contemporary Political Ideology and the Difficulty of Veterans' Policy

Veterans' policy in the United States is administered in a way unlike many other policies providing group-specific benefits. Because of how veterans' benefits historically developed, nearly any piece of legislation that seeks to provide benefits to veterans meets one or more of the following criteria:

1. A program or benefit administered by the federal government
2. A program or directive that spends or redirects federal monies
3. A program that meddles in private industry via veteran-favoring incentives
4. A program that recognizes individual dependency on government assistance

In relating those components to the preferences of major political parties in the United States, we must consider how they comport with the political ideologies of the parties. In academia, the most-often cited way to discriminate against the ideologies of individual legislators is to rely on scoring protocols that place legislators who tend to vote together closer than those who vote less often together along a continuum roughly conceptualized to capture ideology.[2] When discussing what such an ideological continuum represents, scholars offer a fuzzy approximation of ideology as a legislator's taste for government intervention into the economy.[3] The discipline recognizes that many other political issue bundles are also captured into the concept of ideology; since the 1970s, political parties tend to be described as mainly divided along this one-dimensional feature. Let us now consider the ideological differences between the Republican and Democratic parties.

Ideological Underpinnings of the Contemporary Republican Party

In practice, there is no one unified manifesto that describes what Republican ideology entails, but this does not mean there is not a shared understanding that practitioners, politicians, and the public associate with the party. In fact, the modern Republican Party has been found to exhibit higher levels of ideological awareness and cohesiveness among voters than members of the Democratic Party.[4] This cohesiveness around government intervention into the economy as a differentiating element across parties can be observed in the way party elites campaign. Over the past 40 years or so, Republican politicians have increasingly employed broad appeals against federal government spending as a cornerstone of their campaign advertisements and issue framing from within government while Democrats have not.[5]

The post-Nixon Republican Party operates with a set of symbolic tenets attributed to a stylized understanding of Ronald Reagan. These tenets are described as symbolic because they are elastic in interpretation, and both executives and legislators from the Republican Party do not strictly adhere to those tenets.[6] At the core, modern Republican ideology argues for a reduction in government size and reach, a reduction in federal spending, a relaxation of government interventions into private markets, and a desire for individuals to be personally responsible rather than reliant on government in most aspects of life.

Much of this outlook is propagated and re-propagated through a series of extended party networks, including political actors themselves, industry, think tanks, media, and public discourse outside of traditional media. After the 2008 emergence of the "Tea Party," the more anti-government extremist wings of the Republican Party stressing importance of reducing the role of government tended to be privileged in public circles more so than in the past as they spread from smaller fringe outlets to the halls of Congress.

During each presidential race, the parties produce platforms that are meant to centralize what the parties support. These documents do not spell out the intricacies of certain policies although they provide a general sense of party priorities.[7] In the 2016 Republican Party Platform, there were broad sweeping platitudes that make clear the sorts of general ideological approaches of the party. The first pages argue that "government cannot create prosperity, though government can limit or destroy it." The document moves on to describe the economic priority of reducing government spending specifying, "The Republican path to fiscal sanity and economic expansion begins with a constitutional requirement for a federal balanced budget. We will fight for Congress to adopt, and for the states to ratify, a Balanced Budget Amendment which imposes a cap limiting spending to the appropriate historical average percentage of our nation's gross domestic product while requiring a super-majority for any tax increase, with exceptions only for war or legitimate emergencies."

Regarding a commitment to not meddle in private markets, the platform states, "We will end the government mandates that required Fannie Mae, Freddie Mac, and federally insured banks to satisfy lending quotas to specific groups. Discrimination should have no place in the mortgage industry." This position is despite the fact that the veterans' home loan program, which originated in 1944 and is supported by a majority of current Republicans, benefits a specific group and could be considered "discriminatory."

On the care and self-reliance of veterans, the GOP platform indicates that veterans ought to have choices to seek health care outside the VA and urges the private sector to develop solutions for veterans-specific health care needs. This position is in sharp tension with the position of most veterans' groups who argue that more attention should be focused on VA hospitals and providers rather than pushing people to look outside of the system.[8]

Of course, the modern Republican Party is not monolithically against government programs in their discourse. Instead, the party tends to draw distinction around "deservingness." The discursive signals for deservingness are words like "tax-payers," "job-creators," and "contributors" rather than "takers" or "welfare recipients."[9] Veterans are undoubtedly classed in the former bins of government assistance recipients, but this caveat only partially ameliorates the difficulties with squaring veterans' policy prescriptions with GOP ideology. By recognizing a positive role of government in the intervention of individual lives, markets, and health care for a group such as veterans leads to questions about why this would not similarly be the case for other groups who contribute to the well-being of the nation such as miners, teachers, construction workers, and so on.

None of this is to question the wisdom or direction or Republican ideology but merely to show that there is tension with the goals and tenets of Republican ideology and the way that veterans' programs have historically developed in the United States. This difficulty in squaring veterans' policy in practice with the theoretical ideological underpinnings of the modern Republican Party is one reason that we do not observe as much legwork from that side of the aisle as we do from Democrats.

The four elements of veterans' policy are more readily at home with liberal political ideology found in Democratic approaches to governance than in the more conservative, Republican Party approach to social welfare programs. Democratic ideology sees a positive role for government in influencing elements of life that markets may not address equitably. Counter to the most vocal elements of the contemporary GOP, Democrats are more able to commit to increased government spending under appeals to greater egalitarian norms that recognize the limits of what individuals may be able to do. Later in this chapter I consider Democratic ideology in the context of veterans' policy.

In the next section, I detail how the major components of current veterans' policies meet the four criteria laid out previously to make clear the contrast between politics on the ground and political ideology goals.

Federal Administration of Veterans' Programs and Benefits

The current architecture of veterans' policy that has been around for nearly a century is vast. As Chapters 1 and 2 explained, policies and programs are strongly influenced by path dependencies from choices of the past. Rather than pushing off much of the responsibility to states and local administrators as is done for programs such as Medicaid and unemployment assistance, the federal government controls nearly all aspects of veterans' benefits through the federal Veterans Administration (VA).

The Veterans Health Administration

Size and Scope

The Veterans Health Administration (VHA) is America's largest health care system. It controls over 1,200 medical facilities and with over 9 million veterans enrolled who use different services and sites of care each year. The administration employs over 300,000 health care providers and support staff. Additionally, the VHA is the nation's largest provider of graduate medical education. In 2016, there were 127,000 medical students at various stages of their education, led by over 15,000 medical faculty and more than 73,000 volunteers.[10]

The services offered by the VHA are virtually the same as those found in any health system, with additional expertise in physical and mental ailments that are particular to veterans' communities. An integral element of veterans' health care provisions within the VA is continuous assessment. The efforts to track medical practices and health outcomes are perpetually ongoing and add to the vastness of the overall veterans' health care enterprise. The data maintained by the VA on a variety of veterans' health issues are some of the deepest and broadest of any governmental agency.

In 1995, the VHA determined to revitalize the way health care was administered within the VHA system as a response to public criticisms that the quality and timeliness of care were substandard. Part of those efforts involved mandating continued laborious measurement of changes and results in order to create a record of evidence for beneficial changes in health care provision.[11]

After the series of transformations in the VHA in the last 1990s, many facilities reported that demand for services begun to outstrip the ability to supply care in a timely fashion, and thus, the system became somewhat of a victim of its own successes.[12] Despite a somewhat maligned reputation in popular discourse, in some notable ways, the VHA provides health care that outperformed private industry analogues.[13] In a variety of realms such as diabetes care, ambulatory services, and bed management, these data have provided a basis for creating best practices within the VA that then permeated outward to other facilities.[14]

Because practitioners in the system specialize in care primarily administered for military-specific injuries (amputations, chemical exposure, posttraumatic stress disorder [PTSD]) and for ageing populations on account of the number of World War II and Vietnam draftees, veterans seeking health care within the VHA are more likely to be treated by medical staff more attuned to their particular, service-based needs than those who seek treatment privately.

Veterans Education Benefits

Size and Scope

Veterans' education benefits include 19 different types of programs and government-funded reimbursement programs ranging from tuition at traditional four-year colleges and universities to correspondence programs to flight training. These programs are not only available for veterans themselves but are also extended to the dependents and caretakers of veterans in some circumstances. In fact, up to 25 percent of all beneficiaries of veterans' educations programs are nonveterans.[15]

Throughout the United States, every state houses institutions serving veterans and accepting federal funds in the form of veterans' educational benefits. Across all 55 states and U.S. territories, there are over 6,700 four-year colleges and universities, 11,900 noncollege degree-granting institutions of higher education, 18,600 apprenticeship programs, 200 correspondence programs, and 160 flight schools all serving veterans eligible for tuition assistance provided by the federal government.

The Costs of Veterans' Programs and Benefits

Altogether, from 2010 to 2017, veterans' benefits accounted for 4 percent of all annual federal spending. In 2016, the VA reported total spending of $173,685,850.[16] To be sure there are other federal priorities that consume larger shares of the federal budget such as paying off interest on the national debt, active-duty military spending, Medicare, and Social Security, but compared to other sectors veterans receive a decent sum of federal funds. Since 2010, federal spending on veterans' benefits has been greater than spending on agricultural assistance, education, transportation, housing, diplomatic international commitments, energy and environmental efforts, and investments in scientific research. Out of the overall federal expenditures on veterans, the bulk of the dollars go to veterans' pensions, accounting for 48 percent of all VA spending. Following pensions, health care makes up 37 percent of total spending, education accounts for 8 percent, and the remainder is distributed among construction costs, operating costs, insurance, and other expenses.

Costs of Veterans' Health Care

The VHA is financed nearly exclusively through general taxation. In 2018, out of a discretionary budget of over $82 billion, direct medical expenditures on veterans' programs account for $72 billion spent annually.[17] The remaining $10 billion are distributed to programs that support medical care such as research and development, facility construction funds, information technology for enrolling and tracking care, and eventual burial support via the National Cemetery Administration. Put in perspective of total expenditures, the health component of veterans' care accounts for about 2 percent of all government expenditures.

Costs of Veterans' Education

Veterans' benefits that subsidize education are the largest federal program for student aid. Within just one year of implementation of the Post–9/11 GI Bill, the federal government paid out $1.3 billion in benefits to over 170,000 students. Furthermore, educational benefits are the fastest increasing expense for the VA since the implementation of the Post–9/11 GI Bill in 2009.

Federal Interventions into Private Industry on Behalf of Veterans

Government-mandated or government-incentivized preferential treatment of veterans when seeking a job, applying for a home loan, purchasing other retail goods, and so forth is a policy tool used to augment private marketplaces in a way that assists veterans. This strategy of intervention is sometimes costless for the federal government but does require the passage of regulations or directives in order to implement changes. These sorts of provisions range and come in multiple variations. Occasionally there are laws passed that give one-time economic benefits in the form of lump sum payouts to veterans at a cost to the federal government.

One program that veterans have access to is the VA loan guaranty program where the VA acts as a guarantor for veterans seeking to buy, build, or repair their homes. Veterans also have access to retirement plans that offer far lower fees than more traditional 401(k) plans through the Federal Thrift Savings Retirement Plan.[18] While in service, members have the option to put some of their pay in a special Department of Defense Savings Deposit Program that accumulates interest at higher rates than private savings programs, all the way up to 10 percent annually.[19]

Within private industry, there are both federal and state programs to provide preferences in hiring queues for veterans.[20] These statutes came about in a variety of ways. The American Recovery and Reinvestment Act passed during the 111th Congress in 2009 with support from Democrats and Republicans provided businesses a $2,400 tax credit for hiring unemployed veterans.

These benefits exist out of recognition of the costs members bear when they serve and demonstrate a commitment to assisting veterans after active duty. The aforementioned benefits and interventions into economic markets on behalf of a specific group are sometimes in tension with overarching contemporary Republican ideology and thus may be one reason GOP legislators are hesitant to offer legislation to these ends.

Recognition of Individual Dependency on Government

Understanding government benefits demand a bit of detail in assessment. Not all government benefits are the same, and political actors on all sides of the ideological spectrum draw on these nuances to justify inclusion for different policy prescriptions. One difference is earned benefits versus nonearned benefits; the former being offered to individuals who have done something to "earn" the benefits on the front end. For example, a commitment to active service "earns" veterans the benefit of educational reimbursement. Another "earned" benefit—although "earning" is a somewhat inaccurate term—would be lifelong rehabilitation and prosthetic services for a service member who loses a limb in combat. A nonearned benefit would be something like unemployment assistance, which is a benefit paid to someone who is down on his or her luck, rather than a benefit in response to a proactive action.

But even with true sense of earning that veterans do, the programs that exist show that there is a role for government intervention into the lives of individuals. Government can make education more accessible, health care available, job opportunities more attainable, and so forth. This is true in the development and administration of veterans' policy and is at odds with a fundamental Republican principle, which is to stress the supreme role of individuals in determining outcomes and to argue against a role for government to influence individual outcomes.

A Note about Symbolic Legislation

Of course, there are forms of veterans' legislation that do not come into tension with conservative ideology. Like we saw in the previous chapter, legislation can be offered and voted on so that members can *say* they did something on veterans' politics, but nothing in the underlying realm of executable veterans' benefits changes. These symbolic legislative efforts are when Congress passes a resolution publicly honoring veterans of a certain engagement or era. Another way is to name post offices or dedicate commemorative memorials to veterans—again Congress has plenty of these examples.

But when thinking about what matters to change policy, a focus on substantive legislation over symbolic legislation ought to be preferred. This is not to say that symbolic legislation does not serve veterans in any way as these sorts of efforts raise the profile and awareness around veterans' issues. But symbolic legislation is just that, symbolic. They are signals of care, which have some value even when not backed up by stronger pieces of legislation that do the work of actually caring for veterans, but have fewer concrete impacts that aid in the day-to-day life of a veteran.

To be substantive, legislative proposals that change veterans' benefits typically require federal government administration, cost money, intervention into private industry, and recognition that government plays in individual life rather than hoping individuals can be entirely self-reliant.

These tensions are not just quiet undertones. Even before the vocally anti-government, reduced spending demands of the Tea Party, some of the political Right had brought up the uncomfortable reality that government spending on veterans is an area that might be something to revisit and ratchet down. Concerned with growing appropriations for the VHA and aligned with party stances aimed at reducing government spending, some Republicans have argued for tighter eligibility criteria such as restricting access to the VHA to the poor or only those with service-related disabilities.[21]

Contemporary Democratic Ideology and Veterans' Care

I do not as thoroughly consider how veterans' policy interacts with Democratic ideology because there is not as much work to be done describing tensions. Simply put, Democrats recognize and encourage the role of government in providing public goods such as health care and education to people within the United States, veterans included. In their most recent presidential platform, the Democratic Party argued that the government has a role to play in eliminating inequities and stepping in when the free market does not offer solutions for people in an accessible manner.

On health care, the 2016 Democratic Platform reaffirms a commitment to government provisions ensuring health care is provided for all. The role for government in education is to provide and support educational opportunities for all and to spend government funds to achieve both goals as an investment in the U.S. public. There is an upfront recognition that government policies can work in positive ways to influence individual outcomes. Altogether, the ways veterans' programs exist today are more readily rationalizable with contemporary Democratic Party's understandings of government. Therefore, members of the party do not have as many conflicting considerations when introducing legislation on behalf of veterans.

The Resulting Partisan Conundrum

The preceding sections of this chapter describe how Republican ideology is not as aligned as Democratic views are with the way veterans' care is administered today. The contours of modern conservative ideology as manifested within the Republican Party are more at odds with how veterans' policies are implemented in the United States than liberal, democratic ideologies.

Why is it that popular culture and some measurable voting behaviors of veterans indicate that the veteran population tends to support Republicans? How can we explain why the Republican Party is credited with care for veterans and rewarded with veterans' support come election time? In the following section I posit a simple theory that accounts for some of the reasons why we observe this seeming discrepancy.

A Theory of Lip Service over Legwork

Conservative principles and modern Republican Party demands make it harder to actually *legislate* in a way that benefits veterans, but there is no limitation on how much a Republican member of Congress can *say* about the importance of veterans' policy. *Every* member of Congress claims to support and fight for our troops before, during, and after military service. This is not to say there are never partisan differences in approaches to veterans' policy.[22] However, as a group, members of Congress exalt veterans universally in a way unlike the reverence paid to any other group. Despite bipartisan consensus on the status of veterans, there are partisan differences in how much and in what ways members of the two parties pay lip service to veterans.

Compared to congressional Democrats, Republicans are better at mentioning veterans' issues in constituent communications, and the public has little way of distinguishing between such communicative acts and more programmatic legislation. Before describing the specifics, let us first consider the terminology I use through the remainder of the book.

Terminology

I use the shorthand *lip service* to describe statements made by legislators about veterans. Statements made in official communications fit the most common definitions of lip service, "an avowal of advocacy, adherence, or allegiance expressed in words but not backed by deeds" or "support for someone or something that is expressed by someone in words but that is not shown in that person's actions."[23]

For those wary that this characterization sounds unduly pejorative, consider the following facts. During the 111th–114th Congresses, only 171 new laws on veterans' policies were adopted, 3,150 were proposed, and there were over 16,400 official e-newsletters sent by members of Congress referencing veterans. While not all members of Congress simply pay lip service to veterans in communications, a majority of these communications are expressions made with words and not backed by deeds. That is, the level of talk about veterans far outpaces the amounts of legislative attempts to change veterans' policy.

My theory is not entirely novel, but has nonetheless never been put forward as a way to understand the partisan conundrum surrounding veterans politics. I argue that lip service does the heavy lifting in the mind of voters, while actual policy legwork matters less. For instance, on the economy

Blinder and Watson find that while voters think Republican presidents will be better for economic growth, Democrat track records are actually more positive by various metrics.[24] How is that the case? Patrick Egan of New York University details how issues that are "owned" by one party or the other can distort the collective understanding of which party *does* better on an issue versus which party *prioritizes* an issue.[25]

I argue that the Republican Party came to own veterans' policy not through particular legislative victories or prowess but through frequent issue signaling that they care about veterans. Emphasis Allocation Theory, developed by Benjamin Page, argues that each member of Congress has a set amount of time and focus to use, and we can assess differences between members and parties by thinking about how they choose to distribute their focus. In the case of veterans, if Republicans use more of their communications to talk about veterans than Democrats, they are better able to signal an emphasis on veterans. In my further consideration, I make the point that emphasis might not be matched to legislative effort, and that emphasis may be enough on its own.

What is new here is the development of a theory around veterans' politics that can be empirically and robustly tested using data now available. I argue, as others who study political communication do, that the theater of politics has just as much impact as the substance of policy. What differentiates the test of this theory now is that the advent of electronic communications allows for a much more comprehensive and fine-pointed look at how strategic political communications diverge from political actions. After describing more about how lip service works, how voters are ill positioned to know the difference, and how legwork gets lost, I use the next chapter to introduce the data that allow testing these elements in the realm of veterans' politics.

To be clear, it is not my claim that lip service to veterans' issues is the only reason the public associates and veterans tend to prefer the Republican Party. But I do argue that this is an important part of the puzzle. Wielding strategic political communication opportunities to shape a grand public narrative is powerful, and the modern Republican Party is much more adept than the Democratic Party in this way.

How Lip Service "Works"

Studies abound showing the political impacts of "selective exposure," "motivated reasoning," and "cognitive dissonance," but these are distinct from the characterization of lip service here. It's not that Republican members of the public opt in to communications more focused on veterans or that Republicans within Congress tussle with internal cognitive dissonance on the challenges of proposing veterans' policies versus talking about veterans.

A Theory of Lip Service versus Legwork

The mechanism is much simpler. Republicans talk about veterans more than Democrats do.

For veterans' politics and the messaging surrounding it, there is not so much a discrepancy on the truth of the claims made by Republicans and Democrats; rather the greatest differences lie in the volume, amount, and frequency with which members of the two parties refer to veterans. Republicans do it more, way more. Nothing too psychologically intensive is at play here; Republicans pay more lip service to veterans, and that lip service is compelling enough to work in the minds of voters to create a backdrop linking the GOP with veteran interests.

Volume, Repetition, and Framing

We know from decades of marketing research that repetition is a very powerful way to inculcate a belief in a recipient's mind. These sorts of strategies are useful not only in order to sell products to consumers but also in order to create a narrative that people can use when approaching subjects that they might not routinely consider.[26] While the average person might not spend a lot of time considering the topic of political polarization, if a person has been exposed to some theory as to why we see polarization, that theory likely colors the way he or she would approach the topic the next time it came up in conversation. For instance, if someone heard polarization is about economic haves and have-nots based on previous exposure to information on a podcast or radio show relating income inequality and political polarization, then it is reasonable for that person to approach the topic from that perspective in successive encounters.[27]

When the public reviews and internalizes what members of Congress say, it does not necessarily mean that the public digs deeper into those messages. Yet, at a very basic level, repeated narratives make a mental impact. When congressional Republicans talk about veterans more often than Democrats do, no matter the content or underlying legislative reality, Republicans create a narrative reputation associated with veterans. This serves to create a sort of perspective background that the public operates from. For veterans' issues it might not be that the public can articulate what the Republican Party does for veterans, but if there is the general sense of more verbal support from Republicans than Democrats for veterans, then it is more readily understandable why public opinion and veterans' voting patterns generally support the Republican over the Democratic Party.

There are many reasons for why messaging "works" even when that messaging on a certain topic might not comport with the truth of the matter. In many ways messaging can trump substance in the minds of recipients. Decades of work in a host of disciplines speak to the power of framing.[28]

Even when reality may indicate that one thing is true, if there are repeated and consistent *messages* that indicate otherwise, it becomes easier to believe the message rather than the truth.[29] This is not to suggest that members of Congress are not truthful when they positively refer to veterans in official communications. However, this does mean that it is possible for "truth" in legislative effort to be swamped by distorting communications efforts.

We have research that looks at the way voters receive and mentally process such efforts, albeit without clean delineations between talking about policy positions and actually introducing policy. When a legislator cultivates a reputation on a certain topic via repeated emphasis and efforts to display that knowledge to constituents, constituents reward the legislator with policy deference.[30] In fact, the mere act of repeatedly reaching out to constituents can serve to shore up positive perceptions of a legislator.[31] That is, if a legislator can repeatedly and successfully represent himself or herself as someone who cares a lot about veterans' policy, he or she may be perversely released from constituent expectations to legislate for veterans.

Low Information Settings

The power of messaging is especially forceful in low information settings. The overwhelming majority of people do not keep up with politics on a day-to-day basis. The 2016 book, *Democracy for Realists*, provides a comprehensive review of studies on the topic of how little most citizens know about politics.[32] Of citizens who do follow politics keenly, an even smaller set can keep up with any one policy area such as veterans' policies. Of those who keep up with veterans' policies, there are even fewer who have some sort of running tally of which party tends to produce more legislation for veterans.

No one should be faulted for relying on the information short cuts provided in a repetitive narrative. In this sort of low information environment, signaling can be an easy way for a constituent to assess a politician.[33] Legislators know that their words and message strategies matter, and they try to craft reputations with that in mind.[34]

Low to No Cost

Making proclamations supporting veterans is virtually costless for members of Congress. There are no organized anti-veterans movements with any sort of meaningful political clout on the current public stage. The risk of alienating a constituency by promising to work on behalf of veterans is nil. Because of this status quo, the initial determination on whether to talk about veterans' issues or not is quite easy. If a politician has some time or space in an announcement to add an additional point, veterans are an easy pick.

Second, as Chapter 3 shows, the U.S. population feels very positive toward veterans. Bipartisan majorities approve of government-funded programs directed at veterans and their caregivers. Bipartisan majorities view the VA favorably. Even when the VA suffers scandal, there is still a bipartisan agreement that the VA should serve veterans better. While other agencies have persistent differences in both positive and negative assessments demarcated by party, the VA when doing well or poorly is viewed in a lens that seems to transcend partisanship. The consistency of positive public affect, coupled with the absence of any politically organized counter movement, creates a general goodwill within the public toward veterans. This mix of influences provides many reasons that legislators can benefit in the eyes of voters when mentioning veterans.

A final reason why paying lip service to veterans is beneficial in terms of legislator costs is that, compared to other groups, there is evidence that the payoffs might be greater. Veterans vote more often than nonveterans and thus can be a more "useful" constituency to appeal to in an effort to maximize electoral support.[35]

Legislator Awareness

Political actors are aware of the power of controlling a narrative and work hard to do so. If a legislator wants to be known as a supporter of veterans, that legislator ought to describe his or her actions in that way and do it frequently enough to make an impression. This guidance has been empirically established over various political contexts and is known to political practitioners; legislators are strategic in highlighting the things that provide the greatest reputational benefits.[36]

There is even emergent evidence that legislators do not have to discuss their specific positions but simply need to be better known on an issue to cultivate greater levels of public trust and approval.[37] That is, the very style of just talking about veterans and reiterating verbal veneration for veterans can be enough to meaningfully shift public perceptions on policy commitments and ideological understandings.

Deservingness—Why Lip Service Is Possible Even with Ideological Constraints

One concept to note when considering the cognitive congruence between Republican ideology generally and veterans populations specifically is "deservingness." While political actors are generally not keen to make clear different markers or levels of deservingness among their constituencies, when it comes to providing government benefits, veterans occupy a preferred position. Serving the country in the capacity that they do elevates veterans to a more deserving place in the eyes of many when considering who is worthy of government benefits.

Clear examples of the deservingness notion are easy to come by in practice. The very way veterans are referred to in official communications provides ample evidence. The term "veterans deserve" occurs in 640 communications from 2009 until today in instances like "Our veterans deserve the best that our state and our country can provide"[38] and "Our veterans deserve better quality and more prompt care they can trust."[39]

Similar examples of instances speaking to other communities in need of government assistance occur far less frequently. The "poor deserve" was only ever used once in the entire database of legislator to constituent e-newsletters spanning 2009–2017. Even then the full sentence employed a caveat rooted in the notion of deservingness: "The *working* poor deserve a fair chance from government rather than an uncaring system which traps them in poverty" [emphasis added]. Appeals to the deservingness of children are also scant, occurring only 149 times.

The benefits of health care, educational assistance, and other programs extended to veterans exist in various iterations for the disabled, those in poverty, children, and the elderly. Yet debates about expanding social welfare programs to other populations of need are much more ideologically charged than programs for veterans. Part of that is because of a notion of deservingness applied specifically to veterans.

None of this is to imply that veterans are not deserving of the benefits they currently enjoy. In the research and writing of this book, there has been no more compelling takeaway that veterans' service and their continued efforts after active duty does entitle them to services our government promises to deliver. But it is an undeniable fact of modern politicking that the notion of deservingness is quite a powerful way to hedge against other more deeply held ideological principles adhered to by governing party systems.

Lip Service Does Not Necessarily Trade Off with Legwork

A member of Congress could pay lip service to veterans and never attempt to offer legislation. But a legislator could also pay lots of lip service in communications and also do a substantial amount of legislative work for veterans. And, of course, there could be legislators who do lots of legwork on veterans' issues and not much in the way of lip service. Legislators make independent decisions on how much legislating and how much communicating they wish to engage in. However, the role of parties cannot be understated: they provide talking points and policy agreement and therefore play a role in both communication and legislation.

Concluding Thoughts: Why Does Lip Service versus Legwork Matter?

Veterans occupy a small and increasingly smaller share of the U.S. population. Those in the service and their families bear a tremendous burden during and after active duty. They make the lives of everyone in America easier and freer, and, in return, our public and our politicians ought to understand their pain and share the sacrifice. The difference between politicians saying they are committed to veterans and actively doing something within their control to better the lives of veterans merits public scrutiny.

Paying lip service to veterans' issues creates a generally understood public narrative that puts Republicans ahead of Democrats without a deeper understanding of what sorts of legislative efforts each party engages in. Talking about veterans is good, strategic political communication. There are a variety of reasons why a member engages in lip service, and nearly no downside. Writing about veterans allows members to express an opinion with the knowledge that they risk no "anti-veterans" lobby blow back. Furthermore, veterans tend to be more politically active and receptive to such attention, and the public has very little ability or desire to sort talk from action.

Republican Party ideology is harder to square with the introduction and implementation of veterans' policies than the Democratic Party's ideology. In the early chapters I showed that Democrats tend to offer more legislation expanding veterans' benefits than Republicans do. Yet the public and veterans themselves tend to trust Republicans to take care of veterans, and veterans tend to prefer Republicans when electing members to office.

One of the reasons the public and veterans themselves tend to prefer members of the Republican Party is that Republicans do *a lot* more talking about veterans in their public communications. It is challenging for the public to discern the difference between talking about veterans and legislating about veterans, so this strategy is generally successful. This conundrum is not new, but the evidence for this explanation is.

From a volume perspective the public is inured with messages of veterans' support from Republicans at levels that are unmatched by Democrats. Out of the entire set of legislator-to-constituent communications that were sent during the 111th–114th Congresses, 69 percent came from Republicans. Yet out of all the substantive legislation introduced to augment veterans' policies, Democrats offered 60 percent. During the most recent legislative periods, Democrats were left doing the work on behalf of veterans, while Republicans worked to further establish their association with veterans in communications. At the same time veterans voted for Republicans over Democrats by a 20 percent margin in 2014 House and Senate races.[40]

CHAPTER SIX

Lip Service: Legislator Communications about Veterans

In the chambers of Congress, Democrats are more often than not the actors who introduce policies to enhance the benefits for veterans in the United States. But in the collective minds of the public and in the political preferences of veterans, Republicans in Congress are more closely aligned with veterans. Why is that the case? How can legislative efforts be initiated by one party and public opinion benefits be accrued by the other? In the last chapter I argued that this difference came down to lip service over legwork.

There are theoretical reasons to expect that some members approach the issue of veterans in a way that is different than other members. I assess competing theories to get to a better-defined set of considerations that drives the likelihood that some members of Congress focus on veterans in their constituent communications more than others. According to notions of *emphasis allocation theory*, legislators who reference veterans in official communications actively attempt to promote a connection between themselves and veterans' issues in the minds of voters.[1] To better understand why some members put more emphasis on veterans in communications and others in legislation I explore the relationships between a set of plausible variables related to veteran emphasis.

In this chapter, I assess which members of Congress prioritize veterans and veterans' issues in their official communications. I contrast those findings with data on who introduces the most veterans' legislation. The interest is not simply to figure out which members are the most veteran focused but to attempt to identify patterns of communication that contribute to our understanding of why veterans tend to prefer one party over another and why voters associate Republicans with veterans more than the Democrats.

Previous Attempts to Measure Veterans' Focus in Communications

There has been some, but not a lot of, empirical assessment of how often members of Congress discuss veterans in their official capacity. The research to date looks at campaign strategies rather than official declarations of members of Congress. Of the work focused on communicating about veterans, none have yet reported compelling evidence that Republicans do this more than Democrats or vice versa.

In a study of congressional campaign messages aired on TV during the 1998 elections, there were 2,880 ads aired about veterans aggregated across 139 Republican candidates (approx. 21 per candidate) and 2,431 across 129 Democratic candidates (approx. 19 per candidate).[2] While Republicans had a slight numerical advantage, in the context of the greater election and issue prioritization, the author of this study concludes that there was no difference between the two parties on veterans' focus.

In a related campaign analysis, Sides and Karch found that targeted advertising to veterans was not related to significant turnout gains in those populations and report no significant differences across parties in terms of efforts to court such voters.[3] These two studies are the most substantial of all assessments of members of Congress appealing to veterans explicitly in campaigns. But both look at campaign communications, which are different from official communications. In the database of legislator-to-constituent communications, each representative and senator writes in their official capacity as a sitting legislator. In addition to talking about veterans like one might in a campaign capacity, elected legislators engaging in this sort of lip service are also in a position to actually change veterans' policy in ways that candidates cannot.

Congress-to-Constituent Communications: A Way to Assess Lip Service

As the universe of data expands, we have more ways to observe and measure congressional behavior. To measure *lip service* on veterans' issues, I make use of a new database of legislator-to-constituent e-communications. These communications are housed online in the DCinbox database.[4] DCinbox started in 2009 and is the only all-digital, searchable database of every e-newsletter members of Congress send to their constituents. From 2009 until the present day, representatives and senators have sent over 90,000 unique communications to constituents.

This sort of database is preferable to examine the phenomena of interest here for a few reasons. Official e-newsletters are universally available to each member of Congress, supported via official funds and channels, subject to campaign content restrictions, and provide a long-term look at how members of Congress focus their efforts on different topics. Some members send out multiple messages every week, some send one message each week, and some send messages with far less frequency following only breaking national events. While this medium is available to every legislator, every individual member controls how often and on what topics they write to constituents about providing a rich set of data for researchers to pull from.

Lip Service Data

If a member of Congress wants to talk about veterans' issues in official constituent communications, there is virtually no impediment to doing so. Both Republicans and Democrats set up official constituent communications capabilities at similar rates, discussing veterans and veterans' policy on all approved topics for officially sanctioned communications.[5]

As an initial and general test of differential rates of veteran focus in official communications, I queried the DCinbox database for every instance of the word "veteran" and compared the results by the party of the sender.[6] If we expect that all members of the House and the Senate pay equal attention to veterans regardless of party affiliation, then the percentages of veterans mentions official communications would be roughly equivalent to the seat shares held by Democrats and Republicans.

Recall from Chapter 4 that while Republicans won majorities in the 2010 midterm elections, from 2009 to 2016 the overall distributions of seats was 51 percent to Republicans and 49 percent to Democrats. Despite this roughly equal distribution of seats, people who were represented by Republicans in Congress were far more likely to hear about veterans in official communications than those who had Democratic representatives. Figure 6.1 gives the total numbers of official e-newsletters sent by members of the two parties that include the word "veteran(s)" by week from late 2009 to 2017.

Notice that earlier in the database when Democrats held 18 percent more seats than Republicans, the weekly focus on veterans was often equal or near equal in constituent communications across parties. When Republicans took the House in the 2010 election, the volume of communications about veterans did not match the percentage of seats they had newly acquired, but this soon changed. Starting in 2012 Republicans took a lead and focused on veterans at a much greater degree than Democrats did for the duration of the Congresses studied here.

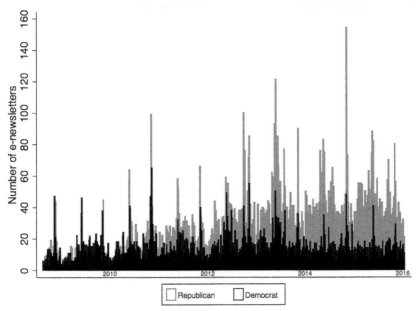

Figure 6.1 Number of official congressional e-newsletters mentioning "veteran" by party by week.

This raw, uncontrolled comparison is illustrative and in many ways makes a necessary point in the lip service versus legwork theory. If talking about an issue or population is a way to signal care or dedication, Republicans were far ahead on veterans from 2011 to 2017, and even when not in the congressional majority in 2009–2010, their lip service counts almost nearly matched Democrats.

Context of Veterans as a Topic in Official Communications

Of all official legislator-to-constituent communications sent during the time period, information about veterans or veterans' policy appears in 22 percent of all messages. To contextualize the frequency of veterans as an e-newsletter topic, the words "economy," "health," and "tax" occur in 45 percent, 38 percent, and 30 percent of all e-mails, respectively, while terms like "sanctions," "same sex," and "marijuana" occur in just 3 percent, 0.3 percent, and 0.3 percent of all communications, respectively. This focus is not simply driven by discussion of veterans on holidays like Veterans Day or Memorial Day but is rather a consistent focus over time. Of the over 2,700 days in the database, only 228 days had no members of Congress mention veterans.

As with legwork measures, I create the measure lip service with a consideration of how long a member served in Congress. The median number of veterans references sent per year in office is 1.5 with a range from 0 to 44. Some of the members who most often mention veterans in their communications are not strictly concerned with policy but rather speak to an interest in listening to the needs of veterans and helping them navigate the bureaucracy.

See this example from Congressman Tim Murphy (R-PA),

> Congressman Tim Murphy will host a Veterans Town Hall Meeting to discuss legislation in Congress and issues that affect the local veterans' community. If you or a family member is interested in attending, please mark the date and time on your calendar.[7]

Many members of Congress advertise events for veterans to either get feedback on how programs are working for them or to expedite the processing of a benefit.

But not all communications about veterans are programmatic or event invitations. Others talk about goals or accomplishments for veterans. In 2015, while writing about the legislative efforts of the Republican majority in Congress, Representative Kevin Yoder (R-KS) had the following to say,

> Thanks to the will of the American people, last November the Republican Party was entrusted with the majority in the United States Senate to go along with our majority in the United States House of Representatives held since 2010.
>
> Altogether, we have responded by being the most productive and bipartisan Congress in years.
>
> . . .
>
> We've sent more than two-dozen bills to the President's desk that he's already signed into law. Bills that will help prevent veterans' suicides, prevent human trafficking, pave the way to American energy independence by building the Keystone XL Pipeline, and help put Americans back to work for the high-paying wages they've been demanding for years.[8]

Representative Yoder is keen to note legislative work on behalf of veterans in the form of policies on suicide prevention. Of the bills passed during the 114th Congress that were aimed at veterans prior to this communication, the only one directed at suicide prevention was H.R. 203 the Clay Hunt Suicide Prevention for American Veterans Act or the Clay Hunt SAV Act. The Clay Hunt SAV Act required annual third-party evaluations of VA's suicide prevention programs, created a website with resources for veterans about a range of mental health services, and required a framework for collaboration on suicide prevention efforts between VA and nonprofit mental health organizations to better serve those seeking care in and outside of the VA system.

Republicans voted for this bill and thus certainly contributed to the passage of such a policy, but the legislation was drafted and written by Representative Timothy Walz, a Democrat from Minnesota. This is not to say that Republicans ought not to publicize their votes for bills that originate from the other side of the aisle. And this is not to say that voting for policies drafted by members of the other party is not critical to legislating. But it is to say that the way messages such as the previously discussed are configured may make it seem like Republicans are doing the work of legislating for veterans or at least make it unclear that a Democrat wrote the bill Representative Yoder is alluding to in his message.

This is an example of fine narrative creation. Of the messages that explicitly talk about veteran suicide and the Clay Hunt SAV Act as a policy attempt to reduce veteran suicides, only 30 percent come from Democrats and 70 percent come from Republicans. Republicans do much more to communicate about veterans even when Democrats have a better claim to legislating on behalf of veterans. While Democrats are willing to put in efforts in creating legislation, they tend to exert less effort in disseminating this information to constituents in the form of lip service.

A Robust Comparison of Lip Service versus Legwork

A more robust comparison of legislator lip service versus legwork requires a more systematic look at how all legislators approach veterans in communications and legislative activities. Recognizing the realities of the data and of Congress, I strive to compare each member as evenly as possible. Members serve different lengths in Congress based on differences in when they enter, if they choose to seek reelection, and if they are successful in that quest. Some move from the House to the Senate, some lose a house race once and then reenter later, and some die in office.[9] The dependent variable of lip service is the number of "veteran(s)" mentions in constituent communications per year in Congress for each legislator. The measure of legwork is the number of legislation offered per year as used in Chapter 4.

In addition to straightforward comparisons of the two outcome measures, in the following sections I consider which institutional, legislator, and constituent characteristics are most associated with the effort to change or communicate about veterans' policy. For each of these explanatory controls, I provide a justification for inclusion and discuss the stand-alone findings relating these variables to the outcomes of interest.

Basic Comparisons of Lip Service versus Legwork

Considering no other influences, the average Democrat in Congress introduces 0.87 pieces of veterans' legislation per year (legwork), whereas the average Republican introduces just 0.55. Each year Democrats send an average 2.59 official constituent communication about veterans (lip service) to the Republican average of 4.26. While this alone serves to show the descriptive differences between the parties, there are other elements at play. Owing to the finding that the share of veterans in a constituency is positively related to the levels of veterans' legislation per year, I consider how constituency demands translate into legwork *and* lip service.

For this exercise the measures of lip service and legwork are mean standardized and then centered at zero resulting in –2 to 2 scales for presentation. I plot smoothed averages of both variables by party. The X-axis in Figure 6.2 represents the different percentages of veterans in a constituency. The lines on the figure are calculated and rendered by party to display comparable measures of lip service and legwork by party.

For both parties, legwork and lip service track each other in similar ways; when veterans' populations increase as a percentage of a legislator's constituency, so too do lip service and legwork measures. But there is an important distinction between the ordering of the lip service (dashed) versus legwork

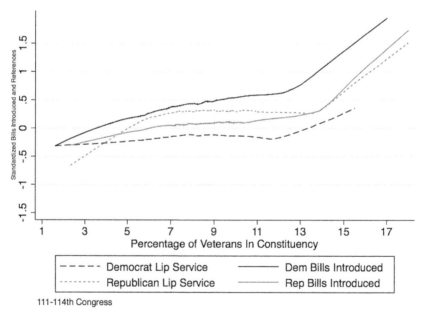

111-114th Congress

Figure 6.2 Veterans' legislation and lip service—standardized comparison of number of veterans' bills introduced per year versus number of references to veterans in communications per year.

Note: Lip service is number of veteran references communication per year. Legwork is number of veterans' legislation introduced per year. Each measure is mean standardized and then centered at zero.

(solid) lines. For Democrats, except at the very low end of veteran populations, legwork is always greater than lip service. That is, Democrats do more legislatively via veterans' policy introduction than they discuss veterans in constituent communications across nearly every sort of district. For Republicans, the opposite is true. Save for the few Republican members with small or very large veterans' constituencies, Republicans talk more about veterans in communications than the amounts of legislation they introduce.

As an additional measure of legwork, one can consider the effectiveness of a legislator by converting his or her introduction into a policy change. Law passage rates compared to lip service are presented in Figure 6.3.

While this is not the preferred measure of legwork because of the many things outside of an individual legislator's control, there are still interesting patterns to observe. Fewer members of Congress can be included in this sort of figure because those who never introduce any veterans' legislation could not possibly pass legislation and are therefore removed when calculating legislative effectiveness per year. When using legislative passage versus lip service to compare parties, the contrast seen in Figure 6.2 is similar, yet starker still in Figure 6.3. Republican legwork surpasses lip service and the low ends of veterans' populations, but in the majority of cases Democrats are more successful in passing policy than Republicans. Democrats show more

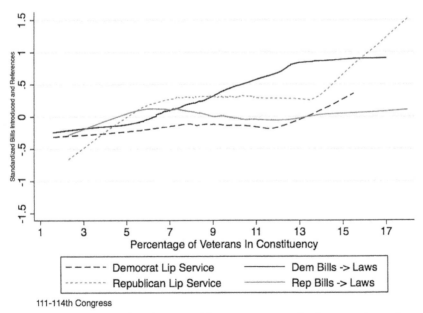

Figure 6.3 Veterans' legislation and lip service—standard comparison of number of veterans' bills that become law per year versus number of references to veterans in communications per year (111th–114th Congress).

ability to pass legislation than their willingness to tout that accomplishment in official communications. Republicans show the opposite trend. As the ability to pass legislation flattens out, the willingness to talk about veterans continues to grow as veterans' constituencies increase as a share of the district or state population.

These figures rely on smoothing the averages across legislators, but they do not necessarily capture all the sources of variation that contribute to different levels of lip service and legwork. Other influences such as a seat on the veterans' affairs committee, or the chamber in which a legislator resides, can augment both the legislative productivity and communication efforts of legislators on veterans' policy. In the next section, I combine each of the explanatory variables introduced to comparatively assess the contributions of each type of influence on the outcomes of interest.

Explanatory Variables

To compare the variety of influences that likely drive veteran focus in communications and legislation, I incorporate a series of independent or explanatory variables. I discuss the theoretical expectations connecting each variable and varying rates of veteran focus in policy and communications. For some variables there are clear hypotheses about what sort of arrangement might lead to more veteran lip service and legwork, but for others the expectations are less clear.

Veterans Affairs' Committee

As the first stop for any piece of veterans' legislation, the Veterans Affairs' Committees in the House and the Senate play a pivotal role in ushering through policy change. In turn, serving on the committee may influence the rate at which a legislator communicates about veterans. Many members tout their veterans' committee roles in constituent communications saying things like, "One of my biggest honors as West Virginia's United States Senator is serving on the Senate Veterans' Affairs Committee"[10] or "It is an honor to serve as Chairman of the House Committee on Veterans' Affairs, which is why I am committed to ensuring our veterans are served with the respect and dignity they deserve."[11]

The work that legislators do on policy development largely takes place in committees. Legislators can tell constituents about committee hearings, markups, votes to get bills out of committees, amendments adopted during the drafting process, and so on. Members who are on Veterans' Affairs Committees will by definition have more to do with veterans' policy and thus have more opportunities to discuss veterans in constituent communications. While members are not in total control of their committee assignments as final determinations come from House and Senate leadership, they do seek certain assignments, and those who seek a seat on Veterans Affairs generally have a greater level of interest in veterans' issues than others. Thus, it is reasonable to expect more interest in talking about veterans with constituents for committee members. Additionally, in Chapter 4 we found that committee membership is related to the number of veterans' bills introduced and passed, providing yet again another link between the work a legislator does and the subject material a legislator could express to constituents.

Being on a veterans' committee is significantly and positively (0.15) related to the number of veteran references made per year. On average, legislators on the committee send 5.66 veterans' references per year while others send 3.15. Given this strong individual relationship, I anticipate that committee status will play a role in the more comprehensive analyses.[12]

Veteran Status

Veterans in Congress may be more likely to discuss veterans' issues in their communications than others by the simple reasoning that they understand the experience more intimately. On the other hand some legislators have noted that they are hesitant to continuously advertise their veteran status in politics and instead prefer to stand alone on their ideas rather than their past. As we found in Chapter 4, veterans did not introduce more veterans' legislation, attract more cosponsors, or pass greater amounts of legislation than non-veterans, but communication styles need not always follow legislative styles.

In the analyses to come, a 1 designates veteran legislators and a 0 designates nonveterans. Veteran status on its own is not significantly correlated to the number of veterans' references per year. The average number of veteran references per year for veterans in Congress is 3.39 compared to 3.44 for nonveterans. While individually this does not support the supposition that veterans are more likely to mention veterans' issues, I keep this variable in the full model because it is theoretically justified and may play more of a role when taken in a context of a greater set of variables.

Veterans in the Constituency

Greater veteran percentages of a constituency ought to increase the importance of veterans' issues for a legislator by the simple fact that more people he or she is tasked with representing hold a shared identity and can call on an established set of interest groups to pressure legislative actors to develop favorable policy. Previous research finds that constituency preferences are related to the ways members communicate; thus, it is conceivable that I find such an influence here.[13]

The average percent of veterans in a given constituency is 8.4 percent with a median of 8.27 percent. Figure 6.4 plots the raw number of official e-newsletters from each state delegation by the number of veterans in each state. As expected, states with more veterans also have legislators who send more messages about veterans when considered as the whole delegation.

Party

Parties prioritize issues in different ways. When discussing policy areas, Democrats and Republicans do not always focus on the same topics. Leadership teams develop and disseminate different talking points to their members. Both Democrats and Republicans in the electorate support veterans in public opinion polls, so from that perspective there is no reason to think that Democrats or Republicans in Congress would talk about veterans in communications in an appreciably different way once other factors are controlled for. Yet, we know public perception links the Republican Party with veterans. I argue that one of the reasons this perception exists is differential levels of lip service or communicative focus on veterans across the parties. Thus, this theory anticipates that even after controlling for other factors related to

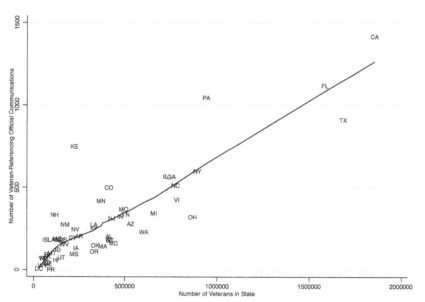

Figure 6.4 Number of veteran referencing Congress-to-constituent communications by veteran population size—state delegations 2009–2016. Without controlling for any other factors and including all members in the database ($N = 825$) the correlation between percentage of veterans in the constituency and references to veterans' issues per year is significant and positive (0.11).

communication strategies, the role of party will contribute to a difference between veterans' emphasis.

In Chapter 4 we saw that party was related to veterans' legwork; Democrats do more legwork than Republicans. In this chapter I find the opposite. There is a significant relationship between legislator party and the number of veterans' references per year. But rather than being the leaders, in terms of communications Democrats send a mean number of 2.59 veterans' referencing communications per year and Republicans send 4.26. These four main explanatory variables, committee status, veteran status, veteran constituency, and party have been the focus thus far. In order to develop a finer test of communication and legislative efforts I now describe and include a set of additional control variables that are common to the discipline and exhibit their own sorts of influences. By combining multiple potential sources of variation the hope is that I can identify the legislator and constituency characteristics that matter most to how legislators deploy communication and legislative strategies for veterans politics.

Additional Controls

I include additional measures to develop a more robust test of the theory of lip service over legwork. Perhaps some other, less obvious phenomena best explain the differences between the legislators who appear the most veteran minded in communications as opposed to those who focus on veterans in legislation. These additional controls are standard variables in many models of legislator behavior such as gender, chamber, seniority, and additional, specifically justified measures. Each of these legislator-specific measures comes from ProPublica, which sources the original information from the official website of the Office of the Clerk of the U.S. House of Representatives, the official website of the U.S. Senate, the Biographical Directory of the U.S. Congress, Congress.gov, which is maintained by the Library of Congress, and the Government Printing Office.

Legislator Chamber

Representatives and senators can send official communications as much as they want. Representatives and senators can also introduce as much legislation as they want. However, there could be differences that relate chamber to policy and communication styles; therefore, I include an indicator to signal which chamber a legislator serves in.

I did not a priori expect that members of one chamber would be more likely to engage in lip service or legwork, yet Chapter 4 showed that senators tend to introduce more veterans' legislation than representatives. For lip service, the measures for representatives versus senators are not statistically different. The numbers of references of veterans per year are 3.57 and 2.76, respectively.

Legislator Gender

There is no immediately obvious reason to suppose men or women do more legwork or lip service on veterans' policy. However, there is research that indicates men and women approach legislating in different ways and communicate to constituents in different ways.[14] Considered alone, legislator gender is not related to veterans' policy introduction or references in communications. Women and men tend to make the same amounts of veteran references per year at 3.23 and 3.46, respectively.

Seniority

The mean number of total years in Congress during the 111th–114th sessions is 12 with a range of 1–59. The longest-serving member in the database is John Dingell (D-MI). We know that there is an expansionary phase in the early career years for members of Congress.[15] But what is less clear is how this relates to communication styles generally and veterans' focus specifically.

One might argue that older members may focus on veterans more because their generations have greater numbers of veterans as a share of the population and therefore a greater familiarity with veterans. Or it could be that longer-serving members have seen more veteran casework in office and are thus more attuned to the needs of veterans. On the other hand, those just starting a legislative career may take note of the power in various veterans' lobbies and thus be more inclined to pay lip service to such an important constituency.

In the context of official e-newsletters generally, there is evidence that members with less seniority and younger members tend to use the medium slightly more often than their more senior, older counterparts; thus, we might expect a finding of fewer communications in all topic areas for more senior members.[16] Without a large line of empirical research relating communication style change and legislative careers, I do not posit a strong theoretical expectation one way or the other for who might most mention veterans.

Independently, I find a negative and significant relationship between the years in Congress a member serves and the number of veterans' references made per year. The correlation of the entire sample is –0.16. That is, considered alone, members who serve in Congress for longer amounts of time tend to send fewer constituent messages about veterans than those who have spent fewer years in Congress.

Veterans' Spending

Districts and states receive different amounts of Veterans Administration (VA) money that can be broken into six constituent parts: compensation and pensions, construction, education and vocational rehabilitation/employment, general operating expenses, insurance and indemnities, and medical care. For each of the models I include the 2010 levels of aggregate funding that flowed from the federal agency to individual districts. In subsequent chapters I isolate specific sorts of funds, but for the assessment of overall veterans' legwork and lip service, I use the aggregate amount. These data are collected and provided by the VA from a variety of sources.[17] Considered alone the total amount of VA spending is positively related to legislation introduced per year (0.09) and shows no correlation with references to veterans per year.

State-Level Effects

There are different pathways that state-level effects could conceivably influence legislative and communicative behavior. There are state-level differences in amounts of veterans, and therefore, demands for veteran benefits' policies are different. Legislators also learn from others in their state delegation about what sorts of strategies and issues play well at home, so some delegations may have folk pathways of knowledge about talking about or legislating on certain issues over others.[18] In the models I control for state delegation effects because the influence may alter both legwork and lip service.

To measure state-level differences, I count the number of institutions that are chartered for VA reimbursement for each state. This count is made of the number of universities, nondegree-granting sites of secondary education, flight schools, and correspondence programs. This might not appear as a directly obvious choice, but a count of institutions is preferable to a measure like dollars spent in the state by the VA or dummy indicators for a few reasons. The numbers of institutions in each state that are eligible for VA dollars serve as a proxy for the total veterans' demands legislators feel. There is a connection between how many voices are clamoring for funding and how many institutions a legislator can please when he or she legislates or talks about veterans.

VA spending per state is not quite appropriate to assess state-level differences because of what VA money is allocated to and to how these costs are different depending on which state the spending takes place in. The authorization of construction projects in different states accounts for some of the variation, but depending on local conditions, construction cost determinations do not cleanly match up across states. More important, legislators themselves cannot influence the count of institutions in their states, but they can more easily influence the amounts of dollars directed to their states.

A count of VA reimbursable institutions is preferable to a fixed effects or indicator style of measurement because it captures the differences across states (all states have a different total number here), but it also provides a way to incorporate important magnitude differences across states.

Theoretically, the measure of veterans demanding institutions per state could be broken into a district-level measure, but in practice this is not feasible. Congressional district boundaries are not natural boundaries and do not always fully encapsulate the institutions covered in this measure. This is especially true with the proliferation of different campus sites for institutions of higher education.

Consider the University of Kansas. Kansas has four congressional districts, and the University of Kansas (KU) has five campus locations: the central campus in Lawrence (district 2), the medical center in Kansas City (district 3), the Edwards campus in Overland Park (district 3), the pharmacy school in Wichita (district 4), and the Salina Campus medical school in Salina (district 1); yet as a count of institutions eligible for federal VA money, all of KU counts as one institution. Rather than attempt to split the measure up, I retain the original counts per state as kept by the VA. By not varying by state, delegates who have otherwise different values are identical by this measure, which provides a way to control for interstate variation while also utilizing a measure of intrastate similarities.[19]

Interactive Considerations

The incentives are certainly in place that a member would want to look active to constituents, and legislation aimed at helping the lives of veterans is generally quite popular. Like with those on Veterans' Affairs Committees, policy authors do more work on veterans' issues and thus may more likely talk about it in constituent communications.

In a causal sense there is a plausible, one-way linkage between legwork and lip service. If a member introduces legislation, that gives cause to discuss legislation in his or her constituent communications. It is reasonable to expect that those who do more legwork may also do more lip service. While the variables are measured simultaneously, the theoretical linkage only flows one way. It is far less justified to think that members of Congress introduce legislation because they talk about veterans rather than the other way around.

In the third version of every model, I include the legwork measure as an explanatory variable for lip service. The correlation between references made per year and legislation proposed per year is just 0.06 (not statistically significant). But as before, I conduct analyses with this variable and others to see if a nuanced contextual relationship emerges.

Results: A Model of Lip Service and Legwork

In this section I compare the competing influences that contribute to the lip service and legwork efforts legislators make for veterans. I model the rate of veterans' legislation introduced per year in service as well as veterans' communications per year as a function of the other variables described previously.

I run three regression models. The first uses the introduction of legislation measure of legwork as the outcome variable. The second uses the lip service measure of veterans' communications per year in service, and the third is the same but includes the legwork measure as an explanatory variable. Owing to the distribution of both the lip service and legwork measures, I use negative binominal regression as my modeling approach. Table 6.1 presents the results from these analyses.

In all of the models, two variables emerge as the primary movers accounting for the differences in legwork and lip service: committee membership and party. The percentage of veterans in a constituency and the seniority of a member, chamber, and state counts of VA-funded sites all show significant relationships in some, but not all, of the models.

In the model of legwork the results look largely like the findings in Chapter 4.[20] All else equal, members on the veterans' committees, those with higher shares of veterans in their districts, senators, and Democrats do more veterans' legwork. Members who come from states with larger numbers of VA reimbursable sites also have high legwork measures. The veteran status and seniority of a legislator measures show no significant relationship with legwork nor does the specific dollar amounts of overall VA spending.

Turning to lip service in the second and third columns, committee membership and partisanship still matter, but the importance of party reverses.[21] Being on the Veterans' Affairs Committee is positively and significantly related to both legwork and lip service. Those members both talk and do more about on veterans' politics than others. However, Republican members are much more prone to talk about veterans in their official communications than Democrats.

Accounting for other influences, how much more do similarly situated Republicans offer legwork and lip service than Democrats? While the results of these regressions are not immediately interpretable from the table, we can use the coefficients to predict how many pieces of legislation a member will offer in a year and how many pieces of communications they will send about veterans in a year. This estimate is an improvement over the raw standardized description provided in Figures 6.2 and 6.3 because this represents a more apple to apples look at how Democrats and Republicans differ, when other explanatory variables are accounted for and held constant.

Lip Service: Legislator Communications about Veterans

Table 6.1 Lip Service and Legwork as a Function of Institutional, Legislator, and Constituency Characteristics (111th–114th Congress)

	Legwork	Lip Service	Lip Service II
On Committee	1.24**	0.56**	0.48*
	(0.14)	(0.15)	(0.18)
Veteran	0.05	−0.06	−0.06
	(0.13)	(0.13)	(0.14)
Veterans in Constituency	0.08**	0.02	0.00
	(0.02)	(0.02)	(0.02)
Democrat	0.45**	−0.48**	−0.47**
	(0.10)	(0.11)	(0.11)
House	−0.63**	0.31	0.24
	(0.16)	(0.19)	(0.14)
Seniority	0.00	−0.02**	−0.02**
	(0.00)	(0.01)	(0.01)
Woman	0.16	0.07	0.04
	(0.11)	(0.13)	(0.13)
Number of VA-Funded Educational Sites (state)	0.00*	0.00	−0.00
	(0.00)	(0.00)	(0.00
FY10 Federal Veterans Funds	−0.00	0.00	0.00
	(0.00)	(0.00)	(0.00)
Number of Bills Introduced per Year			0.06
			(0.05)
Constant	−1.21	1.07	1.36
N	820	819	823
McFadden's Adj R2	0.10	0.02	0.01

Negative binomial regressions with white standard errors in parentheses.
* $p < 0.05$
** $p < 0.00$

A postestimation comparison of means shows that the differences between Democrats and Republicans are statistically significant for both legwork and lip service. Democrats, all else equal, are predicted to introduce 0.87 pieces of legislation, whereas Republicans are predicted to introduce 0.55 pieces and Democrats are expected to send 2.6 communications on veterans to the 4.25 communications expected of Republicans. That is, while Democrats introduce significantly more legislation than Republicans, Republicans reference veterans at a rate that is nearly double of the rate of Democrats on average.

What might surprise some is how little being a veteran seems to relate to either legislating for veterans or talking about veterans. Veteran status does not refer to any innate characteristic of a legislator in the ways that race and gender do. Thus, it is not clear that theories about descriptive representation built looking at those sorts of identities would translate into veteran status. This result is consistent with other research pieces that looked at the propensities for members of Congress to mention Memorial Day holiday celebrations and found that veterans did not do that more than nonvets.[22]

In Figures 6.5 and 6.6, I use the results from models 1 and 2 to present the predicted values of legwork and lip service along with the standard errors for those estimates. I present the data over the share of veterans in a constituency as a way to think about how these patterns vary over different sorts of district contexts. The lines are locally weighted and smoothed. As an additional bit of information, I have overlaid the empirical distribution of veterans' constituencies in each figure so that one can get a sense for how these effects diffuse throughout the majority of legislators in Congress.

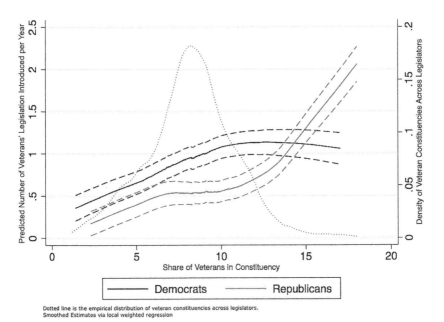

Figure 6.5 Postestimation predicted rate of veterans' legwork per year. Dotted line is the empirical Distribution of Veteran Constituencies across Legislators. Smoothed estimates via local weighted regression.

Lip Service: Legislator Communications about Veterans

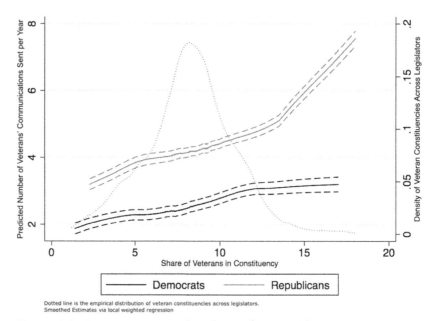

Figure 6.6 Postestimation predicted rate of veterans' lip service per year. Dotted line is the empirical Distribution of Veteran Constituencies across Legislators. Smoothed estimates via local weighted regression.

Notice that for most constituencies, members of the Democratic Party will introduce more veterans' legislation. Even after accounting for other elements of the policy introduction process, these differences are significant across the parties. Toward the right, higher percentage of veterans in a constituency, there is a Republican spike in legwork, but empirically only 10 legislators have constituencies of 15 percent or more veterans, 6 of which are represented by Republicans and 4 by Democrats.

When we look to Figure 6.6, there is a reverse association.

For Republicans and Democrats alike, as the share of veterans in a constituency grows, so too does the number of official communications that mention veterans. Yet, Republicans have nearly double lip service efforts compared to Democrats. Controlling for a host of other variables that could influence communication practices, there is a consistent and significant difference between Republicans and Democrats.

In terms of overall volume, the message is clear; Republicans talk about veterans more than Democrats in the modern Congresses. While some may not find this result surprising, it does represent the first comprehensive, empirical examination of such a phenomenon. Before concluding this chapter I now consider two other features of political communications about veterans. First, I analyze how veteran members themselves refer to their own status and ask if there are party differences specific to self-referencing. Second, I perform some text analyses on the total corpus of official legislator-to-constituent veterans' communications as a way to get a sense of framing or more specific issues foci taken up from one party or the other.

Veteran Legislators Mentioning Their Status

As discussed in Chapter 2, veterans are slightly overrepresented in Congress holding approximately 20 percent of the seats in the House and the Senate but only accounting for about 7–9 percent of the voting age population. Of the 144 veterans serving in the 111th–114th Congresses, 41 percent were Democrats and 59 percent were Republicans.[23] While a majority of veterans in Congress do remind constituents at least once of their military service, a sizeable 43 percent of never made mention of their veteran status in official communications between the 111th and the 114th Congresses. Of those who never discussed, 44 percent were Democrats and 56 percent were Republicans. This split roughly mirrors the overall divisions of veteran legislators in congressional parties.

Despite the fact that being a veteran is nearly universally considered an attribute among voters, some politicians have expressed reservations about referencing their veteran status as a way to score political credibility.[24] Are there differences in which members were most likely to reference their own military service in constituent communications? The theoretical explanation of lip service over legwork expects that Republican members are more likely to talk about veterans than Democrats; however, does that hold true when looking only at military veteran members of Congress?

To assess military veteran legislators and their proclivities to mention their service to constituents, I compiled a count of how often each veteran member made reference to his or her own service in official communications. Every time a legislator sends a communication, he or she has the option of deciding whether or not to remind constituents of his or her service. This is true of both Democrats and Republicans, but the willingness to do this need not be the same across parties.

In this exercise I only assess self-references, but that is not to say that those who are not veterans do not attempt to link their own histories to those of veterans. Women, who historically have had fewer opportunities to serve, will sometimes point to family connections to let constituents know that they understand the challenges of military life and have a personal connection to veterans' policies.

For instance, in a constituent communication sent on November 10, 2016, Democrat Alma Adams (NC-12) wrote,

> As the daughter, granddaughter, niece and sister of veterans, I understand the sacrifices that veterans and their families make and I believe that

support for our troops and their families does not end with the transition out of military service.[25]

Democrat Shelley Berkley (NV-1) sent a similar statement to constituents on May 27, 2011,

> As the wife and daughter of veterans, I understand full well the sacrifices that our military makes, and throughout my time in the U.S. House of Representatives, I have fought to improve the care and benefits for our veterans, as well as those who are currently serving in our armed forces.[26]

Republican Senator Kelly Ayotte made the same sort of connection to veterans' communities through her marriage noting on Veterans Day 2016,

> As the wife of a combat veteran, this day is deeply important to me.[27]

But for this test I only concern myself with members who refer to their own service history. Of those who do mention military veteran status, the rate of self-reference per year ranges from 0.125 to 11.25. The legislator who brings up his service the most, Mike Coffman (R-CO), does so 89 times over his seven years in the database. Recall from Chapter 2, Coffman is also the legislator who most writes about veterans in issues in all of his official communications.

When considering the rates of self-references per year, there are no significant differences between Democrats and Republicans. When considering the other sets of variables discussed previously in relation to self-references, I find the greater number of veterans in a constituency is negatively related to the rate of self-references suggesting that members who are veterans among constituencies who have fewer veterans among them are more likely to remind their audiences of their own military service than others.

The Content of Lip Service

Of all constituent communications about veterans, 34 percent come from Democrats and 66 percent from Republicans. What are members of each party *saying* about veterans? What is the content of constituent communications that discuss veterans' issues? Are there meaningful differences in content as well as in volume of such communications? To compare what members emphasize when talking about veterans in constituent communications, I first conduct a bag-of-words-style text analysis on Republican and Democrat communications.[28] To ensure that I only compare passages that refer to veterans rather than comparing Republican versus Democratic communications generally, I extract every paragraph from each message in the DCinbox database that mentions veterans and only compare those passages that contain the root word "veteran."

Table 6.2 shows the ways members of Congress talk about veterans based on the words that most frequently co-occur in their constituent communications. In instances where single words can be stemmed to a similar root word ("benefit" and "benefits") ("family" and "families"), I present the root word with an asterisk denoting that multiple endings are observed.

When looking at terms of two, three, or four words I do not stem any words and instead keep the terms as is, to more accurately reflect the content of the communications. Veteran is excluded in these counts since I am interested in finding the words that most frequently co-occur with "veteran." Some frequently occurring combinations of common stop words such as "of the" are omitted from Table 6.2 as they do not contribute much to a greater understanding of how parties approach veteran-focused communications in a meaningfully different way.

For the single unigrams that most frequently occur with "veteran" in constituent communications, Democrats and Republicans are very similar. Both use words like "service" or "services" in reference to the military *service* that veterans engaged in while active or messages reference efforts to ensure veterans get the *services* and *care* they need.

Table 6.2 Most Frequently Co-Occurring Words with "Veteran" in Official Communications from Democrats and Republicans

Unigrams

Democrats	*Republicans*
Service*	Affairs
Care	VA
Affairs	Care
Benefit*	Day
Health	Department
Military	Military
Famil*	Service*

Bigrams

Our Veterans	*Veteran Affairs*
Veterans and	Our veterans
Veteran affairs	Of veterans
Of veterans	Veterans and
The veterans	The veterans
For veterans	Department of

(continued)

Table 6.2 (continued)

And veterans	For veterans
Health care	And veterans
The VA	The VA
Veterans Day	Veterans Day
Their families	*The department*
Veterans in	*The House*
To help	Veterans who
Trigrams	
Of veterans affairs	Of veterans affairs
Department of veterans	Department of veterans
And their families	The department of
Veterans and their	Veterans Affairs Committee
The department of	Veterans and their
Men and women	And their families
Our veterans and	For our veterans
For our veterans	Men and women
World War II	Our veterans and
Our nations veterans	Veterans affairs VA
Veterans affairs VA	Of our veterans
To our veterans	Our nations veterans
Of our veterans	World War II
Iraq and Afghanistan	To our veterans
To ensure that	And veterans affairs

* denotes multiple endings.
Italicized words are more uniquely associated with one party.

One difference between the parties is that Republicans use "VA" and "day" as a part of their topmost frequently coincident words with "veteran" and Democrats use "health" and "benefits." During the period of study, Republicans talked about the VA in a variety of ways. Some wrote with a positive spin, such as when a member wrote about how he or she was able to compel the VA to distribute benefits to a constituent who reached out for assistance in navigating the bureaucracy. Sometimes there are critical communications pointing out the scandals or incompetence of different leaders in the VA. In other instances there are more general statements about the work of

Congress to improve the VA such as when Representative Austin Scott (R-GA) wrote,

> This year, the House passed a series of legislation focused on a veteran's transition from active duty to civilian life and holding the VA to higher standards of care by reforming the VA into an organization worthy of the veterans it serves.[29]

The common Republican reference to "day" appears in some messages as a recounting of what a member did on veterans' issues during that day. The other large driver for "day" is messages sent celebrating or commemorating holidays such as Veterans Day and Memorial Day.

The uniquely Democratic words are "benefits" and "health." There is a good deal of casework and procedural references to veterans' benefits. Representative Adam Schiff (D-CA) closes one of his 2016 e-newsletters with,

> Schiff's office helps constituents navigate the complicated immigration and visa system, get back *benefits* for *veterans* or medals they have earned while serving, help with the IRS or Social Security, and much more.[30]

In other cases members of Congress talk about the work they've done securing or providing new benefits for veterans such as when Senator Jon Tester (D-MT) wrote about a bill he supported, the 2017 Military Construction and Veterans Affairs Appropriations Bill, saying,

> this bill did not only *benefit* our veterans, it provides resources and certainty for our active duty troops in Montana and across the globe.[31]

The references to health and veterans range from pedestrian calls for people to support efforts to better deliver health care solutions for veterans to wonky descriptions about how appropriation projects are hamstrung by Republican efforts to obstruct provisions of health care to veterans. For an example of the latter, see Senator Debbie Stabenow's (D-MI) following passage,

> Under current law, the VA must receive specific legislative authorization to lease medical facilities with average annual rental payments in excess of $1 million. However, since 2012, Congress has not, through a regular process, authorized any VA major medical facility leases, hampering the ability of the VA to provide much-needed health care and services to veterans around the country. "Our veterans in Michigan deserve the absolute best health care," said Senator Stabenow. "Our bill would allow the VA to expand much-needed outpatient services in Ann Arbor and Pontiac. No veteran should ever be told they need to wait for quality health care, which is why we need to authorize these leases right away."[32]

Lip Service: Legislator Communications about Veterans

These explanatory links between seemingly disparate government processes are one of the key reasons Congress-to-constituent communications exist. These are inside the beltway stories that rarely get wider media coverage. Members of Congress are in a unique position to relay this information to constituents, and the wide adoption of official e-mail makes doing so much easier.

Moving to two- and three-word phrases, some related partisan differences emerge, but for the most part, language around veterans is quite similar. For two-word bigrams, Democrats continue to have a unique focus on "Health care," and the bigrams "Their families," "Veterans in," and "To help" round out the top of the list. When Democrats reference veterans and families, the term "Their families" appears frequently in Democratic veterans' related e-newsletters as a way to expand the circle of care to family members of veterans, not just veterans themselves. The term is used as an addendum to a sentiment about veterans. This line from Representative Adam Smith (D-WA) is an example,

> Veterans and their families face a unique set of challenges, and Congress must do everything possible to ensure that the men and women who serve our country receive the care and assistance that they earned.[33]

In contrast, uniquely Republican terms include "Department of," "The department," "The House," and "Veterans who." For many the unique terms might not indicate much. But they are quite telling contextually. Republicans were quick to point to shortcomings in the form of The Department of Veterans Affairs to criticize the Democrat-led executive agency of the time. While the GOP was quick to praise veterans generally in communications, they were nearly equally as quick to admonish those tasked with providing care for veterans. See the following from Representative Brad Wenstrup (R-MI) sent on September 11, 2016,

> . . . Affairs healthcare system and provide recommendations for fixing it. In July, the Commission on Care released its 300-page report, confirming what far too many of our veterans know from experience to be true: the VA is plagued by systemic problems.[34]

Messages like these are typical and easier to consume than the one offered by Senator Stabenow. Congress is trying to do right by veterans, but the VA does face some difficulties. This sort of complaint-centered message strategy may be effective, despite the fact that it obscures some important nuances about the VA.[35]

The Democrat focus on veterans and "health care" and "their families" are lip service in their own way. There is not always legislative activity to back up the statements, but the strategy is devoid of a scapegoat in a way that GOP communications tend not to be. Some Democrats do send messages decrying activities at the VA, but many messages are more positive in tone. See the following from Congressman John Sarbanes (D-MD) in May 2016 where he describes a health practice instituted within the VHA that he attempted to expand to the general population via legislation.

> A bill that I authored and introduced, the Co-Prescribing to Reduce Overdoses Act,[36] passed the U.S. House of Representatives on May 11. This bipartisan bill will encourage and train health care providers to prescribe overdose reversal drugs, such as Naloxone, when they prescribe common opioids like pain medication to patients at risk of addiction and overdose. The Veterans Health Administration distributes Naloxone to all veterans in treatment for a substance use disorder or to those who take high doses of opiates and has successfully shown this strategy reduces opioid overdose deaths. The Co-Prescribing to Reduce Overdoses Act would enable more health care providers across the country to implement these kinds of lifesaving co-prescription programs.[37]

This health care and veteran reference highlights a success of the VHA and puts forward a policy proposal to solve a greater problem. This bill did have bipartisan support in the way of a voice vote taken within the House; it was then referred to committee in the Senate and died.

For three-word phrases, systematic differences are fewer and harder to discern. Republicans tend to make more references to variations of Veterans' Affairs Committee work. The only notable nonprocess term that occurs in Democrat communications at a greater frequency is "Iraq and Afghanistan." This term is sometimes used in terms of the pressure group "Iraq and Afghanistan Veterans of America" and in other times referring to the most recent class of veterans to reenter the civilian population from the Iraq and Afghanistan military missions.

Other than the differences in frequencies, there is not great evidence that Republicans and Democrats communicate about veterans in significantly different ways. While there are a few things that are distinct to the parties, generally the language used and the topics mentioned have a good deal of overlap. The greatest difference is the difference in rates with which members of Congress write about veterans' issues in constituent communications.

Concluding Thoughts

Republicans engage in more veteran lip service than Democrats. This is not an issue of content difference but rather a difference in volume. Republicans emphasize veterans more often in their official communications than Democrats do. Knowing nothing more than the count of messages sent by members of Congress to their constituents, it *appears* that Republicans care more about veterans.

Differences in communication styles are not attributable to meaningful differences in types of constituencies. Rather, after having controlled for other factors thought to influence both legislating and communicating priorities, I find the Democrats offer more legwork while Republicans offer more lip service even when these members come from similar sorts of districts. The differences are pretty great in practice. Republican legislators write about veterans nearly twice as often as Democrats.

This amount of Republican lip service overwhelms the legislative efforts expended by members of the party. In the reverse way, Democrats have more room to talk about legislative accomplishments or efforts on behalf of veterans, and yet they do not do so to the extent that their counterparts across the aisle. There are of course many reasons that veterans may prefer Republican politicians.

But what I hope to convince you of is that this cannot be strictly due to the efforts of legislators in their role of crafting governmental solutions. Rather, there is a noticeable and persistent divergence between the parties where Republicans appear to have engendered the respect of veterans and public good despite lagging on legislative efforts. Lip service plays a role in the cultivation of the public narrative, and Republicans are solidly ahead on lip service surrounding veterans. This frequent and public emphasis, empirically established here, is a key part of the reason for the sense and measures that connect Republicans with veterans more than Democrats.

CHAPTER SEVEN

Veterans' Education Policy: The Post–9/11 GI Bill

President Franklin Delano Roosevelt signed the original GI Bill, known as the Serviceman's Readjustment Act, into law in 1944 to provide veterans returning from World War II a stronger foothold in the economy. Since this initial effort to recognize the educational opportunity costs associated with military service, each successive era has seen some form of government educational assistance for returning veterans. In this chapter I discuss the most current version of veterans' educational assistance, the Post–9/11 GI Bill. This bill is considered by many in Congress to be one of the best bipartisan pieces of legislation to pass in recent history.

What is colloquially known as the Post–9/11 GI Bill is referred to by many different names, including the 21st Century GI Bill of Rights, the Webb GI Bill, or the new GI Bill. Formally, the Post–9/11 Veterans Education Assistance Act is Title V of the Supplemental Appropriations Act of 2008, which became law with President Bush's signature on June 30, 2008. The bill was originally drafted to augment Part III of Title 38 of the U.S. Code to include a new provision expanding educational benefits for military veterans who have served since September 11, 2001. The language came from a legislative proposal introduced by Democratic senator Jim Webb of Virginia on his first day in office; hence the occasional reference to the Webb GI Bill. For ease, I refer to the bill passed in 2008 as the Post–9/11 GI Bill.

In what follows I briefly provide the history of past GI bills and situate the current Post–9/11 GI Bill. Next, I describe the legislative path of the bill, the timeline and procedures of implementation, and the congressional reaction to unforeseen hiccups associated with the bill. While heralded as a great success for veterans, the Post–9/11 GI Bill was not without faults. After passage various shortcomings were made apparent, and legislators took to their constituent communications to complain, offer solutions, and remind constituents of the work done on behalf of veterans. With the focus on only one piece of legislation, I provide more detailed examples of the lip service versus legwork phenomena I described in earlier chapters.

A Brief History of Veterans' Education Benefits

Prior to the 1944 law veterans were not provided with widespread formal education benefits by the government. Those returning after World War I in the Progressive Era found that national commitments to both laissez-faire capitalism and a renewed sense of government's responsibility made for a complicated transition to civilian life. Many veterans felt that they ought to be responsible for their own efforts to reintegrate into society after service but lacked the tools to do so.[1] The career opportunity costs that a serviceman paid were realized in underemployment and homelessness of veterans.

In addition, diagnoses of "shell-shock" served to mark men not as just war-wounded but also with a stigma around mental weakness.[2] Public imagination pictured soldiers as strong and self-reliant; when men returned with physical and mental shortcomings, the archetype was challenged, leaving many in a difficult spot. Veterans were told they ought to find a new purpose in life, to reintegrate into civil society, but there was no robust government guidance on how to do so.[3]

Veterans' groups filled this gap by launching political efforts in the form of protests and marches in Washington. The centralizing call was that the government owed veterans some assistance after their return home to ease the transition and recognize the difficulty of returning after war. In response, federal legislators reluctantly passed the World War Adjusted Compensation Act in 1924 to provide a one-time cash bonus to veterans, but the act specified that veterans could not redeem the cash value of the bonus until 1945. This unsurprisingly did not sate the demands of veterans and protest efforts continued. These veteran demands were met with governmental resistance, and in one instance two veterans were shot, who later died, while protesting.[4]

Throughout the 1920s–1940s veterans repeatedly organized to petition the government for benefits and legislators scrambled to put together bonus legislation, budgetary workarounds, and other enticements to placate vocal activists. These strategies of using one-time pay outs to please veterans continue to the current day. As recently as 2009, the U.S. Congress provided a one-time payout of $250 as a part of the American Recovery and Reinvestment Act.

While these protests are a pivotal development in veterans' group consciousness and government response, I do not focus further on these sorts of battles of the early 20th century here. For those seeking more information on the protests of the era, many others have written about the "Bonus Army."[5] In the following section I turn to the history of government's educational benefits for veterans from the first version in 1944 to the most recent version still under implementation today. This history does not include every education program or change instituted by the VA, but rather limits the scope to the two biggest preceding pieces of legislation that gave rise to the Post–9/11 GI Bill.[6]

The Serviceman's Readjustment Act of 1944

The first GI bill, known as the Serviceman's Readjustment Act, passed on June 12, 1944, by a 1-vote margin in the Senate and was signed into law 10 days later by President Franklin Delano Roosevelt. As the close vote indicates, public and political opinions were not as closely aligned behind government programs subsidizing educational opportunities for veterans as they are nowadays.

The VA was not directly tasked with providing higher educational assistance until the 1944 statute. After World War II the amount of government money available to support service members pursuing a college degree led to great enrollment rates among service members. Compared to similarly situated men who did not serve, members who could avail themselves of higher education with government assistance were significantly more likely to do so.[7] For the nationwide graduating class of 1949, 70 percent were veterans.[8] In total this bill sent 2,232,000 veterans to secondary education or apprenticeship programs at the cost of $5.5 billion.[9] While the influx of enrollees overwhelmed some schools and led to increased class sizes, academic administrators at the time generally reported that veterans were a privilege to instruct and good for the university enterprise.[10]

The original GI Bill is credited as a success both because it supported service members and because it provided the overall workforce with a new set of highly trained individuals to support and improve a growing U.S. economy. In many ways the success was not all as expected; legislators were surprised at how many more veterans availed themselves of the benefit than projections predicted.[11]

While a monumental shift in government policy toward veterans, the original GI Bill was rife with problems that simplistic and nostalgic accounts do not always make clear.[12] The bill provided for a lot of local enforcement, and this deferment meant that black veterans were oftentimes excluded from benefits by racially motivated local authorities. The university enrollee surge of veterans with guaranteed, government funding also squeezed out eligible women from attendance spots in higher education. For a comprehensive review of the good and bad of this bill, I direct readers to Frydl's 2009 book, *The GI Bill*.[13] This research shares similarities with the concerns in veteran perception and party efforts, albeit with different methods and focus in time. But nonetheless, it is an excellent example of in-depth, historical public policy research. For now, I briefly describe the change to the VA educational benefits ushered in the 1980s through the most recent, Post–9/11 iteration.

The Montgomery Bill

Facing recruitment shortfalls, in 1984 the original GI Bill was changed under the guidance of Mississippi Democratic congressman Gillespie V. "Sonny" Montgomery. From 1984 to 2008 the statute provided updated and expanded educational benefits to veterans. There is an important distinction to note here: this bill and the later-introduced Post–9/11 GI Bill are categorically different from the original GI Bill in that they were conceived of as incentives for an all-volunteer force rather than the forces of the past that combined volunteers and draftees.

In contrast to the original 1944 bill, the Montgomery GI Bill required service members to contribute $100 each month for their first 12 months of service to be eligible for the benefit after active duty. The payment of $1,200 on the front end could translate into as much as $66,000 on the back end if the veteran opted for an expensive program with the maximum amount of a full-time student payment for the full 36-month limit. The rationale for requiring members to "pay in" was to make the benefit something soldiers had to opt-in to ensure they wanted to pursue higher education after leaving the forces.

For most veterans who availed themselves of the Montgomery Bill, tuition reimbursement was capped at 70 percent of total costs, meaning this bill was a significant aid to veterans but not a guaranteed benefit, as it required ongoing payment from veterans. And as the costs of higher education continued ticking upward through the 1990s, many noted that the bill no longer represented a guaranteed benefit of college education. Yet by 2012, 2.6 million veterans had used the benefit at a price tag of roughly $500 million.[14]

The Post–9/11 GI Bill

The Post–9/11 GI Bill made fundamental changes to the incentives and educational reimbursement opportunities of service members. All told, about 2.1 million veterans were eligible for the new benefits by the time the final bill passed.

Compared to the Montgomery Bill, the Post–9/11 GI Bill is more generous in some ways and more limiting in others. The new bill expanded the definition of who was an eligible veteran, eliminated buy-in provisions, allowed benefits to be transferred to other dependents, increased federal administrative capacities to provide information to veterans, and incentivized colleges to dedicate resources of their own to integrate veterans. But a new limitation of the Post–9/11 Bill was that it did not include a subsidy on the job training and apprenticeship programs that were included in the Montgomery GI Bill.

Under the new bill a veteran pursuing an approved program of education can receive payments covering the program's tuition, up to the cost of the most expensive in state public school where the veteran resides. In addition to that foundation, the new bill offers veterans a set of accessory benefits that were different from previous iterations. I discuss those features in this chapter.

Expanded Eligibility: Veterans and Institutions

One of the largest changes was the expansion of who was considered an eligible veteran. The Post–9/11 Bill includes activated reservists and members of the National Guard who were on active duty for 90 days or more since September 11, 2001, or members who had been discharged with a service-connected disability after 30 days. With the expansion of who could claim veteran education benefits, there was also an expansion of which sorts of higher educational sites worked to recruit veterans. In particular, community colleges played a bigger role than they had under previous GI bills.[15] But the expansion of community college enrollment did not result in a direct trade-off with four-year programs; rather all institutions saw surges owning to the proclivities of different types of veterans. With the expansion to reservists and National Guard veterans, who generally tend to be older than veterans of other branches, there has been an increase in enrollment in four-year schools.[16]

Eligibility Amounts and Time Increased

Another expansion is in the amount of schooling covered. Prior to the Post–9/11 GI Bill, veterans covered under the Montgomery Bill received college tuition benefits amounting up to 70 percent of a public college education; for those using Post–9/11 benefits members serving for three years or more could have 100 percent covered. Not all veterans are given the same education benefits, but rather there are different eligibility bands depending on time served under the Post–9/11 setup. Educational benefits are paid in amounts roughly proportional to time served on active duty, with a maximum entitlement of 36 months of full-time education benefits—the equivalent of a four-year undergraduate degree. Compared to earlier benefits, veterans now have more time to decide if they will pursue higher education.

The Post–9/11 Bill increased eligibility to 15 years, whereas the Montgomery Bill had 10 years' time cap after a veteran left active duty.

Accessory Educational Benefits Included

In the Post–9/11 GI Bill there are provisions to pay for additional educational costs that are not captured in tuition. Each year a veteran can receive up to $1,000 to reimburse expenses on supplies such as books and course-required technologies, as well as for services such as tutoring, testing, and certification fees. In some instances the $1,000 can be used for travel expenses and to cover some costs of relocating to attend school. Depending on the location of the school and local housing costs, veterans are eligible for a monthly housing stipend to cover living expenses.

Transferability

While the provisions permitting veterans to transfer their benefits to other family members are a bit strict, the ability to do so in the Post–9/11 Bill is novel and hailed as a veteran-friendly move to support flexibility in choice. Previous government policies allowed for some limited sorts of educational benefits transfers, but the requirements were very limiting. Not all members who return find that additional schooling is necessary for the sorts of careers they intend to pursue. Some members have spouses who must forego schooling to look after children or work while a service member is on active duty. Others have children who would be better suited to college than a returning veteran. In the Post–9/11 GI Bill, service members who served at least six years and who agree to serve at least for four more years may apply to transfer any of their unused educational benefits to a spouse and/or child. Additionally, all children of service members who died on active duty since 9/11 are eligible for the full education benefit no matter the time in service.

Programmatic Changes in the VA

The Post–9/11 GI Bill created a new program, the Yellow Ribbon Program, in the Department of Veterans Affairs to match any voluntary additional contributions to veterans from institutions whose tuition is more expensive than the maximum educational assistance provided. This meant that private schools that otherwise may be beyond the financial reach of veterans even with Post–9/11 GI Bill benefits could become feasible options if the schools themselves were willing to split the difference of tuition that exceeded reimbursement limitations. While this program is an example of a well-intentioned aim to allow private or public choice, educational administrators warned that this may have a perverse effect of incentivizing for-profit colleges to falsely claim high tuitions, extract the maximum benefits from the federal government, and then underserve veterans.[17] Altogether, about 16 percent of veterans choose to apply Post–9/11 GI Bill benefits to private colleges, which is about the same proportion of civilian students seeking private higher education.[18]

University Guidance: Awareness and Outreach

The bill mandated the printing of a 164-page handbook outlining all of the benefits available for veterans available on the VA website, which was also to be made available in hard copy for purchase from the Government Printing Office for a nominal fee. Veterans and veterans' groups have noted the difficulty in knowing all the ins and outs of how the benefits are meant to be administered, and the bill itself provides guidance for how institutions of higher education can better serve the population in navigating the various elements.[19]

The new bill encouraged colleges and universities to hire dedicated veterans resource officers to assist student veterans. Knowing that many veterans would be first-generation college students, having administrative allies within universities and colleges was an effort to assist veterans in navigating the sometimes-complicated world of higher education. Universities that create roles to coordinate veterans' benefits or dedicated veterans' offices report that they can more easily recruit and retain veterans.[20]

Post–9/11 GI Bill Legislative Path

Similar to the Montgomery Bill, the Post–9/11 GI Bill had more than just education as a goal. In drafting and passing the bill, members of Congress hoped to put reservists and regular members of the armed forces on a more level playing field, increase the ability for the military to recruit high-quality candidates, and provide transferability of benefits as a way to reach different sorts of recruits who may not desire schooling for themselves but rather for a member of their family.

The Post–9/11 GI Bill was created with great intentions and won eventual support from both Democrats and Republicans. Yet, this bill had its difficulties and shortcomings. In this section I describe the path the bill took to pass and then turn the bulk of my focus to the congressional efforts and communications after implementation.

The bill is massively expensive compared to earlier GI bills. Even with uncertainty about how many members would use the benefit, estimates at the time of passage put government costs around $50–60 billion. This was somewhat of a sticking point for congressional Republicans looking to reduce government spending.[21] The level of government spending in the bill was so troublesome for high-profile veteran, Senator John McCain, that he ended up skipping the vote for final passage, and the six senators who voted against the final passage were all Republicans.[22] There were also provisions President Bush wanted to be included such as the transferability of benefits from a would-be veteran to his or her spouse in the event that the service member died in action. Originally the bill did not have such a transferability provision, and President Bush went so far as to say he would veto the bill without it.

The language used to support the Post–9/11 GI Bill by the bill sponsor Jim Webb highlighted the ideological tightrope that some Republicans found themselves on. In press releases and floor speeches, Senator Webb stressed that the Post–9/11 GI Bill represented a commitment to "reclaim economic fairness" in America. One way Webb navigated the criticism of high government costs was to attach the bill to a so-called must pass war-funding bill—FY08 Supplemental Appropriations Bill—so that detractors may be less vulnerable to claims of runaway government spending.

Early support for the bill came almost exclusively from Democrats, with just a few notable Republicans signing on. Similar, but not identical, versions passed the House and the Senate in May 2008. After some weeks of negotiations, more Republican support was secured, and in June 2009, a bipartisan deal was brokered leading the bill to passage as an amendment to H.R. 2642, the FY08 Supplemental Appropriations Bill. The final vote was 416–12 with nine Republicans and three Democrats opposing. A week later, the bill passed the Senate 92–6. President George W. Bush signed H.R. 2642 into law on June 30, 2008.

After passage, both Democrats and Republicans made their victory laps by describing to constituents the positive consequences of the bill. Yet, in the earliest rollout of the bill, unintended consequences and hiccups in administration served as sober reminders that there are limits on the goodness of any one bill. I now discuss the short- and long-term implementation problems for the Post–9/11 GI Bill and utilize a strategy to assess how lip service and legwork from the two major political parties play out in this one specific bill.

Implementation Successes and Setbacks

On paper, the bill pleased many veterans groups, yet in practice the implementation frustrated some veterans seeking to use the benefits. Once implemented, the Post–9/11 GI Bill placed an overwhelming burden on the VA.

Between the formal start of the bill on August 9, 2009, and the due dates for payments at colleges and universities, 300,000 claims were submitted to the VA. Because of the popularity and quick enrollment of the program, there were challenges in back-end processing and payment timing that became apparent at the beginning of the fall 2009 collegiate term. The tight turnaround time, chronic understaffing, and limited funding held up the disbursement of checks to eligible veterans. Some veterans who sought to use the benefit did not receive tuition reimbursement payments in time to meet university-mandated enrollment and pay deadlines.

This understandably resulted in veteran frustration and occasional public excoriation of the VA by legislators. The VA decided in October 2009 to focus on expediting the initial processing and issued emergency checks in the value of $3,000 to veterans in order to cover books and housing allowances as a temporary solution to the processing back order. The initial enrollment and reimbursement challenge was a quickly realized unintended consequence of the bill.

There were other longer-term problems such as system exploitation from veterans as well as from institutions of higher education. Criticisms of the bill targeted government administration as well as outside entities such as for-profit colleges. In 2011, a report discussed by Senator Tom Harkin on the Senate floor indicated that 8 of the top 10 entities receiving Post–9/11 GI funds were for-profit colleges and universities and that these institutions sought to defraud both the government and veterans.[23]

For-Profit Colleges

For-profit colleges aggressively recruit veterans, the colleges are sometimes not accredited, the colleges rarely provide better educational and employment opportunities for graduates than not-for-profit colleges, and oftentimes charge higher tuition than other schools. One of the largest problems is that higher tuition costs at for-profit schools exceed reimbursement maximums allowed under the bill. But that fact is not always made clear and is sometimes intentionally obfuscated to veterans by institutions seeking to use this information asymmetry to their advantage. Once enrolled at a for-profit school, and after realizing the differences in tuition and benefit levels, some veterans take out loans or dip into savings to cover excess costs. Veterans are sometimes misled by for-profit school into thinking the VA will eventually cover the overages, but that this reimbursement will occur over a longer time period. For many for-profit schools, that is not the case because the schools in question are not eligible for additional funds in the first place or the nontuition-based fees exceed the benchmarked limitations under the bill. In this type of situation, veterans are left with hefty, unexpected balances.

For-profit schools make money on increasing enrollments but do not necessarily care about the outcomes or continuation of degree seeking on enrollees after initial tuition bills are paid. For-profit schools are able to get away with such a strategy because they invest heavily in recruitment efforts and there is very little oversight from any governing body. Once a veteran enrolls and pays tuition, he or she sometimes finds out that the structure and demands of for-profit schools are too much to complete successfully. Some veterans enrolled in for-profit school drop out after paying tuition but failing to meet their class obligations. When this happens, a veteran is saddled with debt of his or her own, has used up some GI funds, and cannot transfer the credits to a better institution. It is obvious that this is an undesired outcome, not intended by the originators of the bill.

Many veterans want to start on a degree as soon as possible, and many come from families and communities that do not have an extended history or great knowledge about university enrollments. Owing to these sorts of circumstances, for-profit colleges can dupe veterans. The concern over the influence of for-profit colleges is known within some military realms, yet the flashy promises and aggressive techniques of these schools still work to attract many veterans and drain both government coffers and individual savings at the same time. Robert Songer, the coordinator of all education programs for service members at Camp Lejeune Marine Corps Base in North Carolina, summed up his assessment,

> Some of these schools prey on Marines . . . Day and night, they call you, they e-mail you. These servicemen get caught in that. Nobody in their families ever went to college. They don't know about college.[24]

Legislators responsible for the GI Bill did not intend to fill the bank accounts of companies that run for-profit colleges, but once the bill was enacted, there was very little that could be done to break the abilities of for-profit colleges to entice veterans. Out of the hundreds of millions of dollars in Post–9/11 GI benefits that flowed to for-profit schools just in 2009 and 2010, 69 percent of the funds went to for-profit colleges, whereas just 25 percent of veterans using benefits sought degrees at for-profit colleges.

This shortcoming is something that enraged both Democrats and Republicans. As the full picture became clear, legislators took to their constituent communications to complain about for-profit colleges. But Democrats were far more likely to communicate about the issue in constituent communications accounting for over 90 percent of all mentions of the problem. Early after implementation Senator Tom Carper (D-DE) told the story of one of his veteran constituents to illustrate the problem:

> Last week I heard the most heartbreaking story.
> It was from Sgt. Chris Pantzke, a combat disabled veteran and a true American hero, about his experiences with an unscrupulous online

college. He told me how, after returning from Iraq with a traumatic brain injury and PTSD, he decided to enroll in an online for-profit university to learn photography. From the moment he first called asking about how he could further his education, Sgt. Pantzke was courted and pursued aggressively by the school.

It seems, though, that the school was more interested in securing Sgt. Pantzke's G.I. Benefits than it was in ensuring that Sgt. Pantzke received a quality education and a good paying job after graduation.

Soon after enrolling, Sgt. Pantzke began struggling with his assignments. He asked for help, but his requests went unfulfilled. Two years and $90,000 in G.I. Bill benefits later, Sgt. Pantzke was forced to withdraw from school and begin teaching himself photography.

Sadly, this isn't the first time we've heard of a service member or veteran having an experience like Sgt. Pantzke's. That's where the Senate Homeland Security and Governmental Affairs Committee, which I chair, comes in. I have held multiple hearings on how some schools use some questionable tactics to boost their bottom line while failing our returning heroes. Last week, when we heard from Sgt. Pantzke, we took a hard look at how some for-profit colleges target our nation's veterans for their G.I. Bill benefits but fail to provide a quality education. Not only does this take advantage of a taxpayer funded program, but more importantly it hurts the men and women who have sacrificed so much for our nation. I now intend to work with my Senate colleagues on both sides of the aisle, along with the Obama Administration, to put an end to this disgusting practice and protect our service members and veterans.[25]

In the intervening years there were 44 bill proposals to limit the abilities of for-profit colleges to receive VA funds, but no significant legislation was able to advance to end the problem. All told, of the bills that attempted to curb the abilities of for-profit colleges to deceptively recruit and earn Post–9/11 GI Bill tuition reimbursements, 73 percent came from Democrats. Years after the original implementation and over the calls from private industry, academia, and veterans' groups, for-profit colleges still posed problems for the system. Senator Sherrod Brown (D-OH) had this to say,

Right now, seven of the eight for-profit education companies that receive the most G.I. Bill funds are under federal investigation for their deceptive recruitment tactics. It is despicable enough that these companies are preying on our servicemembers and veterans—and it's beyond the pale that they're doing it with taxpayer funds.[26]

The issue of for-profit colleges is one of the only differences in foci for the parties. Across nearly every other issue, good and bad in the veterans' education policy space, there is substantial overlap.

Overpayment

In addition to these systemic difficulties, the bill had other issues that became apparent as the benefit came online. Like any college enrollees, sometimes veterans using GI Bill benefits enroll for more classes at the start of a term, pay tuition reflecting that credit load, and then drop some of the credits a few weeks in. This results in an overpayment of tuition. Each institution handles this situation differently, but in the instances when the VA directly paid schools and then veteran students were owed a reimbursement for a reduced credit load, the VA directed schools to refund the students instead of returning the money to the VA.[27] This did not result in a free money program for the recipient veterans; rather these veterans were automatically placed in "overpayment status" by the VA, and it became their duty to either return that money back to the VA or risk being considered in debt to the VA. Because of the nonstandardized way the reimbursements flowed from schools to veterans, there were misunderstandings of why or how the money was reimbursed directly to veterans in the first place. Educational institutions did not send tuition reimbursements with accompanying instructions to veterans to repay the VA, and therefore, some veterans mistakenly kept the tuition reimbursements not knowing that this debt to the VA could haunt them in subsequent semesters.

Overpayment as a result of dropping courses can cascade into other benefits if a veteran is no longer considered to be enrolled full-time. If the number of classes dropped shifts a full-time student to part-time status, there is a reduction in the amounts allowed for books and housing stipends. This spillover can catch veterans by surprise after they have already made housing decisions and purchased school supplies. The bill attempted to make clear the details of these sorts of complications in the 164-page book distributed to schools, and with online information available at VA.gov, but these efforts did not reach every eligible veteran.

No Vocational Training Support

Unlike the Montgomery Bill, the Post–9/11 GI Bill did not provide benefits for veterans pursuing vocational, apprenticeship programs, trade school, or flight school. Rather, the Post–9/11 Bill stipulated that nearly all funding had to be used at traditional institutions of higher education. This was known at the time of passage but became a bigger issue as programs that used to permit veterans payment via the Montgomery Bill were denied payment under the new setup.

Use of the Post–9/11 GI Bill

In addition to the programmatic shortcomings of the bill, there are other criticisms about the effectiveness of the bill. The documentation system for the numbers of veterans using the program, years in school, and eventual graduation does not permit the release of any data to show that use of the Post–9/11 GI Bill is related to the likelihood that a veteran graduates from college. In 2012, VA officials indicated that these data are not suited for public release because of inconsistencies in how schools record information and inaccuracies in the data given to the VA.[28] The lack of useable data on the utility of government spending is not only worrisome for public policy reasons, but it also highlights a tension with Republican ideology. If government spending should be avoided in general, to assent to government spending without a way to check on the use of government dollars is a very hard pill to swallow for partisans.

The House Committee on Veterans Affairs reported that 233,424 veteran beneficiaries had taken advantage of the Post–9/11 GI Bill by June 2010. By 2012, that number was estimated to be at 745,000, and by 2013, the number went to 1 million.[29] This number will continue to increase as more service members return from overseas and completed tours. Since the implementation the federal government has paid out roughly $30 billion for the program.

Post–9/11 GI Bill Case Study

To see how lip service and legwork unfold in the area of veterans' education benefits, I limit the focus on bills and communications that explicitly focus on that topic. To narrow the lip service measure, I use the count of all communications that mention the official or commonly used title variations of the Post–9/11 GI Bill. Anytime a legislator writes about the GI Bill to constituents, that number over the number of years served in Congress is the measure of veteran education lip service.

The definition of lip service here encapsulates both positive and negative sentiments a legislator may express. Despite the failure to fix problems in the Post–9/11 GI Bill laying largely with Congress, many members of the House and the Senate spent a good deal of time describing imperfections of the Post–9/11 GI Bill as well as levying blame on executive agencies and the educational system. This sort of complaining is part of the role of being a legislator by identifying problems in existing policy, but complaints without proffered legislative solutions are a version of lip service.

There are also numerous examples of legislators describing the good that the Post–9/11 Gill Bill does for veterans. Some will remind constituents that they worked to pass the initial legislation and tout the numbers of veterans within their districts that benefited from the program. This too is a role of being a legislator, describing to constituents how government can work for them. But again, this is lip service. This sort of communication is positive rather than negative but still does not amount to an effort to institute further governmental change for veterans. Noting the positive forms of this sort of lip service serves as a good reminder that the term is not inherently negative. Rather it serves as a measure of how often members emphasize something in their official communications. And of course, there are legislators that went beyond negative or positive lip service to introduce legwork in the form of legislative solutions to the unforeseen outcomes that became apparent after the passage of the GI Bill.

I use a similar, but somewhat broader, strategy to create a veterans' education legwork score for each legislator. As before, I query the Congress.gov legislation database for the 111th–114th Congresses. If a member proposed a bill that the Library of Congress counts as in the specific subject category—veterans' education, employment, and rehabilitation—I include that piece of legislation as legwork. This strategy admittedly encompasses more than just education. As a second measure I have a narrower count that only considers bills that directly sought to change the Post–9/11 GI Bill. The reason for starting with the broad search is theoretically justified because bills that change the veterans' education landscape without explicitly dealing with the Post–9/11 GI Bill are still efforts in the relevant policy realm. However, noting the potential for overinclusion, I perform analyses with the more narrow measure as well.

The broad scope legwork measure includes some bills that directly augment the implementation of the Post–9/11 GI Bill and others that more indirectly affect educational benefits. For instance, in the database there are examples of bills such as Representative Niki Tsongas's (D-MA) legislation to help college counselors recognize the signs of posttraumatic stress disorder (PTSD) among veterans. This is an effort to allow colleges to better handle the needs of veterans and is made necessary by the anticipated increase in veteran enrollment after the implementation of the Post–9/11 GI Bill.

There are also examples of veterans' education legislation that could be thought of as entirely separate from the GI bills such as the Working to Integrate Networks Guaranteeing Member Access Now Act also known as the WINGMAN Act offered by Ted Yoho (R-FL). This bill attempted to direct the VA to provide data to a congressional employee for each office of a member of Congress anytime a veteran within his or her district submitted a claim for veterans' benefits. A goal of the bill was that each congressional office would have read-only access to all of such veterans' records in the Veterans Benefits Administration (VBA) databases. Presumably, this would have made casework on behalf of veterans easier for legislator staffers, and specifically the bill would permit staff to see eligibility information for different educational benefits.

For legwork each member's score is the number of pieces of legislation that fall into the veterans' education Library of Congress code over the years in Congress. While this is not a clear one-to-one match in focus for the specific lip service terms and the more general legwork search, if anything, the overinclusion of legwork works against the theory of this book. Thus, this approach should offer a more robust test of the theory that some legislators engage in lip service more than legwork.

During the 111th–114th Congresses, there were over 829 references to the Post–9/11 GI Bill in official legislator-to-constituent communications. During that time period, there were 569 veterans' education, employment, rehabilitation bills introduced; 66 specific pieces of legislation introduced to augment the Post–9/11 GI Bill; and 4 specific bills that made it into law.

Modeling Specifics

Like before, I model the lip service and legwork measures as a function of other variables that ought to influence both of these activities. I keep the controls from the original model in place for the educational model, with a few modifications and additions.

First, rather than use the measure of total VA spending per district and state, I use only dollars spent on education, vocational rehabilitation, and employment programs. This measures ranges from a low of $4,230 for Guam in 2010 to a high of $991,205 to the entire state of California. Second, I add a measure of the percent of a constituency that holds a bachelor's degree or higher in each district. These data come from the 2010 Census. This measure is intended to capture differences in educational culture and norms within a district. Veterans who return to places where finishing college is more common may themselves have greater pressures to pursue higher education. The districts with greater levels of education may also be more receptive to legislator messages about the value of a college education, and thus, legislators may focus on the issue more in communications. There is no clean causal, directional claim here regarding how the percentage of college-educated adults in a district relates to the outcomes of interest, but this is variation that is relevant to consider when looking at this specific topic.[30]

Results

Democrats introduced 65 percent of all veterans' education legislation. Using a comparison of means test, the measure of veterans' education legwork for Democrats is 0.17, which is significantly higher than the Republican mean of 0.07. When narrowing the scope to specific legislation seeking to change the GI Bill, there are no significant differences between partisans.[31] On lip service, Republicans have a slightly higher measure of 0.14 to Democrats' 0.12, but this is not significant, and when considering the overall share of messages sent by party, the breakdown is closer to 50:50. That is, while

Democrats appear to be doing slightly more legislating in veterans' education, Republicans do not appear to be doing much more lip service in this case.

Table 7.1 displays the results from the full model for lip service and legwork in veterans' education. I do not include a model for specific GI Bill legislation; there are simply too few people (42) who have nonzero scores for this measure, and the model does not converge. As in Chapter 6, I estimate a model of lip service that includes the measure of legwork and report the results in the final column.

Similar to the findings based on overall legislative activity, being on the veterans affairs committee is significantly and positively related to both talking about the Post–9/11 GI Bill and introducing legislation on veterans' education. Like before, being a veteran is not related to either activity. While there was a relationship between the percentage of veterans in a constituency and overall legislative efforts, for this specific policy space, that is not the case. I find that members of the House are slightly more apt to introduce veterans' education bills than senators and that members whose districts or states receive more VA educational money in the first place are more likely to introduce veterans' education legislation. Across all models, I find that legislators who have been in Congress longer tend to introduce fewer pieces of veterans' education bills and are less likely to mention the topic in communications. In the final model, I find that members who introduced more legislation on veterans' education, all else equal, send greater numbers of communication on the subject.

While the basic comparison of means test indicated that Democrats introduced greater amounts of veterans' education legislation, once other variables are accounted for, these differences appear to be more contributable to other variation between legislators. I also find no difference between the lip service activities of either Democrats or Republicans on the issue of veterans' education. This issue-specific look offers some nuances. It does not appear that Republicans are simply saying more than Democrats in every veteran policy issue space, despite the fact that they generally have more to say about veterans.

Are there differences in the ways Democrats and Republicans talk about veterans' education benefits? To check I perform the same sorts of text analyses from Chapter 6 and report the top five most common words and terms used by members of each party that co-occur in messages about the Post–9/11 GI Bill. Table 7.2 displays the results; I omit the words "post," "9/11," "GI," "bill," and "veterans" from the reporting as they occur in virtually all of the returned texts.

In some ways the results of Table 7.2 are similar to the overall patterns of how Democrats and Republicans discussed all veterans' issues. Democrats consistently talk not just about veterans but also about the veteran families,

Table 7.1 Lip Service and Legwork on Veterans' Education as a Function of Institutional, Legislator, and Constituency Characteristics (111th–114th Congress)

	Legwork	Lip Service	Lip Service
On Committee	0.93*	1.15**	0.67
	(0.37)	(0.34)	(0.35)
Veteran	−0.01	0.01	−0.05
	(0.26)	(0.25)	(0.26)
Veterans in Constituency	−0.07	0.01	−0.07
	(0.06)	(0.04)	(0.05)
Democrat	0.30	0.00	0.22
	(0.23)	(0.20)	(0.25)
House	1.15*	0.62	1.12*
	(0.45)	(0.37)	(0.46)
Seniority	−0.09**	−0.08**	−0.08**
	(0.01)	(0.01)	(0.01)
Woman	0.64	−0.35	0.66
	(0.46)	(0.21)	(0.46)
Number of VA-funded educational sites per state	−0.00	0.00	−0.01
	(0.00)	(0.00)	(0.00)
Percent with college degree	−0.01	0.02	−0.01
	(0.02)	(0.01)	(0.02)
FY10 federal veterans funds' to education	0.00**	0.00	0.00*
	(0.00)	(0.00)	(0.00)
Legislation introduced per year			0.46*
			(0.22)
Constant	−1.19	−2.91	−2.99
N	816	816	816
McFadden's Adjusted R2	0.09	0.07	0.08

Note: Negative binomial regressions with white standard errors in parentheses
* $p < 0.05$
** $p < 0.00$

whereas Republicans tend to bring up the VA in communications about the Post–9/11 GI Bill. Democrats also tend to bring up health and health care when they mention the bill. When Democrats refer to veterans' health care in communications that mention the Post–9/11 GI Bill, the message is typically

Table 7.2 Most Frequently Used Words in Official Communications on the Post–9/11 GI Bill by Party (111th–114th Congresses)

Democrats	Republicans
Unigrams	
Benefits	*Legislation*
VA	*House*
Health	VA
Service	Congress
Congress	Military
Bigrams	
Our Veterans	*The House*
Health Care	*Veterans Affairs*
Their families	Our Veterans
Veterans and	*Of Veterans*
The VA	The VA
Trigrams	
Men and women	*The department of*
And their families	*Of veterans affairs*
Veterans and their	Men and women
Iraq and Afghanistan	Department of veterans
Who have served	*The opportunity to*

something about how well the Post–9/11 GI Bill works and how there is room for improvement in veterans' health care. Legislators recognize that the bill represents a bright example of how the government can assist veterans, yet at the same time veterans' health care is not where it ought to be. This is the point Senator Tom Carper (D-DE) makes when he writes,

> We owe them our sincere commitment to providing them with access to high quality *health* care, ensure they have a place to call home, and offer them skills they need to have a successful life as a civilian.
>
> . . .
>
> The *Post-9/11 GI Bill* affords veterans the valuable opportunity to attain a high-quality education here at home after service. It's a generous benefit that can fully cover the tuition, fees, books, and housing at many of our nation's colleges and universities, like the University of Delaware and Delaware State University.[32]

When using phrases like "their families," Democrats in Congress are again expanding the circle of who the government owes a duty to look after as a part of military service. Not only are veterans themselves to be considered when thinking about the costs of military service but also their families' sacrifice; Democratic legislators make this connection in communications about veterans' educational policy.

Senator Dick Durbin (D-IL) makes this explicit when discussing how for-profit colleges sought to exploit veterans attempting to use their Post–9/11 GI Bill benefits. In an e-newsletter discussing implementation of the bill, Durbin tells constituents about his recent activities to stop for-profit colleges from preying on veterans and their families,

> This week, I joined with nearly two dozen of my colleagues—including Senators Carper and Blumenthal—to help put an end to the for-profit college industry's predatory marketing campaigns and aggressive recruiting of veterans, servicemembers and *their families*.[33]

The more uniquely Republican ways of talking about veterans' educational benefits tend to make linkages between legislative and executive actors. The association of "house" and "the house" is a way that GOP legislators communicate the chamber that they control has done something to assist veterans. This quote from Representative Vicky Hartzler (R-MO) is an example,

> The Department of Veterans Affairs (VA) provides a range of benefits and services to veterans. However, even though they have access to many benefits, veterans may end up misled or exploited, leaving them without adequate assistance. That is why the House voted to reform how the VA administers Post-9/11 Bill benefits.[34]

This bill sought to remedy the confusion of how credits earned with Post–9/11 GI Bill benefits would transfer from one institution to another. Introduced by Representative Jody Hice (R-GA), this is an example of Republican legwork in the realm of veterans' education policy. This bill passed in the House (411–3) but was not considered in the Senate.

When GOP legislators talk about the Department of Veteran Affairs alongside veterans' educational policy, it is usually as a part of a larger communication that discusses updates across many different VA programs. Some of the more explicit links address the issue of oversight and spending on educational benefits. Recall from Chapter 5, one of the greatest difficulties in squaring U.S. veterans' policies with Republican ideology is how programs have generally lacked good oversight mechanisms. Representative Phil Roe (R-TN) wrote to constituents about efforts to increase oversight by discussing a bill called the Veterans Opportunity to Work (VOW) Act.

> It requires reporting of outcomes for students using the Post-9/11 GI bill so the Department of Veterans' Affairs can ensure the oversight and success of the programs implemented through this plan.[35]

Elements of this bill were added to a different bill sponsored by Representative Wally Herger (R-CA), passed by large bipartisan majorities, and President Obama signed the final bill into law in late 2011.[36]

Concluding Thoughts

Veterans' education policy appears to be one of the places with true bipartisan action and attention. Both Democrats and Republicans agreed to pass the Post–9/11 GI Bill. Both parties expressed anger to constituents when the unintended consequence of for-profit colleges sought to bilk the government and shortchange veterans. Subsequently, both Democrats and Republicans attempted to pass other veterans' education legislation during the 111th–114th Congresses. Democrats and Republicans both engaged in similar amounts of lip service on the topic.

There are some partisan differences when looking at the content of the communications on veterans' education, and in many ways, these differences are similar to the overall differences in communicative approaches that were reported in Chapter 6. These nuances are important in developing an understanding of how the different parties frame veterans' educational benefits, but when looking at the volume of efforts legislatively and in communications, the parties are more alike than not.

Unlike in the previous chapter that took a broad look at veterans' legwork and lip service, members of the Republican Party did not clearly write more to constituents about veterans' education and Democrats did not do significantly more legwork. This finding provides an important insight into how the overall pattern of lip service versus legwork unfolds. It is not the case that Democrats simply offer more legislation across all parts of veterans' policies nor do Republican communicate more than Democrats across all veteran domains. Rather, I find that at least when it comes to veterans' education, the two parties are generally quite equal in terms of their legislative and communicative efforts.

CHAPTER EIGHT

Veterans' Health Care and the VA Scandal

In this chapter I focus on veterans' health policy. Health care is one of the most important promises made to men and women who join the service and one of the costliest benefits for the government to deliver. In 2018, approximately $70 million were allocated to VA health care alone.[1] The Veterans Health Administration (VHA) of today provides the central functions that led to the creation of the original Veterans Bureau in the first place—a way to care for veterans who experience traumas different from those associated with civilian life. The VHA does many things well, but there are occasions when it does not and sometimes these turn into full-blown scandals. While the educational benefits from the Post–9/11 GI Bill are considered one of the best government-administered programs for veterans, healthcare provisions are some of the most maligned and scrutinized. In this chapter, I first review the facts surrounding the 2014 Phoenix area VA wait-list scandal and then turn to the congressional response both legislatively and lexically. I present analyses similar to those of the previous two chapters comparing the legwork and lip service efforts of both parties.

Because of the timing of the 2014 scandal, I am able to leverage the official communications data in greater ways than what was possible when considering the Post–9/11 GI Bill. Because the DCinbox database was well established before the 2014 Phoenix VA story, we can look at how members of Congress discussed the VA before the media attended to the wait-list scandal. I find that some Republican legislators started complaining about the VA in constituent communications before the national media turned attention to the scandal. I also find that the Republican legislators were far more likely to turn to constituent communications after the scandal as a way to connect with voters and share in their outrage.

This chapter is somewhat different from the last in that I provide a deeper look at the specific policy solutions offered to improve the VA. After detailing the communication efforts before, during, and after the scandal, I examine the policies introduced as remedies. Using this technique I uncover a strategy that Republican legislators seem to employ more than Democrats. Republican legislators will mention legislation that they introduced or voted for in the past but sometimes use inaccurate tenses around those actions in a way to make it appear that their actions are in response to the scandal. That is, by adopting certain writing techniques to obscure the timing, and likely with the knowledge that constituents will not know any better, some Republican legislators pay lip service to veterans' issues by pulling on their activities of the past and couching those attempts in present-day language to appear responsive. I close this chapter with a look at the legislative leaders in veterans' health care and a detailed look at the policies proposed in the 111th–114th Congresses.

The Phoenix Area VA Scandal

Starting in the 1990s, the VA experienced growth in veteran usage but not necessarily concomitant growth in funding from Congress. From 1990 to 2000 the number of primary care visits increased by 50 percent, whereas the number of primary care providers only increased by 9 percent. Not surprisingly, the system was overworked and wait times ballooned at many facilities.

The economic downturns of the dot-com bubble and the Great Recession of 2008 pushed more veterans into the VA health system. Veterans who might have previously used health care provided through their own or a spouse's insurance instead turned to the VA when economic conditions no longer allowed out-of-pocket expenses or job losses eliminated employer-provided insurance. Between 2002 and 2012, the number of VA health care enrollees expanded to 9 million users, approximately one-third more than in the previous decade.[2]

The VA was well aware of the stress on the system. In 2011 the VA issued guidance that all facilities should strive to see patients within 14 days of a request. With the guidance there is a requirement that each VA facility across the country must send a list of wait times from request until treatment so that the central VA in Washington may assess the performance in different facilities. A subsequent assessment conducted two years after the guidance found that the goal of no more than a 14-day waiting period was met for 60–70 percent of all patient requests system wide.[3]

In the Phoenix VA hospital things were a bit different. In April 2014, Dr. Samuel Foote, who had worked for the Phoenix VA from 1990 until December 2013, brought allegations to Congress that employees in the Phoenix VA

Veterans' Health Care and the VA Scandal

were awarded bonuses for reducing wait times but that wait times were falsely reduced by manipulating data reports.[4]

The data officially reported by the Phoenix VA hospital showed veterans waited an average of 24 days for their first primary care appointment, exceeding targets by just 10 days. However, a subsequent inspector general report indicated that some veterans actually waited 115 days for their first primary care and approximately 84 percent waited more than 14 days.

To pull off this manipulation, the Phoenix VA hospital maintained two lists of patients waiting to be seen for treatment. The first, "real" list recorded the day treatment was initially sought until the day treatment was administered. The executive staff used this "real" list internally to manage treatments.

Executives in Phoenix were aware that their actual wait time would be poorly received in D.C., so they made a falsified second list in the following manner. Once patients were in a 14-day window of getting an appointment, they were then put on the list that is sent to Veterans' Affairs in Washington to make it look like the Phoenix VA hospital was reacting to veterans' needs in a faster way than they were in reality. This was in effect extending the actual wait times of veterans by up to two weeks but making the wait times appear artificially shorter in aggregate reports.

Between 2010 and 2014 at least 40 veterans whose names appeared on waiting lists for care in the Phoenix VA hospital died.

Investigative journalists working for CNN are largely credited with breaking the story of backlogs and wait-list deception occurring at VA hospitals from 2010 to 2014.[5] The first CNN story broke on April 24, 2014. Yet, before the CNN story, some legislators in Congress had heard about the extent of the backlog issues, but media and popular attention were slower to step up coverage.

Recall from Chapter 4 that initially public opinion polls showed that Republicans tended to blame Secretary Shinseki and then Obama, whereas Democrats blamed Secretary Shinseki and then local VA hospitals. That is, originally there was a partisan divide on which actor(s) the public thought was most culpable for the scandal. However, a year later these divisions subsided. Surveys later showed Congress to be the most culpable in the eyes of the public.

A month before Veterans' Day, Fairleigh Dickinson University conducted a survey of a random national sample of 1,026 adults. The survey asked respondents who they thought were most to blame "for not providing veterans with all that they need." Table 8.1 shows the breakdown across the partisanship of the respondent. As mentioned in Chapter 3, this survey did not make an explicit attempt to sample veterans, so results should be considered representative of U.S. adults generally.

Both Democrats and Republicans pointed to Congress as the political actors most responsible for failing veterans. On the heels of the VA scandal in

Table 8.1 Who Do You Think Is the Most to Blame for Not Providing Veterans with All That They Need? (By Party of Respondent)

	All (%)	Party		
		Democrat	Independent	Republican
Congress	42	45	39	44
President	11	9	9	14
VA	29	28	32	28
Public	12	12	17	11
Don't Know/ Refused	6	7	3	4

Source: Fairleigh Dickinson University, PublicMind Poll, USFDU.111015.R04, Social Science Research Solutions (Ithaca, NY: Roper Center for Public Opinion Research, iPOLL [distributor], Cornell University, 2015).

2014, even when other surveys showed that Republican respondents tended to blame Obama more than the GOP controlled Congress, in veterans' politics, the legislative branch bears the brunt of negative public opinion.

The public is not wrong in blaming Congress. While individual VA hospital workers more directly influence what occurs in their facilities, members in Congress can pull many different legislative levers to address these sorts of events preventatively and craft solutions in the face of shortcomings. Rather than immediately drafting legislative fixes to remedy problems in the VA by statute, many in Congress took to expressing their own outrage in constituent communications.

After a month or so of media coverage and increasing pressure from various veterans' policy stakeholders, Secretary Shinseki resigned on May 30, 2014. After the resignation of Secretary Shinseki, Obama nominated Robert McDonald. McDonald was an army veteran who later pursued a 33-year career at Procter & Gamble. McDonald had been retired for about a year before being sworn in on July 30, 2014, as the secretary of Veterans Affairs. This replacement was heralded by many as a successful transition and has brought about meaningful change within the VA. By July 2016 pending claims at VA had fallen by more than 90 percent and by 2017 every VA hospital was set up to offer same-day access to care, while none guaranteed that service in 2014.[6]

Legislator Communications on the Phoenix VA Hospital

The scandal started with a direct focus on Phoenix facilities but quickly expanded to include a host of VA locations with similar problems. A number of different members of Congress indicated similar problems and relaying stories from their own constituents *before* the CNN story.

Internally, the government was already investigating the suspicious wait times. In May 2014, the Office of Inspector General found approximately 1,700 veterans were waiting for primary care appointments at the Phoenix VA but that these names did not appear on the official wait-lists. Instead, members within the system would hold off putting the names of veterans on the official list until their appointments were closer, thereby artificially shortening the wait-time appearance. The Phoenix VA scandal cannot cleanly be blamed on a few bad actors. Hospital underfunding, increases in patients, and an especially intransigent swell of anti-government spending voices in Congress operated in concert to disastrous effects.

The influx of new veterans coming back from Afghanistan and Iraq with long-term physical and mental injuries added to an already-taxed system. Politically, the 113th–114th congressional Republican caucus swelled with newly elected Tea Party members who fought government spending in almost every form. The VA crises were certainly not inevitable, but multiple interactive influences came together in ways that did not serve the interests of veterans or the agency tasked with caring for them.

One of the central problems as to why the VA did not run as efficiently as many hoped was a lack of sufficient financial support. This was and is not a new problem; the VA has a history of underfunding in congressional appropriations. Both Republicans and Democrats decry the financial state of affairs. Yet, as with any complicated policy space involving government spending, compromises are hard to come by. In many instances real change is harder to accomplish and the ability to complain persists. Perversely, complaining about the VA rather than funding hospitals in a more robust manner may actually serve members of Congress by providing a scapegoat to pin responsibility on.

In the next section I present evidence that members of Congress were already aware of the scandal and were actively taking to their constituent communications to complain about elements of veterans care. Using April 24, 2014, the day that the CNN story broke as punctuation in time I analyze the attention in communications and legislative efforts to add another layer to the lip service versus legwork understanding of congressional politicking.

Congressional Communications prior to the CNN Story

Before CNN broke the story on the fatal results of excessive wait times at VA facilities, the House Committee on Veterans' Affairs had launched the VA Honesty Project as an online section of Veterans.House.Gov. This page was meant to highlight claims that the VA lacked transparency with the press and public when information was requested. One of the 70 examples collected by the end of March 2014 detailed a request made by the *Tampa*

Tribune regarding the names of 19 veterans who passed away while awaiting medical procedures.

While both Democrats and Republicans communicated with constituents about providing sufficient veterans' care prior to the larger media attention of the VA scandal, Republicans were the only members talking about the backlog issue specifically. Democrats continued the usual strategy of thanking veterans, soliciting casework for issues dealing with veterans, and discussing legislation, but during the month of March 2014 right before the greater story of the VA scandal broke, no Democrats mentioned anything to constituents indicating they knew of any problems.

On March 27, 2014, Representative John Culberson (R-TX), chair of the Military Construction and Veterans Affairs Appropriations Subcommittee, held a hearing in which Secretary Shinseki testified about the ongoing claims' backlog crises. He wrote to his constituents that 600,000 claims had not been processed and there were excessively long time lags from when a veteran sought medical care, filed a claim to have the VA approve such care, and the eventual processing of that claim.[7] For some veterans the wait lasted over a year. One of the key problems with the system then was that records were kept on paper, and the electronic file program Secretary Shinseki piloted had not yet been widely adopted.

In a communication to constituents on the day of the hearing, Culberson noted, "These are tough budgetary times, but providing for the military and our veterans is a duty that we simply cannot neglect." This tension highlights the Republican straddle of wanting to provide adequate care for veterans while at the same time adhering to core tenets of smaller government and reduced spending.

On March 28, 2014, Congressman Joe Pitts (R-PA), a veteran himself, voiced his concern in a public letter to Secretary Shinseki indicating that more than 377,000 claims had been waiting for upward of 125 days and that the average claims process wait for veterans in Pennsylvania was 309–347 days.[8] A few days later Representative Sean Duffy (R-WI) sent this passage to constituents on March 31, 2014,

> Veterans across the country are being forced to wait weeks, even months, for an appointment. In Marshfield, WI, Roger, a 70-year-old Vietnam War Veteran, sought help from the VA for his hearing loss. He was informed he could not get an appointment for six months. Unfortunately, Roger couldn't wait that long, so he went to his local hearing aid specialist and was seen that day. Roger was willing to pay out of pocket for his hearing aids but that is not an option for many of our Veterans—nor should it have to be.[9]

Duffy reiterated the issue of the claims backlog in a second communication on April 20, 2014, saying he had met with the entire state delegation and all recognized there was a problem and he would work to fix it.[10]

This drumbeat grew a little louder as more and more members of Congress began to air concerns in public. On April 6, 2014, Congressman Jeff Miller (R-FL) sent information to constituents,[11] including (1) a report detailing that the VA paid $200 million for 1,000 veterans' wrongful death claims from 2001 to 2011, (2) a link to the Veterans Honesty Project, (3) an article detailing Florida governor Rick Scott's attempts to get data from the VA, and (4) a news report following the questionable path of repeated hirings and firings of one VA employee. This was all to show that the VA had problems than needed attention.

On April 8, 2014, Senator Bill Nelson (R-FL) indicated things were amiss in the North Florida/South Georgia VA Health System by sending an article from the *Tampa Tribune* detailing three fatalities that occurred due to delays in treatment.[12] On April 9, the House Committee on Veterans' Affairs held a full committee hearing on the topic, "A Continued Assessment of Delays in VA Medical Care and Preventable Veteran Deaths." During this hearing legislators heard stories of delay from veterans. The chairman of the committee, Jeff Miller (R-FL), said that his staff investigators had heard that dozens of Phoenix VA hospital patients died while waiting for care—he also hinted at the two sets of records used to conceal long wait times.

On April 12, 2014, Paul Gosar (R-AZ) sent a communication entitled "I Smell Corruption" to constituents saying he was monitoring reports that as many as 40 veterans died waiting to receive care at the Phoenix VA hospital.[13] He also set forth allegations that the VA kept two sets of records in order to conceal the true length of wait times with one secret list reflective of reality and one alternative list reflective of purposeful changes to mislead the public and investigators. On April 19, 2014, Gosar sent a second communication saying he did not attend a rally meant to protest the delays at the Phoenix VA, but he did reference an editorial in the *Arizona Republic* saying, "It is no secret that the Department of Veterans Affairs is failing countless veterans all over this great nation. . . . The VA's treatment of veterans is unacceptable."[14]

On April 16 Congressman David Schweikert (R-AZ) told constituents that he and 150 veterans and supporters rallied at Steele Indian School Park seeking congressional reform in the VA health care system.[15] Schweikert and others were still reeling from the committee reports that dozens of veterans may have died while waiting for medical care, and he wrote of his marked frustration with the system. On April 19 Paul Gosar (R-AZ) told constituents about another rally to bring attention to mismanagement at the Phoenix VA as well as directing readers to an *Arizona Republic* editorial that contained the line, "Let the heads begin to roll."

Figure 8.1 shows the difference in the frequency with which members of Congress referred to the VA in congressional communications from August 2009 until the end of the Obama term.[16] Notice the telling spike in April 2014 where focus skyrockets for both parties but is markedly more pronounced for Republicans.

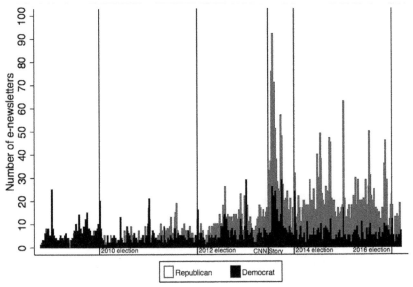

Figure 8.1 Number of official congressional e-newsletters mentioning "VA" by party by week.

In the beginning of the the figure, Democrats are far more likley to mention the VA. Most of this e-newsletter content from the Democrats in 2009–2012 about the VA is about access to VA facilites, benefits for veterans, VA appropriations, the construction of new VA facilites, and increasing funding for VA operations. The pattern of more VA-focused e-newsletters coming from Democrats rather than from Republicans continues for some time even after the Republicans took the House majority in 2010. There is a bit of back and forth on who mentioned the VA more often in 2013 and early 2014, but after the CNN story on April 24, 2014, the attention difference irrefutably switches to Republicans.

Post-CNN Fallout

Despite the fact that veteran issues tend to be bipartisan, the calls against the VA wait-list scandal were dominated by Republicans. Prior to the CNN story, references to the VA were spilt in communications with 57 percent originating from Republicans and 43 percent from Democrats. Members of both parties assumingly disapproved of unnecessary wait times and potential veterans' deaths attributed to those wait times, but Republicans accounted for 78 percent of the mentions of the issue in constituent communications after the scandal broke in the national media. Republicans did a much better job of publicizing their viewpoints than Democrats. The scandal offered a flashpoint that members of Congress used to leverage constituent interest in the media story. Republicans attempted to make a greater political argument that Democrats were uninterested in caring for veterans. In a related way, the VA became an easy launching point to attack President Obama and his administration.

This strategy is related to but somewhat different from the usual lip service offered by Republican members of Congress. The most-often used version of lip service employed by Republicans is supportive of veterans and positive in recognition of their service and committed to having government programs that better serve their needs. The quick pounce on the VA crises and messages that Obama, his administration, and Democrats were to blame for the scandal is an additional reason why overall media narrative intimates that Republicans are better at caring for veterans than Democrats. I now turn to the nuances in this sort of lip service and add in the component of legislative attempts to remedy problems in the VA.

Lip Service after CNN Story

Once the national media reported the story, more legislators began to express their outrage. The first new voice to jump in the fray was that of Representative Bob Goodlatte (R-VA), the day after CNN's coverage by sending a link to the CNN reporting and saying the House was working to monitor and hold the VA accountable.[17] The following day Representative Tom Latham (R-IA) told constituents about the story linking to his Facebook post on the subject and said, "I cannot say this more powerfully; this will not be accepted or forgotten."[18] Congressman Jeff Miller (R-FL) sent a scathing message on April 27 calling for a complete VA inspector general investigation into delays in VA care, not just in Phoenix but department wide.[19] He also routed constituents to a Fox News interview he took with Lou Dobbs on the matter.

When Democrats like veteran Tammy Duckworth (D-IL) wrote about veterans in constituent communications during this time period, there were no references to the VA hospital wait times scandal or backlogs; rather there were generic calls to support our returning heroes and to recognize that veterans ought to have an opportunity to pursue the American dream.[20] Democrats generally appealed to generic veterans' themes rather than particulars regarding the Phoenix area crisis. This was in contrast to the vivid language that appeared in Republican-authored constituent communications.

Republicans were not only more frequent in their references to problems within the VA, but their terminology around the issue was also more dire. On May 2, 2014, Congressman John Carter (R-TX) wrote to constituents, "The big story in Washington this week was the Phoenix VA's secret waiting list, that some would call a death list."[21] The term "death list" had appeared in just two fringe, online outlets prior to Carter's introduction to the vernacular of sitting members of Congress.[22] This example highlights a way that lip service is related to other communication phenomena, using terminology that is particular to and resonates with a partisan constituency in one way that Republicans in Congress can more cohesively create an image linking their goals to the goals of other groups. The use of certain words or tropes signals an "in the know" connection that serves to reinforce ties in a subtle but powerful way.

While the Phoenix area scandal was a concern for Arizona legislators, many others pointed to backlogs as problematic and indicative of a dysfunctional VA at other sites. By June 2014, 42 additional facilities were under investigation by the Office of the Inspector General and 751 were surprised with VA audits. The broad anti-VA zeitgeist transformed from a specific problem in one hospital center to an overall indictment of VA processes and leaders. Legislators from all over the country could point to undesirable wait times in their own districts. As the investigation grew, auditors estimated that 57,000 veterans had waited three months or more for their first appointments. When members of Congress wrote to constituents about the scandal, they expressed outrage, some offered legislative fixes, and nearly all argued that the solution was to remove the top VA administrators.

During the first week of May 2014, Congressman Tom Rooney (R-FL) wrote and published a letter to U.S. attorney general Eric Holder and the state attorneys general in all 50 states urging them to investigate preventable deaths at VA facilities across the country and determine appropriate criminal charges.[23]

Secretary Shinseki vowed to do a face-to-face audit of each of the VA facilities, but this was not enough to assuage the public demands of congressional Republicans. On May 8, 2014, the tone and direction of the rancor changed from general distaste for the VA to a more narrowed focus on Secretary Shinseki. Senator Dean Heller (R-NV) sent a copy of a letter he wrote to Secretary Shinseki to constituents.[24] This letter asks pointed questions and asks for a response within three weeks. That same day the House Veterans' Affairs committee voted to subpoena Shinseki for all e-mails that may have discussed the destruction of a secret list of veterans waiting for care.[25] This sort of move was exceedingly rare, as committees very infrequently subpoena the documents of head secretaries of departments.

The calls inside Congress were echoed outside of Congress. The American Legion called for Shinseki to resign, making that the first time since 1978 that the group had advocated for a public official to leave the VA.[26] On May 9, 2014, Representative Mike Coffman (R-CO), a veteran of both the Gulf War and the Iraq War, sent an e-mail to constituents, saying he wanted Shinseki to resign and if not, he called on the president to fire him.[27] Many other members followed suit.

On May 30, 2014, Secretary Shinseki resigned, but the focus on others working the VA was not over. Internal VA audits led by the Office of

Inspectors General continued and in June 20 senators called for a criminal investigation into VA officials by the Justice Department. On June 11, the FBI launched a probe to determine any criminal wrongdoing.

Following calls from members of Congress, the Office of Inspectors General within Veterans Affairs conducted an investigation of the Phoenix VA hospital.[28] The report did substantiate the claims of excessive wait times for veterans; however, the report did not find that the length of time from care sought to care administered was responsible for the deaths of the 40 veterans from which the original story became a scandal.

Veterans' Health Care Policies: Attempts and Successes of the Contemporary Congress

Amid the calls to reform the VA coming from many members of Congress, there were a few legislative fixes offered after the scandal broke. After April 2014, just one new stand-alone piece of veterans' health care legislation was introduced, and only three new amendments were introduced to remedy the problem in the 113th Congress.

Instead members attempted to win support for legislation already introduced by appealing to the stresses in the VA Phoenix system. The CNN story was to be a jumpstart to the slow moving system of legislative process. Bills that had languished in committees or had been considered in one chamber were given new life.

VA Legislation Introduced prior to the Scandal

Nearly a year before the scandal broke, legislators were working on H.R.2216, the Military Construction and Veterans Affairs and Related Agencies Appropriations Act of 2014[29] by Rep. John Culberson (R-TX). After the scandal broke members who voted for the measure in June of the previous year reminded constituents that this legislation included new reporting requirements for VA facilities and gave Congress better oversight authority. The fact that the congressional actions happened prior to rather than as a result of the Phoenix scandal is muddied in communications. This bill was eventually rolled into H.R.3547—Consolidated Appropriations Act, 2014,[30] which was signed into law on January 17, 2014, roughly three months before the CNN coverage.

Another bill introduced in January 2013, H.R.241, the Veterans Timely Access to Health Care Act by Representative Dennis Ross (R-FL) languished without a vote for months.[31] Congressman Randy Hultgren and others discussed this bill with constituents, as well as another bill, H.R.2189: to improve the processing of disability claims by the Department of Veterans Affairs (VA),[32] which passed the House in October 2013 but was never taken up by the Senate. That is, after mostly giving up on the bill, the scandal provided an opportunity to pay lip service to veterans' issues by mentioning the past movement on the bill.

In May 2013, Representative Dan Benishek (R-MI) introduced H.R.2072, the Demanding Accountability for Veterans Act of 2014. This act offered many programmatic reforms to ensure that the top brass of the VA had clear guidance on how to manage individual hospitals in the face of potential mishaps. The bill required that the VA secretary submit to the inspector general a list of the names of each responsible VA manager and the matter for which the manager is responsible within 15 days of an allegation of misdoing. Rather than other legislation that gave the VA secretary wide leeway in firing lower-level VA officials, this legislation directed the secretary to notify a manager of the claims against him or her, work to craft a plan to remedy those problems, and ensure that no bonuses were awarded to managers who did not make sufficient progress toward rectifying the original complaints. This bill was in the Veteran's Affairs Committee until October and then was moved for a vote after the VA scandal broke. On June 10, 2014, the House passed the bill by a voice vote, but the Senate moved no further.

In October 2013, Representative Harold Rogers (R-KY) introduced H.R.3230, the Veterans' Access to Care through Choice and Accountability Act of 2014. This bill allowed the VA to quickly hire doctors in areas with shortage by fast-tracking authorizations that typically take longer on account of federal government hiring practices; it also expedited the process for firing or demoting current employees. The bill piloted a program to allow veterans to seek private health care if they experienced long wait times for an appointment or lived more than 40 miles from a VA health facility. Lastly, the bill authorized the construction of 26 new VA facilities to deal with a widespread veterans' population.

The bill passed the House a day after introduction by a 265–160 vote.[33] It was not until the CNN story came out that the Senate took up the measure. Senator Bernie Sanders (I-VT) had introduced similar legislation in the Senate, but the chamber voted for an amended version of the House bill on June 11, 2014, with a 93–3 vote.[34] After conference committee work over the summer months, both the House and the Senate agreed to a final version and the president signed this bill into law on October 7, 2014.[35] In the final section of this chapter, I discuss the substantive legislation passed in all realms of veteran health care and note that this was one of the brightest spots of the 113th Congress.

Two months prior to the scandal coverage, Marco Rubio (R-FL) introduced the Department of Veterans Affairs Management Accountability Act of 2014 (S. 2013).[36] This legislation would allow the secretary of the VA to fire or demote any senior executive service employee rather than keep employee protective systems in place. Republicans argued that this sort of swiftness would streamline a burdensome and often prohibitive process by equipping the VA secretary with more power and flexibility to change his employees.

Around the same time Representative Jeff Miller (R-FL) introduced the analogue to the senate bill, H.R.4031, the Department of Veterans Affairs Management Accountability Act of 2014.[37] After the scandal Miller pressed the need to vote to, and he was successful on May 21, 2014, when the House adopted the measure 390–33.[38] Representative John Carter (R-TX) wrote to constituents to discuss his vote on the bill and noted that the bill passed but "with the only 'no' votes coming from Democrats."[39] The callout is another example of how Republicans in Congress do much better strategic lip service. To be sure, Carter is discussing his legwork efforts and that of other Republicans when he mentions this bill, yet the dig at Democrats makes it appear that Democrats are not working to offer legislation to help veterans. As we will see in the subsequent section, that is not the case; like when looking at all veterans' benefits legislation, Democrats outdid Republicans in veterans' health benefits legislation during this time period. But communications like that sent by Representative Carter serve to tell a different story. In this specific case the bill Carter mentions that passed despite some Democrat opposition was then received in the Senate and went no further. He did not send an update noting that detail to constituents.

Another piece of legislation introduced on March 6, 2014, before the scandal broke was the 21st-century Veterans Benefits Delivery Act (S. 2091) by Sen. Dean Heller (R-NV) that followed largely the same route as Representative Carter's bill. This bill focused on empowering patients and other VA bureaucrats by supporting greater veteran outreach to increase awareness about the claims process and claims submission forms as well as imposing a requirement of expedited information sharing between federal agencies and the VA concerning claims and backlogs. Just like with the legislation introduced by Senator Rubio and Representative Carter, members who cosponsored the bill touted it, yet after being introduced in the Senate it went no further.

VA Legislation Introduced after the Scandal

In this section I detail the legwork that can more accurately be characterized as responses to the VA scandal. In the preceding section legislation that was introduced before the scandal was then brought up in constituent communications after the story broke in an attempt to show that legislators were interested in fixing the Phoenix VA issues. Legislators can obscure the timeframes of their actions by not making clear that the bills they reference in these sorts of lip service appeals had already been introduced before any problems in Phoenix were made apparent.

This list of a few notable legislative attempts is not meant to provide a public policy analysis on the suitability of each bill but is merely to provide the reader with a better understanding of what sorts of policy strategies the two parties took when proposing solutions. When discussing these bills, I include information on whether or not the bills were voted on and adopted. Unsurprisingly, most fail at some stage in the lawmaking process.

In late April 2014, Rep. Jeff Miller (R-FL) proposed the Department of Veterans Affairs Management Accountability Act of 2014 along with 151 cosponsors. This bill would give the secretary of the VA the authority to fire an individual from the Senior Executive Service if the secretary determines that person is unqualified for the position—basically relaxing the reasons for which a member may be dismissed. Many of the cosponsors wrote about this bill as a way to show their commitment to fixing problems from the top down. This bill passed the house (390–33) but was not pursued in the Senate.

In late April 2014, the Military Construction and Veterans Affairs Appropriations Act (H.R.4974) passed the House (416–1), and many members pointed to changes included within that piece of legislation as ways to prevent the sorts of secret waiting lists maintained in the Phoenix case. At a top level, the bill offered more money overall for veterans' issues. It increased discretionary funding for veterans' programs by $1.5 billion above the past year, totaling $64.7 billion. Some of that discretionary funding went to existing programs focused on traumatic brain injury, suicide prevention, mental health, and homeless support for veterans. In specific response to the scandal, the bill allocated $173 million for the paperless claims-processing system as an effort to end the disability claims-processing backlog. There was also money supporting the transition to electronic medical records over the traditional paper methods in the form of $20 million for scanning existing records and $344 million for the modernization for the VA electronic health record system.

There were a series of amendments offered and accepted into the final bill. The one that got the most mileage in Congress-to-constituent communications was one that restricted bonus pay for VA executives. An amendment that passed on a voice vote ensured that no taxpayer funding be made available to pay a performance award, or bonus, to senior executives at the VA.

The bill also required the Department of Defense (DoD) and the VA to implement a system to share medical data in a timely and accurate manner—in the hopes that this sort of effort would reduce redundancies in care and aid in timely diagnoses. The onus to adhere to this policy was put on the VA. In the name of accountability, the VA had some funding restricted until they ensured that the VA system would be compatible with the DoD's records. The bill authorized and initiated a VA inspector general's investigation into the Phoenix, Arizona, VA hospital directly.

Many in Congress touted this bill as a way to solve problems within the VA, but the reality is a bit more complicated. This bill was one of 12 appropriations bills that are generally considered and passed annually. This bill was going to be considered whether or not the scandal occurred. There were opportunities to add on additional amendments to the bill, and members of Congress were keen to do that, or cosponsor amendments, or advertise their votes for such amendments. In terms of the major legislative responses to the backlog scandal, this bill did help for sure, but it was not created as a stand-alone problem-solving piece of legislation.

Representatives Kyrsten Sinema (D-AZ) and Matt Salmon (R-AZ) offered an amendment after the CNN story to redirect $1 million in VA general administration funds to the Office of Inspector General. The amendment (H.Amdt.620) was offered to augment the Military Construction and Veterans Affairs and Related Agencies Appropriations Act, 2015 (H.R.4486). The amendment was adopted by a voice vote on April 30, 2014. The larger appropriation bill the new amendment was attached to was introduced a few days before the CNN story on April 17, 2014. Representative Paul Gosar (R-AZ) also offered two amendments that were adopted by voice votes; H.Amdt.635 to increase information technology funds in the VA and H.Amdt.633 to prohibit the use of federal dollars to create or maintain any patient record-keeping system other than those currently approved by the VA Central Office.

The larger bill worked with a system of carrots to get the VA working toward a more streamlined online process for veterans' data. While active, the medical records of our service members are maintained by the DoD. Once those members become veterans, their record must be reentered into the VA systems because the processes used by the DoD are not compatible with those used in the VA. The appropriations bill withheld 75 percent of the VA's information technology funding until the VA made significant progress toward a health records system that both agencies could use. The greater bill was passed on the same day and then later rolled into H.R.83 the Consolidated and Further Continuing Appropriations Act, 2015 offered by Rep. Donna Christensen (D-VI) and signed into law on December 16, 2014.

In May 2014, Representative Jeff Denham (R-CA) introduced H.R.4779, the Veterans Need Timely Access to Care Act.[40] This legislation changed the VA procedures for approving care outside of the VA system by preauthorizing care for a veteran from a doctor or clinic outside of the VA if the wait time for an appointment was longer than the VA's wait time goals of 7 days for primary care and 14 days in the case of specialty care. This bill did not move further than the introduction stage.

In June 2014, Representative Jeff Miller (R-FL) tried to introduce a bill similar to the one offered in May by Representative Denham. H.R. 4810, the Veteran Access to Care Act of 2014, expanded fee-basis, private-sector care for veterans not currently receiving coverage from the VA.[41] This bill was unanimously passed in the House one day after it was introduced and then never taken up by the Senate.

This list of legislation is not exhaustive; it pulls from the legislation members of Congress discussed in constituent communications. It *appears* that Republicans did more legwork based on the previous list of legislation. This is precisely because Republicans more frequently wrote about their legislative activities despite the fact that Democrats actually did more during that time period. Looking just at this case shows one of the very powerful ways in which lip service works. It is hard to know what happens in the halls of Congress and when Democrats fail to talk about an issue or a piece of legislation; it is no fault of the public that there is a general belief that Republicans do more on behalf of veterans. In the next section I present the data and analyses on who introduced legislation on veterans' health benefits and who sent more communications on veterans' health benefits; like in the general case one party seems to do better at legwork and the other excels at lip service.

Lip Service versus Legwork: Veterans' Health Care

Bills that fall under the general category of "Armed Forces and National Security" and secondary category of "Veterans' medical Care" are counted as legwork in the following analyses.[42] I present the number of veterans' health care bills introduced by party by Congress; As before, Democrats introduce more veterans' health care legislation overall and in each individual Congress, save for the 114th.

Looking just at the descriptive results, Democrats overall introduce a majority (58%) of veterans' health bills. But in keeping to the analysis strategy from the last two chapters, I model the legislative legwork effort in comparison to a measure of veterans' healthcare–related lip service.

In order to identify veterans' health care communications, messages had to use the words "veteran," "health," and "Veterans Administration" or "VA." In total, there are over 1,000 messages that meet these criteria. As with the general veterans' focus, Republicans do significantly more lip service on this topic. On average GOP legislators send 0.36 messages on the topic per year in office to Democrats' 0.16.

Table 8.2 Veterans' Health Care Legislative Proposals by Party (111th–114th Congresses)

	Bills Introduced	
Congress	Republicans	Democrats
111th	66	217
112th	84	116
113th	146	197
114th	230	194

Source: www.govtrack.us.

As before, I model the outcomes of interest on variables thought to influence legislative and communicative efforts. In these models, I add two additional controls, the number of dollars spent on veterans' health care in a legislator's district or state, and the total number of unique veteran patients who used those systems.

Perhaps contrary to expectations, the number of patients and the share of veterans in a district are not strongly correlated, and I include both measures in the model. They do capture different theoretical links. The greater share of veterans in a constituency should dictate the level of attention a legislator theoretically pays to veterans' issues, but the number of unique patients in VA hospitals can underlie differences in casework demands and changes for policy as different numbers of people seek services. Table 8.3 provides the results from the legwork and lip service models. All were estimated using the procedures described in Chapter 6.

The results from the health care assessment look similar to that found in Chapter 6. Members on the committee do more for and talk more about veterans' health care. More senior members do the opposite. Democrats offer legislation at rates that are significantly higher than Republicans while Republicans talk about veterans' health care much more frequently. A few new findings emerge in the last model. This is the first time that being a veteran is significantly related to an action either positive or negative. When considering all other variables, veterans tended to pay slightly less lip service to veterans' health care and members who had more federal dollars spent in their districts tended to pay more lip service.

The magnitudes on how much party influences veterans' health care legwork and lip service are substantial. Holding all the other variables at their means, a democratic legislator is expected to introduce roughly one more veterans' health bill per two-year Congress than a Republican legislator. Yet, when looking at lip service, the opposite is true. The average Republican will talk about veterans' health nearly twice as much as the average Democrat, even when all other variables are held constant. Individually, that might not seem so impactful, but when thinking about the size of Congress collectively, there are many more constituents hearing from Republican legislators more often than from Democrats.

To close this chapter, I detail the substantive policies aimed at changing veterans' health care during the time of study. As in education, the numbers of bills that actually make it through the full process are few. In this section I offer one additional look into how lip service manifests itself in official communications. For each policy that passed, I assess the percentage of constituent communications on the bill that came from Republican or Democrat legislators. As is indicated by the theory here, for nearly all policies Republicans tend to do most of the communicating on a given bill despite the fact that Democrats introduce more legislation.

Table 8.3 Lip Service and Legwork on Veterans' Health Care as a Function of Institutional, Legislator, and Constituency Characteristics (111th–114th Congress)

	Legwork	Lip Service	Lip Service
On Committee	1.23**	1.20**	1.17**
	(0.14)	(0.27)	(0.29)
Veteran	−0.25	−0.63	−0.62*
	(0.17)	(0.25)	(0.25)
Veterans in Constituency	0.02	0.01	0.01
	(0.03)	(0.04)	(0.04)
Democrat	0.27*	−0.83**	−0.84**
	(0.14)	(0.22)	(0.23)
House	−0.62**	0.23	0.25
	(0.23)	(0.41)	(0.40)
Seniority	−0.10**	−0.09**	−0.09**
	(0.01)	(0.01)	(0.02)
Woman	0.25	0.66	−0.66
	(0.16)	(0.42)	(0.43)
Number of VA-Funded Educational Sites per State	0.00	−0.00	−0.00
	(0.00)	(0.00)	(0.00)
Number of Unique Patients	0.00	−0.00	−0.00
	(0.00)	(0.00)	(0.00)
FY10 Federal Veterans Funds to Health Care	0.00	0.00	0.00*
	(0.00)	(0.00)	(0.00)
Legislation Introduced per Year			0.05
			(0.14)
Constant	−0.64	−0.64	−0.66
N	818	818	818
McFadden's Adj R2	0.16	0.12	0.12

Substantive Veteran Health Policy Changes during the 111th–114th Congresses

What were the aims of the 13 substantive veterans' health policy changes passed in the 111th–114th Congresses? In this research I have avoided normative judgments on the "goodness" of veterans' legislation. The reason for this is twofold. First, fairly assessing legislation is quite difficult. The task is dependent on which outcomes are desired. There are not easily comparable methods or sensible measures to offer straightforward comparisons if there is no agreed-upon desired outcome. Second, the overall aim of this research project is not so much to address the types of policies that would be best for veterans but rather to address the observed discrepancy between public attributions of responsibility for veterans' policy versus actual legislative action on veterans' policy.

Yet, there is a straightforward comparison to be made from the communication and legislative data used here. In Table 8.4, while presenting the relative amounts of communications that focus on substantive veterans' health legislation passed in the 111th–114th Congresses, I include details on the sponsor, the vote margins for passage, and the share of constituent communications from Republicans versus Democrats that discussed the legislation in terms of the impacts on veterans.[43] The exercise is limited to the bills passed regarding veterans' health care.

There are three big takeaways from Table 8.4. First, of the veterans' health care legislation that passed, more bills were introduced by Democrats than by Republicans. Second, most of the legislation passed unanimously or by great margins, signaling that both parties support the successful veterans' health legislation in most cases. Third, Republicans dominate the constituent communications about veterans' health care bills. In all but the first three rows, Republicans talk more about how policies affect veterans than Democrats do, even when a Democrat proposed specific legislation. Republicans tell constituents about how they were proud to vote for veterans' health legislation and describe the details of legislation. When Republicans do this, they are faithfully signaling their commitment to veterans and pointing to their own votes as evidence. This is all legitimate claiming and is one of the reasons there is a sense that veterans are served well by Republican legislators.

But why don't Democrats do the same? Democrats are working to introduce the legislation in the first place. They vote for final passage just as often as Republicans do; but why don't they take to constituent communications to let those actions be known? These questions are outside of the scope of this book, but in the concluding chapter, I offer a few potential explanations as to why that is the case.

When considering the original questions that drove the genesis of this book, veterans' health care offers compelling evidence for the theory outlined here. Republicans are more often associated with veterans because they more often mention veterans in their official communications. That is, Republicans work to cultivate an impression of connection with veterans more than Democrats do, even when Democrats are the ones putting in effort in creating policy solutions in the first place.

Table 8.4 Substantive Changes to Veterans' Health Care during the 111th–114th Congresses and Partisan Focus in Communications

Legislation	Date Enacted	Sponsor	House Vote	Senate Vote	% Republican Lip Service
H.R.1: American Recovery and Reinvestment Act of 2009	February 17, 2009	Rep. Dave Obey (D-WI)	246–183	60–38	24
H.R.3590: Patient Protection and Affordable Care Act	March 23, 2010	Rep. Charlie Rangel (D-NY)	219–212	60–39	43
S.1963: Caregivers and Veterans Omnibus Health Services Act of 2010	May 5, 2010	Sen. Daniel Akaka (D-HI)	419–0	Unanimous Consent	29
H.R.4505: To enable state homes to furnish nursing home care to parents any of whose children died while serving in the armed forces	September 30, 2010	Rep. Mac Thornberry (R-TX)	420–0	Unanimous Consent	75
H.R.1627: Honoring America's Veterans and Caring for Camp Lejeune Families Act of 2012	August 6, 2012	Rep. Jeff Miller (R-FL)	Voice Vote	Unanimous Consent	83
H.R.3230: Veterans Access, Choice, and Accountability Act of 2014	August 7, 2014	Rep. Harold "Hal" Rogers (R-KY)	420–5	91–3	81
H.R.5099: Communities Helping Invest through Property and Improvements Needed for Veterans Act of 2016	December 16, 2016	Rep. Brad Ashford (D-NE)	Voice Vote	Voice Vote	100
H.R.5392 (114th): No Veterans Crisis Line Call Should Go Unanswered Act	November 28, 2016	Rep. David Young (R-IA)	357–0	Unanimous Consent	98

H.R.5936 (114th): West Los Angeles Leasing Act of 2016	September 29, 2016	Rep. Jeff miller (R-FL)	Voice Vote	Voice Vote	75
H.R.22 (114th): FAST Act	December 4, 2015	Rep. Davis, Rodney (R-IL)	359–65	83–16	67
H.R.4352 (114th): Faster Care for Veterans Act of 2016	December 16, 2016	Rep. Seth Moulton (D-MA)	Voice Vote	Voice Vote	85
H.R.203 (114th): Clay Hunt SAV Act	February 12, 2015	Rep. Timothy J. Walz (D-MN)	403–0	99–0	69
S.2487 (114th): Female Veteran Suicide Prevention Act	June 30, 2016	Sen. Barbara Boxer (D-CA)	Unanimous Consent	Unanimous Consent	75
S.2683 (114th): Federal Aviation Administration Veteran Transition Improvement Act of 2016	October 7, 2016	Sen. Mazie K. Hirono (D-HI)	Unanimous Consent	Unanimous Consent	100
S.524 (114th): Comprehensive Addiction and Recovery Act of 2016	July 22, 2016	Sen. Sheldon Whitehouse (D-RI)	407–5	92–2	90

Veterans' Health Care Policy Changes

As a final note on veterans' health care, I now describe the most recently passed veterans' health legislation. In this section I also provide examples of how members of Congress talk about these accomplishments in constituent communications.

The first big changes during the 111th–114th Congresses are substantively broad and a part of bigger legislative vehicles that many might not associate with veterans' health care. For instance, H.R.1, the American Recovery and Reinvestment Act of 2009, also known as the Recovery Act or Stimulus, that passed shortly after the president took office, changed veterans' health policy in some relatively large ways.

The bill ordered a one-time payment of $250–$500 to eligible veterans currently receiving disability benefits or serving under stop-loss orders. This stimulus was given to 185,000 stop-loss serving members and to nearly 2 million disabled veterans.[44] Second, the bill established a Filipino Veterans Equity Compensation Fund to make payments to eligible individuals and surviving spouses for service members who served before July 1, 1946, as a part the organized military forces of the Philippines while such forces were in the service of the U.S. Armed Forces.[45]

H.R.1 dedicated $1.4 billion to the VA in order to improve medical facilities and allocate grants to states for the construction or improvement of extended care facilities. There was also a provision to allow the VA to hire 1,500 temporary workers to help process backlogged benefits claims.

Owing to the relative unpopularity of the stimulus package to Republicans in Congress, it is not surprising that Republicans were less likely than Democrats to tout the pro-veterans elements of the legislation in constituent communications.

H.R.3950, the Patient Protection and Affordable Care Act, later known as Obamacare, is another highly notable bill out of the first part of the Obama presidency. For veterans' health care this bill mandated that the VA be given access to more data on outside health providers through the newly established National Practitioner Data Bank and required that the VA conduct a study on the efficacy and cost of medical services and drugs provided to veterans inside and outside the system. Again, the majority of those who link the bill to veterans are Democrats, and this is likely because of the GOP distaste for the original bill.

One of largest substantive changes for veterans' health care came in 2010 with the bipartisan, unanimously agreed to Caregivers and Veterans Omnibus Health Services Act of 2010. This bill was substantial; highlights include greater recognition and solutions to the challenges facing family members who act as caregivers for veterans, veterans in rural areas and the attendant difficulties of transportation to health centers, and the different needs of women veterans that current systems oftentimes overlook.

For family members serving as caregivers for veterans, the bill included provisions for training, counseling, health care, support services, and financial assistance. In order to better serve rural veterans, the law ordered the VA to establish a grant program to provide innovative transportation options to veterans in highly rural areas to travel to VA medical centers and to other VA and non-VA facilities for medical care. In anticipation that the numbers of women veterans would increase, this bill provided for a study on barriers to health care access for women, training for mental health care professionals caring for veterans with sexual trauma, and authorized VA to provide health care for newborn infants of women veterans.

It is somewhat curious that we do not observe more Republican messages around this legislation. After all, every Republican supported the final bill. Perhaps because it came from someone of the other party, but even then Senator Akaka (D-HI) was a respected leader on veterans' policy, and he was known as a willing legislator who sought bipartisan compromise.[46] But then again, during this Congress Republicans were quieter on veterans' issues than they were in the 112th–114th.

The final substantive change of the 111th Congress was H.R.4505, which provided for the expansion of use of the State Veterans Home system to parents any of whose children died while serving in the armed forces. Prior laws allowed only veterans themselves to apply for long-term care at these facilities. H.R.4505 was agreed to by unanimous consent in the Senate and by a vote of 420–0 in the House.

The State Veterans Home system varies widely from site to site—some are as small as 60 people and some are much larger facilities caring for over 1,000 veterans and their family members. This bill opened up the eligibility to use such homes for people who were related to a service member who died while on duty. The logic underlying this bill was that seniors oftentimes turn to their children to help pay for the high costs of eldercare in old age. Seniors who lose a child while in the military are thus in a more precarious situation later in life and may find the financial strain of suitable home health care too high. This bill does not guarantee full payment or even partial payment to most parents of veterans who seek to use the Home system, but it does make that possibility an option when it previously was not available. When talking about the bill in constituent communications, Republican legislators noted their support for long-term care for military families as a reason for voting.

The only substantive veterans' health bill of the 112th Congress combined multiple smaller bills into one comprehensive reform (H.R.1627). This reform expanded the definition of persons eligible to make use of the entitlements of veterans, established new regulations for monuments at the Arlington Cemetery, expanded health programs for rural veterans, and made improvements to the disability claims system and the backlogs within.

The expansion of veteran eligibility applied to any person who served at Camp Lejeune, North Carolina, for at least 30 days between January 1, 1957, and December 31, 1987, and their family members. Camp Lejeune is a Marine Corps Base that National Academy of Sciences determined the well-water systems to be highly contaminated by hazardous, carcinogenic chemicals.[47] After all the assessments conducted, the toxicity exposure at Lejeune was the largest recorded environmental and the largest water contamination incident on a domestic DOD installation in American history. The cancer incidences following 30 years of exposure to chemicals such as trichloroethylene, benzene, and vinyl chloride of veterans, works, and related children were recorded, but the VA maintained that these were not covered under the responsibility of care they are meant to provide. Pursuant to that assessment, legislators began arguing that exposed personnel ought to be allowed access to the VA system.

The bill created a pilot program of continuing education efforts to train employees and managers who process veterans' claims and pension benefits on how to increase the efficiency and quality of the claims process. To aid rural veterans, the bill waived telehealth and telemedicine co-payments to incentivize greater use of that system.

When discussing the bill in constituent communications, legislators focused on the new Arlington Cemetery requirements. One change allowed any qualified veteran, regardless of rank, to apply for burial. Another ensured that the funding for new monuments was made more routine, and legislators argued that this act was necessary to ensure that veterans "continue to receive the highest level of respect and reverence the country has come to expect."[48]

The 113th Congress was another gridlocked Congress like the 112th and against only one substantive veterans' health bill passed. Yet, this one law did multiple things. H.R.3230, the Veterans Access, Choice, and Accountability Act of 2014, guaranteed pay to all armed forces in the event of a government shutdown,[49] made steps toward relaxing the exclusivity of the VA in terms of who may provide health care for veterans, put a temporary ban on bonuses for senior-level VA employees until FY 2016, and authorized 27 new VA facilities across the nation.

The bill defined qualifications for when veterans can seek medical care at specified non-VA facilities and still be funded by VA monies.[50] If veterans were unable to receive services within 30 days or if they lived more than 40 miles from a VA medical facility, they could seek health care elsewhere.[51] This was an effort to react to extensive backlogs and pressure from veterans' groups in rural areas to demand closer facilities.

As a measure of transparency, the bill required the VA to establish an electronic waiting list that is accessible online to veterans who have been "unable to schedule an appointment at a VA medical facility within the VHA's wait-time goals so that they can make an informed choice of whether or not to receive care and services at non-VA facilities."[52] There was also a provision requiring an independent assessment of VA medical care.

The Veterans Choice program was not without controversy. By allowing veterans to seek health care outside of the VA system, those in opposition to the bill argued that allowing outside providers reduced the incentives to make internal VA health care better. There was also pushback because funding systems to facilitate choice outside of the system necessarily trades off with funding that could be directed into VA processes. In the original consideration and subsequent re-upping efforts, the Veterans of Foreign Wars, Vietnam Veterans of America, and the Iraq and Afghanistan Veterans Association expressed opposition to this program.

The 114th Congress saw the passage of many veterans' health policies. These pieces of legislation tended to be smaller than the Congresses before and narrower in scope.

The first bill to pass was introduced by Representative Brad Ashford (D-ME). This bill, the Communities Helping Invest through Property and Improvements Needed for Veterans Act of 2016 or CHIP IN for Vets Act, passed both chambers unanimously. This bill established a pilot program for partnership agreements to construct new VA facilities. Rather than the current policy of only allowing the federal VA to purchase and construct VA facilities, this bill allowed nonfederal entities—including state or city governments, nonprofit organizations, and benefactors to donate up to five facilities to VA on a pilot basis.

When discussing the goals of this bill, Republican legislators said the bill would be a way to increase the ability of the VA to deliver health care to veterans. Despite the democratic origins, and the unanimous support of the bill, no Democrats took to their constituent communications to discuss this bill. This silence contributes to the greater understanding of lip service. Republicans do not just do more communicating about veterans; Democrats themselves lag on these measures even when it seems like there is a good opportunity to brag about policy accomplishments on veterans' policies.

In contrast, the next bill that passed, H.R.5392, the No Veterans Crisis Line Call Should Go Unanswered Act, was publicized multiple times by the Republican legislator, Dave Young (R-IA) who introduced it.

Since 2007 the VA has operated a veterans' crisis phone line for veterans and their families to call if they need someone to talk to about any of the difficulties in the transition to civilian life. While the line was intended to be a quick place for veterans to turn in times of stress, these were issues of responsiveness and wait times in the coordination of employees set to answer these calls. In 2014 a VA Office of Inspector General report found that 20% calls were unanswered and were never returned.[53] In 2015, with a 700 percent increase in phone calls, the VA struggled to meet the demands and veterans had to wait on the line for increasingly longer times.[54] The new bill required the VA to develop a quality assurance process and to create and implement a plan to ensure communications on the hotline were quickly routed to a live person. The bill places a 30-second maximum wait-time target in place.

Shortly after introducing the legislation, Representative David Young (R-IA) wrote to constituents to explain why he thought the bill was a good idea and what the bill sought to accomplish and then asked constituents to respond to him with their own opinions on the bill. He updated constituents a week after introduction. The bill quickly passed the House with no opposition. Despite the bipartisan nature of the bill and votes, Republicans in Congress dominated constituent communications, accounting for 98 percent of all communications. Republican legislators wrote about how they proudly voted for the bill and how important it was to serve veterans as quickly as possible. After House passage, the author of the bill wrote constituents again to say he was disappointed that the Senate hadn't yet considered the bill. He blamed the delay on Democrats saying, "Disappointingly, political posturing from one retiring Democrat senior member stands in the way of crucial improvements to a hotline so many veterans in crisis rely on."[55] Two months later, President Obama signed the bill into law after a unanimous consent vote in the Senate. Representative Young sent another communication updating his constituents that his bill had passed.

The West Los Angeles Leasing Act of 2016 (H.R.5936), sponsored by Rep. Jeff Miller (R-FL), was introduced on September 6, 2016, and authorized the secretary of Veteran Affairs "to enter into certain leases at the Department of Veterans Affairs West Los Angeles Campus in Los Angeles, California, to make certain improvements to the enhanced-use lease authority of the Department, and for other purposes." The bill passed both the House and the Senate with a voice vote and was signed into public law by President Obama on September 29, 2016. This bill expanded authorization for non-VA provider care for veterans and allowed the VA to use the West Los Angeles VA campus for housing for homeless veterans. The only Democrat to tout the bill was Ted Lieu from Los Angeles. When he mentioned the bill, he made sure to give credit to Miller for introducing the bill, and he praised the move as a signal that LA would be a more veteran-centric city than before.[56]

Seth Moulton (D-MA) sponsored the Faster Care for Veterans Act of 2016 (H.R.4352) that directed the VA to develop an 18-month pilot program that allowed veterans to use an "internet website or mobile application to schedule and confirm appointments at VA medical facilities." If the program succeeded in its goal of reducing veteran wait times, the scope and duration could be extended. The bill passed both the House and the Senate with a voice vote and was signed into law on December 16, 2016.

Moulton told constituents about his bill in a communication saying he introduced the "bipartisan bill to improve VA health care."[57] A few days later, Republican congressman Erik Paulsen wrote his constituents to say he intended to support the bill and justified that approach by referencing the 2014 VA hospital, scandal noting, "This will help reduce the needless delays and missed appointments that are part of the reason why veterans have had to wait so long to see a doctor."[58] Representative Will Hurd (R-TX) took a more negative tone lamenting that, "the VA has been unable to implement an electronic health record system that is secure and interoperable. Despite billions of tax dollars and reports outlining deficiencies, we have seen little to no improvement."[59] He concluded the communication by saying he would have a hearing on the bill later in the week.

Once the hearing Hurd wrote about occurred, Moulton wrote constituents again to say he was working to get his bill to the whole Congress. Multiple Republican congressmen wrote to constituents indicating their support for the bill; some identified the original sponsor and others did not. Once the bill passed the House via voice vote, Representative Jason Smith (R-MO) told constituents that the bill would cut down on waiting periods for "veterans' accessing the healthcare that they have earned."[60] Other Republicans expressed similar sentiments to their constituents. Despite the bipartisan nature of the bill and the ease with which it passed, no Democrats other than the original sponsor, Seth Moulton, ever mentioned the bill in their constituent communication. Republican legislators sent a full 92 percent of all communications about this bill. Democrats supported this bill, but for some reason they did not take the time to tell constituents. All the while Representative Moulton worked to write and secure passage for the bill.

Introduced by Rep. Timothy Walz (D-MN), the Clay Hunt Suicide Prevention for American Veterans (SAV) Act made sweeping changes to the mental health services offered to service members returning from duty. The bill was named for Clay Hunt, a veteran from Iraq and Afghanistan who committed suicide on March 31, 2011. The act established two pilot programs. The first required the repayment of education loans incurred by individuals who were studying psychiatric medicine and had shown a commitment to working at the VHA. The second improved the access veterans had at obtaining mental health services. Finally, the act required third-party evaluation of the VA's mental health care and suicide prevention programs each fiscal year, the reports of which were to be made available to Congress and the public. The bill passed both the House and the Senate with no opposition and became law on February 12, 2015.

The first member to write about the bill to constituents was fellow Minnesota Democrat representative Collin Peterson. He told constituents that he was proud to support such a bill because of how pressing the issue of veteran suicide was. The original sponsor, Walz, sent the next communication mentioning the statistic that an average of 22 veterans takes their own lives every day.[61] However, when the legislators originally sent these communications, the Congress was in the 113th session, and although the bill was introduced during that Congress, it did not pass.

In the 113th Congress, Senator Tom Coburn (R-OK) blocked the bill saying the efforts were duplicated in other VA systems, and he worried that the $22 million cost was not offset by cuts in another part of the budget.[62] Because of the way the Senate sought to pass bills in the last few days of the 113th Congress, if one member wanted to block unanimous consideration of a bill, it was not possible to consider that bill further; Coburn was successful in this maneuver.

Coburn retired after the 113th Congress, and the bill had to be reintroduced at the beginning of the 114th Congress in January 2015. The bill was reintroduced by Walz and passed unanimously from the House within the first 10 days of the new session. The Senate quickly took up the legislation, and with a 99–0 the bill moved to Obama's desk. Once signed, many Republican legislators took to their constituent communications to talk about the success of the bill. Senator Richard Burr (R-NC), who wrote the companion version to the House bill, wrote, "The Clay Hunt SAV Act will provide much-needed resources to combat the epidemic of veteran suicide. I could not be more pleased to see my legislation signed into law today and I will continue to support efforts to provide care for our nation's heroes."[63] Every single member of Congress at the time supported the bill, yet in a way that characterizes veterans' issue politics. Republicans spoke about the bill and the issue of veteran suicide far more frequently than Democrats did. All told, 91 percent of the messages sent about this bill came from Republicans despite the fact that a Democrat authored it and every Democrat in Congress supported it.

The Female Veteran Suicide Prevent Act (S.2487) was sponsored by Sen. Barbara Boxer (D-CA) and directed the VA to identify mental health care and suicide prevention programs that work best for women veterans. The bill passed both the House and the Senate by unanimous consent and became law on June 30, 2016. The Senate version was ultimately adopted, but there was a companion bill in the House by the same name introduced by Julia Brownley (D-CA). Brownley was the first to discuss the bill in constituent communications, noting the need for the bill as women veterans are six times as likely to attempt suicide than nonveteran women. Both representatives and senators expressed the need for this bill, and unsurprisingly 75 percent of the communications came from Republicans. After the bill was signed into law, military veteran senator Joni Ernst wrote to constituents, saying,

> President Obama signed my bipartisan Female Veteran Suicide Prevention Act into law. I worked on this legislation along with Senators Barbara Boxer (D-CA), Richard Blumenthal (D-CT), Sherrod Brown (D-OH) and Congresswoman Julia Brownley (D-CA) in the House.[64]

Senator Ernst lists four legislators who worked with her on the bill, including the lead sponsor, Senator Boxer. All of the other legislators who drafted and submitted the bill were Democrats, yet only Representative Brownley and Senator Brown ever wrote to constituents about the bill, and many more Democrats said nothing at all about the popular, bipartisan, and uncontroversial bill.

Sponsored by Sen. Mazie Hirono (D-HI), the Federal Aviation Administration Veteran Transition Improvement Act of 2016 required the inclusion of disabled veteran leave in the personal management system of the Federal Aviation Administration. The act passed both the House and the Senate by unanimous consent and was signed into law on October 7, 2016. This bill did not receive as much attention overall as the others from the 114th Congress, with only seven constituent communications versus hundreds for other bills. However, all of the constituent communications were authored by Republican legislators.

The Comprehensive Addiction and Recovery Act (CARA) of 2016, sponsored by Sen. Sheldon Whitehouse (D-RI), authorized the attorney general and secretary of Health and Human Services to award grants "to address the prescription opioid abuse and heroin use crisis, and for other purposes." The act laid out specific treatment services for veterans and allowed the Department of Justice to award grants to state and local governments that expanded or established veterans' treatment courts, peer-to-peer services, and treatment, rehabilitation, and transitional services for incarcerated veterans. The VA was required to expand its Opioid Safety Initiative to all VA medical facilities. Moreover, it ensured that veterans who were at risk of opioid addiction were granted easier access to care, which included lowering the cost incurred by veterans and maximizing the availability to veterans of opioid overdose reversal drugs. The bill also created a faster way for veterans who had already completed military emergency medical technician training to more easily meet civilian emergency medical technician licensure requirements. The bill passed the House by a vote of 407–5 and the Senate by a vote of 92–2. It was signed into law on July 22, 2016.

Many legislators discussed this bill in constituent communications, as every member has constituents suffering with opioid addictions; there are obvious benefits for touting support for legislation that aims to curb drug abuse. By the time the final bill was developed, 18 smaller House bills were rolled together as one big modification to the already-passed Senate version. Despite the spread of opioid addictions to every part of the country, despite the public opinion supporting veterans and antidrug efforts, and despite overwhelming support from Democrats, not one Democratic legislator authored a constituent communication on this Democrat-authored, Democrat-supported bill.

For a lot of the legislation passed in the 111th–114th Congresses, there is broad and sometimes even unanimous support. Yet, even when there is bipartisan or oftentimes unanimous agreement to legislation, Republicans still do more to advertise legislative accomplishments to constituents than Democrats. This is lip service at work. Thinking about political communication as a marketing strategy for politics, it is easy to see why the Republican Party is more closely linked with veterans; Republican legislators talk about veterans and veterans' policy with much greater frequency than Democrats.

Conclusion

In the wake of the 2014 scandal, public opinion on the VA took a dive. And in ways counter to other issues, both Republicans and Democrats assessed the severity of the situation similarly. Yet when looking to who attempted to change policy in a way that serves veterans, the parties took to different tactics. Democrats offered legislation at rates that were significantly higher than Republicans while Republicans talked about veterans' health care much more frequently. This pattern is like the one found in Chapters 4 and 6. In comporting with the overall theory, the greatest VA scandal of the past decade offers an example of how political actors act preventatively and respond retroactively. Democrats worked more than Republicans to better veterans' health care systems before, during, and after the 2014 scandal with the introduction and passage of policies, whereas Republicans took the lead on telling constituents about the failures of the system and how much they *intended* to work to support veterans.

The contours that describe the overall veterans' policy space are sometimes different depending on the specific policy area. In veterans' education Democrats did not perform significantly more legwork, and Republicans did not perform more lip service. Veterans' educational benefits are often considered a high point of overall veteran politics with both Republicans and Democrats agreeing to the goals of bills like the Post–9/11 GI Bill. In contrast, veterans' health benefits are far more contentious, and the policy space is more often marred with scandal. In this setting, the overall pattern of Republican-dominated lip service and Democrat-dominated legwork is observed.

CHAPTER NINE

Conclusions and Directions for the Future of Veterans' Politics and Policies

In this chapter I offer a summary of the major findings of this book and a discussion about where veterans' politics and policies are headed in the future. With the recognition that knowing the past does not provide one with a crystal ball for the future, I hesitate to make claims about the likelihood that specific policies are successful or not. Yet, there are broad shifts on the horizon for veterans' politics and policies that will likely change the way both are done.

The State of Veterans Legwork and Lip Service in the United States

Veterans now enjoy the highest public approval they have at any time in United States' recorded history. Public opinion on Iraq and Afghanistan veterans has remained remarkably high, even as popularity for the wars wanes. The adoration of the public is matched or even surpassed in the official communications of legislators. Compared to other groups of professions mentioned in official congressional communications, veterans are the most often cited and discussed in the highest regard.

In terms of communicative and nonpolicy efforts, veterans are a top priority for many members of Congress. In communications members go to great lengths to communicate their willingness to work on behalf of veterans to help those mired in red tape with the VA, assisting in the awarding of past due medals, and many offer to hold specific veteran-focused listening groups when a legislator is in the district.

In terms of legislative dedication, veterans also receive the greatest amount of support, and there are no indications that Congress seeks to curb the expansion of government benefits. Unlike any other group, the federal government considers and approves benefits for veterans, their spouses, their parents, their children, and their caregivers. In the most recent congress, Senator Tim Kaine (D-VA) proposed a bill, the Military Spouse Employment Act, to address shortcomings in the provision of day care for military families, offer counseling to transitioning military families, expand hiring and career opportunities, and increase access to continuing education programs.[1] The most recent Congress of 2017 has been heralded as one of the most legislatively productive on veterans' policy in recent years, passing policies large and small to benefit veterans.

There are even calls to grant veteran status to others such as nurse cadets who serve those in the military but are not considered to serve in the military.[2] While there have been scandals and setbacks, in terms of public recognition, official expressions of honor, and policy, veterans in the United States today are doing well.

In Chapter 2, we saw that districts with more veterans tended to elect more veterans to Congress, and those veterans tended to be Republicans rather than Democrats. However, there was no evidence that electing veterans to Congress translates meaningfully into increased legislative legwork on veterans' policies. That is, veteran status does not appear to work in the way descriptive representation does for other identities.

Chapter 3 offered an important look at the historical situation of veterans. Veterans today are held in much higher regard than the feared "war cripples" of World War I and World War II and the veterans of Vietnam who were thought to be rabble-rousers. In the post–9/11 era, support for veterans from the public has become the norm with large majorities saying they are proud of veterans, wish the government would focus more on their needs, and are willing to support policies that improve veteran benefits. These sentiments are largely bipartisan. Of those who identify with a major political party in the United States, similar amounts express high levels of support for veterans' benefits. But not all of veterans' politics are outside the grip of politics. In the wake of the 2014 Phoenix VA scandal, Republicans were more willing to blame politicians and the bureaucracy while Democrats focused on individual VA employees and facilities. During the flashpoints of media coverage on the scandal, the partisan flames burned hot, but once some time had passed, the embers of political blame recalibrated back to a bipartisan split. In 2015, majorities of Democrats and Republicans thought that the Congress was at fault when veterans are wronged.

Other than in periods of high tension, public opinion outlooks on veterans' politics and polices are not well defined by any party. Yet, the public opinion of veterans themselves appears to be. Starting in the late 1980s and continuing until today, a majority of veterans identify with the Republican Party and vote for Republican candidates. The majorities among veterans who do so are greater than the majorities of the U.S. public who occasionally prefer Republicans in electoral contest.

Veteran *political* alignment with the Republican Party, both in the general media narrative sense and in the public opinion data and voting sense, would not be exceptionally interesting if not for the veteran *policy* patterns that underlie popular benefits programs. Democratic president Franklin Delano Roosevelt signed the first GI Bill into law. He not only signed this law, but he also conceived of it and proposed it to Congress as a part of other New Deal reforms.[3] Owing to the popularity of the bill, successive Democrats signed Korean and Vietnam War versions of the bill. Then in 1984, Democratic congressman Gillespie (Sonny) Montgomery proposed a new, expanded version of the GI Bill to recruit high-caliber men for the all-volunteer force. Montgomery worked for years to secure passage of his bill, noting that the speed was as slow as a "snail on crutches," but in the end all but two legislators voted for the final passage.[4] In 2008, Democratic senator Jim Webb worked to repeat and expand upon the efforts of Montgomery when he proposed and secured passage of the Post–9/11 GI Bill.

Republicans in Congress do not sabotage veterans' benefits policies; in fact except in rare cases, Republicans join with Democrats for the final passage of the most popular veterans' reforms. But they do not offer nearly as many policy proposals as their Democratic counterparts. A benefit to this strategy is that Republican legislators can tell constituents about how much and how often they support veterans' policies with the knowledge that most voters will not put in the effort to determine who thought of those policies in the first place. Altogether, Republicans do far more of this sort of lip service than Democrats, and that effort is part of the reason that the media narrative linking the Republican Party to veterans persists.

It is important to discern that jumping on at the end or lending a supportive vote is not the same as actively working to create better veterans system. Over the course of the 111th–114th Congresses, even though Republicans held majorities for most of the time, Democrats proposed and successfully passed more veterans' legislation. Of the types of legislation considered, Democrats focused more of their efforts on substantive, stand-alone pieces that translate into meaningful changes in the lives of veterans. At the same time a good deal of Republicans offered legislation as well, but these numbers are fewer than expected by their seat share, at lower levels than that seen by Democrats, and with a greater focus of symbolic legislation.

This general case is not always true in more specific policy areas. In Chapter 7, looking at veterans' education benefits, I found no difference between the legwork levels of Republicans and Democrats and no difference between the lip service levels of members of either party. Both appear to prioritize educational benefits in similar ways, and both discuss their efforts at similar rates in constituent communications.

On veterans' health care, I found quite the opposite. Democrats both introduced and were more successful in passing legislation to enhance veterans' health care in the United States, but Republicans were far more likely to talk about this sort of policy issue in communications. Looking at the 13 specific veterans' health care bills that made it all the way to final passage, the legwork versus lip service distinction is clear. Of the bills authored by Democrats, and supported by Democrats, Republicans tend to take the lead in discussing the positive impacts for veterans in official communications. This lead in lip service for veterans' health care is not slight; there are even instances on certain bills when every official constituent communication comes from a Republican author. When that is the case, it seems as though Republicans do more work on behalf of veterans as they certainly spend more time *talking* about the work they do for veterans than Democrats.

Republicans in Congress simply do not do as much work drafting and securing passage on veterans' legislation as Democrats, yet Republicans still maintain an edge with veterans. Why is this? Why do Republicans not just do more legwork? Why do voters continue to reward Republicans with positive associations with veterans? In offering a theory of lip service versus legwork, I address these questions. Republicans do not offer more veterans' legislation because the way veterans' policies are implemented creates more ideological tension for conservatives than it does for liberals. Notions of small government, reduced spending, free markets, and personal responsibility are all at odds with the way VA health care, educational benefits, employment assistance, and other veterans' targeted policies exist.

These tensions are part of the reason we observe fewer legwork efforts from Republicans, but the reason we see greater association between veterans and the party are because of increased lip service efforts. Republicans spend far greater efforts talking about veterans and veterans' policies than Democrats do, and this sort of lip service works. The public generally and veterans specifically do not have the time and are not really incentivized to care enough to think about who is actually doing the work for veterans. Rather, it falls to the parties to sell their stances to voters and to simplify the ways in which voters perceive partisan actors. By repeatedly emphasizing a commitment to veterans, legislators in the Republican Party bolster the image of being a party that supports veterans. Democrats during the time period of the study offered more veterans' legislation, but they did not communicate those accomplishments or express their interests about veterans in constituent communications as much as Republicans did. There is not a party at *fault* for this state of understanding; there is merely a mismatch in legwork and lip service, and it seems that lip service seems to get the job done in the eyes of voters. If Democrats wanted to be perceived as the party that votes for and legislates on behalf of veterans, they might well be served to better publicize their legislative efforts.

The Future of Veterans' Policy and Politics

Policy

President Donald Trump has proposed continued increases to funding veterans' programs, and Congress seems keen to deliver on those promises.[5] One of early policy achievements of the most recent Congresses builds on the Post–9/11 GI Bill. The Forever G.I. Bill, or Harry W. Colmery Veterans Educational Assistance Act, passed in August 2017 and is set to go into effect by the fall semester of 2018, with other provisions starting thereafter on a rolling basis until 2020. This bill, like the Post–9/11 Bill before it, expands benefits in some ways and pulls back in other ways.

This bill eliminates the 15-year time cap that veterans must adhere to use their educational benefits.[6] This bill also changes the way time in service is calculated for veterans who receive a Purple Heart. All Purple Heart recipients will be eligible for 100 percent of reimbursement no matter the duration of their service.[7] There is also now an option for an additional $30,000 in reimbursement for veterans who choose a STEM field of study. This provision was included to fill a coming gap of STEM professionals and because degrees in those specialties oftentimes take more than four years to complete.

Housing stipends were trimmed in the Forever Bill, but the reduction is just a 1 percent drop in housing allowances. There is more flexibility in how a member transfers benefits to a spouse or child, but there is also a reduction in how much tuition a transferee may be reimbursed for, 36 months versus 45 under the Post–9/11 GI Bill. This reduction was met with some outcry, but the determination was to make transferred benefits more like the original benefits, which are capped at 36 months.[8]

The tension between Republican ideology on government size and spending in contrast to the way veterans' policy is administered in the United States contributed to the fewer numbers of GOP policies in the 111th–114th Congresses, but may not restrict future legislators. The Tea Party is on the wane and members of the Republican Party, who once held views against government spending, seem keen to relax if the spending occurs with a co-partisan as president. In appropriations for 2018, GOP legislators have proposed and supported budgets that would incur over $700 billion in deficit spending for the year, and thus more federal debt for years to come.[9]

With a relaxation of a small government, low government spending outlook and/or an unwillingness of voters to enforce some sort of ideological consistency in candidates, the Republican majorities in Congress could be better suited to offer more veterans' legislation than they have in the past.

As a way to prevent another 2014-style VA crisis, the most recent Congress passed a series of civil service reforms to protect whistle-blowers from within the VA and provide VA management more flexibility in employee terminations. Provisions of this bill had been circulating from the time of the initial scandal and were introduced as a unified bill in May 2017 by Senator Marco Rubio (R-FL). The Department of Veterans Affairs Accountability and Whistleblower Protection Act of 2017 (S. 1094) flew through the Senate with a voice vote and a wide margin in the House before being signed by the president just six weeks after the initial introduction.[10] While there is an obvious lag between the scandal and a policy meant to address some of the greatest causes, this sort of bipartisan legislative solution exemplifies how veterans' politics is somewhat of a bright spot for both parties.

Veteran Recruitment to Congress

Fewer veterans serve in Congress now than at any time in our history, but there are signs of increased interest from both parties and veterans themselves to seek a career in government. From 2008 to 2015, the share of veterans as a part of the federal workforce in the executive branch went from 9 to 19 percent.[11] The majority of these hires went to the Department of Defense, the VA, and the Department of Homeland Security where they perform administrative, technical, and physical jobs that utilize skills honed while serving.

As for elective office, there are multiple groups dedicated to the mission of preparing veterans to run and win seats. Both parties seek to run candidates with credibility and appeal to voters; for that reason veterans are attractive candidate options. Both parties increasingly seek veterans as candidates in the hopes that a history of service will impress voters.[12] One group seeking to increase the share of veterans in legislative politics, With Honor, asks their recruits to sign a pledge that if they are elected, they will work across the aisle and commit to one meeting a month with a member from the other party.[13]

Veteran women are also set to play a larger role in the government. While there are fewer women veterans than men, and only a handful of women veterans ever elected to Congress, the rates at which women seek government careers and elected office after active duty have never been higher. In the 2018 midterm election, Democrats need 24 seats to retake the House from Republicans. By July 2017, the party had recruited and planned to run at least 20 veterans in upcoming races.[14] On their own, over 100 veterans have declared candidacies for the 2018 congressional elections.[15]

Female Veterans

Many of our programs and practices to help veterans are focused on men because of the historical sex division of armed forces. In 2015, women accounted for nearly 10 percent of all veterans, the highest percentage and raw number at over 2 million in U.S. history. By 2043, women are expected to account for upward of 16 percent of all veterans.[16] This increase indicates that there will be a greater need to focus on the particular needs of women veterans.

The group of women veterans is also different than men veterans in a few demographically significant ways. The share of African American women veterans among all female veterans is 19 percent, whereas the general population share is only 12 percent.

African American women are overrepresented in the armed forces as compared to African American men. Hispanic women have a distinction in the opposite way with only 9 percent of all female veterans identifying as Hispanic, whereas the population of women, who are generally Hispanic, is around 16 percent. Women Asians are also unrepresented relative to their share in the general population with a veteran population of just 2 percent compared to a general population share of 5.5 percent.

Despite the demands, relocation, and travel associated with military life, women veterans are more likely to be married at some point than comparably aged civilian counterparts (84% versus 72%), but among married people, women veterans are more likely to experience divorce than civilians (23% versus 13%). Women veterans and nonveterans are roughly equally as likely to have children at some point in their lives. The disparity in divorce rates may speak to greater difficulties in marriage maintenance for units with a women veteran than units without and may therefore signal a place to increase supports for returning veterans in the form of marriage counseling.

The numbers of women using VA-provided benefits continue to rise, and subsequently 34 percent of women veterans complete college compared to 28 percent of nonveteran women, 10 percent of female veterans live in poverty compared to 15 percent in the general population, and only 4 percent of female veterans report not having access to health insurance whereas 9 percent of all other women report not having access to health insurance.

In an attempt to make VA care more suitable and appealing to female veterans, Representative Elizabeth Esty (D-CT) has introduced H.R.2452, the Deborah Sampson Act. This act requires that the VA conduct three-year analyses on a variety of systems and programs in order to better serve women.

Some of those requirements include expansion of a call center hotline, like the one explained in Chapter 8, but with a specific focus on women, a requirement that all VA facilities have at least one full-time or part-time women's health primary care provider, collect and make public data around women's treatments within VA facilities, and an encouragement to create a website to allow for a centralized location for women to access information about all VA offerings. This bill has been referred to the House Committee on Veterans' Affairs where it awaits further action.

Veterans as Political Props

While most might not perceive a difference between lip service and legwork, intensely focused veterans' advocates do. Paul Rieckhoff, founder of Iraq and Afghanistan Veterans of America, routinely makes this point. His argument, like many others, is that the American public generally says it cares about veterans, but when asked anything with more specific content, it becomes clear that veterans act as some sort of placeholder for positive but not well-determined political props.[17]

Veterans are aware that they are used as political props. They are an easy embodiment of all the things that politicians want to project: patriotism, bravery, duty, and so forth. It was not surprising that when candidate Donald Trump skipped a presidential debate and instead held a rally, he dubbed it "A Special Event to Benefit Veterans Organizations." Rather than come off as a dropout from the debate, he got to play champion of veterans with his substitute choice of event.

This sort of political theatrics is not universally appreciated within the veteran community. In the days following this event, it was revealed that candidate Trump had served up one of the greatest versions of deceptive lip service in politics by claiming his foundations had donated over $6 million to veterans' organizations. In reality, his foundations had donated less than half of that amount.[18]

This sort of lip service risks turning veterans against a candidate. In the immediate aftermath, veterans published op-eds against candidate Trump's insincerity.[19] Some veterans' groups sought to distance themselves from the candidate. But when it came time to vote, veterans chose Trump over Clinton with a 60–30 percent margin, whereas the overall popular support was approximately 46 percent for Trump and 50 percent for Clinton.[20]

Discussion

Where do we go from here? The relationships between the public, politicians, and the military are critical underpinnings of a well-functioning

Conclusions and Directions for the Future of Veterans' Politics and Policies

democracy. Each group must rely on each other to deliver on different responsibilities, and each must trust the other to faithfully follow through on their elements of responsibility. This book shows that the ability for different groups to clearly understand the actions versus the statements of others is lacking.

The Republican Party in Congress does a good job of cultivating a sense of respect and reverence for veterans by working to talk about veterans and veterans' policy with great frequency in their official, constituent communications. They do so in a manner that is unmatched by Democrats. Yet, those in the Democratic Party continue to introduce more legislation for veterans in their official capacity as legislators. The public and veterans generally believe that the Republican Party is more in tune with the needs of veterans, and this is no doubt partially attributable to the amount of lip service Republican legislators are willing to send on veterans. They have earned that reputation with their communication focus, but it does not appear that the Republican Party has earned the support of veterans by passing favorable veterans' legislation.

This study is not meant to blame one party over the other or to find fault with veterans or public opinion. Rather the aims of this study have been to explain a seeming contradiction of observations by using empirical assessment of observable actions and recorded words.

In the researching of this book, my own appreciation for veterans has matured and grown. I was in high school when the attacks of 9/11 occurred, and I could not fully appreciate the level of commitment that our active-duty and later veteran families make to the country. I was raised and lived in Kansas when Thomas Frank's book *What's the Matter with Kansas* came out in 2005. His take on the seemingly confusing state of people and politics in Kansas piqued my interest in the study of how actions, words, ideas, and beliefs do not always outwardly align but can be explained with a greater appreciation for the combinations of political forces at play. In that way, it is my hope that this book serves to spread some light on the sometimes-obscured corners of veterans' politics and policies.

Notes

Introduction

1. John R. Petrocik, "Issue Ownership in Presidential Elections, with a 1980 Case Study," *American Journal of Political Science* 40, no. 3 (1996): 825–850; John Sides, "The Origins of Campaign Agendas," *British Journal of Political Science* 36, no. 3 (2006): 407–436; Patrick J. Egan, *Partisan Priorities: How Issue Ownership Drives and Distorts American Politics* (New York: Cambridge University Press, 2013).

2. Jennifer Mittelstadt, *The Rise of the Military Welfare State* (Cambridge, MA: Harvard University Press, 2015).

3. Veterans' legislation being that which the Library of Congress classifies as "Veterans Issues" in legislation tracking data.

4. Patrick Hagopian, *The Vietnam War in American Memory: Veterans, Memorials, and the Politics of Healing (Culture, Politics, and the Cold War)* (Amherst: University of Massachusetts Press, 2009); Wilber J. Scott and John Sibley Butler, *Vietnam Veterans since the War: The Politics of PTSD, Agent Orange, and the National Memorial* (Norman: University of Oklahoma Press, 2004).

5. Gregory B. Lewis, "The Impact of Veterans' Preference on the Composition and Quality of the Federal Civil Service," *Journal of Public Administration Research and Theory* 23 (2013): 247–265.

6. Matt A. Barreto and David L. Leal, "Latinos, Military Service, and Support for Bush and Kerry in 2004," *American Politics Research* 35, no. 2 (2007): 224–251.

7. Jeremy M. Teigen, "Veterans' Party Identification, Candidate Affect, and Vote Choice in the 2004 US Presidential Election," *Armed Forces & Society* 33, no. 3 (2007): 414–437.

8. Nicky Pike, "Stop Using Veterans as Political Pawns," *Havok Journal*, September 26, 2017.

Chapter 1

1. D. L. Leal, "American Public Opinion toward the Military: Differences by Race, Gender, and Class?" *Armed Forces & Society* 32, no. 1 (2005): 123–138.

2. University of Missouri–St. Louis, Eastern Kentucky University, Georgetown Law, SUNY Empire State College, Missoula College of the University of Montana, and the University of Utah.

3. For the pre-1900 expansion of Veterans Assistance, see P. Kelly, *Creating a National Home: Building the Veterans' Welfare State, 1860–1900* (Cambridge, MA: Harvard University Press, 1997).

4. There are many in-depth histories of different elements of U.S. veterans programs. For readers interested in social welfare development of veterans' policy, see A. Campbell, "The Invisible Welfare State: Establishing the Phenomenon of Twentieth Century Veteran's Benefits," *Journal of Political & Military Sociology* 32, no. 2 (2004): 249.

5. U.S. Department of Veterans Affairs. "National Cemetery Administration Fact Sheets," 2017, https://www.cem.va.gov/about/factsheets.asp; M.-W. Sohn, N. Arnold, C. Maynard, and D. M. Hynes, "Accuracy and Completeness of Mortality Data in the Department of Veterans Affairs," *Population Health Metrics* 4, no. 2 (2006): 1–8; National Cemetery Administration, Department of Veterans Affairs, "A Promise Made—A Commitment Kept," Washington, DC, 2000.

6. J. Resch, *Suffering Soldiers: Revolutionary War Veterans, Moral Sentiment, and Political Culture in the Early Republic* (Amherst: University of Massachusetts Press, 2000).

7. L. de Witt Bockstruck, *Revolutionary War Pensions, Awarded by State Governments 1775–1874, the General and Federal Governments prior to 1814, and by Private Acts of Congress to 1905* (Baltimore, MD: Genealogical Publishing Company, 2011).

8. Throughout this book I use the term "veteran" to refer to all service members who are no longer serving active duty regardless of their deployment status, injury status, or branch. This is a simplification, and while the intricacies of combat versus noncombat veteran are important to consider, they are beyond the scope of what I attempt here.

9. J. H. Franklin, "Public Welfare in the South during the Reconstruction Era, 1865–80," *Social Service Review* 44, no. 4 (1970): 379–392.

10. Black veterans were nominally allowed into the system, but within facilities sleeping quarters, meal places, recreation, and medical areas adhered to discriminatory norms of the time of separating races. While 10 percent of the veteran population after the Civil War was black, less than 2 percent of the population in veterans' asylums was black (National Parks Service, History of the National Home for Disabled Volunteer Soldiers, U.S. Department of the Interior, n.d.).

11. R. E. Adkins, "Medical Care of Veterans," *The Veterans Administration*, 1967.

12. C. Edwards, "When the Economy Grows, Lawmakers Should Cut Spending or At Least Hold It Flat," *National Review*, September 4, 2013.

13. R. Holcombe, "Veterans Interests and the Transition to Government Growth: 1870–1915," *Public Choice* 99, no. 3–4 (1999): 311–326.

14. M. B. Wallerstein, "Terminating Entitlements: Veterans' Disability Benefits in the Depression," *Policy Science* 7, no. 2 (1976): 173–182.

15. R. Weigley, *History of the United States Army* (New York: Macmillan, 1967).

16. R. A. Stevens, "The Invention, Stumbling, and Reinvention of the Modern U.S. Veterans Health Care System, 1918–1924," in *Veterans' Policies, Veterans' Politics*, ed. S. R. Ortiz (Gainesville: University Press of Florida, 2012)..

17. S. H. Adams, "The Miracle of Reeducation," *Red Cross Magazine* 14, no. 5 (1919, May): 44.

18. Also known as the Soldier's Rehabilitation Act or the Sears-Smith Vocational Rehabilitation Act.

19. N. B. Young, "Do Something for the Soldier Boys," in *Veterans' Policies, Veterans' Politics*, ed. S. Ortiz (Gainesville: University Press of Florida, 2012), 199–221.

20. This bill is also known as the Servicemen's Readjustment Act of 1944 or the GI Bill of Rights.

21. M. Hindley, "How the GI Bill Became Law in spite of Some Veterans' Groups," *Humanities* 35, no. 4 (2014). https://www.neh.gov/humanities/2014/julyaugust/feature/how-the-gi-bill-became-law-in-spite-some-veterans-groups.

22. U.S. Department of Veterans Affairs, "Education and Training: History and Timeline," November 21, 2013.

23. W. E. Longo, W. Cheadle, A. Fink, R. Kozol, R. DePalma, R. Rege, et al., "The Role of the Veterans Affairs Medical Centers in Patient Care, Surgical Education, Research and Faculty Development," *American Journal of Surgery* 190, no. 5 (2005): 662–675.

24. Nobelprize.org., "Rosalyn Yalow—Biographical," *Nobel Media*, 2014. Nobelprize.org., "Ferid Murad—Biographical," *Nobel Media AB*, 2014.

25. J. Lamoreaux, "The Organizational Structure for Medical Information Management in the Department of Veterans Affairs: An Overview of Major Health Care Databases," *Medical Care* 34, no. 3 (1996): MS31–MS44.

26. Associated Press, "Reagan Would Elevate V.A. to Cabinet Level," *New York Times*, November 11, 1987.

27. B. A. Franklin, "Senate Votes to Elevate VA to Cabinet Status," *New York Times*, July 13, 1988.

28. K. W. Kizer and R. A. Dudley, "Extreme Makeover: Transformation of the Veterans Health Care System," *Annual Review of Public Health* 3 (2009): 313–339.

29. J. Perlin, R. Kolodner, and R. Roswell, "The Veterans Health Administration: Quality, Value, Accountability and Information as Transforming Strategies for Patient Centered Care," *American Journal of Managed Care* Part 2 (2004): 828–836.

30. The Department of Veterans Affairs. "Department of Veterans Affairs—Budget in Brief," 2018 Congressional Submission, 2018.

31. For a detailed and more textured impression of Forbes, see Rosemary Stevens, *A Time of Scandal: Charles R. Forbes, Warren G. Harding, and the Making of the Veterans Bureau* (Baltimore, MD: Johns Hopkins University Press, 2016).

32. In the near 100-year existence of the executive body dedicated to serving veterans, no woman has lead.

33. https://www.vacareers.va.gov/assets/common/print/fs_department_of_veterans_affairs.pdf.

34. S. Julin, "National Home for Disabled Volunteer Soldiers Assessment of Significance and National Historic Landmark Recommendations," National Park Service, 2004.

35. For a detailed historical look at the distribution of the scattered network of Veterans Homes System near the turn of the century, see J. A. Kinder, "Architecture of Injury: Disabled Veterans, Federal Policy, and the Built Environment in the Early Twentieth Century," in *Veterans' Policies, Veterans' Politics*, ed. S. Ortiz (Gainesville: University Press of Florida, 2012), 65–93.

36. G. Bushnell, "Letter to Governor Soldiers' Home, 5 April 1909, RG112, Entry 386, Box 25."

37. R. Stevens, *In Sickness and in Wealth: American Hospitals in the Twentieth Century*, Vol. 2 (Baltimore, MD: Johns Hopkins University Press, 1999).

38. The U.S. Congress, House, Hearings on HR 13026 65th Congress 3rd Session, Assistant PHS Surgeon General, Dr. W. D. Stimpson, Committee on Public Buildings and Grounds.

39. Testimony of Charles M. Griffith, Medical Director, "Hearings," *Veterans' Administration House* 15 (1945): 1607–1608.

40. L. T. Peterson, "Medical History of World War II: Surgery-Amputations-ZI," box 454, RG 112, 1945.

41. The American Legion, "Resolution: Prosthetics Appliances—Artificial Limbs," 24th Annual National Convention, 1942; D. Pearson, "The Washington Merry-Go-Round," *Washington Post*, February 10, 1945, 5; D. D. Bromley, "Army Amputees' Lives Not Bright as Pictured," *Washington Post*, June 17, 1945, B2; E. M. Maisel, "Should Veterans Have Legs?" *Nation*, March 10, 1945, 271–272.

42. A. Jennings, "An Emblem of Distinction: The Politics of Disability Entitlement, 1940–1950," in *Veterans' Policies, Veterans' Politics*, ed. S. Ortiz (Gainesville: University Press of Florida, 2012), 94–118.

43. A. Oliver, "The Veterans Health Administration: An American Success Story?" *Milbank Quarterly* 85, no. 1 (2007): 5–35.

44. S. V. Panangala, "Health Care for Veterans: Answers to Frequently Asked Questions," *Congressional Research Service*, 2016.

45. https://www.va.gov/health/topics/index.asp.

46. For a full listing of VHA in home services, see the VHA website links originating here: https://www.va.gov/HEALTHBENEFITS/access/home_health_care.asp.

47. While some VA programs have limited health provisions for dependents, the primary function of the VHA is to serve veterans themselves. In this chapter, I focus only on care provided to veterans. Care provided through the TRICARE health program is the primary way that families and survivors of active duty and retired members utilize government-funded health provisions.

48. S. D. Durbin, "Expanding the VA Caregivers Program," Official E-Newsletter, Durbin Report, March 15, 2015.

49. U.S. Department of Veteran Affairs, "VA Programs for Homeless Veterans," 2016. https://www.va.gov/HOMELESS/for_homeless_veterans.asp.

50. R. D. Edwards, "U.S. War Costs: Two Parts Temporary, One Part Permanent," *Journal of Public Economics* 113 (2014): 54–66.

51. S. D. Levitt and J. M. Snyder, "Political Parties and the Distribution of Federal Outlays," *American Journal of Political Science* 39, no. 4 (1995): 958–980; W. R. Keech and K. Pak, "Electoral Cycles and Budgetary Growth in Veterans' Benefit Programs," *American Journal of Political Science* 33, no. 4 (1989): 901–911.

52. S. Gelber, "A 'Hard-Boiled Order': The Reeducation of Disabled WWI Veterans in New York City," *Journal of Social History* 39, no. 1 (2005): 161–180.

53. J. Holm, *Women in the Military: An Unfinished Revolution* (Novato, CA: Presidio Press, 1982).

54. Department of Veteran Affairs, *Women Veterans: Past, Present and Future Revised and Updated*, Office of Policy and Planning, 2007.

55. I. Katznelson, *When Affirmative Action Was White : An Untold History of Racial Inequality in Twentieth-Century America* (New York: W.W. Norton, 2006).

56. D. Titus, "Titus Blasts VA for Discrimination against LGBT Veterans." U.S. House of Representatives: Floor Statement, April 30, 2014.

57. U.S. Department of Veterans Affairs, "Incarcerated Veterans," October 22, 2013.

58. This determination holds for Reservists or National Guards people who were recalled to active duty by a federal order (Title 10) and completed the full period for which they were ordered, but not for those Reservists or National Guards people who trained but were never called up.

Chapter 2

1. 1960–2010 U.S. Census Data. Retrieved using factfinder2.census.gov.

2. D. N. Zillman, "Essay: Where Have All the Soldiers Gone II: Military Veterans in Congress and the State of Civil-Military Relations," *Maine Law Review* 58, no. 1 (2006): 135–157.

3. C. Gelpi and P. Feaver, "Speak Softly and Carry a Big Stick? Veterans in the Political Elite and the American Use of Force," *American Political Science Review* 96, no. 4 (2002): 779–793; P. D. Feaver, *Armed Servants: Agency, Oversight, and Civil-Military Relations* (Cambridge, MA: Harvard University Press, 2003). There is also evidence and that veteran preferences may either be caused by or exacerbated by the experience of serving. M. K. Jenning and G. B. Markus, "The

Effect of Military Service on Political Attitudes: A Panel Study," *American Political Science Review* 71, no. 1 (1977): 131–147.

4. 2010 U.S. Census Reports accessible at https://www.census.gov/topics/population/veterans.html.

5. One theorized reason is that the GI Bill provides veterans with the incentives and know-how to better participate in politics. For an analysis on the phenomena see Mettler (2002).

6. C. Clawson, "A Message from the Office of Congressman Curt Clawson," December 19, 2005. The Office of Representative Curt Clawson maintained by DCinbox. In terms of veteran population, Florida-19 consistently has about the 50th highest number of veterans of all 435 congressional districts.

7. J. Serrano, "The Serrano Report—April 26, 2016," April 26, 2016. The Office of Representative Jose Serrano maintained by DCinbox.

8. The territory of the Northern Mariana Islands has the lowest share of veterans (1.2%) for any unit with a representative in Congress.

9. N. J. Ornstein, T. E. Mann, M. J. Malbin, A. Rugg, and R. Wakeman, *Vital Statistics on Congress* (Washington, DC: Brookings Institution, 2014).

10. While the greater analyses of this book indicate that Republicans in Congress talk more about veterans (lip service) and Democrats in Congress do more for veterans (legwork), the partisan makeup of veterans in Congress looks quite the opposite.

11. This relationship holds when controlling for chamber of service as well as party.

12. N. A. Masters, "Committee Assignments in the House of Representatives," *American Political Science Review* 55, no. 2 (1961): 345–357; S. Meinke, *Leadership Organizations in the House of Representatives: Party Participation and Partisan Politics* (Ann Arbor: University of Michigan Press, 2016).

13. Office of the Deputy Assistant Secretary of Defense, "2014 Demographics Profile of the Miliary Community," Department of Defense, 2015.

14. Department of Veterans Affairs, "Fact Sheet: Women Veterans Population," Department of Veterans Affairs, 2016.

15. J. Goldstein, *War and Gender: How Gender Shapes the War System and Vice Versa* (Cambridge: Cambridge University Press, 2001); Department of Defense, "Active Duty Military Personnel by Rank/Grade," 2008.

16. B. Grofman and L. Handley, "Minority Population Proportion and Black and Hispanic Congressional Success in the 1970s and 1980s," *American Politics Research* 17, no. 4 (1989): 436–445.

17. The results are robust to different permutations, eliminations, and additions of demographic controls.

18. Federal Election Commission, "FEDERAL ELECTIONS 2008 Election Results for the U.S. President, the U.S. Senate and the U.S. House of Representatives," Federal Election Commission, Public Disclosure Division, 2009.

19. For instance, we know that the percentage of white voters within a district is related to the likelihood that a white candidate is eventually elected and vice versa with black constituencies and black candidates: K. Hill, "Does the

Creation of Majority Black Districts Aid Republicans? An Analysis of the 1992 Congressional Elections in Eight Southern States," *Journal of Politics* 57, no. 2 (1995): 384–401, as well as greater relationships between the racial composition of a district and congresional liberalism: B. Grofman, R. Griffin, and A. Glazer, "The Effect of Black Population on Electing Democrats and Liberals to the House of Representatives," *Legislative Studies Quarterly* 17, no. 3 (1992): 365–379; C. Sharpe and J. Garand, "Race, Roll Calls, and Redistricting: The Impact of Race-Based Redistricting on Congressional Roll-Call," *Political Research Quarterly* 45, no. 1 (2016): 31–51. And that unemployment rates can have dramatic, if sometimes unpredictable, effects on social political environments: H. Kerbo and R. Shaffer, "Lower Class Insurgency and the Political Process: The Response of the U.S. Unemployed, 1890–1940," *Social Problems* 39, no. 2 (1992): 139–154. We also have research indicating that education levels are related to electoral choice, with those with lower levels prefering Republican candidates: B. Gupta, "People, Parties and Power," *Economic and Political Weekly* 26, no. 15 (1991): 937–939.

20. In the coming chapters I examine the individual preferences of veterans and I report a multitude of measures that indicate that veterans tend to have preferences for Republicans in government. Yet in this chapter, the question is not about the individual preferences of veterans but about the empirical realities relating the share of veterans within a constituency to the legislators of those constituencies.

21. E. Dooley, "Meet the US Military's Three Four-Star Women," ABC News, July 2, 2014.

22. Though this was a nonscientific survey, 61 percent of those polled were either dissatisfied or strongly dissatisfied with the idea of Donald Trump as commander in chief. Marine Corps Times, "Trump or Clinton: For the Military, It's Hardly a Vote of Confidence," *Military Times*, July 23, 2016.

23. I do not present the full results here in the interest of space.

24. The raw data are maintained, categorized, and accessed at Congress.gov.

25. DCinbox is a database started in 2009 that captures every e-newsletter every member of Congress sends to constituents. This database is maintained by the author and a team of research assistants at Stevens Institute of Technology.

26. Not every legislator is in the communications database, as a few still choose not to send official e-newsletter. Of legislators in the database, 16.9 percent are veterans and of the share of veteran-referencing e-newsletters sent from veterans in Congress is 17.4 percent.

27. In subsequent chapters I describe in detail why the introduction of legislation is a better measure than the success rate of legislation as an assessment of effort.

28. N. Himmel, "#VeteranOfTheDay Army Veteran Stephen Earle Buyer," *Vantage Point*, Official Blog of the U.S. Department of Veterans Affairs, November 15, 2016.

29. For a detailed explanation of these sorts of controversies, see Raymond Hernandez, "Candidate's Words on Vietnam Service Differ from History," *New York Times*, May 17, 2010.

30. The distinction between a veteran and a combat veteran as well as an assessment about the attendant social and political grievances are beyond the scope of this book, but that is not to say there are not real nomenclature concerns in this area. The complication of veteran versus combat veteran is taken seriously in some circles, and the issue is a delicate one in crafting eligibility requirements for various policies. For the most part, legislation does not make criteria distinctions based on if someone has seen combat or not. But there are questions around the provision of health care that must consider whether a veteran was injured in combat to determine fee and pay structures. For the purposes of this book, I refer simply to veterans and do not make finer delineations. This is both a matter of practicality and simplicity. Census data and legislator biography data do not make such distinction, neither do I.

31. "Home Style" is a term coined by Richard Fenno in 1978 to describe the particular ways in which legislators relate to their constituents. Some focus on policies, others on district spending, and others on showing connectedness to the district, as well as different variations. R. Fenno, *Home Style: House Members in Their Districts* (Boston, MA: Addison-Wesley Educational, 1978).

32. Office of Representative Mike Coffman, On Education: Parents and Locally Elected School Boards Know Best, Official Constituent Communication, February 28, 2015.

33. S. Hess, "America's Top Dynasty?" *Washington Post*, September 13, 2009.

34. S. Lynn and C. Neihoff, "Field Report 2014: Veterans En Route to the 114th Congress," *Veterans Campaign*, 2014.

35. Veteran counts are maintained via the U.S. Census.

36. G. C. Jacobson, "Strategic Politicians and the Dynamics of U.S. House Elections, 1946–86," *American Political Science Review* 83, no. 3 (1989): 773–793.

37. Zillman, "Essay: Where Have All the Soldiers Gone II," 135–157.

38. S. Watkins and J. Sherk, "Who Serves in the U.S. Military? The Demographics of Enlisted Troops and Officers," The Heritage Foundation: Defense Report, August 21, 2008.

39. Zillman, "Essay: Where Have All the Soldiers Gone II," 135–157.

40. Office of Senator Daniel Inouye, Hauoli Makahiki Hou, Official Constitutent Communication, January 3, 2012.

41. R. Lugar and T. Daschle, "Congress Needs More Veterans: Veterans Can Help Break the Partisan Gridlock Hindering National Security Policy," *U.S. News and World Report*, November 10, 2017.

42. Pew Research Center, "Beyond Distrust: How Americans View Their Government," *U.S. Public and Policy*, November 23, 2015.

43. Pew Research Center, National Election Studies, Gallup, ABC/Washington Post, CBS/New York Times, and CNN Polls, "Beyond Distrust: How Americans View Their Government," Pew Research Center, November 23, 2015.

44. J. Norman, "Americans' Confidence in Institutions Stays Low," *Gallup News*, November 13, 2016.

45. Lynn, Seth. Analysis: Iraq & Afghanistan Veterans Have Begun Reversing the Decades-Long Decline in Congressional Military Service, 2016.

46. For mission and updated membership, see https://www.vfw.org/about-us.

47. Veterans of Foreign Wars, "VFW to Obama: 'No Confused Politics Here,'" Press Release, June 3, 2016.

48. For a full list see Veterans of Foreign Wars, "VFW Legislative Victories Fact Sheet," www.vfw.org, 2017.

49. J. Berry, "VOW (Veterans Opportunity to Work) to Hire Heroes Act of 2011," U.S. Office of Personnel Management, June 15, 2012.

50. U.S. Department of Veteran Affairs, "Veterans Access, Choice and Accountability Act of 2014 ('Choice Act')," Fact Sheet, October 17, 2014.

51. The American Legion, "The Four Pillars of the American Legion," 2010, https://www.legion.org/documents/legion/pdf/four_pillars.pdf.

52. The American Legion, "History of the American Legion," 2017, https://www.legion.org/history.

53. Some research has noted this curious tendency where the American Legion, commonly understood to be a conservative leaning group, assigns higher scores to Democrats than to Republicans, even controlling for other factors that may influence support for veterans' policies in the first place (Schiller 2008).

54. Disabled American Veterans, "Annual Report 2016," 2016.

55. American Veterans, "About Us," AMVETS, 2017.

56. A. Webb, "2016–2017 National Legislative Agenda," American Veterans (AMVETS), 2017.

57. Veterans Campaign, "About Us," 2016.

58. I do not profile all political veterans' groups. Here is a more comprehensive list of those not included: Air Force Association, Air Force Sergeants Association, Association of the United States Navy, Blue Star Families, Got Your Six, High Ground Veterans Advocacy, Military Child Education Coalition, Military Officers Association of America, Military Order of the Purple Heart, National Guard Association of the United States, National Military Family Association, Naval Enlisted Reserve Association, Non Commissioned Officers Association, Paralyzed Veterans of America, The Retired Enlisted Association, Student Veterans of America, Swords to Plowshares, Tragedy Assistance Program for Survivors, Veterans for Common Sense, VetJobs, VetsFirst, and Wounded Warrior Project.

Chapter 3

1. John Sides, "The Origins of Campaign Agendas," *British Journal of Political Science* 36, no. 3 (2006): 407–436; John R. Petrocik, "Issue Ownership in Presidential Elections, with a 1980 Case Study," *American Journal of Political Science* 40, no. 3 (1996): 825–850.

2. Pew Research Center, *Social and Demogrpahic Trends Survey: The Military-Civilian Gap—War and Sacrifice in the Post-9/11 Era* (Archived at the Roper Center, 2011).

3. Nicholas Fandos, "A Bipartisan Congress That Works? Veterans Committees Show How It's Done," *New York Times*, July 10, 2017.

4. WIlliam H. RePass, "Issue Salience and Party Choice," *American Political Science Review* 65, no. 2 (1971): 389–400.

5. Andrew J. Bacevich and Richard H. Kohn, "Grand Army of the Republicans: Has the U.S. Military Become a Partisan Force?" *New Republic*, December 8, 1997, 22–25.

6. Thomas E. Ricks, "The Widening Gap between the Military and Society," *Atlantic Monthly*, July 1997, 66–78; Ole R. Holsti, "A Widening Gap between the U.S. Military and Civilian Society? Some Evidence, 1976–1996," *International Security* 23, no. 3 (1998): 5–42.

7. Peter D. Feaver and Kohn H. Richard, "Digest of Findings and Studies: Project on the Gap between the Military and Civilian Society," Triangle Institute for Security Studies, October 2, 1999, 28–29.

8. Adam Clymer, "Sharp Divergence Is Found in Views of Military and Civilians," *New York Times*, September 1999.

9. Lydia Saad, "Americans Respect the Military, Honor Veterans," *Gallup News*, November 11, 2002.

10. MSNBC, "Bush Calls for a Halt to Swift Boat Veterans' Ads," August 23, 2004.

11. G. Mitchell Reyes, "The Swift Boat Veterans for Truth, the Politics of Realism, and the Manipulation of Vietnam Remembrance in the 2004 Presidential Election," *Rhetoric & Public Affairs* 9, no. 4 (2006): 571–600.

12. Jeffrey M. Jones, "Veterans Solidly Back McCain," *Gallup News*, August 19, 2008.

13. CNN, "McCain Defends Opposition to GI Bill," May 26, 2008.

14. Paul Rosenberg, "Right-Wing 'Superpatriots' Ignore Veterans: The Real VA Scandal No One Will Talk About," *Salon*, June 2, 2014.

15. Michael T. Mcphearson, "Why Do Veterans Support Donald Trump?" Moyers and Company, June 28, 2016.

16. Many explanations can be offered for why the focus of surveys rarely takes up veterans' issues. When veterans' issues are salient, there are incentives to poll about those issues. But for many time periods in our history, veterans' issues are not the focus of general public discourse.

17. These questions usually list a number of government assistance programs and then only offer *yes* or *no* as responses. There is no way to have a finer-grain look at which program the respondents use to try to determine their veteran status. An example of this style, "Please tell me the primary way you paid for . . . in-home care on a regular basis from an aide who helps with such things as bathing, dressing, taking medications, and the like for your close friend or family member. . . . Medicare, Medicaid or MediCal, the government program that provides health insurance for low-income families, Medigap or Medicare Supplement, that is private insurance that supplements Medicare coverage, private health or other insurance, Social Security, your own savings or assets, your

children, relatives beside your children, pension, 401K, or other income, long-term care insurance, some other government source, such as the Veteran's Department of Defense or CHAMPUS (Civilian Health and Medical Program of the Uniformed Services)" AARP, Long Term Care Cost Survey, 2006 (Gfk NOP Roper Public Affairs & Media).

18. Some media outlets such as *Military Times* will poll their readers, most of whom are active-duty or veteran service members, but these polls do not adhere to the scientific practices set out by AAPOR. I do not include them here.

19. The Veterans Administration, *Attitudes toward Vietnam Era Veterans Survey*, Survey (Cornell University, Ithaca, NY: Roper Center for Public Opinion Research, iPOLL, 1979).

20. Bad Robot/Greenberg Quinlan Rosner Research, *Public Opinion Strategies* (Archived at the Roper Center, 2013).

21. Christopher Gelpi and Peter Feaver, "Speak Softly and Carry a Big Stick? Veterans in the Political Elite and the American Use of Force," *American Political Science Review* 96, no. 4 (2002): 779–793.

22. Gallup Organization, *Gallup Poll (AIPO)* (Cornell University, Ithaca, NY: Roper Center for Public Opinion Research, iPOLL, 1946).

23. Pew Research Center, *Pew Social and Demographic Trends Poll: Veterans Survey*, conducted by Social Science Research Solutions (Pew Research Center, 2011).

24. Princeton Survey Research Associates International (2011).

25. Washington Post-Kaiser Family Foundation, "Survey of Iraq and Afghanistan Active Duty Soldiers and Veterans," *Washington Post*, 2013; *Washington Post/ABC News Poll*, "News Poll of U.S. Adults," 2013.

26. Surgeon-General's Office, *Abstracts, Translations and Reviews of Recent Literature on the Subject of the Reconstruction and Reeducation of the Disabled Soldier*, Vol. 4 (Washington, DC, United States, 1918).

27. Nancy Fraiser and Linda Gordon, "A Genealogy of Dependency: Tracing a Keyword of the U.S. Welfare State," *Signs* 19, no. 2 (1994): 309–336.

28. In fact, it is probably more likely that survey makers posed the negative behavior questions so that if they did find differences between how the public thought of veterans and nonveterans, there would be an upside to selling military service as a way to produce upstanding citizens.

29. Of these questions, there were of course people who believed neither group had a stronger claim on the characteristics. Across all the repeated questions, the average response of neither across all the identical questions was 58.8 percent in 1979 and 58.9 percent in 2012.

30. In 1979 people saying veterans had more problems with drug use were 30 percent compared to 7 percent for civilians, suicide was 29 percent to 6 percent, and problems with liquor were 19 percent to 6 percent.

31. In 2012 people saying veterans were disciplined and willing to work to get ahead were 45 percent compared to 4 percent for civilians, suicide was 40 percent, saying they thought veterans were more apt than civilians to attempt (the

wording was slightly different in this question), and having a strong moral character was ascribed to veterans 38 percent of the time and only 4 percent of the time to civilians. The questions on suicide and moral character were not asked in identical formats and make the comparisons a bit more complicated.

32. R. C. Kessler, P. Berglund, O. Demler, R. Jin, K. R. Merikangas, and E. E. Walters, "Lifetime Prevalence and Age-of-Onset Distributions of DSM-IV Disorders in the National Comorbidity Survey Replication," *Archives of General Psychiatry* 62 (2005): 593–602.

33. Karen H. Seal, Greg Cohen, Angela Waldrop, Beth E. Cohen, Shira Maguen, and Li Ren, "Substance Use Disorders in Iraq and Afghanistan Veterans in VA Healthcare, 2001–2010: Implications for Screening, Diagnosis and Treatment," *Drug & Alcohol Dependence* 16, no. 1–3 (2011): 93–101.

34. Pew Research Center for the People & the Press, "Public Praises Science; Scientists Fault Public, Media," 2009.

35. Disabled American Veterans, *Veteran's Health Care Funding Survey*, USBELDEN.08VETHLTH.R11, Belden Russonello & Stewart (Cornell University, Ithaca, NY: Roper Center for Public Opinion Research, iPOLL, August 2008).

36. Andrew Kohut, Carroll Doherty, Michael Dimock, and Scott Keeter, "The People and Their Government DISTRUST, DISCONTENT, ANGER AND PARTISAN RANCOR," Pew Research Center for the People & the Press, April 2010, 2–42.

37. The Veterans Administration, *Attitudes toward Vietnam Era Veterans Survey*.

38. As later chapters show, this 2010 dip is somewhat curious because by measures of legislative efforts, the Congress passed the post–9/11 GI Bill around this time as well as other smaller pieces of legislation to increase benefits to veterans. That is, at the very time the Congress voted for a widely popular, bipartisan bill to help veterans go to college, the U.S. public simultaneously thought political actors were letting veterans down.

39. Chapter 8 presents public opinion data on the Phoenix area VA hospital scandal.

40. Part of the lower levels of assessment could be connected to the 2007 Walter Reed Army Medical Center scandal, in which the *Washington Post* reported that returning veterans were subjected to subpar living and treatment standards. But the timing of the public opinion polls does not permit a clear conclusion that revelations from 2007 would later reduce assessments of effectivess of the VA—which was not in charge of Walter Reed.

41. Gallup Organization, "Gallup Poll," USGALLUP.07MCH026.R12N, 2007.

42. Lyndsey Layton and Jonathan Weisman, "Veterans Group Speaks Out on War," *Washington Post*, February 8, 2007.

43. Pew Research Center, "Chapter 5: The Public and the Military," War and Sacrifice in the Post 9/11 Era, 2001.

44. Moni Basu, "Survey: Veterans Say Afghanistan, Iraq Wars Not Worth It," CNN, October 5, 2011.

45. Scott Clement, "War Vets Miss Commander in Chief George W. Bush," *Washington Post*, April 2, 2014.

46. Paralyzed Veterans of America, *Disabled American Veterans, Healthcare and Veterans Survey, USPSRA.04HLVET.R3* (Princeton, NJ: Princeton Survey Research Associates International, 2004); Disabled American Veterans, *Veteran's Health Care Funding Survey, USBELDEN.08VETHLTH.R03* (Cornell University, Ithaca, NY: Roper Center for Public Opinion Research, iPOLL [distributor], 2008).

47. Phillip Longman, *Best Care Anywhere: Why VA Health Care Is Better Than Yours* (Oakland, CA: Berrett-Koehler Publishers, 2012).

48. Suzanne Gordon, *The Battle for Veterans' Healthcare: Dispatches from the Frontlines of Policy Making and Patient Care* (Ithaca, NY: Cornell Publishing, 2017).

49. Gallup Organization, "Gallup Daily Tracking Survey Sample: Veterans," USGALLUP.070114.R03, 2014.

50. For a detailed meta review of veterans' surveys, see Teryn Mattox and Machael Pollard, "Ongoing Survey Research on Post-9/11 Veterans," RAND Corporation, 2016.

51. It is important to note that when saying the opinions of veterans, this flattens all sorts of people into a label that is lumpy at best. Veterans hold a variety of opinions just as civilian individuals do, and even though veterans share a history of service, those who service in different eras and theaters of war sometimes are found to have systematically different opinions.

52. However, comparing veterans to their similar civilian counterparts in 2004 did not show great differences between the two populations. Jeremy M. Teigen, "Veterans' Party Identification, Candidate Affect, and Vote Choice in the 2004 U.S. Presidential Election," *Armed Forces & Society* 33, no. 3 (2007): 414–437.

53. Of the extant work that specifically considers individual issues and self-identification of veterans, researchers find that veterans are more ideologically conservative and more likely to identify as Republican than nonvets. Jonathan D. Klingler and J. Tyson Chatagnier, "Are You Doing Your Part? Veterans' Political Attitudes and Heinlein's Conception of Citizenship," *Armed Forces & Society* 40, no. 4 (2014): 673–695. This finding is robust to controlling for a host of factors and has been replicated by various scholars and is consistent from 2006 onward.

54. Jeffrey M. Jones, "Veterans Solidly Back McCain," *Gallup News*, August 19, 2008.

55. Frank Newport, "Veterans Give Romney Big Lead over Obama," *Gallup News*, May 28, 2012.

56. Scott Clement, "Veterans Are Voting Republican. And That's Not Likley to Change," *Washington Post*, November 11, 2014.

57. Peter D. Feaver and Kohn H. Richard, "Digest of Findings and Studies: Project on the Gap between the Military and Civilian Society," Triangle Institute for Security Studies, October 2, 1999, 28-29; Donald N. Zillman, "Essay: Where Have All the Soldiers Gone II: Military Veterans in Congress and the State of Civil-Military Relations," *Maine Law Review* 58, no. 1 (2006): 135–157;

Christopher Gelpi and Peter Feaver, "Speak Softly and Carry a Big Stick? Veterans in the Political Elite and the American Use of Force," *American Political Science Review* 96, no. 4 (2002): 779–793; Richard D. Hooker, "Soldiers of the State: Reconsidering American Civil-Military Relations," *Parameters* 33, no. 4 (2003): 4–18.

58. Tim Hsia, "The Role of the Military and Veterans in Politics," *New York Times*, February 1, 2013.

59. U.S. Census, "Statistical Abstract of the United States: 2012," 2012.

60. Jeffrey M. Jones, "U.S. Seniors Have Realigned with the Republican Party," *Gallup*, March 26, 2014.

61. David L. Teigan and Jeremy M. Leal, "Recent Veterans Are More Republican Than Older Ones. Why?" *Washington Post, Monkey Cage*, November 11, 2015.

62. John H. Faris, "The All-Volunteer Force: Recruiting from Military Families," *Armed Forces and Society* 7, no. 4 (1981): 550–554.

63. Peter D. Feaver and Kohn H. Richard, "Digest of Findings and Studies: Project on the Gap between the Military and Civilian Society," Triangle Institute for Security Studies, October 2, 1999, 28–29.

64. Mariann Mankowski, Leslie E. Tower, Cynthia A. Brandt, and Kristin Mattocks, "Why Women Join the Military: Enlistment Decisions and Postdeployment Experiences of Service Members and Veterans," *Social Work* 60, no. 4 (2015): 315–323.

65. Elizabeth G. French and Raymond R. Ernest, "The Relation between Authoritarianism and Acceptance of Military Ideology," *Journal of Personality* 24, no. 2 (1955): 181–191.

66. Marc J. Hetherington and Jonathan D. Weiler, *Authoritarianism and Polarization in American Politics*, 1st edition (Cambridge: Cambridge University Press, 2009).

67. Jeremy M. Teigen, "Enduring Effects of the Uniform: Previous Military Experience and Voting Turnout," *Political Research Quarterly* 59, no. 4 (2006): 601–607.

68. E. M. Schreiber, "Enduring Effects of Military Service? Opinion Differences between U.S. Veterans and Nonveterans," *Social Forces* 57, no. 3 (1979): 824–839.

69. John R. Petrocik, "Issue Ownership in Presidential Elections, with a 1980 Case Study," *American Journal of Political Science* 40, no. 3 (1996): 825–850.

70. Patrick J. Egan, *Partisan Priorities: How Issue Ownership Drives and Distorts American Politics* (New York: Cambridge University Press, 2013).

Chapter 4

1. The main subject category is "Armed Forces and National Security" and the subcategories included in the count are veterans' medical care; veterans' education, employment, rehabilitation; veterans' loans, housing, homeless programs; veterans' organizations and recognition; and veterans' pensions and

compensation. In some Congresses, bills or resolutions will be authored that conceivably fall under the topics listed but are never formally introduced. If a bill or resolution is not formally submitted, it cannot be passed. Therefore, I only consider legislative attempts that meet the minimal formal procedures to effectuate legal changes for veterans.

2. There is no significant relationship between the average number of cosponsors and veteran references or between the legislative success rate of a legislator and the number of veteran references per year.

3. For contemporary takes on majority party privileges, see C. J. Flinocchiaro and D. W. Rohde, "War for the Floor: Partisan Theory and Agenda Control in the U.S. House of Representatives," *Legislative Studies Quarterly* 33, no. 1 (2008): 35–61 and S. S. Smith, I. Ostrander, and C. M. Pope, "Majority Party Power and Procedural Motions in the U.S. Senate," *Legislative Studies Quarterly* 38, no. 2 (2013): 205–236.

4. Gary W. Cox and Mathew D. McCubbins, *Setting the Agenda: Responsible Party Government in the U.S. House of Representatives* (New York: Cambridge University Press, 2005); Sean Gailmard and Jeffery A. Jenkins, "Negative Agenda Control in the Senate and House: Fingerprints of Majority Party Power," *Journal of Politics* 69, no. 3 (2007): 689–700; Eric Schickler and Kathryn Pearson, "Agenda Control, Majority Party Power, and the House Committee on Rules, 1937–52," *Legislative Studies Quarterly* 34, no. 4 (2009): 455–491.

5. E. Scott Adler and John Wilkerson, "The Scope and Urgency of Legislation: Reconsidering Bill Success in the House of Representatives," Annual Meetings of the American Political Science Association, 2005; John Wilkerson, Nick Stramp, and David Smith, "Why Bill Success Is a Lousy Way to Keep Score in Congress," *Washington Post, Monkey Cage*, February 6, 2014. This is not to say I do not look at other measures of legislative effort, but it serves to encourage the reader to think more about introduction as the best measure of individual effort and final passage as a measure of individual effort plus many other influences largely outside the control of the person who initially expended effort on the legislative idea in the first place.

6. Craig Volden and Alan E. Wiseman, "Legislative Effectiveness in Congress," Annual Meeting of the Midwest Political Science Association, 2009; Michele L. Swers, *The Difference Women Make: The Policy Impact of Women in Congress* (Chicago, IL: University of Chicago Press, 2002); Sam Peltzman, "Constituent Interest and Congressional Voting," *Journal of Law & Economics* 27, no. 1 (1984): 181–210; James M. Snyder and Tim Groseclose, "Estimating Party Influence in Congressional Roll-Call Voting," *American Journal of Political Science* 44, no. 2 (2000): 193–211.

7. E. Scott Adler and John S. Lapinski, "Demand-Side Theory and Congressional Committee Composition: A Constituency Characteristics Approach," *American Journal of Political Science* 41, no. 3 (1997): 895–918.

8. Arturo Vega and Juanita M Firestone, "The Effects of Gender on Congressional Behavior and the Substantive Representation of Women," *Legislative*

Studies Quarterly 20, no. 2 (1995): 213–222; Jennifer Lawless, "Female Candidates and Legislators," *Annual Review of Political Science* 18 (2015): 349–366.

9. William Curtis Ellis and Walter Clark Wilson, "Minority Chairs and Congressional Attention to Minority Issues: The Effect of Descriptive Representation in Positions of Institutional Power," *Social Science Quarterly* 94, no. 5 (2013): 1207–1221.

10. To obtain the veteran status of each member of Congress, I used the *Congressional Quarterly*'s Congress Profile Almanac that maintains records of past military service for each member of Congress. In the database that spans October 2009 until the end of Obama's tenure in January 2017, there are 144 veterans who served in Congress, and as a percentage of all members who served during the eight years under study, this accounts for 17 percent of all legislators.

11. Cletus C. Coughlin, "Domestic Content Legislation: House Voting and the Economic Theory of Regulation," *Economic Inquiry* 23, no. 3 (1985): 437–448.

12. Kenneth A. Shepsle, "Can the Government Govern?" in *The Changing Textbook Congress*, ed. John Chubb and Paul Peterson (1989), 238–266; Gary W. Cox and Mathew D. McCubbins, *Legislative Leviathan: Party Government in the House* (New York; Berkeley: University of California Press, 1993); Gary W. Cox and Mathew D. McCubbins, *Setting the Agenda: Responsible Party Government in the U.S. House of Representatives* (Cambridge University Press, 2005).

13. John R. Petrocik, "Issue Ownership in Presidential Elections, with a 1980 Case Study," *American Journal of Political Science* 40 (1996): 825–250; John R. Petrocik, William L. Benoit, and Glenn Hansen, "Issue Ownership and Presidential Campaigning, 1952–2000," *Political Science Quarterly* 118, no. 4 (2003): 599–626; Patrick Egan, *Partisan Priorities: How Issue Ownership Drives and Distorts American Politics* (New York: Cambridge University Press, 2013).

14. For the party measure, the three independents who served during this time period, Joe Lieberman (CT), Angus King (ME), and Bernie Sanders (VT), are considered Democrats as the each caucused with the Democratic Party.

15. For an explanation of how members are incentivized to tout the benefits of, but not necessarily empowered to influence, the outcomes of such appropriation bills, see Justin Grimmer, "Appropriators Not Position Takers: The Distorting Effects of Electoral Incentives on Congressional Representation," *American Journal of Political Science* 57, no. 3 (2013): 624–642.

16. Gregory Koger, "Position Taking and Cosponsorship in the U.S. House," *Legislative Studies Quarterly* 28, no. 2 (2003): 225–246.

17. Some members have exceptionally high numbers of cosponsors and are worth noting if the ability to attract cosponsors is a measure of legislative legwork. There are five representatives who average over 150 cosponsors for their legislation. These members are Tim Bishop (D-NY-1) with 432, Carol Shea-Porter (D-NH-1) with 213, John Culberson (R-TX-7) with 201, Virginia Foxx (R-NC-5), and Gregory Meeks (D-NY-5). During the time of the data, each of the most cosponsored members offered between 1 and 10 pieces of legislation. Given that

there are fewer senators, the numbers of cosponsors possible are fewer. The senators with the highest averages are Chris Dodd (D-CT) with 68.5 and Harry Reid (D-NV) with 61. Three out of the top five most cosponsored members are Democrats in the House, and both are Democrats in the Senate.

18. In the 111th–114th Congresses, Republicans introduced 50 percent of all legislation on areas of finance and the environment, 49 percent of the legislation on international affairs, 48 percent on immigration and law, 47 percent on public lands and resources, 46 percent on animal welfare and Congress, and just 40 percent on veterans.

Chapter 5

1. In many interactions we must make decisions based on what we are told without a full understanding of the underlying reality of a situation. Consider getting to know a new person. If an individual tells you that he or she is very much into caring for animals, wears clothing embroidered with animals, and shows you pictures of their 12 dogs and cats, you may well believe that such an individual has a lot of compassion for animals. But until you have visited his or her home, see how he or she cares for animals, and can ensure that the dozens of cats and dogs are treated as pets rather than puppy and kitty mill wares for sale, the initial assessment of compassion may be misplaced.

2. Keith T. Poole and Howard Rosenthal, "A Spatial Model for Legislative Roll Call Analysis," *American Journal of Political Science* 29, no. 2 (1985): 357–384.

3. Keith T. Poole and Howard Rosenthal, *Congress: A Political-Economic History of Roll Call Voting* (Oxford: Oxford University Press, 1997).

4. Yphtach Lelkes and Paul M. Sniderman, "The Ideological Asymmetry of the American Party System," *British Journal of Political Science* 46, no. 4 (2016): 825–844.

5. William Jacoby, "Issue Framing and Public Opinion on Government Spending," *American Journal of Political Science* 44, no. (2000): 750–767.

6. See, for instance, how states that tend to vote for Republicans take more in federal funds than others. Yphtach Lelkes and Paul M. Sniderman, "Democrats' Policies Are More Popular. But Republicans Are More Ideologically Unified," *Washington Post*, December 16, 2016.

7. Additional limitations are that platforms are not widely read by most supporters, serve career-building functions of the authors, and do not fully capture what the entire ideological pictures contain.

8. From the 2016 Republican Platform: "The level of financial distress and homelessness among vets is a shame to the nation. For a veteran, a job is more than a source of income. It is a new mission, with a new status, and the transition can be difficult. We urge the private sector to make hiring vets a company policy and commend the organizations that have proven programs to accomplish this."

9. Vanessa Williamson, Theda Skocpol, and John Coggin, "The Tea Party and the Remaking of Republican Conservatism," *Perspectives on Politics* 9, no. 1 (2011): 25–43.

10. National Center for Veterans Analysis and Statistics, "VHA FY16 Annual Report," Veterans Health Administration, 2017.

11. Kenneth W. Kizer, John G. Demakis, and John R. Feussner, "Reinventing VA Health Care: Systematizing Quality Improvement and Quality Innovation," *Medical Care* 38, no. 6 (2000): 17–116.

12. P. S. Yaisawarng and J. F. Burgess Jr., "Performance-Based Budgeting in the Public Sector: An Illustration from the VA Health Care System," *Health Economics* 15, no. 3 (March 2006): 295–310.

13. For instance, diabetes care is more effectively administered and monitored in the VHA system than in others. E. A. Kerr et al., "Diabetes Care Quality in the Veterans Affairs Health Care System and Commercial Managed Care: The TRIAD Study," *Annals Internal Medicine* 141, no. 4 (August 17, 2004): 272–281. For a broader comparison of screen, diagnostic, and treatments there is also emerging evidence that the VA outperforms the private market counterparts. See S. M. Asch et al., "Comparison of Quality of Care for Patients in the Veterans Health Administration and Patients in a National Sample," *Annals Internal Medicine* 141, no. 12 (December 2004): 938–945.

14. S. Greenfield and S. H. Kaplan, "Creating a Culture of Quality: The Remarkable Transformation of the Department of Veterans Affairs Health Care System," *Annals of Internal Medicine* 141, no. 4 (2004): 316–318; C. M. Ashton et al., "Hospital Use and Survival among Veterans Affairs Beneficiaries," *New England Journal of Medicine* 349, no. 17 (2003): 1637–1646.

15. U.S. Department of Veterans Affairs, " Education and Training: Education Programs," 2015.

16. Data available by year and state at the VA web portal: https://www.va.gov/vetdata/Expenditures.asp or by e-mailing vancvas@va.gov.

17. U.S. Department of Veterans Affairs, "VA 2018 Budget Request: Fast Facts," 2018.

18. For more details see www.tsp.gov.

19. Defense Finance and Accounting Service, "DoD Savings Deposit Program," December 17, 2017.

20. For a detailed look at employment law regarding veterans, see U.S. Equal Employment Opportunity Commission, "Policy Guidance on Veterans' Preference under Title VII," 1990. There are also provisions within the U.S. federal governments' own hiring practices that give preferential treatment to veterans.

21. E. A. Kerr et al., "Diabetes Care Quality in the Veterans Affairs Health Care System and Commercial Managed Care: The TRIAD Study," *Annals Internal Medicine* 141, no. 4 (August 17, 2004): 272–281.

22. For historical examples of policy debates with Congress about veterans in terms of health care, disability services, race, labor reintroduction, bonuses, pensions, and educational help, see Stephen R. Ortiz, *Veterans' Policies, Veterans' Politics* (Gainesville: University of Florida Press, 2012).

23. *Merriam Webster*, "Lip Service," Merriam-Webster.com, 2017.

24. Alan S. Blinder and Mark W. Watson, "Presidents and the Economy: A Forensic Investigation," Unpublished, Princeton University Department of Economics Brown Bag Seminar, November 2013.

25. Patrick J. Egan, *Partisan Priorities: How Issue Ownership Drives and Distorts American Politics* (New York: Cambridge University Press, 2013).

26. Eleonora Dubicki, "Basic Marketing and Promotion Concepts," *Serials Librarian* 53, no. 7 (2008): 5–15.

27. Experts or researchers on political polarization consider more than the most recent frames or perspectives on the topic of polarization because it occupies more of their day-to-day considerations, and they are exposed to more theories about political polarization to begin with.

28. R. M. Entman, "Framing: Toward Clarification of a Fractured Paradigm," *Journal of Communication* 43, no. 3 (1993); 51–58; H. I. Chyi and M. McCombs, "Media Salience and the Process of Framing: Coverage of the Columbine School Shootings," *Journalism & Mass Communication Quarterly* 81, no. 1 (2004): 22–35; Justin Grimmer, S. J. Westwood, and S. Messing, *The Impression of Influence: Legislator Communication, Representation, and Democratic Accountability* (Princeton, NJ: Princeton University Press, 2014).

29. Vicki R. Lane, "The Impact of Ad Repetition and Ad Content on Consumer Perceptions of Incongruent Extensions," *Journal of Marketing* 64, no. 2 (2000): 80–91.

30. Richard Fenno, *Home Style: House Members in Their Districts* (Boston, MA: Addison-Wesley Educational Publishers Inc, 1978); Jane Mansbridge, "Rethinking Representation," *American Political Science Review* 97, no. 4 (2003): 515–528; Matthew Gabel and Kenneth Scheve, "Estimating the Effect of Elite Communications on Public Opinion Using Instrumental Variables," *American Journal of Political Science* 51, no. 4 (2007): 1013–1028; Christopher F. Karpowitz, Tali Mendelberg, and Lee Shaker, "Gender Inequality in Delibrative Participation," *American Political Science Review* 106, no. 3 (2012): 533–547.

31. David C. W. Parker and Craig Goodman, "Our State's Never Had Better Friends: Resource Allocation, Home Styles, and Dual Representation in the Senate," *Political Research Quarterly* 66, no. 2 (2013): 370–384.

32. Christopher H. Achen and Larry M. Bartels, *Democracy for Realists: Why Elections Do Not Produce Responsive Government* (Princeton, NJ: Princeton University Press, 2016).

33. Monika McDermott, "Voting Cues in Low-Information Elections: Candidate Gender as a Social Information Variable in Contemporary United States Elections," *American Journal of Political Science* 41, no. 1 (1997): 270–283.

34. Lindsey Cormack, "Extremity in Congress: Communications versus Votes," *Legislative Studies Quarterly* 41, no. 3 (2016): 575–603.

35. Jeremy M. Teigen, "Enduring Effects of the Uniform: Previous Military Experience and Voting Turnout," *Political Research Quarterly* 59, no. 4 (2006): 601–607.

36. D. Sunshine Hillygus and Todd G. Shields, *The Persuadable Voter: Wedge Issues in Presidential Campaigns* (Princeton, NJ: Princeton University Press, 2014);

Christian R. Grose, Neil Malhotra, and Robert Parks Van Houweling, "Explaining Explanations: How Legislators Explain Their Policy Positions and How Citizens React," *American Journal of Political Science* 59, no. 3 (2015): 724–743; David B. Holian, "He's Stealing My Issues! Clinton's Crime Rhetoric and the Dynamics of Issue Ownership," *Political Behavior* 26, no. 2 (2004): 95–124.

37. Patrick Tucker, "Legislator Effort and Policy Representation" (presented at the 2018 Annual Southern Political Science Conference, 2018).

38. The total count is 640. Representative David Cicilline, "S.C.A.M," Official E-Newsletter, November 17, 2017.

39. Congressman Michael Fitzpatrick, "Task Force Wrap-Up," Official E-Newsletter, June 26, 2016.

40. Scott Clement, "Veterans Are Voting Republican. And That's Not Likely to Change," *Washington Post*, November 11, 2014.

Chapter 6

1. B. I. Page, "The Theory of Political Ambiguity," *American Political Science Review* 70, no. 3 (1976): 742–752.

2. J. Sides, "The Origins of Campaign Agendas," *British Journal of Political Science* 36, no. 3 (2006): 407–436.

3. J. Sides and A. Karch, "Messages That Mobilize? Issue Publics and the Content of Campaign Advertising," *Journal of Politics* 70, no. 2 (2008): 466–476.

4. The online portal is hosted at www.dcinbox.com.

5. L. Cormack, "Extremity in Congress: Communications versus Votes," *Legislative Studies Quarterly* 41, no. 3 (2016): 575–603.

6. This root query also captures the use of veterans, veteran's, and veterans'.

7. Office of Representative Tim Murphy, E-News from Congressman Murphy, Official Constituent Communication, March 26, 2010.

8. Office of Representative Kevin Yoder, "Continuing Events across the Third District, Opposing the Administration's Nuclear Agreement with Iran," Official Constituent Communication, August 17, 2015.

9. Each member is in the data set only once. There are a few who move from the House to the Senate, and in those instances only one data point is kept using the demographic data of the state as the whole constituency.

10. Office of Senator Joe Manchin, "Senator Manchin's Newsletter—Memorial Day 2017," Official E-Newsletter, May 24, 2017.

11. Office of Representative Phil Roe, "Addressing Veterans Crisis Line Shortcomings," Official E-Newsletter, April 8, 2017.

12. Also potentially related to getting a seat on the committee in the first place is the assessment of "need" for certain types of policy outputs for members of Congress who come from districts with greater demands. Those with more veterans in their constituencies might be more likely to be placed on the Veterans' Affairs Committee in the first place. Previous research has found that for

some committees informational or partisan controls explain much of committee assignment, but for others the demand from constituencies is more important; E. S. Adler and J. S. Lapinski, "Demand-Side Theory and Congressional Committee Composition: A Constituency Characteristics Approach," *American Journal of Political Science* 41, no. 3 (1997): 895–918.

13. L. Cormack, "Extremity in Congress: Communications versus Votes," *Legislative Studies Quarterly* 41, no. 3 (2016): 575–603.

14. M. Swers, "Understanding the Policy Impact of Electing Women: Evidence from Research on Congress and State Legislatures," *PS: Political Science and Politics* 34, no. 2 (2001): 217–220; M. L. Swers, *The Difference Women Make: The Policy Impact of Women in Congress* (Chicago, IL: University of Chicago Press, 2002); C. M. Byerly and K. Ross, *Women and Media: A Critical Introduction* (Hoboken, NJ: John Wiley & Sons, 2008); L. Cormack, "Gender and Vote Revelation Strategy in the United States Congress," *Journal of Gender Studies* 24, no. 5 (2015): 1–15.

15. R. Fenno, *Home Style: House Members in Their Districts* (Glenview, IL: Addison-Wesley Educational Publishers Inc., 1978).

16. L. Cormack, "DCinbox—Capturing Every Congressional Constituent E-newsletter from 2009 Onwards," *Legislative Scholar* 2, no. 1 (2017): 2–36.

17. VA expenditure data sources: Federal Assistance Awards Data System (FAADS) for Compensation & Pension and Education and Vocational Rehabilitation and Employment Benefits; Veterans Benefits Administration Insurance Center for the Insurance costs; the VA Financial Management System for Construction, Medical Research, General Operating Expenses, and certain C&P and Readjustment data; and the Allocation Resource Center for Medical Care costs. Medical care expenditures include dollars for medical services, medical administration, facility maintenance, educational support, research support, and other overhead items. Medical care expenditures do not include dollars for construction or other nonmedical support. Medical care expenditures are based on where patients live instead of where care is delivered.

18. B. Deckard, "State Party Delegations in the U.S. House of Representatives: A Comparative Study of Group Cohesion," *Journal of Politics* 34, no. 1 (1972): 199–222; M. Schwartz, *The Party Network: The Robust Organization of Illinois Republicans* (Madison: University of Wisconsin Press, 1990); B. Knight, "Legislative Representation, Bargaining Power and the Distribution of Federal Funds: Evidence from the US Congress," *Economic Journal* 118, no. 532 (2008): 1785–1803.

19. All the models have been alternatively specific with state-fixed effects, and the results remain the same. Employing this technique allows for more compact result presentations.

20. The model was also run with the legislative success rate per year, and results are as before: committee membership, Democratic Party, and seniority are all significantly and positively related to legislation passage rates.

21. Models 2 and 3 differ only in the inclusion of the legwork outcome variable of model 1, but the results appear impervious to this inclusion. For the remainder of this chapter, I compare model 1 to model 2.

22. K. Kiely, "Most Memorial Day Mentions in Congress Come from Nonveterans," Sunlight Foundation, May 25, 2012.

23. Of veterans serving in Congress, 85 percent choose to set up and send e-newsletters during their tenure. This number is somewhat lower than nonveteran e-mail adoption of 93 percent but is consistent with other research indicating that older members are less likely to set up e-newsletters than younger members. L. Cormack, "DCinbox—Capturing Every Congressional Constituent E-newsletter from 2009 Onwards," *Legislative Scholar* 2, no. 1 (2017): 2–36. Of the Republican veterans in Congress, 94 percent use e-newsletters compared to just 73 percent of Democrat veterans in Congress, which provides evidence that the GOP embraces communications more robustly than Democrats.

24. J. Tsai, "Veterans of Recent Wars Running for Office in Record Numbers," *Stars and Stripes*, November 5, 2012.

25. Office of Representative Alma Adams, "Honoring Our Veterans," Official E-Newsletter, November 10, 2016.

26. Office of Representative Shelley Berkley, "Reply from Congresswoman Shelley Berkley," Official E-Newsletter, May 27, 2011.

27. Office of Senator Kelly Ayotte, "Honoring Our Veterans," Official E-Newsletter, November 11, 2016.

28. A "bag of words" discards the ordering and other context and rather just uses the frequencies of words to assess a given text. This approximating method has been shown to work well across a variety of disciplines and on different corpuses.

29. A. Scott, "2016 Was HUGE," Official Constituent Newsletter—Office of Representative Austin Scott (R-GA), January 1, 2017.

30. A. Schiff, "2016 Year in Review," Official Constituent E-Newsletter, Office of Representative Adam Schiff (D-CA), December 31, 2016.

31. J. Tester, "Delivering for Veterans," Official Constituent E-Newsletter, Office of Senator Jon Tester (D-MT), October 5, 2016.

32. D. Stabenow, "Michigan Brief: Expanding Urban Agriculture," Official Consitutent E-Newsletter, Office of Debbie Stabenow (D-MI), September 30, 2016.

33. A. Smith, "Congressman Adam Smith's Veterans Newsletter," Official Constituent E-Newsletter, Office of Representative Adam Smith (D-WA), November 11, 2016.

34. B. Wenstrup, "9/11 Reminds Us That We Are All Americans," Official Constituent E-Newsletter, Office of Representative Brad Wenstrup (R-OH), September 11, 2016.

35. The Department of Veterans Affairs offers veterans statutory hiring preference. The VA has a workforce of nearly 120,000 veterans accounting for 33 percent of all employment of the department. When the GOP criticizes the VA, they

are not seen as criticizing the veterans that work there, but rather some faceless bureaucrats that seem to muck up tasks. This makes for appealing politics but potentially less than desirable policy.

36. The full text of the bill (H.R.3680—Co-Prescribing to Reduce Overdoses Act of 2016) can be found at https://www.congress.gov/bill/114th-congress/house-bill/3680/text.

37. J. Sarbanes, "Addressing the Nation's Opioid Abuse Epidemic," Official Constituent E-Newsletter, Office of Repsentative John Sarbanes, May 26, 2016.

Chapter 7

1. Col. Ritchie Elspeth Cameron, "Update on Combat Psychiatry: From the Battle Front to the Home Front and Back Again," *Military Medicine* 172, no. 12 (April 2007): 11–15.

2. G. F. Still, "Shell Shock," *British Medical Journal* 2, no. 3216 (1922): 322–323.

3. Jay Winter, *The Cambridge History of the First World War* (New York: Cambridge University Press, 2014).

4. Associated Press, "Veteran Dies of Wounds," *New York Times*, August 2, 1932.

5. For a more comprehensive history of these sorts of legislative battles, interested readers should see Anne L. Alstott and Ben Novick, "War, Taxes, and Income Redistribution in the Twenties: The 1924 Veterans' Bonus and the Defeat of the Mellon Plan," *NYU Tax Law Review* 59 (2006): 373–438; L. G. Telser, "The Veterans' Bonus of 1936," *Journal of Post Keynesian Economics* 26, no. 2 (2003): 227; Stephen R. Ortiz, "Rethinking the Bonus March: Federal Bonus Policy, the Veterans of Foreign Wars, and the Origins of a Protest Movement," *Journal of Policy History* 18, no. 3 (2006): 275–303; Jeff Simmons, *The Bonus: The Veterans March on Washington* (Seattle, WA: CreateSpace Independent Publishing Platform, 2014); Stephen R. Ortiz, *Beyond the Bonus March and GI Bill: How Veteran Politics Shaped the New Deal Era* (New York: New York University Press, 2009).

6. Examples of programs not reviewed here are individual payment rate adjustment legislation, and more specific programs such as the Reserve Educational Assistance Program (REAP) or post–Vietnam Era Veterans Educational Assistance Program (VEAP).

7. John Bound and Sarah Turner, "Going to War and Going to College: Did World War II and the G.I. Bill Increase Educational Attainment for Returning Veterans?" *Journal of Labor Economics* 20, no. 4 (2002): 784–815.

8. "The Class of 1949," *Fortune*, June 1949, 84.

9. P. Timoshenko, Readjustment Training (P.L. 346), file, VA Research Division, Washington, DC (Controller, Division of Veterans Benefits, VA, to Henry T. Tadd, 1960).

10. "Is This Education?" *American Scholar* 16 (1947): 479.

11. Keith W. Olson, "The G. I. Bill and Higher Education: Success and Surprise," *American Quarterly* 25, no. 5 (1973): 596–610.

12. The bill was revised in 1952 and 1966 to address some of these shortcomings. Katherine Kiemle Buckley and Bridgit Cleary, "The Restoration and Modernization of Education Benefits under the Post-9/11 Veterans Assistance Act of 2008," *Veterans Law Review* (Board of Veterans' Appeals) 2 (2010).

13. Kathleen J. Frydl, *The GI Bill* (New York: Cambridge University Press, 2009).

14. Cassandria Dortch, "GI Bills Enacted prior to 2008 and Related Veterans' Educational Assistance Programs: A Primer," *Congressional Research Service*, October 6, 2017; Darryl Kehrer and Michael McGrevey, "The Montgomery GI Bill at 25 Years: A Continuing Legacy of Service," The Ohio Department of Veteran Services, May 23, 2012.

15. Corey Rumann, Marisa Rivera, and Ignacio Hernandez, "Student Veterans and Community Colleges," *New Directions for Community Colleges*155, Fall (2011): 51–58.

16. Andrew Barr, "From the Battlefield to the Schoolyard: The Short-Term Impact of the Post-9/11 GI Bill," *Journal of Human Resources* 50, no. 3 (2015): 580–613.

17. Megan Exkstein, "Colleges Cite Inequities in New Benefits for Veterans," *Chronicle of Higher Education* 55, no. 32 (April 2009).

18. Libby Sander, "Veterans Tell Elite Colleges: 'We Belong,'" *Chronicle of Higher Education* (January 2013). https://www.chronicle.com/article/At-Elite-Colleges-a-Push-to/136459

19. Ravi Shankar, "Post-9/11 Veterans Educational Assistance Act of 2008," *Harvard Journal on Legislation* 46, no. 1 (2009): 303.

20. Tracey L. Moon and Geraldine A. Schma, "A Proactive Approach to Serving Military and Veteran Students," *New Directions for Higher Education* 153, spring (2011): 53–60.

21. Dale Eisman, "Sen. Webb's New GI Bill Gets Overwhelming OK in Senate," *Virginian-Pilot*, June 27, 2008.

22. Roll Call Vote 110th Congress—2nd Session Vote Number: 162 Vote Date, June 26, 2008, 09:42 p.m.

23. Tom Harkin, "For-Profit Education Companies," *Congressional Record* 157, no. 70 (May 2011): S3153–S3160.

24. Daniel Golden, "For-Profit Colleges Target the Military," *Bloomberg Business Week*, December 30, 2009.

25. Office of Senator Tom Carper, "You've Gotta Hear This," Official Constituent E-Newsletter, August 1, 2013.

26. Office of Senator Sherrod Brown, "Ensuring Taxpayer Dollars Are Spent on Education, Not Corporate PR," Official Constituent E-Newsletter, September 2, 2015.

27. John Tester, "Tester Criticizes VA for Mishandling G.I. Bill Overpayments," Senator John Tester Press Releases, April 21, 2010.

Notes

28. Rick Maze, "In 4 Years 745,000 Have Used Post 9/11 GI Bill," *Army Times*, June 29, 2012.

29. Megan Rogers, "1 Million People Have Used Post-9/11 GI Bill," *Inside Higher Ed*, November 2013.

30. A better measure would be a number of veterans matriculating in different districts, but as the data criticism intimated, this sort of information is not available for assessment.

31. Part of this is related to the low sample size. Only 42 members introduced specific post–9/11 GI Bill fixes.

32. Office of Senator Tom Carper, "Upholding Our Commitment to Veterans," Official Constituent E-Newsletter, November 11, 2015.

33. Office of Senator Richard Durbin, "Reining in the For-Profit College Industry & Affordable Care Act Update," Official Constituent E-Newsletter, June 15, 2015.

34. Office of Representative Vicky Hartzler, "Thank You for Contacting Me," Official Constituent E-Newsletter, December 6, 2016.

35. Office of Representative Phil Roe, "We Must Remember Our Veterans & Their Sacrifice," Official Constituent E-Newsletter, October 6, 2011.

36. Public Law 112–56, "VOW (Veterans Opportunity to Work) to Hire Heroes Act of 2011," 2011.

Chapter 8

1. Department of Veterans Affairs, "Budget in Brief," 2018 Congressional Submission, 2018.

2. Brian Mockenhaupt, "Confessions of a Whistleblower: Dr. Sam Foote Reveals How He Went to War with the VA," *AARP Bulletin*, September 2014.

3. Linda A. Halliday and John D. Daigh, "Veterans Health Administration: Review of Veterans' Access to Mental Health Care," Offices of Audits and Evaluations and Healthcare Inspections, VA Office of Inspector General, Department of Veterans Affairs, 2012.

4. Ryan W. Buell, "A Transformation Is Under Way at U.S. Veterans Affairs: We Got an Inside Look," *Harvard Business Review*, 2016.

5. Scott Bronstein and Drew Griffin, "A Fatal Wait: Veterans Languish and Die on a VA Hospital's Secret List," CNN, April 23, 2014.

6. Buell, "A Transformation Is Under Way at U.S. Veterans Affairs."

7. Office of Representative John Culberson, "Veterans Affairs Update," Official Constituent E-Newsletter, March 27, 2014.

8. Office of Congressman Joe Pitts, "My Bill Protecting Seniors Passes the House," Official Constituent E-Newsletter, March 28, 2014.

9. Office of Congressman Sean Duffy, "Our Veterans Deserve Better," Official Constituent E-Newsletter, March 31, 2014.

10. Office of Congressman Sean Duffy, "Happy Easter," Official Constituent Communication, April 20, 2014.

11. Office of Congressman Jeff Miller, "Miller Newsletter—04/06/14," Official Constituent E-Newsletter, April 6, 2014; Howard Altman, "Gov. Scott Asks Answers in VA Hospital Deaths," *Tampa Bay Times*, April 1, 2014; Scott Friedman, "Veterans Administration Hiring Draws Criticism, Sparks Investigation after Death," NBCDFW.com, March 31, 2014.

12. Howard Altman, "VA Releases Findings on Deaths, Injuries from Delayed Tests," *Tampa Tribune*, April 7, 2014; Office of Senator Bill Nelson, "Pushing for Better Care for Our Veterans," Official Constituent E-Newsletter, April 8, 2014.

13. Office of Congressman Paul Gosar, "I Smell Corruption," Official Constituent E-Newsletter, April 12, 2014.

14. Dennis Wagner and Michelle Ye Hee Lee, "Vets Rally in Phoenix to Decry VA Care, Seek Reforms," *Arizona Republic*, April 16, 2014; Office of Congressman Paul Gosar, "Justice and Equality," Official Constituent E-Newsletter, April 19, 2014.

15. Office of Congressman David Schweikert, "ICYMI: This Is about Truth Telling!" Official Constituent E-Newsletter, April 16, 2014.

16. Messages that referred to Virginia by the abbreviation VA were removed.

17. Office of Congressman Bob Goodlatte, "Holding the VA Accountable," Official Constituent E-Newsletter, April 25, 2014.

18. Office of Congressman Tom Latham, "LATHAM REPORT: Taking Action to Support Our Veterans," Official Constituent E-Newsletter, April 27, 2014.

19. Office of Congressman Jeff Miller, "Miller Newsletter—04/27/14," Official Constituent E-Newsletter, April 27, 2014.

20. Office of Congresswoman Tammy Duckworth, "Supporting Our Veterans," Official Constituent E-Newsletter, May 2, 2014.

21. Office of Congressman John Carter, "Judge's Boarding Pass April 28—May 2, 2014," Official Constituent E-Newsletter, May 2, 2014.

22. The first appearance was on April 24 on the online outlet *Veterans Today: A Journal for the Clandestine Community* (http://www.veteranstoday.com/2014/04/24/secret-veterans-death-list-discovered/_) and on April 28 on the blog *DC Clothesline* (http://www.dcclothesline.com/2014/04/28/veterans-die-waiting-months-see-doctor-va-hospitals/).

23. The full text of the letter is available here: https://rooney.house.gov/media-center/press-releases/rooney-calls-for-criminal-investigations-into-va-waiting-list-deaths.

24. The Office of Senator Dean Heller, "E-News from Senator Dean Heller," Official Constituent E-Newsletter, May 8, 2014.

25. David Lawder, "UPDATE 1-VA's Shinseki Gets House Subpoena, Says Will Not Resign," Reuters, May 8, 2014.

26. Richard A. Oppel Jr., "American Legion, Citing Problems, Calls for Veterans Secretary to Resign," *New York Times*, May 7, 2014.

27. Office of Congressman Mike Coffman, "Serving Our Veterans," Official Constituent E-Newsletter, May 30, 2014.

28. Office of Inspector General, "Review of Alleged Patient Deaths, Patient Wait Times, and Scheduling Practices at the Phoenix VA Health Care System," Veterans Health Administration, August 2014.

29. https://www.congress.gov/bill/113th-congress/house-bill/2216.

30. https://www.congress.gov/bill/113th-congress/house-bill/3547.

31. https://www.congress.gov/bill/113th-congress/house-bill/241.

32. https://www.congress.gov/bill/113th-congress/house-bill/2189.

33. http://clerk.house.gov/evs/2013/roll516.xml.

34. https://www.senate.gov/legislative/LIS/roll_call_lists/roll_call_vote_cfm.cfm?congress=113&session=2&vote=00187

35. Public Law 113–146, "Veterans Access, Choice, and Accountability Act of 2014," Page 128 STAT. 1754, August 7, 2014.

36. https://www.congress.gov/bill/113th-congress/senate-bill/2013.

37. https://www.congress.gov/bill/113th-congress/house-bill/4031.

38. http://clerk.house.gov/evs/2014/roll229.xml.

39. John Carter, "Fort Hood Victims Could Soon Receive Purple Hearts," DCinbox: Official E-Newsletters from Congress, May 6, 2014.

40. https://www.congress.gov/bill/113th-congress/house-bill/4779.

41. https://www.congress.gov/bill/113th-congress/house-bill/4810.

42. For an example on the GovTrack URL and interface that provides a full listing of legislation and related information, see this from the 111th Congress: https://www.govtrack.us/congress/bills/subjects/armed_forces_and_national_security/5852#congress=114&terms2=5874.

43. That is, each reference of a bill had to be accompanied by an explanation relating the bill to veterans to be included in the count.

44. Congressman Robert A. Brady, "Happy Veterans Day!" Official E-Newsletter: The Brady Brief, November 11, 2010.

45. This adds very few people to the eligible list of people able to seek veterans' health care, but it is a change in policy.

46. Hawaii News Now, "Murkowski Praises Akaka in Floor Speech," 2012.

47. Senator Richard Burr, "Legislative Update from Senator Richard Burr," Official E-Newsletter, July 20, 2012.

48. Office of Congressman Mike Pompeo, "Heading into Summer," Official Constituent E-Newsletter, May 31, 2011.

49. Some members used the informal bill name, Pay Our Guard and Reserve Act, in constituent communications.

50. The specific rules of eligibility are for one or more of the following conditions: (1) have been unable to schedule an appointment at a VA medical facility within the Veterans Health Administration's (VHA) wait-time goals for hospital care or medical services and such veterans opt for non-VA care or services; (2) reside more than 40 miles from a VA medical facility; (3) reside in a state without a VA medical facility that provides hospital care, emergency medical services, and surgical care, and such veterans reside more than 20 miles from such a facility; or (4) reside within 40 miles of a VA medical facility but are required to

travel by air, boat, or ferry to reach such facility, and such veterans face an unusual or excessive geographical burden in accessing the facility.

51. Importantly, this authority was set to only be in place for two years with the assumption that once the backlog of the VA was eliminated, and procedures became more streamlined, veterans would return to VA-provided care.

52. U.S. Congress, "Public Law No: 113–146: H.R.3230—Veterans Access, Choice, and Accountability Act of 2014," 2014.

53. Department of Veterans Affairs Office of Inspector General, "Healthcare Inspection Veterans Crisis Line Caller Response and Quality Assurance Concerns Canandaigua, New York," Office of Healthcare Inspections, February 11, 2016.

54. Office of Congressman French Hill, "#22PushupChallenge," Official Constituent E-Newsletter, September 27, 2016.

55. Office of Representative David Young, "60 Second Survey—Should the Senate Act?" Official Constituent Communication, October 9, 2016.

56. Office of Representative Ted Lieu, "Rep. Lieu & Mayor Garcetti Statements on President Obama Signing L.A. Homeless Veterans Leasing Act into Law," Official Constituent Communication, September 30, 2016.

57. Office of Representative Seth Moulton, "2016 Got Off to a Busy Start," Official Constituent E-Newsletter, February 19, 2016.

58. Office of Representative Erik Paulsen, "Paulsen Post—February 21, 2016," Official Constituent E-Newsletter, Ferbruary 21, 2016.

59. Office of Representative WIll Hurd, "Faster Care for Veterans," Official Constituent E-Newsletter, March 15, 2016.

60. Office of Congressman Jason Smith, "Congressman Jason Smith Weekly Newsletter," Official Constituent E-Newsletter, December 10, 2016.

61. Office of Congressman Tim Walkz, "Monthly Update from Representative Walz," Official Constituent E-Newsletter, September 3, 2014.

62. Bryant Jordan, "Clay Hunt Veteran Suicide Bill Blocked in Senate by Coburn," Military.com, December 16, 2014.

63. Office of Senator Richard Burr, "Burr: Intel Hearing, ABLE Act, Dean Smith Rememberance," Official Constituent E-Newsletter, February 14, 2015.

64. Office of Senator Joni Ernst, "Bringing Iowans' Values to DC," Official Constituent E-Newsletter, December 28, 2016.

Chapter 9

1. The Office of Senator Tim Kaine, "New Legislation to Support Military Spouses," Official Constituent E-Newsletter, February 8, 2018.

2. "It's Time to Recognize Cadet Nurses as Veterans," *Haverhill Gazette*, February 1, 2018.

3. Meredith Hindley, "How the GI Bill Became Law in spite of Some Veterans' Groups," *Humanities* 35, no. 4 (2014).

4. Suzanne Mettler, *Degrees of Inequality: How the Politics of Higher Education Sabotaged the American Dream* (Lebanon, IN: Basic Books, 2014).

5. Michael D. Shear and Jennifer Steinhauer, "Trump to Seek $54 Billion Increase in Military Spending," *New York Times*, February 27, 2017.

6. Annie Dobler, "New Benefit Bill Could Lead to Surge in Veteran Enrollment, Experts Say," *GW Hatchet*, January 25, 2018.

7. Natalie Gross, "Trump Signed the 'Forever GI Bill.' Here Are 11 Things You Should Know," *Military Times*, August 16, 2017.

8. Davis Louis, "Forever GI Bill Expands Education Chances," *Daily Courier*, January 12, 2018.

9. James Capretta, "Republicans Must Reckon with the Budgetary Reality," *Hill*, February 6, 2016.

10. S.1094–115th Congress (2017–2018).

11. U.S. Office of Personnel Management, "Employment of Veterans in the Federal Executive Branch: FY 2008 to FY 2015," National Center for Veterans Analysis and Statistics, 2017.

12. Stuart Rothenberg, "Republican Recruiting," *Roll Call*, October 8, 2007; Steve Mistler, "With an Eye on the House, Democrats Turn to Veterans for 2018 Races," *All Things Considered*, September 8, 2017.

13. Mike Mullen and Elliot Ackerman, "Can Veterans Rescue Congress from Its Partisan Paralysis?" *USA Today*, February 7, 2018.

14. Emmarie Huetteman, "Democrats Court Military Veterans in Effort to Reclaim House," *New York Times*, July 5, 2017.

15. Rye Barcott and Jake Wood, "Why More Veterans Should Run for Office," *TIME*, November 9, 2017.

16. Maribel Aponte et al., *America's Women Veterans: Military Service History and VA Benefit Utilization Statistics,* Office of Data Governance and Analytics, Department of Veterans Affairs, 2017.

17. Paul Rieckhoff, "A Message to All Candidates: Our Troops Aren't Props," *Huffington Post*, January 10, 2012.

18. David A. Fahrenthold, "What Ever Happened to All That Money Trump Raised for the Veterans?" *Washington Post*, March 3, 2016.

19. For a particularly scathing one, see David Abrams, "Veterans, Patriots and Pawns," *New York Times*, February 4, 2016.

20. CNN Exit Polls, "CNN Politics," 2016.

Bibliography

AARP. *Long Term Care Cost Survey*. Gfk NOP Roper Public Affairs & Media, New York, 2006.

ABC News/*The Washington Post*. "ABC News/Washington Post Poll: 2016 Presidential Election/Hillary Clinton/Veterans Affairs/Global Warming," Langer Research Associates/Capital Insight/Abt SRBI, Inc. New York, NY 2014 USABCWASH2014-1161.

Achen, Christopher H., and Larry M. Bartels. *Democracy for Realists: Why Elections Do Not Produce Responsive Government*. Princeton, NJ: Princeton University Press, 2016.

Adams, Samuel Hopkins. "The Miracle of Reeducation." *Red Cross Magazine*, May 1919, 44.

Adkins, R. E. "Medical Care of Veterans." *Bankers Magazine*, 1919, 96–99.

Adler, E. S., and J. S. Lapinski. "Demand-Side Theory and Congressional Committee Composition: A Constituency Characteristics Approach." *American Journal of Political Science* 41, no. 3 (1997): 895–918.

Alstott, Anne L., and Ben Novick. "War, Taxes, and Income Redistribution in the Twenties: The 1924 Veterans' Bonus and the Defeat of the Mellon Plan." *NYU Tax Law Review*, 2006, 373–438.

Altman, Howard. "Gov. Scott Asks Answers in VA Hospital Deaths." *Tampa Bay Times*, April 1, 2014.

Altman, Howard. "VA Releases Findings on Deaths, Injuries from Delayed Tests." *Tampa Tribune*, April 7, 2014.

The American Legion. "The Four Pillars of the American Legion." 2010. https://www.legion.org/documents/legion/pdf/four_pillars.pdf.

The American Legion. "History of the American Legion." 2017. https://www.legion.org/history.

The American Legion. "Resolution: Prosthetics Appliances—Artificial Limbs." 24th Annual National Convention, 1942.

American National Election Study (Pre-Election). Survey Research Center. University of Michigan, Ithaca, NY: Roper Center for Public Opinion

Research, iPOLL [distributor], Cornell University, 1960. Accessed October 27, 2017.
American Veterans. "About Us." AmVets, 2017.
American Women Veterans. "Home: Mission." 2017. http://americanwomenveterans.org/home/mission/.
Aponte, Maribel, et al. *America's Women Veterans: Military Service History and VA Benefit Utilization Statistics*. Office of Data Governance and Analytics, Department of Veterans Affairs, 2017.
Asch, S. M., et al. "Comparison of Quality of Care for Patients in the Veterans Health Administration and Patients in a National Sample." *Annals Internal Medicine* 141, no. 12 (December 2004): 938–945.
Ashton, C. M., et al. "Hospital Use and Survival among Veterans Affairs Beneficiaries." *New England Journal of Medicine* 349, no. 17 (2003): 1637–1646.
Associated Press. "Reagan Would Elevate V.A. to Cabinet Level." *New York Times*, November 11, 1987.
Associated Press. "Veteran Dies of Wounds." *New York Times*, August 2, 1932.
Bacevich, Andrew J., and Richard H. Kohn. "Grand Army of the Republicans: Has the U.S. Military Become a Partisan Force?" *New Republic*, December 8, 1997, 22–25.
Bad Robot/Greenberg Quinlan Rosner Research. *Public Opinion Strategies*. Archived at the Roper Center, 2013.
Barcott, Rye, and Jake Wood. "Why More Veterans Should Run for Office." *TIME*, November 9, 2017.
Barr, Andrew. "From the Battlefield to the Schoolyard: The Short-Term Impact of the Post- 9/11 GI Bill." *The Journal of Human Resources* 50, no. 3 (2015): 580–613.
Barretto, Matt A., and David L. Leal. "Latinos, Military Service, and Support for Bush and Kerry in 2004." *American Politics Research* 35, no. 2 (2007): 224–251.
Basu, Moni. "Survey: Veterans Say Afghanistan, Iraq Wars Not Worth It." CNN, October 5, 2011.
Berry, J. "VOW (Veterans Opportunity to Work) to Hire Heroes Act of 2011." U.S. Office of Personnel Management, June 15, 2012.
Binder, S., E. Lawrence, and F. Maltzman. "Uncovering the Hidden Effect of Party." *Journal of Politics* 61, no. 3 (1999): 815–831.
Blinder, Alan S., and Mark W. Watson. "Presidents and the Economy: A Forensic Investigation." Unpublished, Princeton University Department of Economics Brown Bag Seminar, November 2013.
Bound, John, and Sarah Turner. "Going to War and Going to College: Did World War II and the G.I. Bill Increase Educational Attainment for Returning Veterans?" *Journal of Labor Economics* 20, no. 4 (2002): 784–815.
Bronstein, Scott, and Drew Griffin. "A Fatal Wait: Veterans Languish and Die on a VA Hospital's Secret List." CNN, April 23, 2014.
Buckley, Katherine Kiemle, and Bridgit Cleary. "The Restoration and Modernization of Education Benefits under the Post-9/11 Veterans Assistance Act of 2008." Veterans Law Review (Board of Veterans' Appeals), 2010.

Buell, Ryan W. "A Transformation Is Under Way at U.S. Veterans Affairs. We Got an Inside Look." *Harvard Business Review*, 2016.

Bureau of Labor Statistics. Table A-5. Employment Status of the Civilian Population 18 Years and over by Veteran Status, Period of Service, and Sex, Not Seasonally Adjusted. United States Department of Labor, 2017.

Burnett, K. D. Congressional Apportionment. 2010 Census Briefs, 2011.

Bushnell, George. "Letter to Governor Soldiers' Home, 5 April 1909, RG112, Entry 386, Box 25."

Business Week/Harris Poll. *Business Week* Jan. Louis Harris & Associates. Ithaca, NY: Roper Center for Public Opinion Research, iPOLL [distributor], Cornell University, 1995.

Byerly, C. M., and K. Ross. *Women and Media: A Critical Introduction*. Hoboken, NJ: John Wiley & Sons, 2008.

Cable News Network. *CNN/Opinion Research Corporation Poll*. Ithaca, NY: Roper Center for Public Opinion Research, iPOLL [distributor], Cornell University, 2009.

Campbell, A. "The Invisible Welfare State: Establishing the Phenomenon of Twentieth Century Veteran's Benefits." *Journal of Political & Military Sociology* 32, no. 2 (2004): 249–267.

Capretta, James. "Republicans Must Reckon with the Budgetary Reality." *Hill*, February 6, 2016.

Carter, John. "Fort Hood Victims Could Soon Receive Purple Hearts." DCinbox: Official E-Newsletters from Congress, June 5, 2014.

CBS News. "CBS News Poll: Veterans Administration. USCBS2014–05D." Social Science Research Solutions, 2014.

Center for Responsive Politics. "Influence & Lobbying." OpenSecrets.Org, 2017.

Childers, Travis W. "Veterans Day: Honoring Those Who Served Our Country." Official E-Newsletter, November 11, 2009.

Chyi, H. I., and M. McCombs. "Media Salience and the Process of Framing: Coverage of the Columbine School Shootings." *Journalism & Mass Communication Quarterly* 81, no. 1 (2004): 22–35.

Clawson, C. "A Message from the Office of Congressman Curt Clawson." The Office of Representative Curt Clawson maintained by DCinbox, December 19, 2015.

Clement, Scott. "Veterans Are Voting Republican. And That's Not Likely to Change." *Washington Post*, November 11, 2014.

Clement, Scott. "War Vets Miss Commander in Chief George W. Bush." *Washington Post*, April 2, 2014.

Clinton/Veterans Affairs/Global Warming. Conducted by Langer Research Associates/Capital Insight/Abt SRBI, Inc., 2014.

Clymer, Adam. "Sharp Divergence Is Found in Views of Military and Civilians." *New York Times*, September 1999.

CNN. "McCain Defends Opposition to GI Bill." May 26, 2008.

CNN Exit Polls. "CNN Politics." 2016.

CNN/ORC International Poll. *Government Veterans Leaders.* USORCCNN2014–006. Ithaca, NY: Roper Center for Public Opinion Research, iPOLL [distributor], Cornell University, 2014.

Cormack, L. "DCinbox—Capturing Every Congressional Constituent E-newsletter from 2009 Onwards." *Legislative Scholar* 2, no. 1 (2017): 2–36.

Cormack, L. "Extremity in Congress: Communications versus Votes." *Legislative Studies Quarterly* 41, no. 3 (2016).

Cormack, L. "Gender and Vote Revelation Strategy in the United States Congress." *Journal of Gender Studies* 24, no. 5 (2015): 1–15.

Coughlin, Cletus C. "Domestic Content Legislation: House Voting and the Economic Theory of Regulation." *Economic Inquiry* 23, no. 3 (1985): 437–448.

Cox, Gary W., and Mathew D. McCubbins. *Legislative Leviathan: Party Government in the House.* Berkeley: University of California Press, 1993.

Cox, Gary W., and Mathew D. McCubbins. *Setting the Agenda: Responsible Party Government in the U.S. House of Representatives.* New York: Cambridge University Press, 2005.

de Witt Bockstruck, Lloyd. *Revolutionary War Pensions, Awarded by State Governments 1775–1874, the General and Federal Governments prior to 1814, and by Private Acts of Congress to 1905.* Baltimore, MD: Genealogical Publishing Company, 2011.

Deckard, B. "State Party Delegations in the U.S. House of Representatives: A Comparative Study of Group Cohesion." *Journal of Politics* 34, no. 1 (1972): 199–222.

Defense Finance and Accounting Service. "DoD Savings Deposit Program." December 17, 2017.

Department of Defense. "Active Duty Military Personnel by Rank/Grade." 2008.

Department of Veterans Affairs. "Budget in Brief." 2018 Congressional Submission, 2018.

Department of Veterans Affairs. "Fact Sheet: Women Veterans Population." 2016.

Department of Veterans Affairs. *Women Veterans: Past, Present and Future Revised and Updated.* Office of Policy and Planning, 2007.

Department of Veterans Affairs Office of Inspector General. "Healthcare Inspection Veterans Crisis Line Caller Response and Quality Assurance Concerns Canandaigua, New York." Office of Healthcare Inspections, February 11, 2016.

Disabled American Veterans. "Annual Report 2016." 2016.

Disabled American Veterans. *Veteran's Health Care Funding Survey.* USBELDEN.08-VETHLTH.R03. Ithaca, NY: Roper Center for Public Opinion Research, iPOLL [distributor], Cornell University, 2008.

Dobler, Annie. "New Benefit Bill Could Lead to Surge in Veteran Enrollment, Experts Say." *GW Hatchet*, January 25, 2018.

Dooley, E. "Meet the US Military's Three Four-Star Women." ABC News, July 2, 2014.

Dortch, Cassandria. "GI Bills Enacted Prior to 2008 and Related Veterans' Educational Assistance Programs: A Primer." *Congressional Research Service*, October 6, 2017.

Dubicki, Eleonora. "Basic Marketing and Promotion Concepts." *Serials Librarian* 53, no. 7 (2008): 5–15.

Durbin, Senator Dick. "Expanding the VA Caregivers Program." Official E-Newsletter, Durbin Report, March 15, 2015.

Eckstein, Megan. "Colleges Cite Inequities in New Benefits for Veterans." *Chronicle of Higher Education* 55, no. 32 (April 2009).

Edwards, Chris. "When the Economy Grows, Lawmakers Should Cut Spending or At Least Hold It Flat." *National Review*, September 4, 2013.

Edwards, Ryan D. "U.S. War Costs: Two Parts Temporary, One Part Permanent." *Journal of Public Economics* 113 (2014): 54–66.

Egan, Patrick J. *Partisan Priorities: How Issue Ownership Drives and Distorts American Politics*. New York: Cambridge University Press, 2013.

Eisman, Dale. "Sen. Webb's New GI Bill Gets Overwhelming OK in Senate." *Virginian-Pilot*, June 27, 2008.

Ellis, William Curtis, and Walter Clark Wilson. "Minority Chairs and Congressional Attention to Minority Issues: The Effect of Descriptive Representation in Positions of Institutional Power." *Social Science Quarterly* 94, no. 5 (2013): 1207–1221.

Entman, R. M. "Framing: Toward Clarification of a Fractured Paradigm." *Journal of Communication* 43, no. 3 (1993): 51–58.

Fahrenthold, David A. "What Ever Happened to All That Money Trump Raised for the Veterans?" *Washington Post*, March 3, 2016.

Fairleigh Dickinson University. *PublicMind Poll. USFDU.111015.R04*. Social Science Research Solutions. Ithaca, NY: Roper Center for Public Opinion Research, iPOLL [distributor], Cornell University, 2015.

Fandos, Nicholas. "A Bipartisan Congress That Works? Veterans Committees Show How It's Done." *New York Times*, July 10, 2017.

Faris, John H. "The All-Volunteer Force: Recruiting from Military Families." *Armed Forces and Society* 7, no. 4 (1981): 550–554.

Feaver, P. D. *Armed Servants: Agency, Oversight, and Civil-Military Relations*. Cambridge, MA: Harvard University Press, 2003.

Feaver, Peter D., and Kohn H. Richard. "Digest of Findings and Studies: Project on the Gap Between the Military and Civilian Society." Triangle Institute for Security Studies, October 2, 1999, 28–29.

Federal Election Commission. "FEDERAL ELECTIONS 2008 Election Results for the U.S. President, the U.S. Senate and the U.S. House of Representatives." Federal Election Commission. Public Disclosure Division, 2009.

Fenno, R. *Home Style: House Members in Their Districts*. Boston, MA: Addison-Wesley Educational Publishers Inc., 1978.

Finocchiaro, C.J., and D.W. Rohde. "War for the Floor: Partisan Theory and Agenda Control in the U.S. House of Representatives." *Legislative Studies Quarterly* 31, no. 1 (2008): 35–61.

Fortune. "The Class of 1949." June 1949, 84.

Fox News. Conducted by Anderson Robbins Research/Shaw & Co. Research. USSFOX.060414.R40, Roper iPOLL, 2014.

Fraiser, Nancy, and Linda Gordon. "A Genealogy of Dependency: Tracing a Keyword of the U.S. Welfare State." *Signs* 19, no. 2 (1994): 309–336.

Franklin, Ben A. "Senate Votes to Elevate VA to Cabinet Status." *New York Times*, July 13, 1988.

Franklin, John Hope. "Public Welfare in the South during the Reconstruction Era, 1865–80." *Social Service Review* 44, no. 4 (1970): 379–392.

French, Elizabeth G., and Raymond R. Ernest. "The Relation between Authoritarianism and Acceptance of Military Ideology." *Journal of Personality* 24, no. 2 (1955): 181–191.

Friedman, Scott. "Veterans Administration Hiring Draws Criticism, Sparks Investigation after Death." NBCDFW.com, March 31, 2014.

Frydl, Kathleen J. *The GI Bill*. New York: Cambridge University Press, 2009.

Gabel, Matthew, and Kenneth Scheve. "Estimating the Effect of Elite Communications on Public Opinion Using Instrumental Variables." *American Journal of Political Science* 51, no. 4 (2007): 1013–1028.

Gailmard, Sean, and Jeffery A. Jenkins. "Negative Agenda Control in the Senate and House: Fingerprints of Majority Party Power." *Journal of Politics* 69, no. 3 (2007): 689–700.

Gallup Organization. "Archived by the Roper Center." 1946.

Gallup Organization. "Gallup Daily Tracking Survey Sample: Veterans." USGALLUP.070114.R03, 2014.

Gallup Organization. *Gallup News Service Poll: November Wave 1 [USAIPOGNS2000–49]*. Ithaca, NY: Roper Center for Public Opinion Research, Roper Express, Cornell University, 2000.

Gallup Organization. *Gallup Poll (AIPO)*. Ithaca, NY: Roper Center for Public Opinion Research, Cornell University, 1940.

Gallup Organization. *Gallup Poll (AIPO)*. Ithaca, NY: Roper Center for Public Opinion Research, iPOLL [distributor], Cornell University,1946.

Gallup Organization. *Gallup Poll (AIPO)*. Ithaca, NY: Roper Center for Public Opinion Research, iPOLL [distributor], Cornell University, 1950.

Gallup Organization. *Gallup Poll (AIPO)*. Ithaca, NY: Roper Center for Public Opinion Research, iPOLL [distributor], Cornell University, 1953. Accessed October 27, 2017.

Gallup Organization. "Gallup Poll." USGALLUP.07MCH026.R12N, 2007.

Gallup Organization. *Gallup Poll. USGALLUP.070114.R01*. Ithaca, NY: Roper Center for Public Opinion Research, iPOLL [distributor], Cornell University, 2014.

Gallup Organization. *Military Pensions/Unions/Politics/Electric Power Companies*. Ithaca, NY: Roper Center for Public Opinion Research, Cornell University, 1938.

Gallup Organization. *Spending Defense*. Ithaca, NY: Roper Center for Public Opinion Research, iPOLL [distributor], Cornell University, 1950.

Gallup Organization. "USGALLUP.042990.R21." 1990.

Gallup Organization. "USGALLUP.922019.R21D." Ithaca, NY: Roper Center for Public Opinion Research, iPOLL [distributor], Cornell University, 1990.

Gallup Polls. Archived by the Roper Center. 1946.

Gallup Polls. Archived by the Roper Center. 1947.

Gelber, Scott. "A 'Hard-Boiled Order': The Reeducation of Disabled WWI Veterans in New York City." *Journal of Social History* 39, no. 1 (2005): 161–180.

Gelpi, C., & P. Feaver. "Speak Softly and Carry a Big Stick? Veterans in the Political Elite and the American Use of Force." *American Political Science Review* 96, no. 4 (2002): 779–793.

Golden, Daniel. "For-Profit Colleges Target the Military." *Bloomberg Business Week*, December 30, 2009.

Goldstein, J. *War and Gender: How Gender Shapes the War System and Vice Versa*. Cambridge: Cambridge University Press, 2001.

Gordon, Suzanne. *The Battle for Veterans' Healthcare: Dispatches from the Frontlines of Policy Making and Patient Care*. Ithaca, NY: Cornell Publishing, 2017.

Greenberg Quinlan Rosner Research and Public Opinion Strategies. "A New Generation of Leaders: A Report on America's Perceptions of Iraq and Afghanistan Veterans." June 13, 2012.

Greenfield, S., and S. H. Kaplan. "Creating a Culture of Quality: The Remarkable Transformation of the Department of Veterans Affairs Health Care System." *Annals of Internal Medicine* 141, no. 4 (2004): 316–318.

Grimmer, Justin. "Appropriators Not Position Takers: The Distorting Effects of Electoral Incentives on Congressional Representation." *American Journal of Political Science* 57, no. 3 (2013): 624–642.

Grimmer, Justin, S. J. Westwood, and S. Messing. *The Impression of Influence: Legislator Communication, Representation, and Democratic Accountability*. Princeton, NJ: Princeton University Press, 2014.

Grofman, B., and L. Handley. "Minority Population Proportion and Black and Hispanic Congressional Success in the 1970s and 1980s." *American Politics Research* 17, no. 4 (1989): 436–445.

Grofman, B., R. Griffin, and A. Glazer. "The Effect of Black Population on Electing Democrats and Liberals to the House of Representatives." *Legislative Studies Quarterly* 17, no. 3 (1992): 365–379.

Grose, Christian R., Neil Malhotra, and Robert Parks Van Houweling. "Explaining Explanations: How Legislators Explain Their Policy Positions and How Citizens React." *American Journal of Political Science* 59, no. 3 (2015): 724–743.

Gross, Natalie. "Trump Signed the 'Forever GI Bill.' Here Are 11 Things You Should Know." *Military Times*, August 16, 2017.

Gupta, B. "People, Parties and Power." *Economic and Political Weekly* 26, no. 15 (1991): 937–939.

Hagopian, Patrick. *The Vietnam War in American Memory: Veterans, Memorials, and the Politics of Healing (Culture, Politics, and the Cold War)*. Amherst: University of Massachusetts Press, 2009.

Halliday, Linda A., and John D. Daigh. "Veterans Health Administration Review of Veterans' Access to Mental Health Care, Offices of Audits and Evaluations and Healthcare Inspections, VA Office of Inspector General." Department of Veterans Affairs, 2012.

Harkin, Tom. "For-Profit Education Companies." *Congressional Record* 157, no. 70 (May 2011): S3153–S3160.

Harvard School of Public Health. "Harvard Debating Health: Election 2008 Survey." SHARRIS.08DEBHLTHAP.R02, Harris Interactive. Ithaca, NY: Roper Center for Public Opinion Research, iPOLL [distributor], Cornell University, 2008.

Hawaii News Now. "Murkowski Praises Akaka in Floor Speech." 2012.

Henry J. Kaiser Family Foundation, Harvard School of Public Health. "Knowledge of Medicare and Support for Policy Proposals Survey." USHARRIS1995-MED001, Louis Harris & Associates, 1995.

Hernandez, R. "Candidate's Words on Vietnam Service Differ from History." *New York Times*, May 17, 2010.

Hess, S. "America's Top Dynasty?" *Washington Post*, September 13, 2009.

Hetherington, Marc J., and Jonathan D. Weiler. *Authoritarianism and Polarization in American Politics*. 1st edition. Cambridge: Cambridge University Press, 2009.

Hill, K. "Does the Creation of Majority Black Districts Aid Republicans? An Analysis of the 1992 Congressional Elections in Eight Southern States." *Journal of Politics* 57, no. 2 (1995): 384–401.

Hillygus, D. Sunshine, and Todd G. Shields. *The Persuadable Voter: Wedge Issues in Presidential Campaigns*. Princeton, NJ: Princeton University Press, 2014.

Himmel, N. "#VeteranOfTheDay Army Veteran Stephen Earle Buyer." *Vantage Point*. Official Blog of the U.S. Department of Veterans Affairs, November 15, 2016.

Hindley, Meredith. "How the GI Bill Became Law in spite of Some Veterans' Groups." *Humanities* 35, no. 4 (2014).

Holcombe, Randall. "Veterans Interests and the Transition to Government Growth: 1870–1915." *Public Choice* 99, no. 3–4 (1999): 311–326.

Holian, David B. "He's Stealing My Issues! Clinton's Crime Rhetoric and the Dynamics of Issue Ownership." *Political Behavior* 26, no. 2 (2004): 95–124.

Holm, Jeanne. *Women in the Military: An Unfinished Revolution*. Novato, CA: Presidio Press, 1982.

Holsti, Ole R. "A Widening Gap between the U.S. Military and Civilian Society? Some Evidence, 1976–1996." *International Security* 23, no. 3 (1998): 5–42.

Hooker, Richard D. "Soldiers of the State: Reconsidering American Civil-Military Relations." *Parameters* 33, no. 4 (2003): 1–14.

Hoover, Herbert. "Executive Order 5398—Establishing the Veterans' Administration." Online by Gerhard Peters and John T. Woolley, The American Presidency Project, July 21, 1930.
H.R. 5600–114th Congress. No Hero Left Untreated Act. www.GovTrack.us, 2016.
Hsia, Tim. "The Role of the Military and Veterans in Politics." *New York Times*, February 1, 2013.
Huetteman, Emmarie. "Democrats Court Military Veterans in Effort to Reclaim House." *New York Times*, July 5, 2017.
"It's Time to Recognize Cadet Nurses as Veterans." *Haverhill Gazette*, February 1, 2018.
Jacobson, G. C. "Strategic Politicians and the Dynamics of U.S. House Elections, 1946–86." *American Political Science Review* 83, no. 3: 773–793.
Jacoby, William. "Issue Framing and Public Opinion on Government Spending." *American Journal of Political Science* 44, no. 4 (2000): 750–767.
Jenning, M. K., and G. B. Markus. "The Effect of Military Service on Political Attitudes: A Panel Study." *American Political Science Review* 71, no. 1 (1977): 131–147.
Jennings, Audra. "An Emblem of Distinction: The Politics of Disability Entitlement, 1940–1950." In *Veterans' Policies, Veterans' Politics*, edited by Stephen Ortiz, 94–118. Gainesville: University Press of Florida, 2012.
Jones, Jeffrey M. "Veterans Solidly Back McCain." *Gallup News*, August 19, 2008.
Jordan, Bryant. "Clay Hunt Veteran Suicide Bill Blocked in Senate by Coburn." Military.com, December 16, 2014.
Julin, Suzanne. "National Home for Disabled Volunteer Soldiers Assessment of Significance and National Historic Landmark Recommendations." National Park Service, 2004.
Kaiser Family Foundation/Washington Post Poll. "Political Parties [USICR2012-WPH031]." Conducted by Social Science Research Solutions (SSRS), 2012.
Kammerer, Gladys. "The Veterans Administration in Transition." *Public Administration Review* 8, no. 2 (1948): 103–109.
Karpowitz, Christopher F., Tali Mendelberg, and Shaker Lee. "Gender Inequality in Deliberative Participation." *American Political Science Review* 106, no. 3 (2012): 533–547.
Katznelson, Ira. *When Affirmative Action Was White : An Untold History of Racial Inequality in Twentieth-Century America*. New York: W.W. Norton, 2006.
Keech, William R., and Kyoungsan Pak. "Electoral Cycles and Budgetary Growth in Veterans' Benefit Programs." *American Journal of Political Science* 33, no. 4 (1989): 901–911.
Kehrer, Darryl, and Michael McGrevey. "The Montgomery GI Bill at 25 Years: A Continuing Legacy of Service." The Ohio Department of Veteran Services, May 23, 2012.
Kelly, Patrick. *Creating a National Home: Building the Veterans' Welfare State, 1860–1900*. Cambridge, MA: Harvard University Press, 1997.

Kerbo, H., and R. Shaffer. "Lower Class Insurgency and the Political Process: The Response of the U.S. Unemployed, 1890–1940." *Social Problems* 39, no. 2 (1992): 139–154.

Kerr, E. A., et al. "Diabetes Care Quality in the Veterans Affairs Health Care System and Commercial Managed Care: The TRIAD Study." *Annals Internal Medicine* 141 (August 17, 2004): 272–281.

Kessler, R. C., P. Berglund, O. Demler, R. Jin, K. R. Merikangas, and E. E. Walters. "Lifetime Prevalence and Age-of-Onset Distributions of DSM-IV Disorders in the National Comorbidity Survey Replication." *Archives of General Psychiatry* 62, no. 6 (2005): 593–602.

Khadduri, Jill, Dennis Culhane, Meghan Henry, Rian Watt, Lily Rosenthal, and Azim Shivji. "The 2016 Annual Homeless Assessment Report (AHAR) to Congress." The U.S. Department of Housing and Urban Development Office of Community Planning and Development, 2016.

Kiely, K. "Most Memorial Day Mentions in Congress Come from Non-veterans." Sunlight Foundation, May 25, 2012.

Kinder, John A. "Architecture of Injury: Disabled Veterans, Federal Policy, and the Built Environment in the Early Twentieth Century." In *Veterans' Policies, Veterans' Politics*, edited by Stephen Ortiz, 65–93. Gainesville: University Press of Florida, 2012.

Kizer, Kenneth W., John G. Demakis, and John R. Feussner. "Reinventing VA Health Care: Systematizing Quality Improvement and Quality Innovation." *Medical Care* 38, no. 6 (2000): I7–I16.

Kizer, Kenneth W., and R. Adams Dudley. "Extreme Makeover: Transformation of the Veterans Health Care System." *Annual Review of Public Health* 3, no. 30 (2009): 313–339.

Klingler, Jonathan D., and J. Tyson Chatagnier. "Are You Doing Your Part? Veterans' Political Attitudes and Heinlein's Conception of Citizenship." *Armed Forces & Society* 40, no. 4 (2014): 673–695.

Knight, B. "Legislative Representation, Bargaining Power and the Distribution of Federal Funds: Evidence from the US Congress." *Economic Journal* 118, no. 532 (2008): 1785–1803.

Koger, Gregory. "Position Taking and Cosponsorship in the U.S. House." *Legislative Studies Quarterly* 28, no. 2 (2003): 225–246.

Kohut, Andrew, Carroll Doherty, Michael Dimock, and Scott Keeter. "The People and Their Government: Distrust, Discontent, Anger and Partisan Rancor." Pew Research Center for the People & the Press, April 2010.

Lamoreaux, Jan. "The Organizational Structure for Medical Information Management in the Department of Veterans Affairs: An Overview of Major Health Care Databases." *Medical Care* 34, no. 3 (1996): MS31–MS44.

Lane, Vicki R. "The Impact of Ad Repetition and Ad Content on Consumer Perceptions of Incongruent Extensions." *Journal of Marketing* 64, no. 2 (2000): 80–91.

Lawder, David. "UPDATE 1-VA's Shinseki Gets House Subpoena, Says Will Not Resign." Reuters, May 8, 2014.

Lawless, Jennifer. "Female Candidates and Legislators." *Annual Review of Political Science* 18 (2015): 349–366.

Layton, Lyndsey, and Jonathan Weisman. "Veterans Group Speaks Out on War." *Washington Post*, February 8, 2007.

Leal, David L. "American Public Opinion toward the Military: Differences by Race, Gender, and Class?" *Armed Forces & Society* 32, no. 1 (2005): 123–138.

Leal, David L., and Jeremy M. Teigan. "Recent Veterans Are More Republican Than Older Ones. Why?" *Washington Post, Monkey Cage*, November 11, 2015.

Lelkes, Yphtach, and Paul M. Sniderman. "Democrats' Policies Are More Popular. But Republicans Are More Ideologically Unified." *Washington Post*, December 16, 2016.

Lelkes, Yphtach, and Paul M. Sniderman. "The Ideological Asymmetry of the American Party System." *British Journal of Political Science* 46, no. 4 (2016): 825–844.

Levitt, Steven D., and James M. Snyder. "Political Parties and the Distribution of Federal Outlays." *American Journal of Political Science* 39, no. 4 (1995): 958–980.

Lewis, Gregory B. "The Impact of Veterans' Preference on the Composition and Quality of the Federal Civil Service." *Journal of Public Administration Research and Theory* 23, no. 2 (2013): 247–265.

Longman, Phillip. *Best Care Anywhere: Why VA Health Care Is Better Than Yours*. Oakland, CA: Berrett-Koehler Publishers, 2012.

Longo, Walter E., et al. "The Role of the Veterans Affairs Medical Centers in Patient Care, Surgical Education, Research and Faculty Development." *American Journal of Surgery* 190, no. 5 (2005): 662–675.

Los Angeles Times/Bloomberg Poll. Bloomberg, November. Ithaca, NY: Roper Center for Public Opinion Research, iPOLL [distributor], Cornell University, 2007.

Louis, Davis. "Forever GI Bill Expands Education Chances." *Daily Courier*, January 12, 2018.

Louis Harris & Associates. Harris Poll, August. Ithaca, NY: Roper Center for Public Opinion Research, iPOLL [distributor], Cornell University, 1989.

Louis Harris & Associates. Harris Survey. Ithaca, NY: Roper Center for Public Opinion Research, iPOLL [distributor], Cornell University, 1984.

Louis Harris & Associates. Harris Survey, January. Ithaca, NY: Roper Center for Public Opinion Research, iPOLL [distributor], Cornell University, 1985.

Louis Harris & Associates. Harris Survey, May. Ithaca, NY: Roper Center for Public Opinion Research, iPOLL [distributor], Cornell University, 1985.

Louis Harris & Associates. *National Organization on Disability. Public Attitudes toward People with Disabilities*. Ithaca, NY: Roper Center for Public Opinion Research, iPOLL [distributor], Cornell University, 1991.

Louis Harris & Associates. "National Organization on Disability." USHARRIS.91DISB.RD04, 1991.

Louis Harris & Associates. *Topics: Defense Veterans*. Ithaca, NY: Roper Center for Public Opinion Research, iPOLL [distributor], Cornell University, 1982.

Louis Harris & Associates. *Topics: Veterans Spending Defense*. Ithaca, NY: Roper Center for Public Opinion Research, iPOLL [distributor], Cornell University, 1984.

Louis Harris & Associates. USHARRIS.121878.R06. Ithaca, NY: Roper Center for Public Opinion Research, iPOLL [distributor], Cornell University, 1978.

Lugar, R., and T. Daschle. "Congress Needs More Veterans, Veterans Can Help Break the Partisan Gridlock Hindering National Security Policy." *U.S. News and World Report*, November 10, 2017.

Lumina Foundation for Education. USGALLUP.040714.R21D. Gallup Organization, 2013.

Lynn, S. "Analysis: Iraq & Afghanistan Veterans Have Begun Reversing the Decades-Long Decline in Congressional Military Service." Veterans Campaign, 1–6.

Lynn, S., and C. Neihoff. "Field Report 2014: Veterans En Route to the 114th Congress." Veterans Campaign, 2014.

Maisel, Edward M. "Should Veterans Have Legs?" *Nation*, March 10, 1945, 271–272.

Mankowski, Mariann, Leslie E. Tower, Cynthia A. Brandt, and Kristin Mattocks. "Why Women Join the Military: Enlistment Decisions and Postdeployment Experiences of Service Members and Veterans." *Social Work* 60, no. 4 (2015): 315–323.

Mansbridge, Jane. "Rethinking Representation." *American Political Science Review* 97, no. 4 (2003): 515–528.

Marine Corps Times. "Trump or Clinton: For the Military, It's Hardly a Vote of Confidence." *Military Times*, July 23, 2016.

Market Strategies. *Americans Talk Security. Peace Dividend as the Public Sees It Survey*. Ithaca, NY: Roper Center for Public Opinion Research, iPOLL [distributor], Cornell University, 1990.

Masters, N. A. "Committee Assignments in the House of Representatives." *American Political Science Review* 55, no. 2 (1961): 345–357.

Mattox, Teryn, and Michael Pollard. "Ongoing Survey Research on Post-9/11 Veterans." RAND Corporation, 2016.

Maze, Rick. "Bill Would Boost Education Payments for Some." *Army Times*, September 18, 2009.

Maze, Rick. "In 4 Years 745,000 Have Used Post 9/11 GI Bill." *Army Times*, June 29, 2012.

McDermott, Monika. "Voting Cues in Low-Information Elections: Candidate Gender as a Social Information Variable in Contemporary United States Elections." *American Journal of Political Science* 41, no. 1 (1997): 270–283.

Bibliography

Mcphearson, Michael T. "Why Do Veterans Support Donald Trump?" *Moyers and Company*, June 28, 2016.

Meinke, S. *Leadership Organizations in the House of Representatives: Party Participation and Partisan Politics*. Ann Arbor: University of Michigan Press, 2016.

Mettler, S. "Bringing the State Back in to Civic Engagement: Policy Feedback Effects of the G.I. Bill for World War II Veterans." *American Political Science Review* 96, no. 2 (2002): 351–365.

Mettler, Suzanne. *Degrees of Inequality: How the Politics of Higher Education Sabotaged the American Dream*. Lebanon, IN: Basic Books, 2014.

Miller, Thomas E. *The Praeger Handbook of Veterans' Health History, Challenges, Issues, and Developments*. Santa Barbara, CA: Praeger, 2012.

The Mission Continues. "A New Generation of Leaders: Public Opinion Strategies." Bad Robot/Greenberg Quinlan Rosner Research. Archived at the Roper Center, 2012.

Mistler, Steve. "With an Eye on the House, Democrats Turn to Veterans for 2018 Races." *All Things Considered*, September 8, 2017.

Mittelstadt, Jennifer. *The Rise of the Military Welfare State*. New York: Harvard University Press, 2015.

Mockenhaupt, Brian. "Confessions of a Whistleblower: Dr. Sam Foote Reveals How He Went to War with the VA." *AARP Bulletin*, September 2014.

Moon, Tracey L., and Geraldine A. Schma. "A Proactive Approach to Serving Military and Veteran Students." *New Directions for Higher Education* 153, spring (2011): 53–60.

Mother Jones. USGREEN.04MOTHERJ.R074. Greenberg Quinlan Rosner Research, 2004.

MSNBC. "Bush Calls for a Halt to Swift Boat veterans' Ads." August 23, 2004.

Mullen, Mike, and Elliot Ackerman. "Can Veterans Rescue Congress from Its Partisan Paralysis?" *USA Today*, February 7, 2018.

National Cemetery Administration, Department of Veterans Affairs. "A Promise Made—A Commitment Kept." Washington, DC, 2000.

National Center for Veterans Analysis and Statistics. "VHA FY16 Annual Report." Veterans Health Administration, 2017.

National Conference of Christians & Jews. *Racial & Religious Minorities & Women*. Louis Harris & Associates, USHARRIS.78NCCJ.R17FBB. Louis Harris & Associates [producer]. Ithaca, NY: Roper Center for Public Opinion Research, iPOLL [distributor], Cornell University, 1978.

National Park Service. "History of the National Home for Disabled Volunteer Soldiers." U.S. Department of the Interior, n.d.

Newport, Frank. "Veterans Give Romney Big Lead over Obama." *Gallup News*, May 28, 2012.

Nobelprize.org. "Ferid Murad—Biographical." *Nobel Media AB*, 2014. "Rosalyn Yalow—Biographical." *Nobel Media*, 2014.

Norman, J. "Americans' Confidence in Institutions Stays Low." *Gallup News*, November 13, 2016.

Odegard, Peter H. "Is This Education?" *American Scholar* 16, no. 4 (1947): 479.
Office of Congressman Bob Goodlatte. "Holding the VA Accountable." Official Constituent E-Newsletter, DCinbox, April 25, 2014.
Office of Congressman David Schweikert. "ICYMI: This Is about Truth Telling!" Official Constituent E-Newsletter, DCinbox, April 16, 2014.
Office of Congressman French Hill. "#22PushupChallenge." Official Constituent E-Newsletter, DCinbox, September 27, 2016.
Office of Congressman Jason Smith. "Congressman Jason Smith Weekly Newsletter." Official Constituent E-Newsletter, DCinbox, December 10, 2016.
Office of Congressman Jeff Miller. "Miller Newsletter—04/06/14." Official Constituent E-Newsletter, DCinbox, April 6, 2014.
Office of Congressman Jeff Miller. "Miller Newsletter—04/27/14." Official Constituent E-Newsletter, DCinbox, April 27, 2014.
Office of Congressman Joe Pitts. "My Bill Protecting Seniors Passes the House." Official Constituent E-Newsletter, DCinbox, March 28, 2014.
Office of Congressman John Carter. "Judge's Boarding Pass," Official Constituent E-Newsletter, DCinbox, April 28–May 2, 2014."
Office of Congressman Mike Coffman. "Serving Our Veterans." Official Constituent E-Newsletter, DCinbox, May 30, 2014.
Office of Congressman Mike Pompeo. "Heading into Summer." Official Constituent E-Newsletter, DCinbox, May 31, 2011.
Office of Congressman Paul Gosar. "I Smell Corruption." Official Constituent E-Newsletter, DCinbox, April 12, 2014.
Office of Congressman Paul Gosar. "Justice and Equality." Official Constituent E-Newsletter, DCinbox, April 19, 2014.
Office of Congressman Robert A. Brady. "Happy Veterans Day!" Official E-Newsletter: The Brady Brief, November 11, 2010.
Office of Congressman Sean Duffy. "Happy Easter." Official Constituent Communication, April 20, 2014.
Office of Congressman Sean Duffy. "Our Veterans Deserve Better." Official Constituent E-Newsletter, DCinbox, March 31, 2014.
Office of Congressman Tim Walz. "Monthly Update from Representative Walz." Official Constituent E-Newsletter, DCinbox, September 3, 2014.
Office of Congressman Tom Latham. "LATHAM REPORT: Taking Action to Support Our Veterans." Official Constituent E-Newsletter, DCinbox, April 27, 2014.
Office of Congresswoman Tammy Duckworth. "Supporting Our Veterans." Official Constituent E-Newsletter, DCinbox, May 2, 2014.
Office of Inspector General. "Review of Alleged Patient Deaths, Patient Wait Times, and Scheduling Practices at the Phoenix VA Health Care System." Veterans Health Administration, August 2014.
Office of Representative Alma Adams. "Honoring Our Veterans." Official E-Newsletter, November 10, 2016.
Office of Representative David Young. "60 Second Survey—Should the Senate Act?" Official Constituent Communication, October 9, 2016.

Bibliography

Office of Representative Erik Paulsen. "Paulsen Post—February 21, 2016." Official Constituent E-Newsletter, DCinbox, February 21, 2016.

Office of Representative John Culberson. "Veterans Affairs Update." Official Constituent E-Newsletter, DCinbox, March 27, 2014.

Office of Representative Kevin Yoder. "Continuing Events across the Third District, Opposing the Administration's Nuclear Agreement with Iran." Official Constituent Communication, August 17, 2015.

Office of Representative Mike Coffman. "On Education: Parents and Locally Elected School Boards Know Best." Official Constituent Communication, February 28, 2015.

Office of Representative Phil Roe. "We Must Remember Our Veterans & Their Sacrifice." Official Constituent E-Newsletter, DCinbox, October 6, 2011.

Office of Representative Seth Moulton. "2016 Got Off to a Busy Start." Official Constituent E-Newsletter, DCinbox, February 19, 2016.

Office of Representative Shelley Berkley. "Reply from Congresswoman Shelley Berkley." Official E-Newsletter, May 27, 2011.

Office of Representative Ted Lieu. "Rep. Lieu & Mayor Garcetti Statements on President Obama Signing L.A. Homeless Veterans Leasing Act into Law." Official Constituent Communication, September 30, 2016.

Office of Representative Tim Murphy. "E-News from Congressman Murphy." Official Constituent Communication, March 26, 2010.

Office of Representative Vicky Hartzler. "Thank You for Contacting Me." Official Constituent E-Newsletter, DCinbox, December 6, 2016.

Office of Representative Will Hurd. "Faster Care for Veterans." Official Constituent E-Newsletter, DCinbox, March 15, 2016.

Office of Senator Bill Nelson. "Pushing for Better Care for Our Veterans." Official Constituent E-Newsletter, DCinbox, April 8, 2014.

Office of Senator Daniel Inouye. "Hauoli Makahiki Hou." Official Constituent Communication, January 3, 2012.

Office of Senator Dean Heller. "E-News from Senator Dean Heller." Official Constituent E-Newsletter, DCinbox, May 8, 2014.

Office of Senator Joni Ernst. "Bringing Iowans' Values to DC." Official Constituent E-Newsletter, DCinbox, December 28, 2016.

Office of Senator Kelly Ayotte. "Honoring Our Veterans." Official E-Newsletter, November 11, 2016.

Office of Senator Richard Burr. "Burr: Intel Hearing, ABLE Act, Dean Smith Remembrance." Official Constituent E-Newsletter, DCinbox, February 14, 2015.

Office of Senator Richard Burr. "Legislative Update from Senator Richard Burr." Official E-Newsletter, July 20, 2012.

Office of Senator Richard Durbin. "Reining in the For-Profit College Industry & Affordable Care Act Update." Official Constituent E-Newsletter, DCinbox, June 15, 2015.

Office of Senator Sherrod Brown. "Ensuring Taxpayer Dollars Are Spent on Education, Not Corporate PR." Official Constituent E-Newsletter, DCinbox, September 2, 2015.

Office of Senator Tim Kaine. "New Legislation to Support Military Spouses." Official Constituent E-Newsletter, DCinbox, February 8, 2018.

Office of Senator Tom Carper. "Upholding Our Commitment to Veterans." Official Constituent E-Newsletter, DCinbox, November 11, 2015.

Office of the Deputy Assistant Secretary of Defense. "2014 Demographics Profile of the Military Community." The Department of Defense, 2015.

Oliver, Adam. "The Veterans Health Administration: An American Success Story?" *Milbank Quarterly* 85, no. 1 (2007): 5–35.

Olson, Keith W. "The G. I. Bill and Higher Education: Success and Surprise." *American Quarterly* 25, no. 5 (1973): 596–610.

Opinion Research Corporation. *ORC Public Opinion Index*. Ithaca, NY: Roper Center for Public Opinion Research, iPOLL [distributor], Cornell University, 1952.

Oppel, Richard A., Jr. "American Legion, Citing Problems, Calls for Veterans Secretary to Resign." *New York Times*, May 7, 2014.

Ornstein, N. J., T. E. Mann, M. J. Malbin, A. Rugg, and R. Wakeman. *Vital Statistics on Congress*. Washington DC: Brookings Institution, 2014.

Ortiz, Stephen R. *Beyond the Bonus March and GI Bill: How Veteran Politics Shaped the New Deal Era*. New York: New York University Press, 2009.

Ortiz, Stephen R. "Rethinking the Bonus March: Federal Bonus Policy, the Veterans of Foreign Wars, and the Origins of a Protest Movement." *Journal of Policy History* 18, no. 3 (2006): 275–303.

Ortiz, Stephen R. *Veterans' Policies, Veterans' Politics*. Gainesville: University of Florida Press, 2012.

Ossad, Steven L. *Omar Nelson Bradley: America's GI General*. Columbia: University of Missouri Press, 2017.

Page, B. I. "The Theory of Political Ambiguity." *American Political Science Review* 70, no. 3 (1976): 742–752.

Panangala, Sidath Viranga. "Health Care for Veterans: Answers to Frequently Asked Questions." *Congressional Research Service*, 2016.

Paralyzed Veterans of America, Disabled American Veterans. *Healthcare and Veterans Survey*. USPSRA.04HLVET.R3. Princeton Survey Research Associates International, 2004.

Parker, David C. W., and Craig Goodman. "Our State's Never Had Better Friends: Resource Allocation, Home Styles, and Dual Representation in the Senate." *Political Research Quarterly* 66, no. 2 (2013): 370–384.

Pearson, Drew. "The Washington Merry-Go-Round." *Washington Post*, February 10, 1945, 5.

Peltzman, Sam. "Constituent Interest and Congressional Voting." *Journal of Law & Economics* 27, no. 1 (1984): 181–210.

Perlin, J. B., R. M. Kolodner, and R. H. Roswell. "The Veterans Health Administration: Quality, Value, Accountability and Information as Transforming Strategies for Patient Centered Care." *American Journal of Managed Care* 10, no. 2 (2004): 828–836.

Peterson, Leonard T. "Medical History of World War II: Surgery-Amputations-ZI." Box 454, RG 112, 1945.
Petrocik, John R. "Issue Ownership in Presidential Elections, with a 1980 Case Study." *American Journal of Political Science* 40, no. 3 (1996): 825–850.
Petrocik, John R., William L. Benoit, and Glenn Hansen. "Issue Ownership and Presidential Campaigning, 1952–2000." *Political Science Quarterly* 118, no. 4 (2003): 599–626.
Pew Research Center. Archived at the Roper Center, 2011.
Pew Research Center. "Beyond Distrust: How Americans View Their Government." *U.S. Public and Policy*, November 23, 2015.
Pew Research Center. "Chapter 5: The Public and the Military." War and Sacrifice in the Post 9/11 Era, 2001.
Pew Research Center. *Pew Social and Demographic Trends Poll: Veterans Survey.* Conducted by Social Science Research Solutions, Pew Research Center, 2011.
Pew Research Center. *Social and Demographic Trends Survey: The Military-Civilian Gap—War and Sacrifice in the Post-9/11 Era.* Archived at the Roper Center, 2011.
Pew Research Center for the People & the Press. "Pew Research Center for the People & the Press Poll, Jan, 2017." USPSRA.011917A.R01H, 2017.
Pew Research Center for the People & the Press. *Pew Research Center for the People & the Press Poll. USPSRA.041810A.R03LF2.* Princeton Survey Research Associates International, 2010.
Pew Research Center for the People & the Press. *Pew Research Center Poll: January 2015 Political Survey. USPEW2015–01POL.* Ithaca, NY: Roper Center for Public Opinion Research, Roper Express, Cornell University, Princeton Survey Research Associates International, 2015.
Pew Research Center for the People & the Press. *Pew Research Center Poll: October 2013 Political Survey.* USPEW2013–10POL, ABT SRBI, Inc., 2013.
Pew Research Center for the People & the Press. *Pew Research Center: October 2016 Political Survey [USPEW2016–1025].* Princeton Survey Research Associates International, 2016.
Pew Research Center for the People & the Press. "Public Praises Science; Scientists Fault Public, Media." 2009.
Pew Research Center for the People & the Press. USPSRA.031098.R10AF1. Princeton Survey Research Associates, 1998.
Pew Research Center for the People & the Press. USPSRA.041810A.R03LF2, Princeton Survey Research Associates International, 2010.
Pew Research Center, National Election Studies, Gallup, ABC/*Washington Post*, CBS/*New York Times*, and CNN Polls. "Beyond Distrust: How Americans View Their Government." Pew Research Center, November 23, 2015.
Phillips, Dave. "Coming Home to Damaging Stereotypes." *New York Times*, February 5, 2015.
Pike, Nicky. "Stop Using Veterans as Political Pawns." *Havok Journal*, September 26, 2017.

Poole, Keith T., and Howard Rosenthal. *Congress: A Political-Economic History of Roll Call Voting.* Oxford: Oxford University Press, 1997.

Poole, Keith T., and Howard Rosenthal. "A Spatial Model for Legislative Roll Call Analysis." *American Journal of Political Science* 29, no. 2 (1985): 357–384.

Public Law 112–56. "VOW (Veterans Opportunity to Work) to Hire Heroes Act of 2011." 2011.

RePass, William H. "Issue Salience and Party Choice." *American Political Science Review* 65, no. 2 (1971): 389–400.

"Representative Mike Kelly's Weekly E-Newsletter," Official Constituent E-Newsletter, DCinbox, May 2, 2014.

Resch, John. *Suffering Soldiers Revolutionary War Veterans, Moral Sentiment, and Political Culture in the Early Republic.* Amherst: University of Massachusetts Press, 2000.

Reyes, G. Mitchell. "The Swift Boat Veterans for Truth, the Politics of Realism, and the Manipulation of Vietnam Remembrance in the 2004 Presidential Election." *Rhetoric & Public Affairs* 9, no. 4 (2006): 571–600.

Ricks, Thomas E. "The Widening Gap between the Military and Society." *Atlantic Monthly*, July 1997, 66–78.

Rieckhoff, Paul. "A Message to All Candidates: Our Troops Aren't Props." *Huffington Post*, January 10, 2012.

Ritchie, Elspeth Cameron. "Update on Combat Psychiatry: From the Battle Front to the Home Front and Back Again." *Military Medicine* 172, no. 12 (April 2007): 11–15.

Rogers, Megan. "1 Million People Have Used Post-9/11 GI Bill." *Inside Higher Ed*, November 2013.

Roper Organization. "Roper Report 85–8, Aug." Ithaca, NY: Roper Center for Public Opinion Research, iPOLL [distributor], Cornell University, 1985.

The Roper Organization. *Roper Reports # 1983–08: Trade/Politics/Consumerism.* Ithaca, NY: Roper Center for Public Opinion Research, Roper Express, Cornell University, 1983.

Roper Organization. *USRPRR1986–08 Roper Reports 1986–08: Children/Health/National Issues.* Ithaca, NY: Roper Center for Public Opinion Research, Roper Express, Cornell University, 1986.

Rosenberg, Paul. "Right-Wing 'Superpatriots' Ignore Veterans: The Real VA Scandal No One Will Talk About." *Salon*, June 2, 2014.

Rothenberg, Stuart. "Republican Recruiting." *Roll Call*, October 8, 2007.

Rumann, Corey, Marisa Rivera, and Ignacio Hernandez. "Student Veterans and Community Colleges." *New Directions for Community Colleges* fall, no. 155 (2011): 51–58.

S.1094–115th Congress (2017–2018). "Congress.gov." 2018.

Saad, Lydia. "Americans Respect the Military, Honor Veterans." *Gallup News Service*, November 11, 2002.

Sander, Libby. "Veterans Tell Elite Colleges: 'We Belong.'" *Chronicle of Higher Education*, January 2013.

Sarbanes, J. "Addressing the Nation's Opioid Abuse Epidemic." Official Constituent E-Newsletter, DCinbox, Office of Representative John Sarbanes, May 26, 2016.

Schickler, Eric, and Kathryn Pearson. "Agenda Control, Majority Party Power, and the House Committee on Rules, 1937–52 Authors." *Legislative Studies Quarterly* (2009): 455–491.

Schiff, A. "2016 Year in Review." Official Constituent E-Newsletter, DCinbox, Office of Representative Adam Schiff (D-CA), December 31, 2016.

Schiller, N. "Examining Veterans' Interest Groups: Understanding Success through Interest Group Ratings." *Res Publica—Journal of Undergraduate Research* 13, no. 1 (2008): 64–76.

Schreiber, E. M. "Enduring Effects of Military Service? Opinion Differences between U.S. Veterans and Nonveterans." *Social Forces* 57, no. 3 (1979): 824–839.

Schwartz, M. *The Party Network: The Robust Organization of Illinois Republicans.* Madison: University of Wisconsin Press.

Scott, A. "2016 Was HUGE." Official Constituent Newsletter, Office of Representative Austin Scott (R-GA), January 1, 2017.

Scott, Wilber J., and John Sibley Butler. *Vietnam Veterans since the War: The Politics of PTSD, Agent Orange, and the National Memorial.* Norman: University of Oklahoma Press, 2004.

Seal, Karen H., Greg Cohen, Angela Waldrop, Beth E. Cohen, Shira Maguen, and Li Ren. "Substance Use Disorders in Iraq and Afghanistan Veterans in VA Healthcare, 2001–2010: Implications for Screening, Diagnosis and Treatment." *Drug & Alcohol Dependence* 16, no. 1–3 (2011): 93–101.

Serrano, J. "The Serrano Report—April 26, 2016." The Office of Representative Jose Serrano Maintained by DCinbox, April 26, 2016.

Shane, Leo. "Poll: Civilians Believe Veterans Are Valuable, but Lack Education and Suffer PTSD." *Stars and Stripes*, June 13, 2012.

Shankar, Ravi. "Post-9/11 Veterans Educational Assistance Act of 2008." *Harvard Journal on Legislation* 46, no. 1 (2009): 303.

Sharpe, C., and J. Garand. "Race, Roll Calls, and Redistricting: The Impact of Race-Based Redistricting on Congressional Roll-Call." *Political Research Quarterly* 45, no. 1 (2016): 31–51.

Shear, Michael D., and Jennifer Steinhauer. "Trump to Seek $54 Billion Increase in Military Spending." *New York Times*, February 27, 2017.

Shepsle, Kenneth A. "Can the Government Govern?" in *The Changing Textbook Congress*, edited by John E. Chubb and Paul E. Peterson, 238–266. Washington, DC: Brookings Institution, 1989.

Sides, J. "The Origins of Campaign Agendas." *British Journal of Political Science* 36, no. 3 (2006): 407–436.

Sides, J., and A. Karch. "Messages That Mobilize? Issue Public and the Content of Campaign Advertising." *Journal of Politics* 70, no. 2 (2008): 466–476.

Simmons, Jeff. *The Bonus: The Veterans March on Washington.* Charleston, SC: CreateSpace Independent Publishing Platform, 2014.

Smith, A. "Congressman Adam Smith's Veterans Newsletter." Official Constituent E-Newsletter, DCinbox, Office of Representative Adam Smith (D-WA), November 11, 2016.
Smith, S. S., I. Ostrander, and C. M. Pope. "Majority Party Power and Procedural Motions in the U.S. Senate," *Legislative Studies Quarterly* 38, no. 2 (2013): 205–236.
Snyder, James M., and Tim Groseclose. "Estimating Party Influence in Congressional Roll-Call Voting." *American Journal of Political Science* 44, no. 2 (2000): 193–211.
Sohn, Min-Woong, Noreen Arnold, Charles Maynard, and Denise M. Hynes. "Accuracy and Completeness of Mortality Data in the Department of Veterans Affairs." *Population Health Metrics* 4, no. 2 (2006): 1–8.
Spiegel, Alex. "What Vietnam Taught Us about Breaking Bad Habits." National Public Radio, January 2, 2012.
Stabenow, D. "Michigan Brief: Expanding Urban Agriculture." Official Constituent E-Newsletter, DCinbox, Office of Debbie Stabenow (D-MI), September 30, 2016.
Stevens, Rosemary. *In Sickness and in Wealth: American Hospitals in the Twentieth Century*. Vol. 2. Baltimore, MD: Johns Hopkins University Press, 1999.
Stevens, Rosemary. *A Time of Scandal: Charles R. Forbes, Warren G. Harding, and the Making of the Veterans Bureau*. Baltimore, MD: Johns Hopkins University Press, 2016.
Stevens, Rosemary A. "The Invention, Stumbling, and Reinvention of the Modern U.S. Veterans Health Care System, 1918–1924." In *Veterans' Policies, Veterans' Politics*, edited by Stephen R. Ortiz, 11–38. Gainesville: University Press of Florida, 2012.
Still, G. F. "Shell Shock." *British Medical Journal* 2, no. 3216 (1922): 322–323.
Surgeon-General's Office. *Abstracts, Translations and Reviews of Recent Literature on the Subject of the Reconstruction and Reeducation of the Disabled Soldier*. Vol. 4. Washington DC: American Red Cross, 1918.
Swers, M. L. *The Difference Women Make: The Policy Impact of Women in Congress*. Chicago, IL: University of Chicago Press, 2002.
Swers, M. "Understanding the Policy Impact of Electing Women: Evidence from Research on Congress and State Legislatures." *PS: Political Science and Politics* 34, no. 2 (2001): 217–220.
Swers, Michele L. *The Difference Women Make: The Policy Impact of Women in Congress*. Chicago, IL: University of Chicago Press, 2002.
Teigen, Jeremy M. "Enduring Effects of the Uniform: Previous Military Experience and Voting Turnout." *Political Research Quarterly* 59, no. 4 (2006): 601–607.
Teigen, Jeremy M. "Veterans' Party Identification, Candidate Affect, and Vote Choice in the 2004 U.S. Presidential Election." *Armed Forces & Society* 33, no. 3 (2007): 414–437.

Telser, L. G. "The Veterans' Bonus of 1936." *Journal of Post Keynesian Economics* 26, no. 2 (2003): 227.

Tester, J. "Delivering for Veterans." Official Constituent E-Newsletter, DCinbox, Office of Senator Jon Tester (D-MT), October 5, 2016.

Tester, John. "Tester Criticizes VA for Mishandling G.I. Bill Overpayments." Senator John Tester Press Releases. April 21, 2010.

Testimony of Charles M. Griffith, Medical Director. "Hearings." *Veterans' Administration House* (1945): 1607–1608.

Timoshenko, P. Readjustment Training (P.L. 346). File, VA Research Division, Washington, DC, Controller, Division of Veterans Benefits, VA, to Henry T. Tadd, 1960.

Titus, Dina. "Titus Blasts VA for Discrimination against LGBT Veterans." U.S. House of Representatives: Floor Statement, April 30, 2014.

Tsai, J. "Veterans of Recent Wars Running for Office in Record Numbers." *Stars and Stripes*, November 5, 2012.

Tucker, Patrick. "Legislator Effort and Policy Representation." Presented at the 2018 Annual Southern Political Science Conference, 2018.

U.S. Census. "Statistical Abstract of the United States: 2012." 2012.

U.S. Census Bureau. "2010 Census Shows Nation's Population Is Aging." 2011.

U.S. Congress, House. Hearings on HR 13026 65th Congress 3rd Session. Assistant PHS Surgeon General, Dr. W. D. Stimpson, Committee on Public Buildings and Grounds, 1989.

U.S. Department of Veterans Affairs. "Education and Training: Education Programs." 2015.

U.S. Department of Veterans Affairs. "Education and Training: History and Timeline." November 21, 2013.

U.S. Department of Veterans Affairs. "Incarcerated Veterans." October 22, 2013.

U.S. Department of Veterans Affairs. "National Cemetery Administration Fact Sheets." 2017. https://www.cem.va.gov/about/factsheets.asp.

U.S. Department of Veterans Affairs. "PTSD: National Center for PTSD." Public Section Home, October 3, 2016.

U.S. Department of Veterans Affairs. "VA Programs for Homeless Veterans." 2016. https://www.va.gov/HOMELESS/for_homeless_veterans.asp.

U.S. Department of Veterans Affairs. "VA 2018 Budget Request: Fast Facts." 2018.

U.S. Department of Veterans Affairs. "Veterans Access, Choice and Accountability Act of 2014 ('Choice Act')." Fact Sheet, October 17, 2014.

U.S. Office of Personnel Management. "Employment of Veterans in the Federal Executive Branch: FY 2008 to FY 2015." National Center for Veterans Analysis and Statistics, 2017.

"U.S. Seniors Have Realigned with the Republican Party." *Gallup*, March 26, 2014.

USABCWASH2014–1161, Langer Research Associates/Capital Insight/ABT SRBI, Inc., 2014.

Vega, Arturo, and Juanita M. Firestone. "The Effects of Gender on Congressional Behavior and the Substantive Representation of Women." *Legislative Studies Quarterly* 20, no. 2 (1995): 213–222.

The Veterans Administration. *Attitudes toward Vietnam Era Veterans Survey*. Louis Harris and Associates. Ithaca, NY: Roper Center for Public Opinion Research, iPOLL [distributor], Cornell University, 1979.

Veterans Campaign. "About Us." 2016.

Veterans of Foreign Wars. "VFW Legislative Victories Fact Sheet." 2017. www.vfw.org.

Veterans of Foreign Wars. "VFW to Obama: 'No Confused Politics Here.'" Press Release, June 3, 2016.

Veterans Today: A Journal for the Clandestine Community (http://www.veteranstoday.com/2014/04/24/secret-veterans-death-list-discovered/_) and on April 28 on the blog *DC Clothesline* (http://www.dcclothesline.com/2014/04/28/veterans-die-waiting-months-see-doctor-va-hospitals/).

Vietnam Veterans of America Foundation. Global Engagement Survey. USGREEN.01GLOBE.R009, Greenberg Quinlan Rosner and Public Opinion Strategies, 2001.

Volden, Craig, and Alan E. Wiseman. "Legislative Effectiveness in Congress." Annual Meeting of the Midwest Political Science Association, 2009.

Wagner, Dennis, and Michelle Ye Hee Lee. "Vets Rally in Phoenix to Decry VA Care, Seek Reforms." *Arizona Republic*, April 16, 2014.

Wallerstein, Mitchel B. "Terminating Entitlements: Veterans' Disability Benefits in the Depression." *Policy Science* 7, no. 2 (1976): 173–182.

Washington Post/ABC News Poll. "News Poll of U.S. Adults." 2013.

Washington Post-Kaiser Family Foundation. "Survey of Iraq and Afghanistan Active Duty Soldiers and Veterans." *Washington Post*, 2013.

Watkins, S., and J. Sherk. "Who Serves in the U.S. Military? The Demographics of Enlisted Troops and Officers." The Heritage Foundation: Defense Report, August 21, 2008.

Webb, A. "2016–2017 National Legislative Agenda." American Veterans AMVETS, 2017.

Weigley, Russell. *History of the United States Army*. New York: Macmillan, 1967.

Wenstrup, B. "9/11 Reminds Us That We Are All Americans." Official Constituent E-Newsletter, DCinbox, Office of Representative Brad Wenstrup (R-OH), September 11, 2016.

Wilkerson, John, Nick Stramp, and David Smith. "Why Bill Success Is a Lousy Way to Keep Score in Congress." *Washington Post, Monkey Cage*, February 6, 2014.

Williamson, Vanessa, Theda Skocpol, and John Coggin. "The Tea Party and the Remaking of Republican Conservatism." *The Tea Party and the Remaking of Republican Conservatism* 9, no. 1 (2011): 25–43.

Winter, Jay. *The Cambridge History of the First World War*. New York: Cambridge University Press, 2014.

WNBC/Marist Poll. *WNBC. Apr. Marist College Institute for Public Opinion*. Ithaca, NY: Roper Center for Public Opinion Research, iPOLL [distributor], Cornell University, 2007.

Yaisawarng, P. S., and J. F. Burgess Jr. "Performance-Based Budgeting in the Public Sector: An Illustration from the VA Health Care System." *Health Economics* 15, no. 3 (March 2006): 295–310.

Young, Nancy Beck. "Do Something for the Soldier Boys." In *Veterans' Policies, Veterans' Politics*, edited by Stephen Ortiz, 199–221. Gainesville: University Press of Florida, 2012.

Zillman, Donald N. "Essay: Where Have All the Soldiers Gone II: Military Veterans in Congress and the State of Civil-Military Relations." *Maine Law Review* 58, no. 1 (2006): 135–157.

Index

ABC News, 58
Affirmative action, 71, 85–86
Afghanistan, 19, 42, 47, 69, 91, 165, 168, 188, 195, 215, 217, 221, 228
Air force, 29, 36, 239
Alcoholism, 65
Amendments, 110–11, 151, 201, 204–5
American Legion, 43–44, 46, 200
American Recovery and Reinvestment Act, 132, 172, 210, 212
American Veterans (AMVETS), 46–47
American Women Veterans (AWV), 48–49
Amputations, 8, 19, 130
Apprenticeship, 131, 173, 175, 182
Appropriation(s), 6–7, 37, 46, 69, 110–12, 134, 166, 171, 178, 195–96, 198, 201, 204–5, 225
Arizona Republic, 197
Army, 5, 7, 14–15, 21, 29, 36–37, 40, 173, 194
Asylum, 6, 15
Authorization, 110–12, 156, 166, 202, 216

Backlog, 193, 196, 199–200, 203–5, 212–14
Balanced Budget Amendment, 128
Benefits, 2, 4–5, 7, 9–10, 14, 16, 21–22, 37, 40, 44–46, 50, 53, 66–68, 71–72, 81, 84, 86–90, 108, 110, 112–13, 125–35, 139–41, 143, 156, 163–66, 171–82, 184, 186–91, 198, 203, 206, 212, 214, 220, 222–25, 227; benefits transfers, 176
Bills: American Recovery and Reinvestment Act, 132, 172, 210, 212; Caregivers and Veterans Omnibus Health Services Act, 210, 212; Clay Hunt Suicide Prevention for American Veterans (SAV) Act, 44, 47, 147, 217; Communities Helping Invest through Property and Improvements Needed for Veterans Act of 2016, 201, 215; Comprehensive Addiction and Recovery Act, 185, 211, 219; Deborah Sampson Act, 211, 219, 227; Demanding Accountability for Veterans Act of 2014, 202; The Department of Veterans Affairs Accountability and Whistleblower Protection Act of 2017, 226; Department of Veterans Affairs Management Accountability Act of 2014, 202–4; Faster Care for Veterans Act of 2016, 112, 211, 216; Federal Aviation Administration Veteran Transition Improvement Act of 2016, 211, 219; Female Veteran Suicide Prevention Act, 47, 211,

218; Military Construction and Veterans Affairs and Related Agencies Appropriations Act, 201, 205; Military Spouse Employment Act, 222; The National Asylum for Disabled Volunteer Soldiers Act, 6; National Defense Authorization Act, 111; No Veterans Crisis Line Call Should Go Unanswered Act, 210, 215; Patient Protection and Affordable Care Act, 210, 212; Post–9/11 GI Bill, 55, 132, 171, 173–78, 181–91, 220, 223, 225; Post–9/11 Veterans Education Assistance Act, 171; Serviceman's Readjustment Act, 171, 173; 21st Century GI Bill of Rights, 171; 21st-Century Veterans Benefits Delivery Act, 203; The Veterans Access, Choice, and Accountability Act, 18, 44, 210, 214; Veterans' Access to Care through Choice and Accountability Act of 2014, 202; Veterans Need Timely Access to Care Act, 205; Veterans Opportunity to Work (VOW) Act, 190; Veterans Timely Access to Health Care Act, 201; Vocational Rehabilitation Act, 7–8; West Los Angeles Leasing Act of 2016, 211, 216; Working to Integrate Networks Guaranteeing Member Access Now Act, 184; World War Adjusted Compensation Act, 172
Black veterans, 9, 21, 173
Bonus Army, 173
Brookings Institute, 26–27
Bush, George H. W. (1989–1993), 10, 12–13
Bush, George W. (2001–2009), 13, 44, 55, 69–70, 87, 89, 171, 178
Buy-in, 174

Camp Lejeune, 44, 180, 210, 214
Caregivers, 18–19, 66, 72, 90, 139, 210, 212–13, 222

Caregivers and Veterans Omnibus Health Services Act, 210, 212
Cash bonus, 172
Center for Responsive Politics, 42, 103
Civil War, 6–8, 14, 17
Clay Hunt Suicide Prevention for American Veterans (SAV) Act, 44, 47, 147, 217
Clinton, Bill (1993–2001), 13
Clinton, Hillary, 33, 95, 228
CNN, 193, 195, 198–202, 205
Coast guard, 29
Committee on Veterans' Affairs, 26–29, 35–37, 53, 99, 102–4, 108–9, 111, 114–21, 151–54, 157–59, 165, 168, 183, 186–87, 195–97, 200–202, 207–8, 228
Communities Helping Invest through Property and Improvements Needed for Veterans Act of 2016, 201, 215
Community college, 175
Comprehensive Addiction and Recovery Act, 185, 211, 219
Construction, 37, 46, 131, 156, 166, 196, 198, 201–5, 212
Continuing education, 214, 222
Correspondence programs, 131, 156
Counseling, 213, 222, 227
Crisis phone line, 215

DCinbox, 34, 144–45, 163, 191
Death list, 199
Deborah Sampson Act, 211, 219
Defense spending, 85–86
Demanding Accountability for Veterans Act of 2014, 202
Department of Defense (DOD), 10, 36, 68, 132, 204, 226
The Department of Veterans Affairs Accountability and Whistleblower Protection Act of 2017, 226
Department of Veterans Affairs Management Accountability Act of 2014, 202–4
Deservingness, 5, 20, 128, 139–40

Index

Disability, 5, 9, 175, 201, 204, 212–13
Disabled American Veterans (DAV), 42, 45, 89–90, 110

Education, 2–10, 34, 40, 44, 54, 58, 60, 66, 71–72, 81, 85–86, 92, 98, 102, 107, 126, 130–34, 140, 156–59, 171–90
Electronic medical records, 36, 196, 204, 217
Eligibility, 3, 5, 17, 21, 36, 44, 108, 134, 175–76, 184, 213–14
Emphasis allocation theory, 136, 143
Employment, 9, 34, 47, 66, 90, 98, 126, 156, 179, 184–85, 222, 224

Fairleigh Dickinson University, 193
Faster Care for Veterans Act of 2016, 112, 211, 216
Federal Aviation Administration Veteran Transition Improvement Act of 2016, 211, 219
Federal Thrift Savings Retirement Plan, 132
Feeling thermometer, 88
Female Veteran Suicide Prevention Act, 47, 211, 218
Filipino Veterans Equity Compensation Fund, 212
Flight school, 131, 156, 182
Foote, Dr. Samuel, 192
Forever G.I. Bill, 225
For-profit colleges, 177, 179–81, 189–90
Four-year colleges, 131, 175
Framing, 127, 137, 162

Gallup, 55, 58, 66, 72
GI Bill(s): Forever G.I. Bill, 225; Harry W. Colmery Veterans Educational Assistance Act, 225; Montgomery GI Bill, 174–77, 182, 223; Post–9/11 GI Bill, 55, 132, 171, 173–78, 181–91, 220, 223, 225; Post–9/11 Veterans Education Assistance Act, 171; Serviceman's Readjustment Act, 171, 173; The Webb GI Bill, 171
Government spending, 6, 37, 54, 67, 84, 127–29, 134, 178, 183, 195, 225

Harry W. Colmery Veterans Educational Assistance Act, 225
Health care, 3, 5, 9, 11, 16–18, 38, 44, 47, 72–73, 89, 92–93, 98, 107, 110–12, 126, 128–34, 140, 165–68, 187–88, 191–220, 224
Holder, Eric, 200
Homelessness, 172
Housing, 9, 14, 18, 34, 36, 75, 98, 131, 176, 179, 182, 188, 216, 225

Ideology, 43, 75, 120, 139; Democrat Party ideology, 134; Republican Party ideology, 126–29, 132–33, 141, 183, 189, 225
Iraq, 19, 29, 40, 69, 90–91, 165, 168, 181, 188, 195, 200, 217, 221
Iraq and Afghanistan Veterans of America (IAVA), 42, 47, 168, 215, 228
Issue ownership, 53–54, 82, 106

Kaiser Family Foundation, 58, 88
Kerry, John, 55

Legislator-to-constituent communications, 24–25, 34–36, 51, 56, 109, 126, 135, 141, 143–46, 148, 150–51, 153, 157, 162–64, 167–68, 172, 180, 185, 191–92, 194–95, 198–99, 203–4, 206–9, 212–16, 218–19, 224–25, 229
Legwork, 4, 20, 27, 97–115, 117–20, 123, 125–37, 139–41, 143, 146, 148–51, 154–62, 169, 172, 178, 183–91, 195, 203, 206–8, 220–25, 228
Library of Congress, 34, 98, 126, 154, 184
Lip service, 4, 20, 27, 125–27, 129, 131, 133, 135–37, 139–41, 143–46,

148–51, 153–63, 165, 167–69, 172, 178, 183–87, 190–92, 195, 199–200, 202–3, 206–8, 210, 215, 220–21
Loan guaranty, 9, 132
Loans, 21, 34, 98, 126, 179, 217

Marches, 172
Marine Corps, 29, 49, 180, 214
McCain, John, 31, 55, 77, 111, 178
McDonald, Robert, 13, 37, 194
Memorial Day, 146, 160, 166
Mental health, 2, 16, 19, 44–47, 90, 147, 204, 213, 217–18
Military budget, 87
Military Construction and Veterans Affairs and Related Agencies Appropriations Act, 201, 205
Military Spouse Employment Act, 222
Montgomery GI Bill, 174–75

The National Asylum for Disabled Volunteer Soldiers Act, 6
National Cemetery Administration, 5, 131
National Defense Authorization Act, 111
National guard, 175
Navy, 29
No Veterans Crisis Line Call Should Go Unanswered Act, 210, 215
Noncollege degree-granting institutions of higher education, 131

Obama, Barack (2009–2017), 13, 18, 26, 30–33, 40, 44, 46, 55, 68–70, 73–74, 77, 92–94, 181, 190, 193–94, 197, 199, 212, 216, 218
Obamacare, 212
Office of Inspector General, 195, 199–200, 202, 204–5, 215
Opioid Safety Initiative, 219
Overpayment status, 182

Party platform, 128
Patient Protection and Affordable Care Act, 210, 212
Pension, 5–9, 34, 84, 86–87, 98, 102, 126, 131, 156, 214
Pew Research Center, 58, 68
Phoenix, 15–16, 68, 72, 191–95, 197, 199, 201, 203–4, 222
Political communication, 19, 21, 34, 136, 141, 161, 220
Political participation, 80
Poll, 32, 55–56, 58–62, 66, 68, 72, 74–79, 153, 193–94
Post–9/11 GI Bill, 55, 132, 171, 173–78, 181–91, 220, 223, 225
Post–9/11 Veterans Education Assistance Act, 171
Posttraumatic stress disorder (PTSD), 19, 65, 90, 130, 181, 184
Presidents: Bush, George H. W. (1989–1993), 10, 12–13; Bush, George W. (2001–2009), 13, 44, 55, 69–70, 87, 89, 171, 178; Clinton, Bill (1993–2001), 13; Obama, Barack (2009–2017), 13, 18, 26, 30–33, 40, 44, 46, 55, 68–70, 73–74, 77, 92–94, 181, 190, 193–94, 197, 199, 212, 216, 218; Reagan, Ronald (1981–1989), 10, 12, 127; Roosevelt, Franklin D. (1933–1945), 9, 12, 171, 173, 223; Trump, Donald J. (2017–), 11, 13, 56, 95, 225, 228
Privatization, 18
ProPublica, 154
Protests, 172
Public opinion, 1, 20, 53–54, 53–79, 81, 83, 137, 143, 153, 193–94, 219–21, 223, 229
Purple Heart, 225

Reagan, Ronald (1981–1989), 10, 12, 127
Record-keeping system, 205

Rehabilitation, 7–8, 18–19, 34, 44, 60, 98, 133, 156, 184–85, 219
Research and development, 131
Reservists, 21, 175, 177
Roosevelt, Franklin D. (1933–1945), 9, 12, 171, 173, 223
Rural veterans, 213–14

Scandal, 6, 11–15, 44, 67–68, 72, 74, 125, 139, 165, 191–205, 207, 209, 213, 215, 217, 219–20, 222, 226
Seniority, 98, 154–55, 158–59, 187, 208
Serviceman's Readjustment Act 171, 173
Shell-shock, 172
Shinseki, Eric, 13, 44, 73–74, 92–94, 193–94, 196, 200
Small government, 54, 224, 226
State Veterans Homes, 17
Stop-loss, 212
Substantive legislation, 112–13, 133, 141, 202
Suicide prevention, 44, 46–47, 147, 204, 211, 217
Supplemental Appropriations, 171, 178
Swift Boat Veterans for Truth, 55
Symbolic legislation, 110, 112, 133, 223

Tampa Tribune, 197
Tea Party, 128, 134, 195, 225
Trump, Donald J. (2017–), 11, 13, 56, 95, 225, 228
Tuition reimbursement, 174, 179, 181–82
21st Century GI Bill of Rights, 171
21st-Century Veterans Benefits Delivery Act, 203
Twitter, 42

Unemployment, 9, 32, 129, 133
U.S. Census, 25–26, 185

VA, the: Veterans Administration (VA), 1–21, 40, 57, 62, 73, 74, 86, 90, 92–94, 129, 156; Veterans Affairs (VA), The Department of, 5, 13, 26, 35, 88, 92–93, 165, 167, 176, 188–90, 193–94, 197, 201–2; Veterans Benefits Administration (VA), 5, 184; Veterans Bureau, 4–5, 9, 11–13, 50, 191
VA Honesty Project, 195
Veteran members of Congress, 29, 34–35, 104–5, 114–16, 118–20, 125, 152
Veteran populations, 23, 25–29, 33–35, 37–51, 61, 65, 75, 150
Veteran status, 3, 21, 25–29, 36, 57, 104–5, 114–16
Veteran women, 78, 218, 226–27
The Veterans Access, Choice, and Accountability Act, 18, 44, 210, 214
Veterans' Access to Care through Choice and Accountability Act of 2014, 202
Veterans' Affairs Veteran Data Portal, 26
Veterans Campaign, 26–27, 43, 49
Veterans Choice program, 215
Veterans Day, 10, 38, 146, 163–66, 193
Veterans' groups: American Legion, 43–44, 46, 200; American Veterans (AMVETS), 46–47; American Women Veterans (AWV), 48–49; Disabled American Veterans (DAV), 42, 45, 89–90, 110; Iraq and Afghanistan Veterans of America (IAVA), 42, 47, 168, 215, 228; Veterans Campaign, 26–27, 43, 49; Veterans of Foreign Wars (VFW), 42–43, 47, 215; Vietnam Veterans of America (VVA), 46, 215; VoteVets, 43, 47–48, 69
Veterans Health Administration (VHA), 5, 13, 16, 18, 129–31, 134, 168, 191, 214, 217
Veterans homes, 8, 14–15, 17

Veterans Integrated Service Networks, 11, 112
Veterans Need Timely Access to Care Act, 205
Veterans of Foreign Wars (VFW), 42–43, 47, 215
Veterans Opportunity to Work (VOW) Act, 190
Veterans' studies, 4
Veterans Timely Access to Health Care Act, 201
Veto, 7, 109, 178
Vietnam Veterans of America (VVA), 46, 215
Vietnam War, 10, 19, 35, 39, 67, 87–88, 196, 223
Vocational Rehabilitation Act, 7–8
Vocational training, 6, 8, 102, 182
VoteVets, 43, 47–48, 69

Wait times, 14, 44, 74, 93, 192–93, 195, 197–202, 215–16

Wait-list scandal, 191, 198
Walter Reed National Military Medical Center, 68
Washington Post, 58, 73
The Webb GI Bill, 171
West Los Angeles Leasing Act of 2016, 211, 216
Widows, 84
With Honor, 41, 226
Working to Integrate Networks Guaranteeing Member Access Now Act, 184
World War Adjusted Compensation Act, 172
World War I, 7–9, 21, 39, 59, 65, 172, 222
World War II, 9, 21, 36, 39, 41, 65, 67, 84, 130, 165, 171, 173, 222
www.govtrack.us, 98

Yellow Ribbon Program, 176

About the Author

Lindsey Cormack, PhD, is assistant professor of political science and the director of the Diplomacy Lab at Stevens Institute of Technology in Hoboken, New Jersey. She created and maintains the database of official Congress-to-constituent e-newsletters at www.dcinbox.com. Her research on congressional communications has been published in peer-reviewed journals such as *Legislative Studies Quarterly* and *Gender Studies* as well as in popular outlets including the *New York Times*, the *Washington Post*, and the *Hill*.